Rowan
University

The

Domosh

Collection

A Gift

The Twenty-first Missouri

CONTRIBUTIONS IN MILITARY HISTORY

THE
TWENTY-FIRST
MISSOURI

From Home Guard to Union Regiment

LESLIE ANDERS

Contributions in Military History, Number 11

GREENWOOD PRESS
Westport, Connecticut • London, England

Library of Congress Cataloging in Publication Data

Anders, Leslie.
    The twenty-first Missouri.

    (Contributions in military history; no. 11)
    Bibliography: p.
    Includes index.
    1. United States—History—Civil War, 1861-1865—
Regimental histories—Missouri Infantry—21st.
2. Missouri Infantry. 21st Regt. I. Title. II. Se-
ries.
E517.521st.A52   973.7'4778   75-64
ISBN 0-8371-7962-9

Library of Congress Catalog Card Number: 75-64
ISBN:0-8371-7962-9

First published in 1975

Greenwood Press, a division of Williamhouse-Regency Inc.
51 Riverside Avenue, Westport, Connecticut 06880

Printed in the United States of America

Contents

Preface

The Twenty-first Missouri Volunteer Infantry was formed on December 31, 1861, when the understrength First and Second Northeast Missouri Volunteers merged. The parent outfits had formed in that anxious summer when Northerners came to a realization that secession's flames could not be extinguished, in William T. Sherman's phrase, "with a squirt gun." Veterans forming the new regiment had gained combat experience suppressing Confederate insurgency in northeastern Missouri, and many had fought victoriously on August 5, 1861, at Athens, Missouri, in the war's "northernmost" battle thus far west of the Mississippi.

Following muster in at Canton, the new outfit left for the lower Mississippi valley. It was the first Union regiment fully engaged at Shiloh, and, after a severe mauling, it went on to participate in both battles of Corinth, Mississippi, later that year. Other campaigns and battles followed, including skirmishes and scouting in western Kentucky and Tennessee, Sherman's Meridian expedition, the battle of Tupelo, the Price raid into Missouri, the battle of Nashville, and the siege and assault of April 9, 1865, on Mobile's Fort Blakely—where the Missourians were first to plant colors on the captured works. Then, for a year after the close of hostilities, the regiment was a mainstay of federal authority on Alabama's Gulf coast.

Readers still believing that Fort Sumter instantly separated "good" from "bad" guys will find here small comfort for such outmoded fancies. Writers of the past generation have analyzed for us the tangled emotions afflicting the famous and powerful, but it seems ever more certain that we cannot understand fully the *ordinary* American—Northerner or Southerner—of that terrible time without delving more deeply than we have into his feelings and circumstances. Subjected to such microhistoriography, many long-held and comfortable assumptions may well pass away: that the sectional conflict purely and simply polarized Americans, that Yankees flocked to the colors from simple patriotism or to end the scandal of black servitude just as Southern poor whites presumably offered up their lives to preserve more fortunate neighbors' stakes in the peculiar institution, or that the boys in blue all came home to join the Grand Army and vote the Republican ticket come rain or shine.

Because many Americans have come to see in the Civil War their own folk epic, they have developed a fascination for this bloodiest of the nineteenth-century wars. The reasons for this preoccupation are as numerous as Civil War buffs. Yet, if one motive clearly penetrates the whole, it is the unspoken faith that studying those complex ancestors helps us to know ourselves better as a people. And it is not alone for the "amateur" that the war bulks so large: the current text prescribed for the Reserve Officers Training Corps, the first to be written solely by professional historians, devotes more than a sixth of its narrative to this four-year conflict. Interestingly, this work frowns on the traditional obsession with the war in northern Virginia and reminds us that "it was the Union armies west of the Appalachians that struck the death knell of the Confederacy."

Acknowledgments

Very special assistance with source materials was provided by Dr. Richard S. Brownlee, director of the State Historical Society of Missouri at Columbia, his associate Dr. James W. Goodrich, reference librarian Goldena Howard, and newspaper librarian Alma Vaughan; Elmer O. Parker, chief of the Old Military Records Branch, National Archives; Jack L. Best, the archivist whose efficient counsel was a constant blessing to the writer's work in the archives; Captain Clyde B. Martin, administrative officer to the Adjutant General of Missouri; John Batsel, Jr., and Jean Jernigan, librarian and assistant librarian of the Garrett Theological Seminary of Evanston, Illinois; William Keller, newspaper librarian, and Paul Spence, curator of manuscripts, Illinois Historical Library, Springfield; Martha E. Wright, reference librarian, Indiana State Library, Indianapolis; Lida Lisle Greene, reference librarian, Mrs. J. M. Love and John Robison of the newspaper division, Iowa Department of Archives and History, Des Moines; Mrs. George Hawley, librarian, Kansas State Historical Society, Topeka, her assistant Mrs. Jack Toma; and Thomas Turinsky, of the newspaper division; Frances Stadler, manuscript librarian of the Missouri Historical Society, St. Louis; Luella Harlan, librarian of the Peoria (Illinois) Historical Society; R. Philip Morris, librarian of Central Methodist College, Fayette, Missouri; Dr. A. Sterling Ward, professor, and Dr. W. D. Sparks, librarian, Saint Paul's School of Theology, Kansas City, Missouri.

Invaluable official documentation was furnished by Paul C. Brown, probate judge of Adair County, Kirksville, Missouri, and his clerk, Marguerite H. Price; William D. Dreyer, probate judge of Knox County, at Edina; John F. McElfresh, clerk of the circuit court, Edina; William D. Orcutt, probate judge of Clark County, Kahoka, and his clerk Allen L. Horton; Wilma L. Plant, clerk of the circuit court at Monticello, Lewis County; Birney O. Reeves, probate judge of Scotland County, Memphis, and his clerk Vera Turner; Donald L. White, probate judge of Franklin

County, Kansas, at Ottawa, and his clerk Kathy Tevis; David W. Wilson, probate judge at Monticello, and Nimmie Jean Humphrey, his clerk.

It is further incumbent upon the author to express gratitude for substantial aid and encouragement from others. Mardellya Soles Anders, the authentic Missourian in this transplanted Kansan's house for over three decades, was unsparing in her encouragement, untiring in newspaper research supporting the work, and unerring in her advice on how "Missourians look at things." Dr. Theron F. Swank, director of instructional resources at Central Missouri State University, loaned projecting equipment to facilitate microfilm research. Larry C. Melton, instructor in social studies at the Smith-Cotton High School of Sedalia, Missouri, prepared the maps. Reading the manuscript and commenting on it most helpfully were the author's colleagues: Dr. Claude H. Brown, dean emeritus of the Central Missouri State University School of Arts and Sciences; Dr. Perry McCandless, professor of history; and Dr. Guy Griggs, assistant professor of history. Useful though their suggestions were, imperfections surviving in the book remain chargeable to the author alone.

For specific acts of assistance, the writer is indebted also to Flora E. Angell, past president, Missouri Department, Daughters of Union Veterans; Robert Anthony, Fort Madison, Iowa; Henry B. Bass, Enid, Oklahoma; Ray F. Brookhart, Carlsbad, California; Postmaster and Mrs. Donald Downing, Edina; George Fisher, editor of the *Fort Madison Evening Democrat;* Miss Eve French and Mrs. Ethel French Collins, Farmington, Iowa; Milton Garber, editor of the *Enid News;* Dr. Carl W. Hagler, Quincy, Illinois; Hiram Hiller, Kahoka; Alice Downs Hoyes, La Grange, Missouri; Ethel J. Hunt, Paola, Kansas; Harry Killen, Knox City, Missouri; Colonel and Mrs. Glenn Kisling, Cedar Rapids, Iowa; Helen E. Kohlenberg, vice-president, Miami Publishing Company of Paola; Douglas Lamont, managing editor, *The Daily Gate City,* Keokuk, Iowa; Carl Landrum, Quincy; H. C. McComb, Bonaparte, Iowa; the late James H. McWilliams, Kahoka; Harry Matlick, Newkirk, Oklahoma; Thorpe Menn, book review editor of *The Kansas City Star;* Allin C. Morton, Pleasant Hill, Missouri; Paul C. Rowe, editor of the *Kahoka Gazette-Herald;* the late F. E. Schofield, editor of *The Edina Sentinel;* Paul V. Sellers, Lewistown, Missouri; Evelyn Sheets, Trenton, Missouri; Ruth Skeens, secretary of the Athens Park Development Association; Geroldine Wagner, Donnellson, Iowa. Still others will find their acknowledgments in the bibliographical essay.

Leslie Anders
Warrensburg, Missouri

The
Twenty-first
Missouri

1

D. Moore, Union

"And by the Gods!" yelled the rangy six-footer backing down the ladder, "if I had more room I would add 'Now and Forever'!" Several muttering neighbors, passing his general store, had seen David Moore retouching that sign over the entrance, and they were not surprised he had painted out "Wrightsville" and replaced it with bold black letters spelling out "U N I O N." Damned, infernal Yankee . . .

Political fevers were high in northeastern Missouri, and most of Dave's acquaintances were of a different mind from his. But he had no second thoughts: *they* were countenancing treason in their cheers for Jefferson Davis, but *he* had worn captain's bars under Old Glory in the Mexican War–and it was not for him to flinch in this hour of peril. Rare indeed were Wrightsvillians anxious to take on the owner of that unruly black hair and those crimson-lined hazel eyes. To be sure, some brave soul had pinned a note on his door telling him to "get out"; well, this new sign over the door was his answer.

Dave had been born in eastern Ohio on July 3, 1817, son of John and Sarah Clark Moore, immigrants from Ireland. Descended from hard-bitten Scots of the Ulster Garrison, it was only natural for John to shoulder a musket in 1812, as did his son in 1846. Dave, married to Diademia Schnabel before the war and a family man, developed western fever after coming home from service. In 1850, he bade goodbye to his sister and brother at Wooster, loaded Diademia and their four sons and small daughter into a wagon, and headed west to Clark County, Missouri. After farming, he went into pork packing and storekeeping at Wrightsville.

Old settlers found him cantankerous. One remembered him as a man "who could get madder and swear longer without repeating himself than any man I ever knew." The coming of the Republicans had made no impression on him, or on most Missourians. He found his political solace in Stephen A. Douglas' "popular sovereignty" wing of the Democracy, but this was the source of his political troubles now. The settlers of the region, descended mostly of Tennessee, Virginia, and Kentucky families, leaned toward states' rights views of the sectional controversy. Compounding Dave's torments, Diademia and the older boys leaned that way, too. Community folklore has it that Dave's horsewhip kept down his domestic dissidence, but it is known that the oldest son, William, served in 1860 as

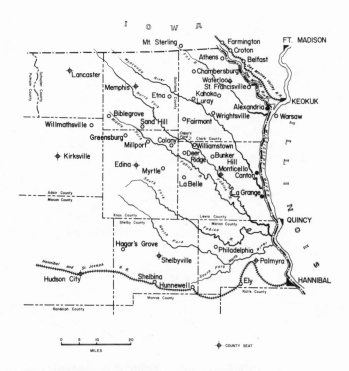

NORTHEAST
MISSOURI
1861~62

musician for the Hickories of Alexandria, a Douglas-for-President club of
which David Moore was captain.

This was a land of broad prairies, grassy hills drained by deep-set creeks
and branches, and woodlands of ash trees, oaks, hickories, hard and soft
maples, black walnuts, elms. The principal rivers—Fox, Wyaconda, various
forks of the Fabius (pronounced "Fabbius" locally)—flowed to the south
through Lewis, Clark, Scotland, and Knox counties to empty into the
Mississippi above Canton. There was frequent flooding in the Mississippi
bottoms, from Alexandria down to La Grange. The humorist Mark Twain,
journeying up the river in 1872, "missed Alexandria; was told it was under
water, but would come up to blow in the summer." Throughout the region,
the fences were either hedges or "staked and ridered" Virginia—or zigzag—
affairs, ordinarily made of oak or walnut and six feet high.

Visitors found that the people were prone to "reckon" if they agreed,
"pack" instead of carry, and feel "peart" when in good health. An eastern
traveler said of these Upper South folk that they dressed "to a great extent
in dyed blue or butternut. Put one of the natives in a butternut coat, and
vest, with blue pants, and you have a good idea of that backwoods fashion.
The cut does not change. Frock coats are universal. I do not remember seeing a sack coat made of homespun, even the little boys just in their teens
are dressed in the inevitable frocks, they have a prematurely old appearance, but one more article is wanted, and that, a 'stove pipe' hat."

If the back country of this four-county region was settled by old-stock
Protestants of the Upper South, the situation differed in some of the towns.
At Edina, seat of Knox County, a thriving Irish community had taken root
since 1842. In the next decade, Germans had come to La Grange, a major
landing on the Mississippi in southeastern Lewis County. The Irish of Edina
were all Roman Catholic, but Germans along the river were, by and large,
Methodists, thanks to a German-Jewish physician, Ludwig S. Jakobi, a convert who had done missionary work along the Mississippi from St. Louis
to Keokuk since 1841. Although the Germans were antislavery Unionists,
observers were uneasy about the Irish, whose voting habits betrayed no
warmth toward a Republican movement whose nativist Know-Nothing
elements the Irish were bound to distrust.

The election of 1860 presaged stormy times. The bitter drama played
out in an atmosphere of ideological and sectional animosity. Offered four
tickets, Missourians rejected the extremes—the pro-Southern slate headed
by Vice-President John C. Breckinridge and the black-abolitionist candidacy
of Abraham Lincoln. Voters of the four-county area gave a thin edge to
John Bell's Constitutional Unionism in the only state Douglas carried.

This election, says William E. Parrish, "clearly indicated that the great majority of Missourians were conservative and desired no extreme solution to the slavery question."

Northeastern Missourians were subjected to constant journalistic incitements. Ranging from "conservativism" to downright disunionism was a vigorous outstate press, led by the *Hannibal News, Palmyra Spectator,* Edina's *Knox County Herald,* and the *National Democrat* of Memphis. These were ably backed by the *Missouri Republican* of St. Louis, the *Herald* of Quincy, Illinois, and the *Daily Journal* (later *Constitution-Democrat*) of Keokuk, Iowa. Some of these would suffer repression for excesses, but others would repair to carefully chosen "Conservative-Union" positions. Opposing them were such major "radical" organs as James B. Howell's *Daily Gate City* of Keokuk, the *Anzeiger des Westens,* and *Missouri Democrat* of St. Louis. The fanatical Dr. Charles Elliott, through the columns of the "northern" Methodists' *Central Christian Advocate,* lent a prophetic note to the Radical-Union barrages, overshadowing by his ferocity the conservatism of David R. McAnally's *St. Louis Christian Advocate,* a Southern Methodist paper published in the same building. A big gun of northern Missouri's Radicalism was Charlton Howe's *National American* at La Grange.

Elections over, Missourians experienced an abatement of partisan passions. But then the secessions came, first South Carolina in December, then other cotton states in the weeks following. Missourians, viewing matters through the newspapers and personal leanings, beheld with rising excitement the rending of their country. Hotbeds of secessionism existed in various localities, but the greatest were in Lewis County and the little Dixie area to the south and southwest. Here Confederate recruiters would find happy hunting-grounds, forest recesses and brush-country for guerrilla hideaways or training camps.

Much depended upon the presumably pro-Douglas governor lately elected, Claiborne Fox Jackson, and his wing of Democracy dominating the statehouse. His inaugural address on January 5, 1861, hardly masking his sympathies with the rebelling South, stressed his feeling that the North was obligated to go a second—or third—mile in composing differences with states noisily renouncing ties with the Federal Union. Those who hoped to keep Missouri within the Union took little comfort from the fact that the general assembly, woefully unrepresentative to be sure, was under the sway of Southern sympathizers. Lieutenant Governor Thomas C. Reynolds, one of the state's loudest secessionists, presided in the senate, and an outspoken Breckinridge man was speaker of the house. Nor could Unionists hide their jitters over Jackson's call for a state convention to decide "future relations" with other states. By late January, federal officials and their Missouri supporters sensed they were faced with a calculating enemy in Jefferson City.

Elections to the convention rekindled political rancors. The tiny Republican faction in the legislature shared the national stereotype of Missouri as a den of secessionists. The statehouse gang believed it, too, but the voters on February 18 fooled everyone. About 110,000 votes were cast for Unionists of varying fervor, while open secessionists could find but 30,000. The Union men gasped in disbelief, while their enemies hollered "foul!". A Quincy editor crowed, "There will not be ten secessionists" in the ninety-nine man convention.

Former Governor Sterling Price, a Mexican War hero afflicted with "conditional Unionism" and getting vague about his conditions, was called by a decisive majority to preside over the convention. Meeting February 28 in the Cole County Courthouse in Jefferson City, the delegates felt that their environment was decidedly unfavorable, so they promptly repaired to a more "loyalist" setting at the Mercantile Library in St. Louis, where they remained in session, off and on, for three years.

During that stormy political winter, David Moore of Wrightsville completed his ideological journey from Douglas Democracy to black abolitionism. Surviving records suggest few milestones of this pilgrimage, and we are left to conjecture that, given his hair-trigger temper and Scots-Irish sense of personal honor, his Republicanism had been hammered out on a forge of heated contention with his neighbors.

Soon after Jackson's inauguration, Congressman Frank Blair came to the conclusion that Union men had better arm and organize. There was no better place to start than with the Germans of St. Louis, and he began forming them into reliable Home Guards. Captain Nathaniel Lyon, a fanatical abolitionist commanding the St. Louis garrison, arranged for muskets in February, and alarmed Southern men in the city set up minutemen units. Blair saw to the establishment of a "Committee of Public Safety" in St. Louis to direct and propagandize for the Union cause.

The most worrisome fly in Blair's ointment was Brigadier General William S. Harney, commanding the Department of the West. Poor Harney, torn between his Southern sympathies and his sworn obligations to the President, could have been counted upon to come down on the side of duty, but neither Blair nor Lyon dared bet Missouri's future on that. They saw eye to eye: only force and firmness of purpose could intimidate rebels and keep the state in the Union. Harney, however, was averse to harshness and seems to have believed that a conciliatory policy and willingness to negotiate could save Missouri from Jefferson Davis. That Jackson and

Price might string him along to gain time and strength for seceding, Harney evidently did not suspect. Blair did—and his connections in Washington served him well as he strove to avert the consequences of appeasement and to promote the rise of Lyon. After all, Frank was chairman of the House Committee on Military Affairs, and his brother would be Lincoln's Postmaster-General.

The rebel attack on Fort Sumter caused a fresh spasm of Confederate enthusiasm that April. Blood was spilled, and the nation was coming to civil war. Lincoln called on the states for volunteer troops to assist his tiny regular army in suppressing the insurrection, but Governor Jackson, treasonably in Blair's judgment, hotly spurned the call and summoned his general assembly to put the state on a war footing. The purpose in view, it was officially given out, was to safeguard the state's neutrality. Secretly, however, an appeal went out to Jefferson Davis for Confederate intervention.

In early May there assembled in St. Louis, near the arsenal at a tent city called "Camp Jackson," several hundred militiamen called by the governor. This intensified feelings: the secessionists thrilled that action was near, Blair and Lyon fretful the rebels would seize the arsenal. Confederate flags in the camp and the naming of its streets for famous rebels disturbed Unionists. Harney felt that Washington could never tolerate the likes of the camp. Rightly or wrongly, Lyon and Blair decided to act.

For Lyon it was high time. Blair, conniving backstage, had gotten Harney called east for consultations, but he was due back any day. Harney, the negotiator, a contemporary said, was oppressed at "how dreadfully excited the secessionists were; how desirous the great majority of the people were for peace; how a 'careful, prudent policy' might keep thousands from joining the rebels."

Harney's absence had given Lyon and Blair time to muster into the United States Volunteers four regiments of German Home Guards, with which muscle Lyon occupied Camp Jackson on May 10 and arrested its garrison. Then, as the prisoners were being led off, the pro-Southern crowd became embroiled with the guardsmen. In an exchange of various flying objects and harsh words, the "damned Dutch" turned muskets on their tormentors and littered the street with twenty-eight dead and many more wounded. Anger swept the city: the bloodshed of Sumter had reached its boulevards.

Two days later, Price was in Jefferson City to accept the rank of "major general commanding" in the Missouri State Guard. The angry lawmakers passed a "military bill," making the governor a dictator and handing him the state treasury. Branded by Harney as an "indirect secession ordinance," it was a mandate to "put down rebellion and repel invasion"—even if it involved killing fellow-Missourians or firing on the United States Army. The eight congressional districts were declared military regions.

Missourians as a whole evidently yearned to sit out the Civil War in blissful neutrality. This, to state guardsmen forming in northeastern Missouri, meant that "Lincoln's hirelings" had to be taught their place, exterminated, or expelled. The level of terrorism mounted during May, and journalists from Iowa and Illinois noted with rising indignation and fear that Union men were rapidly being harassed into flight. The *Whig-Republican* of Quincy reported on May 14 that forty had crossed into Illinois in one day. The paper almost daily thereafter provided accounts of scores fleeing Clark, Scotland, Schuyler, and other counties.

The last straw, so far as the Blair-Lyon camp was concerned, was the Harney-Price agreement of May 21, which in essence left the maintenance of order "within the state and among the people thereof" with Jackson and Price. That they were already angling for Confederate aid and instigating anti-Union violence still escaped Harney's suspicions. He *could* have known, for the papers—and his ears—were full of tales of mob violence against Unionists in many areas. But he stood by his conviction that a passive Union military posture would prevail.

Blair secured from the War Department on May 20 a secret order dismissing Harney but deliverable at Blair's option. Now he chose, and on May 30 told Harney he was being unhorsed for a newly created brigadier general of United States Volunteers, "N. Lyon." Blair and Lyon would handle Jackson, Price, and company *their* way.

There was no time to lose. Rural outstate Union men were cowed. Charlton Howe might tell readers that Satan himself was "the first secessionist," but such bravado was galvanizing few to action. Alexandria men happily organized a state guard company, and David Moore dropped by to stand for its captaincy. But they would not buy *that* captain. "Why, this 'nigger lover' would have us shootin' down our Southern neighbors before you could say 'Jack Robinson'," someone jeered. And so Dave Moore went back to Wrightsville and laid aside his old uniform.

Over at Memphis, the seat of Scotland County, insurgents hoisted a rebel flag when the circuit court opened. Judge Thomas S. Richardson liked that. But a gigantic North Carolinian by the name of Ellsberry T. Small did *not*. He rallied a handful of reckless friends to put up Old Glory on the far side of the courthouse square. "Southern men" assembled to tear it down, but the irate giant soon convinced them that someone was likely to die if "the starry emblem of liberty" was touched. Editor Howell sounded an ominous note from Keokuk: "Secessionists will not be allowed, after attacking Union men, to take shelter behind any stupid prattle about 'invasion' or State lines. The people of Iowa will stand by the Union men of Northern Missouri."

Blair and Lyon, preparing the showdown with Jackson, made ready for a test of arms with Price. Through the Committee of Public Safety, they knew the leaders around whom loyal forces could be built outstate. William Bishop, a wealthy Virginian and commodity speculator up at Alexandria, knew his way around the northeastern counties. Out at Edina, Dr. Samuel M. Wirt would do his part in organizing Union strength in Knox. And at Canton, Lewis County, there was an elderly attorney, Stephen W. B. Carnegy, past grand master of Missouri Masons and a Kentuckian so proud of his Scottish forebears that as a surveyor he had given Scotland County its name and awarded the townsite of Edina the classical name of Scotland's capital. Indeed, Knox County owed its name to this white-maned patriarch born in the administration of George Washington.

Lyon offered Bishop on June 6 "power to enlist as many as is thought advisable to serve the Government for as long a period as will be necessary. The enlisted men to keep up a thorough organization for discipline and drill, at the same time to attend to their usual avocations." Four days later the bewhiskered Virginian was in St. Louis, a colonel of United States Volunteers. General Lyon told Bishop to hurry home to organize, equip, and swear into service home guardsmen. Those who enlisted, he vowed, "and *render service* to the General Government, will have a claim against it, and I shall use my endeavors to have provision made for ample remuneration at the earliest period."

Boarding his packet, Bishop pondered where to start. Carnegy would handle Lewis County, and Wirt was his man in Knox. If rebel ruffians did not pick them off, they would do "to tie to." However, Bishop thought, first things first—he would get his friend Dave Moore started. If anybody would respond to his trumpet, it was the Wrightsville superpatriot. In fact, Dave was already sounding out acquaintances, and four dozen were ready.

On Friday, June 14, Moore put on his old uniform of 1847 and rode into Alexandria to take the oath that returned him to duty as a captain of volunteer infantry. His blood was up, and he was prepared for action. The editor of Alexandria's *Delta* produced the handbills, and the captain galloped away to spread his word:

THE UNDERSIGNED IS AUTHORIZED TO RAISE A COMPANY OF VOLUNTEERS IN THIS COUNTY FOR UNION SERVICE. ALL

WHO ARE WILLING TO FIGHT FOR THEIR HOMES, THEIR COUN-
TRY, AND THE FLAG OF OUR GLORIOUS UNION ARE INVITED
TO JOIN HIM, BRINGING WITH THEM THEIR ARMS AND AMMUNI-
TION..UNTIL THE GOVERNMENT CAN AID US, WE MUST TAKE
CARE OF OURSELVES.
SECESSIONISTS AND REBEL TRAITORS DESIRING A FIGHT
CAN BE ACCOMODATED [sic] ON DEMAND.

D. MOORE.

Meanwhile, Lyon was settling accounts with the governor, seeing in
him what the *Gate City* had labeled "a dastardly and pettifogging traitor."
On the evening of June 11, Jackson and Price visited the Planters House
in St. Louis and tried to persuade Lyon to honor the Harney-Price arrangement. "N. Lyon," fierce-eyed and distrustful, rebuffed attempts to "dictate
to my Government in any matter however unimportant" and boldly threatened war if Jackson persisted. The governor and General Price hurried off to
Jefferson City, cutting telegraph lines and burning bridges over the Osage
and Gasconade rivers.

"This means war." Lyon, having tried to tell them, now set forth
to prove his point. On June 13, the trusty German volunteers boarded
river transports for a quick move on the capital. Anticipating them, Jackson issued a call for fifty thousand state guardsmen and left for Boonville,
some forty miles up the Missouri, where several hundred were assembled.
Quincy's *Whig-Republican,* never at a loss for words where Jackson was
concerned, fancied that he was "getting to be rather more of a scoundrel
than his friends can bear." Lyon occupied Jefferson City on June 15 and
marched on Boonville two days later with two thousand Germans. The
ill-trained guardsmen counterattacked, but Lyon made short work of
them. The rebels scattered, and Jackson fled with his pro-Southern legislators toward the southwestern counties bordering Confederate Arkansas.

The witches' brew was spilling into northeastern Missouri. Following
Lyon's lecture to the governor at Planters House, the Sixteenth Illinois
Infantry entered Hannibal to fasten a grip on the Hannibal & St. Joseph
Railroad. The *News* was shut down, its prorebel editor arrested for hailing
the Illinoisans as "this most infamous body of men." Colonel Samuel R.
Curtis' Second Iowa Infantry came next, proof that the federals meant
business. Local secessionists, a contemporary lamented, had done too
much threatening and not enough organizing. Colonel Cyrus Bussey, aide
to Governor Samuel J. Kirkwood of Iowa, wrote to his chief on June 15
that he was certain of "trouble in the northern counties of Missouri, which

may extend to Iowa." Jackson's recent behavior would induce a "more
dangerous and insulting" mood among "traitors" of border areas.

Bishop was learning that "only the truest men and the most fearless"
would make common cause with him. It was a time "when to talk and
act treason was popular." Many were hard put to untangle their emotions
and make a stand. The issue of states' rights had a fascination that men of
today cannot appreciate, and using Missourians for coercion of other Americans had no attraction for hard-working settlers on the prairies of northern
Missouri. Moreover, while rebels were starting "depradations" in many places,
Union men were yet in grave doubt over the Lincoln administration's will
to assert itself. To be sure, these considerations were affected by a hope
that the fighting would go away and leave Missouri alone.

Consequently, most Missourians entered this summer of violence as conditional Union men—or, as some were calling themselves, "conservatives."
They had little enthusiasm for a sudden release of the servile population.
Missouri had had trouble enough getting *into* the Union, wrote Congressman James S. Rollins, "but our calamities will be a thousandfold greater
if we should get out." Some, Charlton Howe among them, were proposing
in early spring a "central Confederacy" of border states to keep the North
and South apart. This proved only an intriguing chimera that later would
haunt its champions. To others grown "Radical" on the sectional issue,
conservatives were "half-and-half" sympathizers with "the Southern side
of every national issue." But this view showed little understanding of the
anguish felt by Conservative-Unionists and voiced by Palmyra's *Spectator:*
"Citizens of Missouri, your position is an embarrassing and fearful one.
You cannot raise your hand against your Southern brethren, for it is unnatural. You cannot raise your hand against your Government, for it is
self destruction. . . . 'Stand still and see the salvation of the Lord.'"

After Moore's little band materialized into a company of fifty-four
guards, Bishop rode away on June 15 to find others worthy of confidence.
That very day, he swore in as captains William Jackson of Waterloo and Thomas
Hughes Roseberry of St. Francisville. Roseberry had lately gained notori-
ety by ripping a rebel bears-and-bars flag off the courthouse at Waterloo
despite the threats of onlookers, and now he was ready to rekindle the
martial fires of his younger days in Pennsylvania, where he had served
as a captain of volunteers in the Mexican War. Dr. Oliver B. Payne, a thirty-
nine-year-old Connecticut Yankee practicing at St. Francisville, thought he
could organize a company, and Bishop swore him in to try it. On June 16
Bishop was at Fairmont, in western Clark County, swearing in Ohio-born
Peter S. Washburn and an upstate New Yorker named Aaron Mattley. Until

recently, Washburn had been a prominent contractor at Cincinnati. Mattley, having delivered the first "unconditional Union" speech in Scotland County during the last election, was confident he could raise a mounted unit in the eastern townships. The next day Bishop was in Alexandria swearing in Henry Putnam Spellman of Warsaw, Illinois, whose later record with the Seventh Missouri Cavalry would win him a major's commission and praise as "every inch a soldier." Out at Luray, one of Bishop's deputies was giving the oath to yet another willing captain, Hartwell Silver.

On June 18, Bishop reached Athens, about twenty miles above Keokuk and just across the Des Moines River from the Lee County, Iowa, town of Croton, a station on the Des Moines Valley Railroad. Here he swore to service a local farmer, Barton P. Hackney, and an earnest young immigrant Ulsterman, James S. Best, then running a forge over at Memphis. Four days later, Daniel F. Hull, a veteran of the Mexican War dreaming of a cavalry career, came in and raised his hand for Colonel Bishop.

Carnegy's prestige was on the line in seething Lewis County, and before the end of June five captains were recruiting. First to organize a company was a bush-bearded Kentuckian, Felix Scott, at the village of Deer Ridge in northwestern Lewis County's "Breckinridge country." At work since early June, Scott won his captaincy by election June 22, and Carnegy was only too happy to ratify. A wealthy farmer, Thomas J. Cochran, and a Methodist Episcopal minister, William B. Moody, sought out loyal men in other rural areas. John F. Grigsby, assisted by Frederick Leeser, agitated among the Germans of La Grange. Charles Yust, a veteran sergeant of the Prussian regular army, organized Germans at Canton.

Carnegy's strong right-hand man was Humphrey Marshall Woodyard, another Kentuckian, lawyer, and Whig of statewide reputation. A pioneer member of the county bar, Woodyard had been a member of the general assembly in 1849-1850. He had proved "Radical" on slavery and secession, and two angry legislators had branded him, Edward Bates, and James Rollins as the truly dangerous free-soilers of Missouri. In 1856, the American (Know-Nothing) party had nominated him for the state public works commission. He lost but prospered as an attorney and real-estate developer. By 1860, he owned more than four thousand acres in Lewis County. So great was Carnegy's esteem for him that Woodyard would soon be a regimental commander of Home Guards.

Wirt, due a colonelcy himself, was busy out at Edina. On June 7, Milton Hendrick of Novelty in southwestern Knox County organized a Unionist rally, at which a Union guard company "formed on the spot." He was, he wrote, "of Southern parentage, and [hoped] to see this Union preserved."

Elias V. Wilson, an Edina lawyer and the son of a Kentucky sheriff, had already started a transition to Republican Radicalism by abandoning the Democracy to vote Constitutional Union in 1860. Now he was raising an Edina legion that would checkmate the state guard unit captained by his partner, John T. Davis. The two companies drilled on the same field at times, without violence but with no end of "jawing." Fears the local Irish would follow their Democratic voting habits into the rebel camp proved groundless, probably because of Father Bernard McMenomy of St. Joseph's Church. From the onset of the crisis, he had set his face against any truck with slavocracy—and parishioners drew their own conclusions.

Two companies formed in northern Knox County under Wirt's auspices. On June 5, a secret meeting of Union men was held at Millport, up on the middle fork of the Fabius, and the *Herald* pouted that nobody else was "permitted to know of it until it was past." This was the work of a forty-eight-year-old farmer, Nicholas W. Murrow, who had come from Kentucky more than twenty years before. Within a few weeks, he would present Wirt a company of Knox County guards. Around Colony, to the east of Millport, Benjamin F. Northcutt, a Kentuckian residing in Missouri since boyhood, was putting together another guard unit. Working the northwestern townships was Gilbert E. Murray, who had sold his store at Quincy in 1855 to farm at Greensburg. By mid-July, Wirt would be able to show Bishop encouraging results.

Up in Scotland County, Jim Best and Aaron Mattley were inspiring others. Thomas McAllister, a farmer, was organizing, as was William Harle, a prominent merchant of Memphis. In the southwestern part of the county, another unit came into being under a miller on the Fabius, Simon Pearce, handsome native of Mansfield, Ohio, with relatives along the Knox-Scotland line. Ellsberry Small was also scouting for followers, in the southern parts of the county.

By late June, Bishop had a three-thousand-man guard, but he could entertain few illusions that it was yet much of an army. Nor could he delude himself that pure patriotism was bringing these men to the colors. The plain truth was that most were escaping the terror by banding together, and the flag-waving patriotism would only come with experience in fighting and marching. Would these guardsmen be enough to intimidate terrorists and guerrillas? Time would tell. In any case, short on experience and dependable firearms, they would need a lot of training and equipping. Some were Mexican War veterans and, much less importantly, alumni of various state militias required by Congress since 1792 but long since degenerated in many places to social organizations. Dan Hull, with twenty

revolvers, rifles, and shotguns in a company of forty-two horsemen, leveled a written demand for regulation arms before the rebels could exploit
his situation: "If wee had armes I think it would hav an attendency to do
the cose a gradeel of [good]. They ar makeing many hard thretts, &c. . . .
sens they hav armes and wee hav not."

Like most other Americans, these Missourians were incapable of Old
World reverence for military usages. They preferred going to war part-
time—and on horseback. Oaths of enlistment weighed lightly; of the fifty-
five vowing to stand with Milton Hendrick in defense of home and country
in June, only eight could be accounted for upon disbandment in September. Some had fled the state with their families and portable possessions;
some had simply "relieved themselves from duty"; others had blithely
enlisted elsewhere as fancies shifted. Like other Americans, they cherished
a jack-of-all-trades assumption that leadership traits displayed in civil life
could transplant easily to the military. After all, their heroes were not professionals but amateurs like Washington, Jackson, Mad Anthony Wayne,
and John C. Frémont.

Political arguments ranged on in the northeastern counties, as rebel
agitators carried on their propaganda to persuade "conservatives" that
the "Lincoln gang" had neither the will nor means to defend its partisans.
The patrol on the Hannibal & St. Joseph they discounted as a nuisance
operation, and Union men could not blink the fact that pleas for weaponry were too often answered with federal exhortations to "arm yourselves."
Some comfort! Barton Hackney, once sworn in, could find but 28
guns among his 105 men. A St. Louis newspaper felt the time near when
Jackson's minions would have "a favorable opportunity to commence an
indiscriminate rout, or slaughter, of all opposed to their infamous plots
and traitorous purposes."

Enrolled as a private with Hackney was the Reverend John H. Cox,
Methodist Episcopal pastor at Chambersburg. It is improbable that men
of the "Prairie Home Guard" foresaw the likelihood that this lean and
homely but intense circuit rider would soon be hailed publicly by Dr.
Elliott as a "noble young preacher" and leave an indelible mark on the
religious, military, and political history of Missouri. Whether he would
have cut such a swath through the Civil War turmoil if his disaffected
neighbors had shown him more respect, no one can know. However,
many Methodists and other local folk worked up a perfect horror at
Brother Cox's "abolitionism" and harping on "disloyalty" in "M. E.
South" ranks. To his way of thinking, *those* Methodists would have
been right at home "with Judas." Born in Virginia in 1833, he had

learned the printer's trade at South Bend, Indiana, working as a teen-
ager for Schuyler Colfax, destined for national prominence as U. S.
Grant's Vice-President. Before Cox was twenty-three, he was ordained
to the "northern" Methodist ministry by Bishop Thomas A. Morris.
After two years in Indiana, Cox entered the Missouri-Arkansas conference in 1860. The next year, he began work in Clark County, where
furious neighbors were soon spreading word that "if I attempt to preach
again, they will take me out and attend to my case." Well, Cox decided,
after the mobocrats were subdued, he *would* preach, "for I was sent here
by the Lord and Bishop Morris to preach the Gospel and by the grace of
God and Colt's arguments I'll try to fill the bill." He would indeed, and
Hackney would have a first sergeantcy for an educated young man with
such spirit.

A most inviting feature of volunteer companies was the fellowship
they afforded with familiar creatures. In Washburn's outfit, for example,
were most of the able-bodied men at Fairmont. There were the Webers,
headed by First Sergeant Daniel Weber, Sergeant Leroy, and brothers
Thomas, Dudley, and Edmund. The captain himself enlisted his wife's
young brother, Wilbur F. Davis, and his own elder son, Marion. He also
had a restless fourteen-year-old son, George Putnam Washburn, who
could not see staying on the farm with a stepmother when there was
going to be such excitement where his father went. Washburn understood this and permitted the lad to come along as general roustabout.

Other youths with interesting backgrounds and potentialities were
entering Bishop's swelling ranks. Best's younger brother Joseph signed
on with him, scarcely dreaming that his casual enrollment would lead
the thin and serious boy to a colonelcy in four years. Brought to America as a baby, Joseph had been educated at Quincy and had become a
bricklayer. He joined his widowed mother and two older brothers at
Memphis in 1859. A thirty-three-year-old native of Lincolnshire, England,
William French, joined Captain Jackson at formation of the Kahoka Home
Guards. Married to a woman from the Old Country, French had been farming near Athens in recent years. In time, the young Briton would be Moore's
orderly.

With June fading into July, sentiment grew among Bishop's captains
to form a regiment of Scotland and Clark County companies. To that
end, troops raised by Moore, Silver, Hackney, Jackson, Washburn, Payne,
Roseberry, Hull, Mattley, Spellman, Best, Small, and Harle assembled at
Kahoka, in the heart of Clark County, Thursday morning, July 4. Such
a gala Fourth the little town had never seen in its square! Festivities began

in midmorning with a demonstration drill by several outfits under Hackney's direction. After a picnic lunch, a drum and bugle corps played patriotic airs. The musicians were mostly young men of the Roseberry family, sons of Captain Tom and his brother John, who had both come out in the 1850s and become leading farmers. Young Thomas Hughes Roseberry, the captain's nephew known as "Hughes," led the group, which included his brother James and their cousins Matthias and Rees.

The rest of the day was given over to a "speaking." Hackney and Moore spoke in turn. Other addresses, equally unconditional in tone, were given by a young attorney from Athens, Hiram Hiller, and by the Methodist Protestant pastor from Winchester, in the lower part of the county, Charles Stuart Callihan. The latter made a special impression; although he was from an old Virginia slaveholding family, he was a devotee of Frederick Douglass, apostle of Afro-American freedom. Perhaps of more interest now was Callihan's reminder that he had once been a West Point cadet. Folklore has it that he claimed to be a graduate, but the truth is that he dropped out before his class of 1841 graduated (a French course was the root of his trouble).

Climaxing the program was a caucus of captains to choose field officers for the regiment. David McKee of Athens, thirty-eight, second lieutenant of Hull's company, emerged as major, provoking Hull's refusal to continue as company commander. "We're not legally organized," he spluttered; what he meant was that it had taken loads of gall for those fellows to pass over Dan Hull and elect a lieutenant. The captains bestowed the lieutenant colonelcy on Callihan. For the colonelcy there was a brief holding action by supporters of Bishop, but they lost to the merchant of Wrightsville. "D. Moore, Union" could embroider silver eagles on those shoulder straps now, but it would be up to Bishop to persuade state or federal authorities to make it all "regular." It was only a home guard colonelcy that came this day to Moore, but it was a sweeter prize than the lost captaincy of Alexandria Secesh.

Before calling it a day, Colonel Moore announced other appointments. Sylvanus Hicks, second-in-command of the Wrightsville Guard, became adjutant of the "First Northeast Missouri Home Guards." Emery P. Slate, a Waterloo farmer of Massachusetts lineage, accepted the quartermaster's post. Dr. Wilfred M. Wiley of Edina assumed the duties of surgeon, with Dr. Andrew Clark of Kahoka as his assistant. Ultimately casting a greater shadow than all of these was the original quartermaster sergeant, Aaron Ward Harlan. This goateed patriarch from Croton had joined Captain Joseph T. Farris' Croton Guards after spring planting. Born in 1811 on the White River in eastern Indiana, he had been in Lee County since 1834 and had captained the first steamboat up the Des Moines to Keosauqua in 1837. During the spring and summer of 1850, he had gone with a party of prospectors across the Rockies to the Nevada gold fields. He was farming on both sides of the Des Moines around Athens and Croton, and it attests to his civic prominence that this remarkable Hoosier had named Sweet Home Township, in which Athens lies. Poet, farmer, boatman, prospector, historian—he savored life to the full.

They had a different kind of Fourth of July down at Canton, carried by Breckinridge in 1860 and living up to a reputation as "a hard secession hole." Here was a concentration of Union Home Guards put together by Carnegy, including two companies raised north of town by Captain John Howell. Tempers exploded on this day, and a wave of rioting erupted. A rebel hotelkeeper shot and killed Howell, and his terrified followers ran for cover. Former United States Senator James S. Green of Canton, "leaning secesh" a little too loudly for his own good, took off for the countryside during the night when word came that Colonel John M. Palmer's Fourteenth Illinois Infantry was crossing over from Quincy to crack down on the rebellious elements around Canton.

Fleeing into the brush country along the North Fabius above Monticello was the Senator's older brother, County Judge Martin E. Green. Since early June, he had been organizing a state guard company for Governor Jackson. Hearing of Palmer's approach, he concluded the time for action had come and repaired to his Horseshoe Bend camp. Moore said years later that Green "was not a brilliant man like his brother, but was regarded as a very worthy citizen. . . . He had no knowledge of military tactics or evolutions." Green and Moore would soon get to know each other—and the people of Illinois, Iowa, and Missouri would remember them both for a long time.

With widespread popular anticipation that the war would prove a brief affair and cause no lasting scars, Lincoln and Davis strove to prepare for the test. Both had to build armies virtually from scratch, inheriting fragments of the minuscule regular army. Strategies had to be fashioned. Lieutenant General Winfield Scott, a relic of the War of 1812 now commanding the United States Army, preferred a strategy of safeguarding Washington, D.C., blockading the Confederacy, and building Union strength for drives aimed at splitting the Confederacy in pieces. Davis, conversely, trusted that the hemisphere's newest republic could with a strategy of "repulse and riposte" wear down Yankee determination and compel Washington to let the South go. To this end, Davis ordered a strong concentration in northern Virginia near Manassas Junction. To Lincoln's circle, this force was a threat to Washington, and Yankee newsmen howled louder each passing week for a victorious march to "squelch out" the "rebellion." Brigadier General Irvin McDowell assembled a collection of regulars and short-term volunteers north of Manassas to see what he could do for Lincoln and the editors.

2

Boldness in the Day of Judgment

Governor Jackson's flight had left a vacuum, and it was time to decide
if Missourians would pass under military rule or pretend Jackson was still
there. Creation of a provisional administration proved a more attractive,
if compromise, alternative. After heated debate, the convention dumped
the old regime on July 30 by a vote of 56 to 25. Among stargazers trusting
the governor to come back and behave was Emilius K. Sayre of Monticello
a New Jersey-born lawyer opposed to "the use of force to set the slaves
free." Indeed, Sayre and his comrades from the northeast, Henry M. Gorin
of Memphis and Nathaniel F. Givens of Waterloo, took unyielding positions
on the Southern side of issues before them. But their protests availed them
little. The provisional government, wrote William E. Parrish, "constituted
a unique experiment, the only government in the entire history of the
United States to be established by a convention legally in existence for
an entirely different purpose."

On July 31, the convention called to the governorship a conservative
old Whig, Hamilton R. Gamble. Born and educated in Virginia, he had
practiced law in St. Louis since the 1820s. Brother-in-law of Lincoln's
Attorney General Bates, he had been chief justice of Democratic Missouri
in the 1850s. Now sixty-three and frail in health, he was emerging into a
political arena he had generally shunned, and he would find the challenge
of his life in this struggle to vindicate Missouri's sovereignty against both
Lincoln and Davis while soothing passions endangering public peace.

News reached St. Louis on July 25 that the army had named Illinois
and the region between the Rockies and the Mississippi as the Western
Department. Chosen to head it was the legendary path-finder of the
West, Frémont. Missouri's Conservatives, fearful of Lyon's radical zeal,
had engineered the move. Frémont seemed to possess ideal qualifications.
Besides his western expeditions, he had been the Republican presidential
candidate in 1856; in short, he was a big name, whose coming signified
Lincoln's concern for Missouri's internal struggle. Indeed, the new "major

general commanding" was the son-in-law of Missouri's ex-Senator Thomas Hart Benton.

Frémont secured the Joshua Brant mansion on Chouteau Avenue for his headquarters, staffing it with an exotic set of swashbuckling figures with "outlandish" names and uniforms. It did not take him long to start coordinated efforts to check the rebel threat. On July 29, Brigadier General John Pope organized the District of North Missouri, embracing the right-of-way of the Hannibal & St. Joseph Railroad. Brigadier General Stephen A. Hurlbut, an Illinois lawyer, came in to command three Illinois regiments detailed to hold the railway.

Nathaniel Lyon's entry into Springfield on July 13 was almost overlooked in the discouragement seeping westward in the last days of July. The battle of Bull Run on July 21 ended in a dismaying defeat for McDowell's attempt to lower the boom on secessionists congregating in northern Virginia. Conservative hopes for reconciliation or, at worst, a short war to restore order were dashed in the dust. McAnally's *St. Louis Christian Advocate* recklessly hailed the news as "thrilling and important," and another journalist sensed the mood gripping the North: "On every brow sits sullen, scorching, black despair."

On July 15, Carnegy turned over to Woodyard the rolls of his "Lewis County Home Guard," four companies aggregating some three hundred men. At his age, Carnegy preferred to yield the colonelcy to his younger colleague. Appointed as lieutenant colonel to Woodyard was Barnabus B. King of Canton, Carnegy's son-in-law. New Jersey-born Barney, now forty, had in his youth operated the first ferry on the Mississippi at the Marion City settlement above Hannibal and had served as the Whig sheriff of Marion County. He had been a commission merchant in Canton in recent years. Woodyard's battalion had an interesting composition. The companies of Captains Cochran and Scott were "native American" in origin, but the other two were less so. The Reverend Mr. Moody found it difficult to get much of a native company at Williamstown, and Grigsby, working around La Grange, found himself captain of a unit fully a third German. These forces merged under Grigsby. Captain Yust encountered no difficulty at Canton in raising a company almost wholly German, except for two lads named Kelly and Wesley.

Among the young men enlisting was a tough farmer in Cochran's company, Asa D. Starkweather of Canton, who hailed from New York. He joined as a buck private, but was destined for prominence, some of it unwelcome. A Chicago newsman reported on August 6 that he had been hanged by Green's men. For a man with nearly forty years to live, this was a trifle "previous."

Yust, the old Prussian *feldwebel*, whose name had been "Just" until he entered English-speaking society, took into his company his brother Frederick and the latter's son Frederick Junior. Young Fred, like many of the others, had been born in Gräfenhainichen, near Wittenberg. When he was eleven, in 1855, his family had followed "Uncle Karl" and his people to New York and preceded them to Canton. Enlisting with Fred was another boy his age, Louis F. Koch, a Württemberger soon picked by Woodyard to be his orderly.

Assisting Grigsby with the La Grange Germans was a gray-eyed teamster, Frederick Leeser. The thirty-four-year-old Waldecker became Grigsby's second-in-command and later succeeded him to the captaincy. Privates under them included John and Henry Klusmeier, sons of a Prussian *soldat* in the last campaign against Bonaparte. Henry was only sixteen, but the Klusmeiers shielded Woodyard from the unwelcome news. Older than the Klusmeiers was a Swiss-born drummer, Stephan Werly, born July 4, 1824, and proud of his birthday throughout his adult life. "Converted" by Brother Jakobi at Quincy in 1849, Werly was intensely religious. A granddaughter later said of this patriotic Republican Methodist that he was a "man of few doubts."

The Knox County Home Guards took shape as the various captains finished their companies. Hendrick's Novelty Guard swore in July 15 at Edina, as did Vick Wilson's men. Murrow's Millport Guard was sworn in by Northcutt July 15, and Northcutt's men took the oath July 24. As the guardsmen concentrated at Edina, they were joined by a company under Captain Murray of Greensburg. (It is impossible to know the size of Murray's force or the date of its formation, as he died before he could make official rolls.)

On July 2, there rode into Alexandria a prosperous farmer from Willmathsville, in Adair County. Joseph Story, grandson of a Revolutionary War soldier of Scottish birth, was native to New Jersey. He had come west in the 1840s with his brother Alfred's family. Joseph himself had gone over to Jersey County, Illinois, where he enlisted in Company I, First Illinois Volunteers, in 1846. After his return from service, he married an Illinois woman of Southern parentage and moved out to Willmathsville. He was anxious for duty again, and Bishop was ready to accommodate him. Four days later, Captain Story gave the oath to his lieutenants, Lucius D. Woodruff and Edward Fox, and to thirty-two enlisted men, including First Sergeant Jeremy Hall, husband of his niece Victoria. The little company was very much a Willmathsville affair, and Story proudly reported it for duty at Edina two weeks later.

At his Kahoka encampment, Moore struggled with twin frustrations.

Men available far outnumbered weapons, and the variety of guns on hand made it unthinkable to depend upon military sources for munitions. What Moore thought he needed was five hundred of those "caliber .58" Springfields, rifled muskets then in use by the regulars. Dave's other problem was his "Bishop faction," headed by Major McKee and Captain Spellman, ever willing to snipe at his authority. Not only did this clique challenge Moore, but it found added grist for its mill in a scandalous rumor, soon proved true, that the Colonel's older sons Bill and Gene had gone off to Horseshoe Bend! Was Moore not the man who had offered to command that secesh outfit at Alexandria? Was he not the husband of a secesh wife? Could he be depended upon under fire?

The colonel was neither deaf nor blind, however, and about July 10 he killed two birds with one stone. David McKee and Henry Spellman suddenly learned they were members of a delegation to go *away* to St. Louis to seek the muskets Moore wanted.

McKee arranged to "stay gone," for Bishop was organizing his own "Black Hawk Cavalry" and needed recruiters. Spellman, however, came back on July 17—with 250 rifles. Bishop, on grand jury duty in St. Louis, helped arrange for the guns and for rations and clothing to come later by rail to Croton. They could not get Moore ready for action too soon, for the *Gate City* was convinced that the secesh of northeastern Missouri were "busy as the devil in a thunderstorm."

Moore was soon ready. Messengers rode to Keokuk and Quincy for reinforcements. Hurlbut, then at Quincy, authorized Captain George W. Coster's "Warsaw Greys," a small company of infantry, to go to Kahoka July 20 for action with Moore. Similar help came from the Keosauqua and Croton Guards after Moore appealed to Governor Kirkwood to "pleas scend 500 men armed and Equipt with two Days rasions to cooporate with my Reg home gards. I hope they will march amediately."

Meanwhile, at Horseshoe Bend, a thousand mounted state guardsmen were also about ready. In mid-July they elected Green as their colonel, with Joseph C. Porter his lieutenant colonel. Near Etna, in eastern Scotland County, Benjamin W. Shacklett had a thriving camp of rebels putting the fear of Jeff Davis into local farm families, and it was thought politic to elect him major of Green's legion. Porter was farming near Newark, and Shacklett was a slaveholding Kentuckian prominent in Scotland County since 1853. Green was acutely aware that time was on the Yankee side. As Richard S. Brownlee has said, in his *Gray Ghosts of the Confederacy,* "General Lyon's strategy paralyzed State Guard recruiting. Many State Guard companies . . . in north Missouri were stranded."

Moore was feeling a bit stranded himself. Provisions and munitions would be coming up to Croton very soon, he heard, and it made sense to retire on the village of Athens to be as close as possible to Croton. But dare he turn his back on rebels at Etna, fourteen miles to his west? Scouts were bringing reports of a mounted troop under Shacklett and a "secession flag" atop the "Liberty Pole" at Keller's tavern.

The Greys came in from Warsaw, under an impression that theirs was a defensive mission. Before daybreak Sunday, they beheld the entire camp bestirring itself. That the Sabbath was for resting just never occurred to Moore. Shortly, the First Northeast Missouri was on the march, five hundred strong, with Captain William McKee's horsemen and the Greys leading. When they reached Etna late in the afternoon, McKee saw Shacklett's riders. Moore gave the order to charge, and the guardsmen rushed in, McKee to the front. The rebels were unnerved. "After delivering one volley they fled," Farris reported. No one was hit on Moore's side, for the defenders had fired too high. One of Shacklett's men, seriously wounded, died in the tavern after dark. Several prisoners were taken to the colonel and ordered held.

News of Moore's bold thrust electrified Union men of the region. The *Gate City* "discovered" the colonel, and thereafter its columns were filled with news about him. A German paper in St. Louis reported with enthusiasm that his troops *"griffen das Rebellenlager an, . . . und trieben die Secessionisten auseinander* [seized the Rebel camp and scattered the Secessionists]."

Now the guardsmen could retire on Athens without fear of harassment, and they began the twenty-mile trek across Clark County. There was plenty of work for mounted pickets under McKee, Spellman, and Harle. One of McKee's men, young Frenchman Joseph Grade, told of the "hard and hazardous" scouting done by Moore's riders, "practically without any equipage, no tents, no blankets and no means of going from place to place, only as provided by ourselves." Until August, the men subsisted on "such as we could pick up by foraging in a country where we knew not if we were surrounded by friends or enemies."

Pickets rustled up no end of frightening reports. At Nick Conkle's, in the Little Fox bottoms north of Luray, some of them jumped a squad of secesh, killed four or five, and suffered one minor wound in the fracas. Other scouts brought rumors that Green was on the move, north to Luray. There arose in the colonel's mind the spectre of a rebel pincers from the southwest and northwest corners of the county—closing in on the rear of his column. His answer was to post a three-hundred-man detachment under Callihan, including horsemen and Peter Washburn's infantry, at Luray to cover the rear. After camping overnight at Luray, the main body proceeded on to Athens.

When Moore reached Athens, Captain Farris reported, "All the rebels that had not fled previously were arrested." Moore apparently "confiscated everything he might need in the way of food, clothing, forage for horses, and shelter for his troops. He, as far as possible, . . . discommoded the Southern sympathizers first," and there were "far more of these in the Athens vicinity than pro-unionists." W. H. Spurgeon got sad news that his long brick drygoods store would be a military hospital. Former County Judge William Baker's home, Widow Jane Gray's farm at the south edge of town, and various other residences were also commandeered for billets.

Successful though Moore might be at confiscating private foodstuffs, there was need for substantial purchases through commercial channels. Slate rode up to Farmington, a few miles up the river from Athens, and negotiated purchase of nearly seven tons of ham and pork shoulders, for which department headquarters received a bill for $524.20. The happy proprietors of the Shreve & Scott commission firm also became regular suppliers of produce and clothing for Moore's hospital.

Moore decided to stir up the Keokuk fellows a bit more. He wrote to the Committee of Public Safety July 23 to demand reinforcements from the local militia: "We must have them. . . . Our men are worn out. We have marched forced marches for three days. We ask much of you. Our cause is the same. My men are destitute. Can you send me 200 blankets and some bread or crackers? . . . We have just received a despatch from Memphis, they have a force of 1,000 men at that point. We can take them with 700 men. Send us one piece of artillery."

There was friction aplenty as the Athenians adjusted to the loyalist roughnecks quartered on them. The squad at Baker's house ransacked it, but the host kept his tongue and therewith his life. A guardsman at Widow Gray's discovered the "Sunday suit" belonging to Barney, her elderly house servant. "Such an outcry!" the widow's niece recalled. "I fancy Barney had an inkling that he was what the fight was all about and felt safe in raising hail Columbia." The widow squawked to Colonel Moore, who decided things in Barney's favor as soon as the culprit could be corraled. "Use your own clothes!" he scolded, confident the army would send more suitable garments anyhow.

The Keokuk committee appealed to Governor Kirkwood for arms and troops to sustain Union men on the Missouri border, but the governor was unable to offer immediate aid. Colonel Bussey, learning at his home in

Bloomfield that Frémont was in St. Louis, resolved to go "immediately to lay the facts before General Frémont, and to ask him for arms to arm a force large enough to meet Green."

Before Bussey could reach Frémont, Green moved out from Horseshoe Bend. Early on July 30, his mounted state guards cantered westward, and wild rumors of his coming spread across Knox County. A quick huddle of Wirt's officers took place, and a "Knox County Guard Regiment" resulted. The captains chose Wilson as "colonel," Murray as "major." And then they formed on Troublesome Creek, three miles east of Edina.

It was about dark when Green's force reached the creek, and several volleys were exchanged. Colonel Wilson took counsel with his officers. Advised to retreat, he led the group in a hasty flight forty miles south to Macon City, on the railroad and under Colonel Palmer's protecting guns. Two years later, sensitive to widespread ridicule, Wilson tried to unload the blame on a dead man, Gilbert Murray. Unfortunately for Wilson's imputation, it was known that Murray declined to have any part in the retreat and marched off to Canton for service with Woodyard, while Joe Story and his boys stomped back to Willmathsville "madder'n hornets." They were dressed up for a fight, not what happened on Troublesome Creek.

Secessionists of Edina welcomed the state guard the morning of July 31. Iowans now grew fearful of Green's designs, suddenly recalling that Croton had been a station of the "underground railroad" for fugitive black Missourians, and remembering dire threats from aggrieved slaveowners. Would the valley of the Des Moines now be ravaged by Confederate foragers? Some contemporaries were sure he was mainly out to "get Dave Moore" or Moore's supplies, while others held that the powder and lead stored at Keokuk were the principal attractions. A young attorney wrote that in Keokuk Green's foray "was believed to be, primarily, to defeat and disperse Moore's command and thus establish the supremacy of the rebel cause in that portion of northern Missouri, and secondarily, to cross the Des Moines River, invade Iowa, and capture the supplies then stored at Croton."

Southern men at Athens were also taking alarm at the prospect of violence. On July 25, a deputation met with Moore at Joseph Benning's house to implore the colonel to "stack arms" and thus earn the community's gratitude for averting "an effusion of blood." They argued that if the home guards would lay those guns away, Green's men would be morally obligated to do the same.

Moore cut them off with a rejoinder that "if Mart Green desires to

avoid the shedding of blood, he had better keep his men beyond the
range of my muskets!" A reporter had written him down as "a rough,
not over bright, but withal a well-meaning and brave old soldier." Moore
may not have been an intellectual, but horse sense told him that "peace"
purchased through unilateral disarmament could be an intolerable travesty.
Many of the men, however, failed to share their commander's sense of
urgency, and some captains permitted them to go home on weekends.

Cyrus Bussey, combining gall with luck, intervened to buttress Moore
with material aid. Toward midmorning on July 30, he met with Frémont
and asked for rifles to accommodate the Missourians and the border militia.
Frémont could not "spare one gun." Bussey then asked for fifty thousand
rounds of .58 ammunition, on hand at the arsenal—and shipped up the
river that very night. Before leaving, Bussey reminded Frémont that Colonel William H. Worthington's Fifth Iowa Infantry and Colonel C. D. Mc-
Dowell's Sixth Iowa were at Burlington. In his view, Iowa would be a lot
"safer" if they were moved to Keokuk. Frémont gave him orders to move
them if he wished.

In the early afternoon of August 2, making rounds in Keokuk, Bussey
learned that a thousand Springfield muskets had just arrived on a Rock
Island freight. They were consigned to Colonel Grenville M. Dodge's
Fourth Iowa, forming out west at Council Bluffs. Here were the desperately needed weapons! Unfortunately, they were legally beyond his grasp,
but Bussey "at once decided to seize these arms, and use them to arm the
people for their own protection." After all, rebels were thicker around
here than at Council Bluffs.

Such short-stopping made no comrade of Dodge, and even Kirkwood
frosted over until explanations cleared the air. Loading the muskets on a
special train, Bussey headed up the Des Moines valley to share them. Two
hundred guns went to Captain Hugh W. Sample's mounted "Keokuk Rangers" and William W. Belknap's "City Rifles," two hundred to Dave Moore
at Croton, and the rest to militia companies up the Des Moines. The cause
might yet fail, but Bussey was doing his best.

As hysteria and violence mounted in the countryside around Athens,
David Moore kept up his guard. On August 2, Green issued at Edina a
proclamation of amnesty to all men submitting to the "*lawful militia* of
Missouri." Then his force rode off the next morning for Scotland County.
Passing over the Middle Fabius below Millport, Green moved through
Etna to the Wyaconda. Meanwhile, rations and clothing promised Moore
had arrived in Croton, thirty-five tons in all. Farris posted a watch over
the goods as well as an assortment of "rebels" Moore was keeping in cus-

tody. Callihan's detachment had rejoined from Luray. Civil War was coming with a vengeance to Clark County.

On Sunday, August 4, the rebel host forded the Wyaconda and passed through Luray to bivouac on the Fox near Chambersburg, seven miles from Athens. Informants estimated Green's strength as high as four thousand. On Sunday night, a young son of the Reverend Jabez Harrison, chaplain to Moore, brought word that an assault on Moore's camp was impending. A farm wife down by Belfast, Iowa, wrote her father that "the secessionists kept sending word for several days that they were coming to Athens for dinner on the 5th." Sensing fire in all this smoke, Moore on Sunday night ordered out Harle's mounted pickets to patrol the Fox.

Given the presumed vastness of the rebel horde, Moore sent to Keokuk for help. John M. Hiller, his judge advocate, took a handcar from Croton and was in the Gate City before 9:00 P.M., but, said Hiller, "as they had been alarmed frequently on false reports succeeded only in getting some 75 or 80 men," in Sample's City Rangers and Belknap's City Rifles. They were at Croton by midnight, but the captains were afflicted with "states' rights" and "would not pass over the river." Other militiamen were alerted at Farmington and Keosauqua.

It was not quite 5:00 A.M. when Harle rode in with news that "Green could be upon us in fifteen minutes." Drummers sounded the "long roll," and the First Northeast Missouri Home Guards rose to early reveille. Cooks started preparing flapjacks and coffee, and some breakfasts were indeed eaten. Joseph McGowan, Best's teamster, got orders to take the sick and injured across the river to Croton. The Des Moines was very low this hot and dry summer, so fording was no great problem.

Toward 5:30, the state guards appeared on the bluff, a small flank force north of town and a larger one under Shacklett coming up below the cemetery ridge toward WidowGray's. Moore promptly redeployed to meet them. Hackney moved off toward Stallion Branch, in the brush and woods north of town. Callihan took charge of the left flank, leading Small's infantry and Spellman's riders down to the widow's cornfield. James Kneisley, postmaster at Palmyra until a German Republican got his job, parked his artillery battery on the cemetery ridge to command the main road. It was a nondescript outfit, including a nine-pounder and six-pounder poured at Hannibal, and a hollowed log. Kneisley had a little "solid shot," but his men had spent the night at a Chambersburg blacksmith shop breaking chains and bolts for scattershot.

Unknown to the guardsmen, the Confederates were on the verge of panic. Green had not, said a follower, expected to find Moore here. The last thing he wanted was to take his undisciplined mob into a pitched battle with Moore. Bill and Gene had warned rebel brass of their father's ferocity, I. M. Walters said, and when Green found him before Athens, "it caused considerable consternation. We knew he would fight and that his men had better arms." Yet, the rebel leaders felt incapable of evading the collision, convinced "a retreat without an effort" would have wrecked state guard morale.

Pacing up and down his line of battle, Moore told Payne to take a squad of McKee's horsemen and his own for a last-minute look at the enemy deployment. But when these scouts saw Kneisley's battery, Payne ordered a retreat. Back down the road they came, and, as one of Best's disgusted riflemen said later, "quietly rode past our line, down the hill and across the river, many of them never to come back." This performance must have affected many a soldier in the line, for one called out to Moore: "Colonel, I can't stand it. I've got to go!" Snarled Moore, "Damn it! you've *got* to stand it!" To another lad worried over that rebel artillery, the colonel was heard to scoff: "Say, whoever heard of anybody being killed by a cannon!"

Keokuk had spent the night in an uproar. A messenger raced in at dawn with news that an attack on Athens was about to start. Colonel Worthington deemed it urgent to get help to the threatened point and forthwith ordered the Sixth Iowa to the scene. "We swallowed our breakfast as quick as we could," wrote one of McDowell's men, "and marched down to headquarters to get a musket and cartridge box apiece." The Committee of Public Safety decided to send Dave Moore a six-pound brass cannon and a consignment of powder and shells. By 8 o'clock, the men and munitions were ready to leave.

Long before the Sixth Iowa cleared the railway yards, action had started at Athens. Green's opening artillery shot came about 5:30; it went over the heads of the defenders, cleared the river, and wrecked the Croton railroad station. Another shot, wide instead of high, struck the Benning house, entering next to the door-casing and whizzing through a kitchen wall before dropping into the Des Moines. The "log cannon" promptly flew to pieces at the first attempt to scatter "shrapnel" over Spring Street. Kneisley's battery needed practice, but it was making authentic battlefield noises.

Small-arms firing spread from the center of the opposing lines out to the flanks. Up in the woods to the north, Hackney's men drove the rebels back from Stallion Branch. It was different, however, down in Gray's cornfield, when Callihan beheld Shacklett's line. "Come on, men!" he yelled, whirling his horse around toward the river. "We'll never stop 'em!" And he spurred his mount toward the ford, with Spellman's riders charging in be-

hind him. To the southeast they thundered, into Lee County, and were
soon lost to sight.

As Moore said later quite pointedly, "Captain Small and his men stood
just where they were posted." By this time, the City Rifles had come down
to the opposite bank and begun to fire a few rounds at the cornfield. The
stationmaster at Croton, however, thought Belknap's men were "making
no great effort to 'reinforce'—just sniping a little from behind trees on
the opposite side of the river." But it was soon evident to Moore that his
flanks would hold.

Before long, the Confederate lines began to ravel. Shacklett suffered a
severe neck wound, and his demoralized men fell back in confusion. It
seemed to Moore the time to wind things up had come. He passed orders
down the line to fix bayonets. Then came the command in that bullhorn
voice the boys would never forget: "Forward! Charge! Bayonets!"

Up Thome Street, across yards and gardens they came. Green's line began to waver. Kneisley's battery hauled its two remaining guns frantically
out of sight and took off for the Fox River. Seeing the disorder, the home
guards decided to rush the rebels despite Moore's orders to hold to common
time. The Confederates bolted for the rear, so panic stricken that many fled
without their horses. A general retreat developed, but the victorious Unionists, short of cavalry, only pursued for a mile or so. It had taken Martin
Green a week to get to Athens, Dave Moore less than two hours to turn
him around.

Lending a comic note was the experience of the Sixth Iowa on its way
to the rescue. "When we had got about half way there," a soldier wrote,
"we met a couple of horsemen coming full speed for help. They told us
for god's sake to hurry up, that the Union men were almost surrounded."
Officers interrogating civilians south of Croton found it "difficult to obtain intelligent or reliable information from them, but all agreed that the
Union forces were being . . . cut all to pieces." One of Belknap's men, coming up tardily with the Sixth Iowa, arrived certain that "the whole country
around Croton and Athens [was] dripping with gore and that the grass
and woods were full of dead men." Callihan's hysterical warnings that
Dave Moore had "sold out to the traitors" were heard all the way across
Lee County as far as Montrose, on the Mississippi, before noon, and the
Iowa volunteers had little hope of finding anything at Athens save a
ghastly slaughter pen.

"Rescuers" crossing the Des Moines now learned that the dreaded rebel
host was a fugitive mob. One of Moore's hands thought it "hardly necessary
to add that the Colonel's bravery and loyalty were never questioned after

that day." The famished victors were soon "feasting on the meats, chickens, pies, and cakes" that local sympathizers had intended for Green's men. Cyrus Bussey, arriving at Croton around 10:00, ordered the Fifth and Sixth Iowa to assist Moore's pursuit. After a sortie toward Luray, the Iowans returned Tuesday evening to board a train for Keokuk. Though Bussey and others around him tried for years to claim credit for the victory at Athens, a Chicago reporter in the area concluded that "the Union Home Guards of Clark and Scotland Counties, almost unaided, put to flight the combined secession forces of half a dozen counties and, for the present at least, hold the complete ascendancy."

The casualty toll suggested no decisive engagement. Moore figured Green's losses at thirty-one killed and wounded, his own at twenty-three. Three Union men were dead. First to die was an elderly onlooker, William C. Sullivan, a veteran of the War of 1812. Jabez Harrison, dismounting to help him, was struck in the mouth by a musket ball and perished soon afterward. One of Spellman's men, William Sprouse, wounded in the flight across the river, died in a first-aid station at Croton after the battle ended.

In the absence of the regular surgeons, Dr. William Aylward of Memphis treated the wounded of both sides in Spurgeon's drygoods store. Among these were six of Roseberry's men, First Sergeant George W. Newmyer and Privates Andrew Fogleman, Matthew Woodruff, Isaac N. Longcor, Sanford Huston, and Foster Fuller. The latter, who lost a leg, was the most seriously wounded. Two Scotland County boys suffered hits, Lieutenant Ralph C. Dougherty of Best's company and First Sergeant Jeremiah Hamilton of Harle's. Several wounded in the battle were taken elsewhere. Joe McGowan, who caught a bullet in his shoulder while taking the sick across the river, went to an Iowa doctor to have it removed, while young James Kisling of Best's company was taken by his mother to their home in Scotland County, forty miles away. Believed mortally wounded was Captain Mattley. Aylward found his lungs punctured and abandoned hope for the fiery ex-schoolmaster; however, Mattley recovered that autumn—and lived another twenty-seven years.

Because of fragmentary records, one cannot pinpoint Confederate losses. Despite Moore's figures, there were rumors long after that graves of "upwards of forty dead Confederates" were seen on a farm some fourteen miles from the battlefield. Oliver Boardman of the Sixth Iowa felt the rebels had no fewer than twenty dead. "They took care not to have it known how many of them were killed," he claimed. "Several saw them hauling them off by the wagon load." All Moore could be certain of was that into his hands fell twenty prisoners, "four hundred and fifty horses, saddles and bridles complete, hundreds of arms, and a wagon load of long knives."

Before resuming operations, Moore had to take stock of his regiment..
There was no future here for Callihan, who properly kept his distance. Nor
did Spellman or the McKees, fancying themselves in Black Hawk livery,
try to stay. Making up for such defections, however, was the steadfastness
of Washburn and Roseberry, rising popular enthusiasm, the willingness of
Iowans like Farris to stand by the colonel, and the certainty that Simon
Pearce, Tom McAllister, and Joe Story would rally hundreds more to his
standards. Then, too, Moore had the material support of department headquarters and Keokuk's stalwart committee.

Casting a wide net, Moore started for Memphis on Thursday evening,
August 8. His force camped at Etna the first night out and spent Friday
scouting the area. On Saturday, the regiment entered Memphis, only to
find that known secesh folk had gone off in haste for rural scenery. Moore,
said a newsman, had his "invincible" brass cannon along. "The rebels will
undoubtedly keep at a safe distance."

Just the same, loyal Memphians were sure that at least four hundred
rebels were patrolling the local countryside, and Moore sent one reconnaissance after another to "flax them out." Several of Green's scouts, captured on these forays, wound up in the county jail, where David Moore
could spend some quiet moments with them. By Monday, August 12, news
was out that the terrible battle at Wilson's Creek, below Springfield, had
resulted in the death of General Lyon. It seemed afterward to Governor
Jackson's aide that Lyon, by "wisely planning, by boldly doing, and by
bravely dying" had assured the Union's ultimate victory in Missouri. But,
for the time being, there were lively fears that Sterling Price would soon
be marauding in central and northern Missouri.

General Hurlbut, hoping Green could be "treed" in northwestern Lewis
County, issued orders on Sunday, August 11, for Woodyard to join Moore
for action against the wily Confederate. Woodyard prepared to march out
from Canton, while Moore sent messengers to the county seats of southern
Iowa. Bells rang and drums beat, and nearly four hundred militiamen from
Iowa headed toward Memphis. Farris' Croton Guards crossed the Des Moines
heading for Memphis Monday morning. At Bloomfield, however, the tidal
wave of support for Missouri's Union men was deflected. A thousand Iowans
assembled in the square to march to Moore's aid, but Captain H. H. Trimble
of the local militia dissuaded them. Branding Moore as a cutthroat heading
a band of predatory ruffians, the Bloomfield lawyer proclaimed that the
Constitution and laws of the land prohibited Davis Countians from med-
dling in Missouri's internal affairs. Such high-principled oratory took the
starch out of that crowd.

Editor Howell was incensed: "We have no patience with the squeamish sentimentalism which stands by and closes its ears to the anxious cry of Union men for help against traitors, on the plea that there is no authority for them to cross the State line." Like all radicals grown suspicious of stuffy hankerings for principle over action, Howell was scornful of "fine-spun technicalities, the purpose of which is to make out Colonel Moore a lawless desperado, and those who . . . fly to his rescue, simply marauders and murderers."

Moore's troops left for Edina, more than twenty miles south of Memphis, on Monday morning. Certain the rebels were thick along the Middle Fabius, the guards camped at Sandhill and Millport to scout the wooded "bottoms." The Johnnies stayed out of their way, and on Thursday morning the First Northeast Missouri marched into Edina, "the old flag flying, the drums beating, and the soldiers cheering." During the reception, nobody noticed several of Green's officers in the crowd, sizing up the regiment and identifying fellows whose homefolk might be living on farms not too well protected after dark. Father McMenomy made the richly symbolic gesture of inviting Colonel Moore to stay at the parish house. Since a priest would hardly have sat down to dinner with an "Orangeman" in the Old Country, this seemed a refreshing dividend of Americanization.

Word came in the night that Porter was marauding between Fairmont and the Wyaconda. Woodyard, a messenger said, was out to catch him; and bright and early on Wednesday, Moore started for Clark County. On the way, however, the colonel got news that Woodyard had overtaken Porter and routed him the night before at Clapp's Ford, on the North "Fabbie" at the Clark County line. Murray, whose men were in the scrap, estimated that Porter had lost fifty-three dead, but in reality his death toll stood at *one.* Woodyard also had one man dead of wounds. Following this skirmish, Woodyard pulled back to high ground on the Clapp farm while Porter retreated several miles upstream before recrossing to join Green east of Edina.

Farris failed to make contact with Moore. The Croton boys reached Memphis Wednesday morning, August 14, and found a crowd of "strangers" on horseback and in wagons, just pulling out. Who were they? Farris discreetly avoided inquiring. But while his Iowans were warming rations, the word came that local rebels were gathering outside town to capture them, mainly to get their weapons. Union men offered little hope that Farris could get to Moore, as "800 rebels had encamped between Memphis and Sandhill." The Croton Guard, twenty strong, took the advice of friends and lit out for home.

Meeting Woodyard's Second Northeast Missouri Home Guards at Fairmont, Moore took the combined force on to Athens by way of Waterloo, on August 18. Together they were about a thousand strong. Sterling Price was in Springfield again, and if he made it back to the Missouri River, Green might try to break out through the federal cordon and join him. John Pope was determined to stop rebel recruiting north of the river, and the regiments under Moore and Woodyard figured prominently in his calculations.

These days at Athens were hectic. With his bodyguards, Moore could be seen riding out daily for Keokuk, Waterloo, or Croton. There was correspondence with Pope, necessitated by the coming chase after Green. And there were "domestic" worries. When he reached Athens, Farris was waiting with the infuriating news that Bishop had held hearings for Moore's prisoners—and turned them loose after giving them the oath of allegiance. Boldly revealing Moore's sentiments, Farris warned in the *Gate City* that though Bishop might "consider himself the Great Pacificator, there are places where he will be safer, and meet with more respect than in Athens."

Moore was capable of dishing out retribution on "both sides of the fence." He stopped in Waterloo to see the postmaster, Isaac Fields. "Ike," he hissed, "it has come to my ears that you are sending word of my movements to old Pap Price. . . . I warn you that it's got to stop, or I'll have you in irons before a court martial." Ike kept his own counsel, however, only to find himself on September 10 a "guest" of Frémont's provost marshal.

Another problem concerned a small "La Grange Home Guard" that came to join up at Athens. Editor Howe, known to be a good Union man, was its captain. But he and Moore failed to hit it off, for Dave thought those fellows oversupplied and suspected that "jayhawking" was more their style than the genuine soldiering he had in mind.

His suspicions were confirmed to his satisfaction on August 24, when an urgent call came from Kirksville: Hurlbut was surrounded and ordered Moore to his rescue. The La Grange boys balked. They assembled and adopted resolutions rejecting Moore's authority and vowing to march to "Camp Carnegy, Canton, Mo." A journalist related that "Col. Moore immediately surrounded and disarmed them and sent them home, as he did not want that kind of assistance." The offenders were dumped onto the deck of the *Menominee* that night in Keokuk and sent to their blessed "Camp Carnegy."

Moore and Woodyard left for Kirksville Tuesday afternoon, August 27. Two days later, they were in Edina, where they learned that Hurlbut was breaking out of Kirksville heading south. Pope was nearly out of patience with Hurlbut, under fire in the press for drunkenness, aversion to fighting, and maltreatment of citizenry along the Hannibal & St. Joseph. "I cannot conceive how you could have remained ten days at Kirksville and allowed Green's forces to interrupt travel and commit outrages unopposed all through Marion County," Pope scolded. "Break up your camp at once and march on Palmyra." Converging also on Palmyra would be Moore's regiments and Bussey's newly formed Third Iowa Cavalry. With Hurlbut already were Colonel R. C. Smith's Sixteenth Illinois and part of Colonel Nelson G. Williams' Third Iowa Infantry.

Indeed! If Green was in Marion County, that was where all hands under Pope should go. And go they did, Moore and Woodyard marching toward a rendezvous with Hurlbut on the North River at Bethel, twenty-five miles south of Edina in Shelby County. On Sunday, September 1, the union of all forces took place. Here, Hurlbut directed the home guards and the six- teenth Illinois to proceed east, since "my information . . . was that Green was at Philadelphia." With his artillery and the Third Iowa Infantry, Hurl- but proceeded south to Shelbyville and Shelbina. Moore and Smith contin- ued to Philadelphia, where they camped the next morning. By the time Moore and Smith reached Palmyra, the afternoon of September 3, Green had escaped across the railroad some fifteen miles to the southwest at Monroe City.

Pope finally got his fill of Hurlbut in a ridiculous affair at Shelbina. Williams, coming from Hannibal on September 3 with a force made up of his own regiment and the Second Kansas Infantry, found Green in force waiting for him. Telegraph wires were out, and Hurlbut had fallen back to Brookfield, more than fifty miles west. By daybreak Green had the town invested, and Kneisley's battery was all set to show what it had learned since August 5.

Kneisley's bombardment rattled the Kansans, however, and they per- suaded Williams to evacuate toward Macon City, twenty-two miles to the west. Hurlbut, having promised "immediate relief," managed to get to Macon City, where he met the Iowa colonel and "demanded the reasons for the withdrawal." One reporter claimed Hurlbut had overindulged in "Secesh whisky," but after interviewing concerned officers, Hurlbut re- ported to Pope that the guilt for the loss of Shelbina "does not rest . . . on any of the officers and men of my command."

Pope would see about that in due time, but for the moment he was in hot pursuit of Green. On the evening of September 6, he ordered Hurlbut and Moore to close in on Green's camp, believed to be at Florida on the Salt River down in Monroe County. Moore pushed his home guards, with Washburn's men out front, down through Hunnewell toward Florida. Pope's aides were all over the area, frantically urging the various regiments

on to Green's lair. Quartermaster Slate reported in Keokuk that Green
was doomed, "completely trapped south of the railway." Hurlbut, he
declared, would have caught the slippery rebel at Shelbina "had he been
half a *General*, instead of a drunken loafer."

The combined assault on Green's sanctuary miscarried on Sunday, September 8. Green had cleared out toward the west. A couple of sleepy
recruits, a mountain of fodder, and the provisions lost by Williams at
Shelbina—that was nearly Pope's total catch. But not quite all: Ordering
the troops to bivouac in the rebel camp, Pope turned on Hurlbut and
Williams, ordering them to St. Louis for a hearing into that malodorous
Shelbina affair. An amused Aaron Harlan told friends that Pope had
arrested "two drunkards and a coward."

To everyone's amazement, a party of Green's recruits appeared in camp
at daybreak Monday. Moore, standing in the picket line, waited until they
were fifty yards away before challenging. The group leader, sensing an
error, shouted orders to escape. Moore, turning to the Sixteenth Illinois,
called for a quick volley at the fleeing Johnnies. The Illinoisans refused to
obey a mere home guard officer. Suddenly, Dave grabbed one boy's Springfield, blazed away, and picked the leader off his horse. Thanks to the legal
sensitivities of the Sixteenth Illinois, the others made good their escape.

Pope's command withdrew to Hunnewell. On the morning of September 11, he briefed the colonels, explaining that Price was approaching Lexington (on the river in western Missouri) and that Green was heading for an
early linkup with him. The Illinois and Iowa regiments would go west immediately, but the home guards were returning home. Frémont had just given
the home guards a "get-in-or-get-out" order: either muster-in as United
States Volunteers or disband. As neither Moore nor Woodyard preferred
the latter, they could recruit their units up to strength for an early muster
in to "three-year service."

The home guards set out for Canton, apprehensive of further skirmishes,
since some of Green's men were still believed skulking in the area. Sure
enough, an encounter did come at Ely Station, ten miles southwest of
Palmyra. The place itself was "merely a side track on the open prairie . . .
near which is an old affair dignified with the name of house." About
4 P.M. a group of some forty rebels, having lain in the brush to catch
Moore's wagon train, suddenly galloped up to the roadside.

Captain W. J. Livingston, a Mexican War pensioner, demanded of the
train guards: "Who are you?"

"Union men!" somebody told him.

"Well," Livingston snorted, "you march damned loose for Union men."

And his party rode away without a further word.

"This equivocal remark," Aaron Harlan said, "did not remove the doubts of some of our boys." Some thought the strangers Union men from Adair County, but others blazed away at them. In the exchange of shots that followed, one of Woodyard's men got a buckshot in the cheek. Harlan thought five of Livingston's men were wounded. The whole thing was over before Moore even knew about it.

The rest of the march to Canton was a triumphal procession. At Palmyra, reporters professed astonishment that anyone could have thought Moore "disloyal," considering the "reputation which he bears among secessionists." His command, it was noted, "has done more marching in the same time than any two regiments in Northern Missouri." The boys camped at La Grange from September 12 to 14, and here they learned that Martin Green had succeeded in crossing the Missouri to join Price.

September 15, a Sunday, saw the grand march-in at Canton. The entire outfit took up quarters in the "large and commodious Christian University" (present-day Culver-Stockton College), situated on the bluff above town. The artillery battery sounded a thirteen-gun salute, and to the accompaniment of wild cheers from troops and onlookers the "starry flag" was "planted on the dome of the University." An observer said of Woodyard and Moore that "had it not been for such men Northeast Missouri would be in possession of the rebels."

The stay at Canton was brief but explosive. On Monday morning, while Woodyard was working over political captives, word came that hostile riders had been sighted near Monticello. True to his nature, Moore within minutes had a line of three hundred horsemen riding toward the county seat. "The rebels, as usual, tried their speed in running," a reporter said. Dave brought in six more prisoners and a herd of horses. Before returning, he came to an agreement with civic leaders, promising to leave them unmolested so long as his troops enjoyed similar treatment.

The same day, Harle's company went on a scout to Fairmont. A handful of guerrillas, hiding in a blacksmith shop there, opened up with a volley from behind the scouts. Thomas Benton Harle, seventeen-year-old son of the captain, fell with a bullet beneath his shoulder blade. His companions whirled around and charged back. In the fusillade that followed, they riddled the shop and gunned down the malefactor who shot young Harle. Surgeons in Keokuk said "Bent" would live but carry the bullet to his grave. It had lodged too near the heart to be removed.

Moore could see that his campaign to squelch out secession was far from an end. Learning that Captain Howell's killer was running loose in

Canton, he ordered the man arrested and packed off to St. Louis. And
friends were coming in daily to report that rebels around Athens had
grown bolder by the hour in Dave's absence. Keokuk was having one
"Athens scare" after another. At length, the colonel concluded he must
march on Memphis, where worse outrages were reported. On Tuesday
morning, September 17, he told Woodyard their combined force would
leave for Scotland County.

Humphrey Woodyard objected. General Pope had *released* him from
Moore's command to come home and recruit. Well, that was not the way
Moore understood it, and he would abide no insubordination. Since Wood-
yard was adamant, Moore placed him under arrest. Picked squads of the
First Northeast Missouri disarmed and arrested Woodyard's regiment
within an hour. It was a tense morning at Canton.

That evening, Woodyard broke arrest and rode down to Quincy to see
Brigadier General Benjamin M. Prentiss. This officer, who had recently
come off second best in a similar squabble in southeastern Missouri with
a brigadier named Ulysses S. Grant, had just arrived in Quincy to command
federal operations in northeastern Missouri. He at once took Woodyard's
side and dispatched orders to Canton for Moore to report without delay
to account for his behavior.

When the courier reached Canton Wednesday morning, September 18,
he learned that Moore's troops, including some of Woodyard's men unwilling to tamper with the Clark County colonel, had left. The next day, however, there came the horrifying news that Lexington, and thirty-five hundred
Union soldiers, had fallen into Price's hands. Suddenly the crimes of David
Moore paled to insignificance.

There was a four-day stop at Kahoka, during which Moore brought the
regimental staff back to full strength. Jesse H. Holmes, a Keokuk man who
had been a captain in the Seventh Missouri Infantry, arrived to become
lieutenant colonel, transferred by state orders. The major's slot was filled
when Moore appointed Murray and thereby secured his company to the
regiment. Brother Cox, lately conducting "political warfare" on a lecture
tour up the Des Moines valley, rejoined also, as chaplain.

Moore also visited Etna. One foraging party called on a secesh farmer
north of Luray and "borrowed" three wagons, teams, and harness. This,
Harlan waggishly explained, was "what we call 'interesting' the rebels in
support of the Government." Another squad called at Shacklett's estate
near Etna, got the corn and hay Moore sent for, and then improved on
his orders by adding a carriage and four hundred pounds of bacon. A farm-
hand concealed in the brush tried to scare the boys off by sounding "charge"

on a bugle. Moore overlooked that stunt and returned the bacon and carriage; he knew the difference between foraging and plundering.

While the regiment was at Etna, a Keokuk reporter came by and interviewed several boys. Moore, he proclaimed, "is the Marion of North Missouri, and strikes terror into the hearts of the Rebels everywhere. He comes upon them like a thief in the night, as the Good Book says, and . . . they are growing every day more humble."

Reaching Memphis on Thursday, September 26, Moore billeted his men in shops and vacant houses while quartering the staff in the "M. E. South" church. Captain McAllister and several others rode out west of town the next afternoon, taking groceries to relatives they had not seen since mid-August. In a patch of woods two miles out, they ran into an ambush. McAllister was hit in the right leg; Private David Justice toppled to the ground with fourteen wounds. Leaving him for dead, his comrades fled the scene. Captain John McCully, the guerrilla leader, emerged from the brush, removed the cartridge box and belt from the body, and rode away.

Dave's mother, seeing it all, refused to accept that her son was dying. With the help of neighbors, she moved the boy to town. Dr. Aylward extracted one minié ball and a few buckshots, then gave up and told the distraught mother it was hopeless. Much to his puzzlement and the woman's delight, the patient was still breathing the next morning. In fact, six decades would pass before David Justice's funeral.

Less fortunate was Tom Weber, bushwhacked at Fairmont that weekend while recruiting for Captain Washburn. The sorrowing relatives laid the twenty-nine-year-old sergeant to rest in the town cemetery.

Meanwhile, Woodyard was trying to reach the 845-man "minimum" for volunteer regiments. Aided by Carnegy and Vick Wilson, he staged a "speaking" to kindle patriotism. His officers, however, were finding Lewis County a barren ground for recruiting, and one staged a visit up in Lee County a barren ground for recruiting, and one staged a visit up in Lee County, Iowa, netting over fifty enlistees. Department headquarters was so optimistic that Woodyard and Barney King received appointments as colonel and lieutenant colonel on October 7. Both should have been commissioned by Governor Gamble, but Frémont was no stickler.

Moore had another idea for filling ranks. At Memphis on October 3 he published "General Order 15," commanding men on "furlough" to Iowa and Illinois to "report themselves for duty immediately" and threatening to publish a "complete list of their names" if any failed to appear in six days. This brought on a squabble among his partisans in Iowa. So many Hawkeyes were fascinated with Moore and Woodyard—and Bishop's Black

Hawk Cavalry—that recruiters trying to fill Iowa's quota for volunteers
were getting frustrated. Iowa, said one, wanted "credit for the volunteers
furnished, also to keep them in shape that they may be protected by all
laws . . . passed by the State for . . . the families and volunteers of the State."

On October 11, therefore, Governor Kirkwood forbade Iowans to join
units of other states. Moore's recruiters, including Farris, were hastily
ushered out of Lee and Van Buren counties. This protective reaction was,
however, counterproductive. Moore's friends loudly denounced the state
government for undercutting the heroic protector of southern Iowa, and
within a month the governor felt compelled to make a temporary exception in David Moore's case.

As if Moore did not have his hands full already, one calamity followed
another during the stay at Memphis. In early October, rumors spread in
Keokuk that he was selling government horses and pocketing the money.
Moore's blistering rebuttal in the *Gate City* quickly drove gossipers to
cover. Then, on October 12, he found himself without a quartermaster,
for Woodyard had arrested Slate at Quincy and sent him to Keokuk to
face "a number of srious charges." Details of the complaint and the character of Slate's dismissal are veiled in mystery, but Moore was soon hunting
for a replacement.

While Moore was away in St. Louis, disaster struck at Memphis. On Sunday night, October 13, there was sporadic picket firing around town, and
during one alarm a soldier's musket discharged accidentally, shattering
Major Murray's right leg below the knee. Doc Aylward, fearing irreparable
damage, amputated on Thursday. Then Colonel Holmes, scouting in the
countryside, fell from his horse on Friday and broke a leg.

Moore galloped into Memphis on Monday, October 21, to learn that
Murray had died the previous day. As the widow preferred not to bury her
husband amid the desolation of the homestead down at Greensburg, his
company took the major back to Quincy for a stately funeral with "a large
concourse." Murray left four children, including a daughter yet unborn. It
took military bureaucrats fifteen years to acknowledge the nation's obligations to the widow and her children.

Since rebel activity had faded and recruiting was drying up around Memphis, Moore's regiment returned to Athens October 22. Three days later,
Captain Charles C. Smith, mustering officer at Keokuk, arrived to muster
every company that was full. Moore reported 750 enlistments. This did
not fill up the regiment, but the companies of Harle, Pearce, and Roseberry were big enough. Jackson and Farris were told they were short.
Daniel M. Wooley, trying to assemble a company from the remnants of

defunct Clark County Guards, was in the same shape. Captain George F. Pledge, an old soldier with artillery know-how, came up from Canton to organize the battery of artillery, now swollen to four guns with the addition of a twelve-pounder sent from St. Louis; however, this valuable company never filled.

Mattley had a full company, but his boys wanted no part of an outfit that might leave Missouri. *Their* war was here, they insisted. The regional press had been bombarding Iowans with promises that by joining Moore "they can be near home and do their service under an honorable and brave man." Moore struck back on two fronts. He arrested Mattley, then made the boys a speech vowing that "if this regiment is ever ordered south of the Hannibal & St. Joe I will raise perfect hell." Mattley refused to "come around right," and resigned. His men followed suit. For the time being, Moore had to get along with a fragmentary regiment. Woodyard was having no better luck, thanks to the "closed season" in Iowa applied to his recruiters.

It was time to appoint a staff for the First Northeast Missouri Volunteer Infantry. George Z. Streaper of Burlington, late of the disbanded First Iowa Infantry, came in as adjutant. Of course, the zealous Chaplain Cox stayed. Joining as quartermaster was a wealthy grocer from Keokuk, Daniel W. Pressell. This forty-year-old Marylander would "go the duration" with Moore. Dr. Joseph K. Rickey, a Keokuk dentist, secured the sutler's appointment and gave his son Joe charge of the business.

Exceptional enlisted men were showing up in the new regiment. New York-born Henry M. Kilmartin enlisted as chief musician, having been a fifer of the First Iowa, veterans of Wilson's Creek. Joining Farris' company was a young Dutchman, Gerrit Jan Stegeman, who had enlisted already in the Fifteenth Iowa. However, those rascally farm boys had found his name and accent all too entertaining, played practical jokes on him and shouted "Stiggaman!" whenever he came in sight. His craw full of it, "Stiggaman" was changing outfits.

Terrorism was getting out of hand in Schuyler County, and Prentiss wanted Moore and Woodyard to pacify it. On October 29, the First Northeast Missouri marched down to Alexandria and went into camp. Here, a *Gate City* reporter found the regiment in new uniforms, good health, and good spirits. "Col. Moore is never idle," the visitor noted, although he did pity the colonel because his wife, "as we learn, is a rebel."

Moore's coming complicated matters for the Black Hawk Cavalry across the river at Warsaw. Within a few days, about fifty of Bishop's men, un-mustered, came across to Alexandria and enlisted with Moore. Colonel Bishop was having a wretched time of it anyhow, unable to get supplies, horses, weapons. None of his companies was ready to muster, and Moore's magnetic presence was no help. In exasperation, Bishop made bold to write directly to Lincoln, "desiring to know whether [I] will be sustained in [my] appointment and in the subsistence of the Regt., etc." The White House bucked the "out-of-channels" letter to St. Louis, and Bishop got a withering reminder that "the difficulty with your regiment has been that nothing has been known about it."

On November 5, Moore's troops moved to "College Hill" in Canton, preparing to move on Schuyler County. Captain McCully was out there recruiting, and federal officials heard he was doing very well. On Thursday, November 14, the combined Northeast Missouri regiments marched up the Fabius watershed toward Memphis. The wagon train, escorted by Harle to Williamstown, took a more northerly route.

Leaving the wagons, Harle moved rapidly on Memphis, under orders to carry out a ticklish operation—the selective arrest of Southern sympathizers. There was a delay, east of town, when three rebel scouts got in the way and drew Harle's fire. One was shot in the lung and captured, but the others vanished; however, Harle still had time to stake out the town before daylight.

Among the prisoners taken in was an old friend of the colonel's, Judge Richardson, a forty-two-year-old Kentuckian who had read law with Senator Green and served in both houses of the general assembly before taking over the Fourth Judicial Circuit in 1859. "He was a Secessionist," a contemporary said, "but not a rebel." This, the judge appreciated, was a feat of ideological gymnastics beyond a simpler patriot's comprehension, and it is for that reason that Richardson, fearing for his safety, asked for protective custody during the stay of the Unionists.

On Saturday, a delegation of Schuyler County Conservatives showed up at Memphis with that shopworn plea of "live-and-let-live," begging Richardson to keep Moore's disturbing presence out of Schuyler. The judge called Dave in and tried to dissuade him from stirring up those peace-loving neighbors, a waste of everyone's time.

Then, on Monday evening, came a disaster that nearly wrecked Moore's career. Richardson, trying to lift a window in the county clerk's office, was shot in the forehead by someone outside. He fell backward and died without a word. Colonel Moore rode to the Richardson home to convey the news to the widow. That done, he huddled with Adjutant Streaper to prepare a prompt notification to Prentiss and a campaign to catch the perpetrator of a "a most foul and cowardly murder." Dave's personal honor was on the line, and he was obsessed with capturing the killer. After consulting

E. K. Sayre, he offered "one thousand dollars in gold," half from Sayre and half from his own pocket, for "information that will lead to the apprehension and conviction of the person or persons implicated." Nothing came of it, and the judge remained another statistic in the catalog of violence wracking northeastern Missouri. Department headquarters sent a three-man board of inquiry from the Third Missouri Cavalry to Memphis for hearings. Although Moore branded the inquisitors as "bitterly opposed" to him personally, they were unable to lay any guilt on him.

Frémont's empire collapsed on November 2, with Lincoln's order of dismissal. The death of the "Martyred Lyon," loudly charged to Frémont's neglect, rankled many Union men, and Conservatives were livid at his recent attempt to start emancipating Missouri's slaves. "Frémont's arrival in Missouri," wrote an adversary, "was a national disaster, resulting in the loss of Lyon . . . and Price's undisturbed march of triumph and desolation through Missouri." On November 19, Major General Henry W. Halleck assumed charge of the "Department of the Missouri," and a week later Prentiss took control of northern Missouri. Halleck was both a West Pointer and a lawyer, and his writings had long since won him the nickname of "Old Brains." In this cauldron, he would need all the brains God had given him.

Moore decided to assail the rebels over in Schuyler, considered by Pressell as one of Missouri's "rankest rebel holes." Guerrillas were having a field day stealing horses, robbing farmhouses, and chasing loyal men to Iowa. Sending to Canton for a mounted company Woodyard had left there, Moore alerted his troops to march at daybreak, November 24, to Lancaster, twenty miles west.

"We got within two or three miles of the town," wrote Chaplain Cox, "when we were fired into from the brush by a party of brushwhackers, the result, we returned the fire and captured three horses." Harlan reported four rebels killed, none of Moore's men. On approaching Lancaster, Moore learned that the horsemen from Canton were already there—but surrounded by a much larger contingent of the enemy.

Seeing Harle's cavalry and Pledge's gunners coming up, the Confederates fell back to the west. The First Northeast Missouri paused by the courthouse while Moore waited for Harle's report. Soon scouts were back with news that the state guards had formed in the brush west of town.

The troops under Moore and Woodyard met the rebels "on their own ground and fought them in their own way," Cox explained, "and when they played 'quits' by skidaddling we found the game resulted in four dead rebels—which we brought to camp, leaving Captain Harle and his brave men to pursue the running rascals." Harlan placed the Confederate dead at thirteen, in a fight lasting half an hour and ending at sunset: "Col. Moore does not fight according to European tactics. He led a portion of his infantry as near the fighting brush as they could get in good order, and on quick time formed them as a reserve, gave some hurried instructions, then pitched into the brush himself among the scouts who engaged hand to hand." All in all, Pressell thought Moore had given the guerrillas "such a castigation as they have not had before even in Northeast Missouri."

Union casualties were scanty. Joseph Garrison of Harle's company was killed, and it was thought for a time that Philip Adams of the same outfit would die. Shot out of his saddle in the evening's fight, Adams had crawled to a fence and fired his musket once before growing too weak to handle it. But, Harlan exulted, he was "much too game to die." DeWitt Gallup, of Pledge's cannoneers, was less seriously wounded. Captain Pearce got a buckshot below one eye, and that was about the extent of the damage done the victors.

But great was the jubilation when they found John McCully among the enemy dead! Justice's cartridge box and belt were recovered from the body. McCully had been active in the "M. E. South" church, Cox could not forbear reporting. Harlan noted with mock indignation that McCully had used strips of the *St. Louis Christian Advocate* as wadding in his shotgun: "No wonder that their own shotguns play them false when wadded with such infernal lies," he quipped. Two sons of the state guard captain were also dead, as was a son-in-law—which prompted the chaplain's vindictive observation that "our boys completely 'cleaned out' one traitorous family."

This latest Confederate disaster, Pressell thought, had just about convinced local rebels that "secesh is no go." Moore was promising that "if they would come to our camp, lay down their arms, take the oath of allegiance, . . . he would protect them against federal troops." Moreover, as discouraged guerrillas came in to surrender, they were presented rations from Pressell's wagons for their destitute families. Indeed, Cox said of the colonel that though "he is as severe as Nero with the enemy . . . when he conquers, he transforms himself into an angel of mercy."

Such praise was not universal. One reporter, conceding that "the enemy have a perfect dread of him," alluded to "bitter and hostile feeling . . . toward him from Union men. The Colonel has acted very indiscreet at times." Some journalists were irked by his secrecy, and it is likely that reportorial hostility lay behind occasional false rumors of "defeats" suffered by Moore's troops in distant places—and even of his "arrest" by various generals.

By the end of 1861, Cox fancied his colonel in the "noontime of as much glory perhaps as any other officer of the same rank, . . . for the reason that he has never been whipped." His physique, the chaplain said, was "symmetrical as the 'Greek Slave.' He is as 'straight as an arrow.' And his gait is surpassingly beautiful, partaking of the military 'common time.' " He was always clean-shaven. Cox found him in good society as "polite as a 'French schoolmaster,' and as popular as sin. When on duty he is colonel, when off, but a common soldier." Editor Howell rapturously hailed Moore as "the Ethan Allen of 1861."

Moore and Woodyard found it impossible to fill up the regiments. Halleck, therefore, decided to take a hand, since there were numerous fragmentary units around Missouri that could be amalgamated into fewer but "regulation" units. Old Brains was appalled at Frémont's permitting units to take on designations from *sections* of a state or names like "Black Hawk." These fellows would shape up as "Missouri Volunteers" or he would disband them. On December 31, Governor Gamble issued "Special Order 15," directing consolidation of the First and Second Northeast Missouri Volunteers into a "21st Missouri Volunteer Infantry." Woodyard and King, stepping down to lieutenant colonel and major, were posted to the new regiment. But in Halleck's estimation, the colonelcy could only belong to "D. Moore, Union."

3

"Well, This Is What They Call War!"

The winter was fairly quiet in the East, as the contenders prepared for the bloody work ahead. A strong concentration of Confederate troops wintered in northern Virginia under command of General Joseph E. Johnston, late quartermaster general of the "Old Army." Southern forces west of the Alleghenies, holding a long, thin line running through Kentucky to the Ozarks, were under General Albert Sidney Johnston. Major General George B. McClellan, summoned by Lincoln after Bull Run, rose to commander-in-chief over federal armies in November 1861 and remained in the East. Major General Don Carlos Buell, on the Ohio River, watched the Confederates in Kentucky, while Halleck's department anchored the west end of the Union line.

While the federals were blockading or occupying a few Southern ports, such as Jacksonville, Florida, and New Berne, North Carolina, major action before spring came in the West. Here, troops under Grant broke the rebel grip on the lower Ohio's confluences with the Cumberland, Tennessee, and Mississippi. To Grant and Halleck, these "river roads" were keys to victory. With a fleet of transports and armored vessels operating out of St. Louis, they could carry on amphibious warfare against the vitals of the Confederacy. Such strategy would interdict the defenders' use of their rivers and, ultimately, many railroads.

During February 1862, Grant's troops in western Kentucky seized Fort Henry on the Tennessee and Fort Donelson on the Cumberland, rupturing the Confederate line west of the Alleghenies. Sidney Johnston fell back on Corinth, Mississippi, while forces under Grant and Buell flowed into Tennessee toward an inevitable confrontation with Jeff Davis' western army. In Missouri, Price's sojourn at Lexington had ended in late September with his retirement to the southwestern corner of the state. Sam Curtis, Moore's regimental commander in the Mexican War and now risen to major general of United States Volunteers, began assembling an army in the Ozarks to chase Price on to Arkansas.

Robert Peel Guthrie, of Dan Wooley's company, was troubled during the Christmas holidays. To his father William, an Edina attorney, he confided fears in the regiment that Colonel Moore was on the verge of dismissal. The elder Guthrie reported the rumor to Halleck, ignorant of plans the latter had for the colonel. By late January, after learning the general "had never heard such report," the Guthries were satisfied that Moore was enjoying excellent credit in St. Louis.

However bitter Woodyard's feelings about subordination to David Moore, he had no choice but to quit or get busy with consolidating the companies into a single regiment. Some officers would indeed grasp the opportunity to quit; others, like Wooley, Pledge, and Northcutt, would be be squeezed out. Still others, like Washburn, would accept reduction in rank. There were two categories of enlisted men to deal with,—those mustered in with the Northeast Missouri Volunteers and those since "enlisted" but not mustered. The former were obligated to abide by the transfer, but the latter would still renege. Weeks of pleading and downright browbeating would go into completing the new regiment.

Moore and Woodyard viewed this unit as a combat team in a rather modern sense of the word, with seven companies of infantry, two of cavalry, and one of artillery; however, when they petitioned Halleck's approval, they provoked a harsh rejoinder that Old Brains would "have nothing to do with these attachments of artillery and cavalry. These men must enlist as infantry in Col. Moores regiment in which case they will be paid for their past services, otherwise not."

Two problems delayed retirement on Canton to effect the merger: Bill Dunn, Scotland County's peskiest bushwhacker, and a measles epidemic, which by mid-January had about a hundred soldiers under treatment in Memphis. Time and Doc Aylward would take care of the measles, but it was up to Moore to look after Dunn.

On Saturday evening, January 18, the colonel handpicked 170 men for a protracted scout. A foot of snow covered the area, and those without horses came along on sleighs. Entering Schuyler County the next afternoon, they flushed out Dunn and eighty guerrillas in a barnyard. Dunn fled, Harlan related, "but was so hard pushed by Geo. Wilson that he had no time to take his saddle from his tired horse, . . . so he lost his tired nag and rode his race horse barebacked thro' the brush." Still, Moore captured nearly everyone else at the affair. He lined the captives up for drill, but finding that most did not know how, he gave them the oath and freed them. A dozen others, more proficient, came along under constraint.

Before withdrawing, Moore visited Bryan's Mills, "situated in a deep hollow, surrounded by thick brushwood." The little distillery there was a hangout for Dunn and his friends, Harlan heard. "It so happens in Missouri that brushy land breeds secesh," he noted, especially when combined with effects of "bad whisky." The colonel decided to "cut off the supply by ordering the distillery burned, and while the flames were curling beautifully around the chimney he practiced his artillery on the still standing chimney, and all is now leveled down. The curling flames consuming bad whisky, the crackling of timbers, . . . the wo-begone countenances of the secesh prisoners, made a very striking scene."

At last, on Tuesday, January 28, the First Northeast Missouri was able to repair to Canton. Harlan later told Howell that "many of our young men had but partly recovered from the measles; the weather was cold and all the trees and fences covered with ice; a North wind helped us along the road, but the exposure sent many of our young men back to the hospital."

The assembling of the two understrength regiments on College Hill at Canton was complete the morning of February 1, with Leeser's company B, Second Northeast Missouri, marching up from La Grange. If the other companies were as much in the dark about what was happening as Leeser's men were, all hell must have broken loose. Prentiss showed up to deliver a masterpiece of patriotic oratory, but popular enthusiasm for his inspiring message dwindled when he rhetorically unveiled the ulterior purpose of these proceedings.

Thinking they were being called together only to be paid for their earlier service, the men now learned the governor had ordered them merged into an infantry regiment for a three-year term. Gunners and horsemen alike screamed bloody murder. Nearly a hundred Iowans protested they had joined up on Kirkwood's approval to serve *only* in northeastern Missouri. Many Missourians, understanding that the old regiments were to stay in Missouri, developed doubts this new outfit would. Stephan Werly and others of Leeser's company recalled with pious shudders that Colonel Moore was "a man who did not seem to know any religion and who would swear and curse and mistreat his troops."

A rangy mustering officer, British-born Lieutenant Edwin A. Moore of the Sixteenth Illinois, was in town to start the mustering. Before the day was over, eight companies had come to agreement and were lettered A through H. Two others, under Harle and Leeser, stood their ground, and Prentiss and Moore went after them with mailed fists. Prentiss offered two choices: muster in as ordered, or he would see to it that they "would not be able to get any pay for what they had done and . . . they would be sent to St. Louis to work on fortifications." That is the way George Nightingale of Drakesville, Iowa, in Harle's company, heard it. And it was the essence of Werly's recollections that "there was no other way, without perhaps being taken away under guard for a long time and . . . dragged around as prisoners." Lieutenant Moore said later that those not previously mustered were given their choice, but in the case of those mustered into the old regiments who tried backing out, "I arrested them."

Perhaps with tongue-in-cheek, Aaron Harlan noted that the two intransigent companies soon "came along," a tribute he thought to what "love of a republican government and obedience to orders will do." At any rate, by February 12, the President's birthday, the ten-company Twenty-first Missouri Infantry was mustered, 962 men in all. Within half a year, more than a hundred of them would lie in graves from Keokuk to Georgia.

By and large, the staff was composed of men well known to Moore. He could not do much about Woodyard and King, thrust upon him by higher authority. Charles C. Tobin, a merchant from Quincy, was his new adjutant. Pressell stayed as quartermaster, but there was no chaplain. There was an irksome furor over the surgeon's job when department headquarters named Dr. Rufus H. Wyman of Keokuk, a forty-five-year-old New York lately of Belknap's City Rifles. Moore had promised the spot to his chief Iowa recruiter, Dr. William H. Davis. After some confusion, Gamble settled the matter in Wyman's favor. Davis rejecting the assistant's post, Dr. Joseph H. Seaton of Keokuk volunteered for it.

The enlisted staff positions went to men congenial to Moore. The sergeant-major's office went to Joseph G. Best. A young construction engineer from Canton, Charles W. Tracy, became quartermaster sergeant, and Harlan stayed as commissary sergeant. Dr. George S. Carnahan of Canton, a fifty-year-old Ohioan and friend of Carnegy and Woodyard, came in as hospital steward. Drum major was young Hughes Roseberry, while Kilmartin served as fife major.

Continuing essentially as a German unit was Captain Yust's Company A. Privileged to wear gold bars as Yust's first lieutenant was another German, Henry Menn, twenty-nine, a carriage painter of Canton. Edwin Turner, also twenty-nine, wore the unadorned shoulder straps of second lieutenant. First Sergeant Charles Lannig, like the Yusts and others of his company, was a native of Gräfenhainichen.

An entirely different sort of man for Company A was William Rolen, or Rowland, or Roland; he was an illiterate former slave, had invented his name, and had no idea how to spell it. Fair-haired and blue-eyed, he was not sure when or where he had been born, but he understood it was about 1825 near Lexington, Kentucky. During the previous summer, Roland had been the *cause celèbre* in one of the most bizarre incidents in the history of slavery. An honorable citizen of Quincy for eighteen years, he was arrested as a fugitive slave while escorting an insane woman to her relatives near Brookfield. His "owner," Samuel Kennon of Boone County, had gotten wind of Roland's coming into the state and conspired to have him taken off the train at Macon City. This unveiled Roland's past, and neighbors learned that he had escaped in 1843, fled south into Osage County, adopted a new name, married a white woman, and passed as white. He later took his wife to Quincy, where he became a Douglas Democrat safely resident on the free soil of Illinois. Now, returning in arrest to Boone County, Roland made a bargain to deed over his Quincy home to Mr. Kennon and serve three more years in slavery. Then, with agitated Quincyites hanging on every word of his case, Roland took off for Illinois after less than two days back in the toils of the peculiar institution.

Story's Company B retained a Willmathsville flavor, even after taking in some Iowans, transfers from Northcutt's outfit, and recent recruits. Story and his lieutenants, Lucius D. Woodruff and Edward Fox, were neighborhood friends, and one of the corporals was the captain's nephew, John D. Story. On the threshold of a memorable career was Sergeant Josiah W. Davis, born in 1840 the son of a leading physician of Clay County, Indiana.

Magnificent, blonde-bearded Simon Pearce got a full Company C together, even if it took a bit of fibbing. Michael Cashman, a man of fifteen, stepped right up to say he was nineteen. Born in Connecticut, he had come to Quincy as a small boy with his parents. The landmark event of his childhood, he would always say, was the Lincoln-Douglas debate in Quincy on October 13, 1858. When the war came, Mike "took the fever"; but since the elder Cashman would not let him enlist, the lad ran off, with a half-dollar in his pocket, to Scotland County, Missouri—and into Company C. Twins Edwin and Edward Smith allowed that they had just turned seventeen, and Pearce believed them. Born at Oxford, Ohio, they had come with their parents to Clark County when very small. A relative always thought the boys a bit overoptimistic about their ages, however. Pearce was less in doubt about his lieutenants, a thirty-four-year-old Scotland County farmer named William Lester and a forty-seven-year-old Virginia-born carpenter of Memphis, Thomas H. Richardson.

Murrow's Company D inherited many of Northcutt's and Wilson's men. Wilson's first sergeant, a young Pennsylvanian named Henry McGonigle, stepped up to first lieutenant, and an immigrant Irish farmer, Lewis Ainslie, became second lieutenant. The first sergeant was a son of English gentry from Manchester; he was Charles C. Morrey, born thirty years before in Ohio. Timothy W. Holman, seventeen-year-old son of an old Kentucky sheriff enlisted from Sandhill. The boys would never forget Tim, who became one of the foremost historians chronicling their martial deeds.

Wilford Cunningham, Murrow's original second lieutenant, did not stay, but his younger brother John Henry rose to become a sergeant of the new company. Harvey Cunningham, though older than John, served as corporal. These young men, Indianans, were sons of "Old Bob" Cunningham, a strong-willed Radical farmer of the Millport neighborhood. Elias B. Davidson, husband of the boys' late sister Lucinda, had been Murrow's first sergeant in the old outfit, but the bereaved young farmer remained in the company as a duty sergeant.

Among those serving with Murrow was William H. Matlick, son of Zachariah Matlick of Sandhill and great-grandson of a Scot who had migrated to Pennsylvania before the Revolution. William was sixteen, with an older brother Edgar, in Company E, who preferred spelling his name "Matlock" (there was no consensus in the clan about it). There also came to the company a steely-eyed farm lad from Colony, William R. Killen, whose forebears included the William Killen who had been Delaware's first chief justice.

Fundamentally a Knox County unit also was Company E, made up of some men formerly serving with Vick Wilson or more recently enlisted. Its commander was George W. Fulton. The sombre-visaged captain, a native of Pennsylvania, was an Edina carpenter. His lieutenants, farmers near Edina, were the twenty-seven-year-old Hoosier Tobias McQuoid and the thirty-one-year-old Kentuckian William J. Pulis. McQuoid had been Wilson's second lieutenant, and Pulis had come to know him through his work in the Masonic lodge at Edina. Enlisting with Pulis was his New York-born father John S. Pulis and his younger brothers Reuben and Robert.

Also a family affair was the enlistment of the Roseberrys—William, James, Thomas, and David—of Knox County, sons of the Kentuckian Nathan Roseberry who had also served in Wilson's home guard but did not stay on for the volunteer service. The boys, born in Indiana and Missouri, boasted parents who qualified as Old Settlers. They were apparently unrelated to the Roseberrys of St. Francisville.

A slender, black-eyed Irish youth going on sixteen also signed with Fulton. He was Martin N. Sinnott, born in County Wexford and brought to America at the age of three. Although he entered service as a private, this child of people driven from Ireland by the great famine would make a splendid impression on the captain and prosper himself in uniform.

The Croton Guards, mustered as Company E of the First Northeast Missouri, became Company F. Farris, profiting from Kirkwood's dispensation to bring in more Iowans, still needed remnants of companies gathered by Moody, Cochran, Jackson, and Scott to finish Company F. His first lieutenant was Alexander F. Tracy, younger brother of the quartermaster sergeant. Frank Whittemore of Kahoka, twenty-two-year-old veteran of Jackson's home guards, became second lieutenant.

Among the enlisted men were several who would assume great significance as the years advanced. Corporal Henry D. Wellington, twenty-four, had come from Massachusetts. He had been associated at Memphis in the furniture and carpentry business with his father, Darius ("Duke") Wellington, a prewar mayor of the town and a leader in Masonic affairs. Duke, at fifty-six, was one of Pledge's gunners, but he stayed in the regiment as a private of Company H. Nehemiah D. Starr, a Pennsylvania Quaker reared in Ohio and teaching at Canton since 1859, was signed as one of Farris' original sergeants. Among others was Isaac C. Schram, one of Moore's "old originals," a short, thirty-eight-year-old New Yorker farming near Winchester. Before peace returned, the boys would be saluting "Ike" Schram and "Nick" Starr.

Five of the six men wounded in Roseberry's line at Athens mustered for Company G. Foster Fuller, minus his leg, could not come along. First Sergeant George Newmyer, a twenty-two-year-old Pennsylvanian living at Winchester, accepted a reduction to private. Two men from St. Francisville, both thirty-two, also mustered: Sanford Huston, born a Virginian, and Andrew Fogleman, a Marylander. Isaac Longcor, eighteen, a farm boy from Belfast, Iowa, was also among the wounded of Athens coming back for more. Last, there was Matt Woodruff, Ohio-born and nineteen, who would rise to top sergeant.

As neither of Roseberry's original lieutenants cared for the new ser-

vice, it was necessary to find new officers. First Lieutenant Edward K.
Blackburn was an Ohioan, just turned twenty-one, a bookkeeper at
Waterloo. Second Lieutenant Daniel Reece Allen, twenty-two, was a
Kentuckian lately farming near St. Francisville.

Chaplain Cox, responding to popular clamor in Company H, reluc-
tantly laid aside his ministerial gown, buckled on a revolver, and took
command. Peter Washburn, able to hold but seventeen of his men to
service, accepted the first lieutenancy. William Penn Rickey, twenty-
six, a Canton dentist and son of the sutler, became the other lieutenant
in a company composed of remnants from commands raised by Washburn, Pledge, and Wooley.

Several farmers from Chambersburg made valuable enlisted men.
There was James Cameron, born in Pennsylvania in 1812, and his Ohio-
born son Joseph, eighteen, who had come with the family to Clark
County in 1845. Two other Cameron boys, Alfred and Samuel, would
join later. Old Jim let on that he was only forty-five, but he was to
find that few men pushing fifty could long masquerade as infantrymen.
Coming to Clark County shortly after the Camerons was Philarmon Reynolds, another young Ohioan of whom much more was to be heard in
years ahead.

William Harle, captain-presumptive of Company I, needed a few days
to persuade his remaining holdouts to come down off their horses and
serve the cause as foot soldiers. By February 5 their objections were
sufficiently overborne to enable Lieutenant Moore to resume mustering.
Harle's first lieutenant was a fellow-Virginian, thirty-six-year-old Joseph
J. Oliver. Hudson Rice, thirty-one, Oliver's brother-in-law and also a
farmer, had gone west to Scotland County from Kentucky in the prewar decade.

Among the sergeants of Company I was the captain's younger brother Wilson, a bear of a man conscious of his strength and fearless in
using it. Also, there was Cyrenus Z. Russell, a veteran of Athens like
the Harles. He was twenty-one, son of a Disciples of Christ minister
and a relative of Secretary of State William H. Seward. The slim and
austere sergeant was native to Peoria, Illinois, and had moved to Scotland County with his parents not long before the war.

It took yet another week to hush the angry voices of dissent among
Leeser's Germans. Company K's first lieutenant was the balding and
rugged Starkweather, the second lieutenant a youthful butcher from
La Grange, George M. Davis. Typical of the rank and file were hardy
young Germans such as First Sergeant Louis Puster, twenty-nine and

a family man; and William Smith, born Wilhelm Schmidt twenty years before at Lashorst, Prussia, but Americanized in 1856. Steve Werly, subordinating personal desire to public good, stayed with the boys as their drummer.

A younger brother of Charles Blines, Murrow's company, later said of Moore's troops that most "were from rural homes and were of the hard working common classes, real pioneers in the settlement of northeast Missouri. They were used to severe struggles with hard labor in plowing the tough sod of the prairies, felling the choice forests, making rails for fencing, building log cabin homes, wooden bridges across the local streams, long journeys to markets and custom mills."

Sergeant Major Best was coming to believe "a soldier's life is not the thing it is cracked up to be." The pleasures of this calling he likened to "angels visits, few and far between." To a cousin he described the routine of soldiers: "When they return to their Quarters to lay down on dirt and frost and many things not prudent to commit to writing and again when you are a sleep some soldier comes in and commences the usual inquiry whose got my Blanket, in morning have a fight about a wash pan or who'll stand at the fire and when you get your breakfast issued to you you must hugg it like . . . an arm full of corn." Still, his discomforts were small when balanced against the honor of supporting "as great and good a government as this." He foresaw the Union's triumph across "fields that are now stained and are to be stained with *Blood.*" Death in this cause he considered "dying like a Christian. But think for a moment of a Traitor's Grave, those who fill them leave their friends and all that's dear to them their Families disgraced and I dare say are disgraced in the Lower Regions, the future home of many who are engaged in advancing this foul Rebellion."

His suspicions that the regiment would soon "receive orders for Kentucky" were intensified on Monday, February 17, when Colonel Moore issued "General Order 4," calling for a dress parade at 3:00 P.M. In guarded language, Moore told the boys to prepare to march at a moment's notice. Starr jumped to the conclusion that "our gallant Col. MOORE, after killing secession in N. E. Mo., is needed south." Rumormongers went to work, speculating that the Twenty-first Missouri would help Ben Prentiss assault Columbus, Kentucky. "Wiser heads" saw General Order 4 as a ruse to keep the boys off Canton's streets.

Moore turned the troops out in marching order the next morning. The colonel leading, they tramped "up Fourth St. to Clark; thence to Front; down Front to Lewis; thence back to Fourth; when our departure became apparent." Moore was taking them away from College Hill. "We waved our caps to the ladies of Canton," Starr said, ". . . and left with regret."

That afternoon, the regiment halted at La Grange. The city's hotel was available to out-of-town men, but local boys had more pleasing prospects. Here, Werly observed gratefully, "I could pass again a night with my family and rejoice in their midst and have the pleasure to join in family prayer." But daybreak came all too soon, and it was time to march the seventeen miles to Palmyra. Assembling before the hotel, the regiment received a banner made by Mrs. Charlton Howe's ladies' association. The ladies "received our cheers and heartfelt thanks," Starr said, but he conceded that the euphoria faded on the day's hike "tedious and tiresome to troops unaccustomed to marching."

Colonel John M. Glover's Third Missouri Cavalry welcomed the regiment to Palmyra and saw to its billeting. Farris' Company F and Leeser's Company K slept in the "M. E. South" church, the sanctuary of which had been heated for a prayer meeting. Werly was too tired to brood over the "heart rending departure from my family." Starr thought Company F would surely emerge from a night's sleep "in the sacred chamber" with a reputation for piety. Yust's and Pearce's companies did not get to enjoy Palmyra's hospitality, however, as the former was sent on by train to Hannibal to prepare for the regiment's arrival, while the latter moved to the Salt River, below Hannibal, to patrol and to construct a blockhouse at the railroad bridge.

The next afternoon, the main body reached Hannibal. Here the troops took quarters in a cantonment erected by the Twenty-sixth Illinois and named for its commander, Colonel John M. Loomis. Harlan described its accommodations as "pine scantling frames covered with pine lumber, making a building about as close as barns are generally. They . . . include a square piece of ground, of about four acres as a parade ground on a South hill-side, near one mile from the steamboat landing." Werly was gratified by the presence of a German Methodist congregation, Starr thankful the boys had been paid for the "1861 services," since pies, cakes, cigars, apples, and newspapers were available to the lucky holders of "a few dimes."

The colonel announced a severe regimen of training, which included five hours of company drill a day. Kilmartin would sound reveille at daylight, lights out at 9:05 P.M. In a letter to Henrietta Headley of Canton, of whom his heart was growing fonder in this enforced absence, Starr confided a wishful belief that Moore's troops would be distributed around Hannibal to guard bridges and public property.

There was excitement at regimental headquarters. Colonel Bishop, arrested at Hudson City February 20 on a variety of charges, was due in Palmyra for trial. Woodyard, an experienced lawyer, was called to Palmyra to serve on the court. The case against Bishop was a strange fabric of alleged shortcomings in training and administering the Seventh Missouri Cavalry, formerly his Black Hawk outfit. Viewed in retrospect, the affair smacks of an administrative maneuver to purge an amateur from command of the Seventh Cavalry.

Acting Governor Willard P. Hall having set February 24 as the date for electing a successor to Judge Richardson, the Twenty-first Missouri took an avid spectator interest in the campaign. The post went to a Canton attorney, James Ellison, a native of northern Ireland with service in the state legislature. The new circuit judge advertised himself "a firm Union man," but his Unionism was of the Conservative strain.

Along about March 1, a Baptist preacher, William Cleaveland, found himself in Moore's doghouse. For this, the portly old fellow had Barney King to thank. The good major had accused Cleaveland of preaching a revival for Green's men at Horseshoe Bend, and Moore drew ominous conclusions. On Monday, March 3, Mr. Cleaveland was routed out of his cell "by my reverend persecutor, 'Captain Cox,' and his insolent myrmidons" to face the scourge of northeastern Missouri secessionists, "surrounded by an ill-mannered, ruffian-like multitude who stared and sneered as if I were a curiosity on exhibition."

"Are you a rebel?" Moore opened.

The pastor mumbled something about having rebelled against Satan.

"The hell and damnation you have!" the colonel interrupted.

"I am a minister of the gospel, sir," Cleaveland persisted, "and it is my business to make war against the kingdom of Satan."

"Are you a Southern man?"

"I was born in the South," replied Cleaveland, "raised and educated there, and my sympathies irresistibly lead me in that direction."

"Other men control their sympathies!" Moore retorted. "Why can you not do the same and harmonize with the North as well as the South?"

As Cleaveland insisted on the impossibility of this, Moore took another tack: "How do you like old Abe?"

"In some respects," Cleaveland obliged him, "well enough; in others, not so well. On the whole I don't endorse him as a President."

"The hell you don't!" bellowed Moore furiously to the accompaniment of sustained laughter among his staff. After further thrusts and parries, he directed Cox to return the man to his cell for nine days of "coarse fare." And if we may credit the indignant prisoner's later recollections, Cox forced him to offer morning prayers for "old Abe" while standing on a cannon. Whatever the truth of the matter, there is little question that Moore and his prisoner were much inflamed by their encounter.

Triumph and tragedy mixed with rancors as the days sped by at Hannibal. On March 4, one of Company A's recruits, James Oboy of Hancock County, Illinois, lost control of a team in a runaway, fell in front of his wagon, and suffered fatal injuries. Then, on Sunday afternoon, March 9, news came that Curtis, pursuing Price and Ben McCulloch into northwestern Arkansas, had bested them in a hard-fought battle at Pea Ridge and sent the rebels scurrying on toward Little Rock. Sharing in the defeat were luckless Martin Green and his Athens veterans. Colonel Moore jubilantly ordered Company H, which had custody of those field pieces, to fire a salute. As luck would have it, one cannon misfired while Private Charles H. Dietz, a young German potter from Memphis, was ramming the load. The thumber may have been careless. At any rate, the load went off and ripped away much of the flesh of Dietz' left arm as well as the thumb and two fingers of his right hand. Wyman removed the mangled limb, bringing the war to a sudden end for Charles Dietz.

On the Sunday Dietz was injured, Woodyard returned from Palmyra. The court-martial had heard the lengthy case against Bishop, including an attack by William McKee on his fitness to command, but on March 8 the judges found the colonel "not guilty" on all counts and ordered him to "resume his sword." What this meant is rather unclear, since a new commander had taken over the Seventh Cavalry in Bishop's absence. Pridefully refusing the lieutenant colonelcy, Bishop was mustered out with no formal notification.

On March 17, the Twenty-first Missouri suffered another kind of loss. Three men left to accept offices in the Scotland County courthouse. Wilson Harle became sheriff, and the county clerkship went to the first sergeant of Company C, William W. Purmort of Memphis. John W. McIntyre, upstate New Yorker, left Company I to become circuit clerk at Memphis. None of the three, appointed by Governor Gamble, had much Radicalism in his bloodstream, needless to say.

There were interludes in the training schedule. On Wednesday, March 12, Moore and King led a party of enlisted men down to the caverns below Hannibal since enshrined in American fiction by Twain. Werly was ecstatic: "The cliffs on both sides of the grotto look like beautiful clouds, projecting above one another from the mountains with sharp points." Here, he wrote, "God's children can see the wonderful creation and the almightiness of God, that [what] everyone is seeing has been made out of nothing through the word of God 'It be.' "

Sutler Rickey arrived in Keokuk on March 17 with news that the Twenty-first Missouri "has been ordered south." His foster son, Rufus Wilsey, made ready to go with the regiment as Doc's representative. The ice was breaking up on the Mississippi, following recent heavy rains, and river traffic was about to resume.

The steamer *Die Vernon,* a 578-ton craft just three years old, tied up at Hannibal's levee on Tuesday afternoon, March 18, to take Moore's regiment on board. The men were loaded by nightfall for the first of many voyages. Indeed, while the great rebellion lasted, they would spend three months on the decks of such vessels.

As the *Die Vernon* pulled into St. Louis the morning of March 19, Moore's troops could sense that they were part of a vast tide of bluecoats flowing toward western Tennessee. The Department of War had lately confided the entire battle line in the Mississippi valley to Halleck and designated his expanded domain as the Department of the Mississippi. Buell's Army of the Ohio had just passed through Nashville, while Grant's Army of the Tennessee was already at a place called Pittsburg Landing, on the west bank of the Tennessee just above the Mississippi state line. As the boys read their St. Louis newspapers, they could see the outlines of a mighty collision between Grant and Sidney Johnston somewhere in northern Mississippi or southern Tennessee.

The soldiers spent a night in the comfort of Benton Barracks, but on March 20 they got the sad news that their stay there was a short one. Colonel Moore, appearing at Halleck's headquarters the afternoon before, received Special Orders 21 directing him to "proceed forthwith and report to Maj. Gen. U. S. Grant, touching at Fort Henry for orders."

The next afternoon the regiment boarded the steamer *T. C. Swan,* an older and lighter craft than the *Die Vernon.* Pulling out of St. Louis at 5:00 P.M., they were at Cairo, Illinois, twenty-four hours later. Leaving Cairo the evening of March 22, the boat proceeded up the Ohio to Paducah, Kentucky. Aaron Harlan, going ashore to supervise loading of rations, "saw a large amount of cannon balls, shells, shot, telegraph wires and . . . cotton bales that had received many shots—all of them trophies from the late battles of Forts Henry and Donelson." Soon he and others were listening in rapture to an extended lecture by an elderly slave about the nature and sources of these mementoes, and the commissary sergeant could not help thinking over and over to himself: "A. W. Harlan receiving knowledge from a negro!"

The *Swan* proceeded from Paducah up the Tennessee that morning and docked at Fort Henry in the evening. Harlan was enthralled: "The river is generally twice as wide as the Des Moines; that is, . . . from six to eight hundred yards, remarkably straight, and I know by the shape of the willows on the banks that the shores do not wash much. At present it is very high, being from three to four feet over the banks. The bottoms are narrow, say from quarter to half a mile, but seldom more. . . . The timber on the hills is generally oak, and looks finely. On the bottoms there is sweet gum, gray ash, hickory, and beech."

But if he found nature's prospects pleasing, he found the human condition vile aboard the *Swan*. There had been cloudiness and damp weather all the way, and nearly a hundred men were either under the surgeon's care or "complaining." Dysentery, as W. W. Belknap later said, was "that disease, the terror of all camps, whose wasting weakness, as our surgeons said, outrivals shot and shell." Harlan placed much of the blame on the victims themselves, believing that "whisky and large amounts of fruit with which some of the men gorge themselves, are worse than secesh in the open field."

It must have been an anxious trip for Lieutenant Washburn. Son George had been impatient to rejoin his father. Not long before the regiment left Hannibal, Washburn wrote the lad to come on to Camp Loomis. But the boy failed to appear, and until and unless he reached Tennessee his father could only worry about him.

George was taking good care of himself. Arriving at Loomis March 19, he learned the Twenty-first Missouri was at Benton Barracks. True enough, but it was gone when George got there. "I enjoyed the scene at Benton Barracks," he later recalled, "and resolved then and there to be a soldier." He remembered walking over to a cannon, leaning on it, and saying to himself, "Well, this is what they call war!"

The *Swan* reached Pittsburg Landing Tuesday, March 25, at 4:00 P.M., but the regiment did not unload until morning. As the boys made ready to go ashore to make camp, the boat carrying the Twelfth Michigan arrived, with George P. Washburn on board. "My father and brother were overjoyed to see me," George said. "We soon disembarked and moved out about one mile on the Corinth road and went into camp. It kept running through my mind, 'And this is war.' "

David Moore was experiencing little jollity. Wyman reported that

Lieutenant Lester, down with typhoid, was sinking. He died March 28.
Private Sam Jolliffe of Company E was fatally wounded by jittery guards
the first night in camp. Serious also was a visit from Grant's provost
marshal, informing Moore that Grant was incensed over word that the
Twenty-first Missouri's conduct on its trip had been "infamous." Grant
understood that "a constant fire was kept up all the way, . . . and in some
instances the citizens on shore were fired at." Grant wanted Moore held
for trial—and as the evening shadows lengthened across the Tennessee,
Humphrey Woodyard must have sensed that the mills of military justice
might yet restore those silver eagles to his shoulder straps.

4

The Lion and the Adder

As the twenty-first Missouri camped near Pittsburg Landing, General Prentiss came up to organize the Sixth Division of Grant's Army of the Tennessee. Troops on hand or promised would suffice for two four-regiment brigades, satisfying regulations governing divisional organization. Enough regiments were at hand to form a First Brigade for Colonel Everett Peabody. Available immediately to the colonel were the Twelfth Michigan, Sixteenth Wisconsin, Twenty-first Missouri, and his own Twenty-fifth Missouri.

Peabody, after checking with Prentiss and Grant's representative, Brigadier General William T. Sherman, went into camp along a line stretching west from the Eastern Corinth Road at a point one and a half miles southwest of the landing. It was imperative, Sherman said, that the Sixth Division take up its line right away, for units coming in would need room near the landing. On Sunday, March 30, Woodyard ordered the tents struck for a move down across Oak Creek. Werly found it "very disagreeable to me to . . . pass Sunday in such a manner." A German Methodist evangelist was holding forth in a regiment near by—and Werly had intended to be there. "But in time of war," he lamented, "they don't care for that."

Back at army headquarters in the Cherry Mansion at Savannah some nine miles north of the landing, things were out of joint. Grant had gotten into deep trouble with Halleck by failing to answer several telegrams and, worse yet, going to Nashville without permission to confer with Buell. Jumping to the conclusion that Grant's former "bad habits" were back, Halleck on March 4 had relieved him and given the army command to Brigadier General Charles F. Smith. Days passed before Grant realized he was suspected of tippling, and he was left sulking at Fort Henry baffled by Old Brains' wrath. The President, however, got wind of Halleck's treatment of the rising national hero and demanded an accounting. Halleck pulled in his horns. Running the matter through as demanded, he discovered that thanks to a "rebel" telegrapher many of his communications had never reached Grant. On March 13 he promised to restore his victim's command.

In the meantime, General Smith had scratched his shin while jumping into a boat. The abrasion developed an infection, and Smith took to bed with a fatal case of blood poisoning. Grant resumed command on March 17, uncertain of his future. Word came that Halleck would soon reach Savannah to command all forces, and orders were for Grant to avoid any general engagement until Buell could get over from Nashville and Halleck would make his appearance.

Moving down the Eastern Corinth Road, Woodyard ordered tents pitched in an area "covered with woods," as John Codman Ropes said a generation later, "with large cleared spaces between, and which was

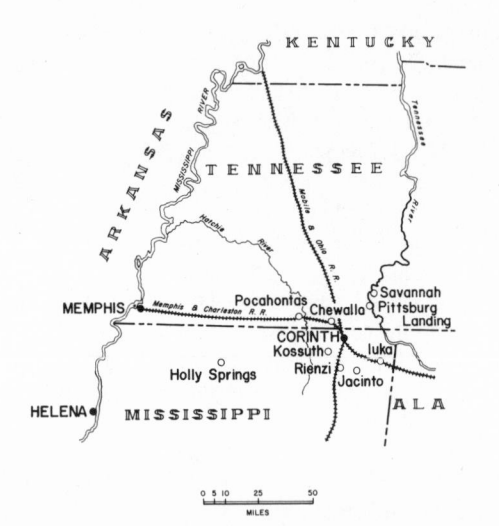

WEST   TENNESSEE
&
NORTH MISSISSIPPI
1862

intersected by deep ravines." Verdant oaks dominated the landscape, with occasional hickories, gums, cedars, and other trees lending variety. Redbuds and dogwood highlighted the underbrush grown luxuriant in the warm rains of early spring.

Camped between Woodyard and the Eastern Corinth Road was Colonel Benjamin Allen's Sixteenth Wisconsin, and on the immediate west was the Twelfth Michigan, commanded by Colonel Francis Quinn. Peabody's Twenty-fifth Missouri, farther west, held the brigade right, with Lieutenant Colonel Robert T. Van Horn in command. East of the road the Second Brigade formed, under Colonel Madison Miller, whose Eighteenth Missouri stood in line with the Sixty-first Illinois and Eighteenth Wisconsin. Prentiss set up his command post on a wooded knoll a few hundred feet behind the Second Brigade and within easy reach of the Eastern Corinth Road.

Three-quarters of a mile to the northwest of Woodyard's camp and overlooking Oak Creek was a little Methodist meetinghouse known as Shiloh Church. Here was Sherman's Fifth Division, or at least its main body. One of his brigades, under Colonel David Stuart, was standing on the Hamburg Road, not quite a mile east of Prentiss' headquarters and probably a half-mile from the river. Just behind Sherman was Major General John A. McClernand's First Division, and a half-mile to the north of Prentiss were the nearest elements of Hurlbut's Fourth Division. Farther back, west of the landing, was Brigadier General William H. L. Wallace's Second Division, and to the north at Crump's Landing was Brigadier General Lewis Wallace's Third Division. The army had not yet quite concentrated, and few commanders seemed to think there was any hurry.

On Friday, April 4, Woodyard learned he was not going to command the Twenty-first Missouri just yet. The court-martial for Moore, convening at Savannah that morning, cleared him. That evening, at a retreat formation, Prentiss ceremoniously restored the colonel's sword. As a newsman recorded the event, the colonel proceeded to deliver a "very brief, but characteristic speech, . . . which, however, we cannot repeat."

Saturday was a balmy spring day, but George Washburn sensed a nervousness in camp. A soldier of the Twelfth Michigan recalled his lieutenant colonel's feeling "some unseen impending danger." High time! By noon a line of rebel infantry, four brigades strong, had snuggled down in the brush two miles from Shiloh Church.

Johnston's forty-thousand-man army, after struggling along "narrow wheelways, . . . traversing a densely-wooded country" well soaked by

recent showers, was getting into position to fall on the weaker Army of
the Tennessee before Buell could reinforce. By sundown, Johnston and
his deputy, the flamboyant General Pierre G. T. Beauregard, would
have three heavy lines of infantry ready to move in on the exposed
Yankees.

It was about 5 P.M. when Prentiss rode into Moore's camp to order
out a reconnaissance. Captains Pearce, Cox, and Harle turned out with
their companies, and with Moore at their head trudged south down a
well-beaten trail leading to Eastern Corinth Road, a half-mile from camp.
Then proceeding west for a mile to the Fraley farm, just beyond the
Western Corinth Road, Moore still found no evidence other than fresh
hoof-prints of a rebel presence. Concluding that the enemy horsemen
might be near, he returned to camp at 7 P.M. and so reported. Prentiss
immediately doubled his "grand guard," and sent Captain Edward Saxe's
Company A, Sixteenth Wisconsin, to picket nearly a mile southwest of
camp.

Throughout that rainy night there were enough bursts of picket firing
to keep the camp on edge. Before snuffing out his candle for the night,
Orderly French consoled himself in the colonel's tent by reading from
Psalms 91, which assures the keeper of the covenant that

Thou shalt not be afraid for the terror by night,
Nor for the arrow that flieth by day,
Nor for the pestilence that walketh in darkness
Nor for the destruction that walketh at noonday.

The psalmist further promises that the faithful shall "tread upon the
lion and the adder" without fear. Moore's dutiful bodyguard would
find himself reflecting often on these comforting lines in later years.

Down on Lick Creek, Colonel Nathan Bedford Forrest's Confederate
horsemen were trading lead with Stuart's outposts. By midnight, Saxe's
men had fired so many rounds toward the Bark Road that Prentiss decided to have his front reconnoitered again. Some time before 3:00 A.M.,
Major James E. Powell took three companies of his Twenty-fifth Missouri
and elements of the Twelfth Michigan up to Saxe's picket line. The general hoped that this force might overpower and capture a marauding patrol—for an intelligence coup of historic magnitude.

At 4:55 A.M., in the Fraley field, Powell drew the fire of Major Aaron
B. Hardcastle's Third Mississippi Infantry. After a brief exchange, Powell
withdrew his line and re-formed under cover of adjoining woods. Had
it occurred to him the rebels were skirmishers of Major General William

J. Hardee's corps, the withdrawal would certainly have covered more mileage. As the gray line came on, Powell chose to fight a delaying action and send back for help.

Prentiss was ready to reinforce. Riding up to Peabody's camp—"very leisurely," thought George Washburn—he called for Moore to take half of the Twenty-first Missouri and give Powell the backing needed to hold the enemy. Summoning companies A, C, D, H, and I, Moore strode off to Powell's rescue around 5:20. An aide to Prentiss dashed off to tell Saxe to call in the pickets. Moore's column grew as he marched. Saxe, followed by his company, joined the Missourians along the road east of the Rhea field. Moore told him to "fall in on the right or left of my regiment." Throwing his coat to the ground, Saxe chose to fall in on the right, in order, as he yelled to his men, to "head them out!"

The Twenty-first Missouri had hardly right-faced and started on before Powell's retreating detachment came into view, bringing its wounded. Moore, said a Michigan soldier, "rated us cowards for retreating." As Dave himself put it, "Those who were able for duty I ordered and compelled to return to their posts." Powell warned of trouble ahead, but the caustic merchant of Wrightsville thought he had seen worse in north Missouri and had no intention of slinking off into the brush. He did take Powell's admonition sufficiently to heart to send Lieutenant Menn back to urge Woodyard forward on the "double-quick" with the rest of the Twenty-first Missouri.

Prentiss, conferring with Peabody when the breathless Menn burst out of the woods, instantly authorized Woodyard to go. These Missourians, he knew, had been long since "blooded," and he did not hesitate to commit them. "Now the 'long roll' beat," said George Washburn, "and there was a great excitement in camp and I felt sure that I was going to see a sure enough battle. . . . I busied myself in opening cartridge cases and filling cartridge boxes."

It was about 5:45 when Woodyard's riflemen came jogging down the trail to join Moore at the crossing of the east branch of Shiloh Creek. "We marched some 300 yards together . . . in a nearly westerly direction by flank movement, four ranks, when the head of the column came to the northwest corner of a cotton field," Woodyard said later. To the south and west it appeared the woodlands were crowded with Johnnies, but few in Moore's column thought they were about to open fire. Their confidence was misplaced, however, for musketry suddenly blazed along the rail fence on the north side of the Seay farm. A line of rebels bolted from the fence toward woods on the west, as Captain Saxe and one of his sergeants collapsed along the road with fatal wounds.

Some Yankees "laid down in the road," one lad remembered, "others got behind trees and commenced firing." His voice rising above the commotion, Moore shouted orders to get through the fence to form a firing line in a corner of the Seay field. His Missouri farmers dismantled the fence in short order, and it was Moore's pleasure to open fire on the Eighth and Ninth Arkansas Infantry forming at the south end of the field. Moore "thought he could whip the whole Southern Confederacy with the Twenty-First Missouri," one admirer said, and Dave confessed later his exhilaration at that first volley across Seay field. His regiment, he claimed, "appeared like a volcano in full blast. The enemy's lines presented the appearance of a line of fire; the air was filled with lead and iron." Indeed, the commander of the Ninth Arkansas was impressed with the sharp firing that marked his initial encounter with the Missourians. An officer of Miller's brigade noted afterward that the "almost incessant roar of musketry . . . told the desperate character of the contest being waged between the rebels and the 21st Missouri."

The nature of Moore's thrills soon changed, as the growing rebel line began giving better than it got. Brave boys who had come a long way with Moore began falling. Hugh Shirkey of Company D fell, and the dying youth was carried into woods north of the road on the strong back of Sergeant John H. Cunningham. Just twenty, Hugh was a Knox County lad, and the tragic distinction of being the first in the regiment to die on the field of Shiloh would enshrine him in the memory of comrades grown old and gray. Private Gustav Berner of Company H, stepping out to get "a better shot," suddenly spun around to the sodden ground behind him, his life's blood spurting from an ugly neck wound. He was a German-born watchmaker of Keokuk, and Cox said of him that "his name deserves to be embalmed in the hearts of his countrymen and ours, and his grave is worthy of a marble monument." Lieutenant Menn, grazed, was borne insensate to the rear. And then a minié ball struck Colonel Moore's right leg, below the knee.

Orderly French summoned Mike Cashman and Peter Klein to bear the dazed colonel to safety beyond the branch to the northeast, and Woodyard took command. It was nearly six, and sunlight streaming through the upper branches of taller trees lent an eerie glow to patches of fog hugging the ground in the densest woods. The firing from the south end of Seay's was dying away; however, fresh enemy formations soon appeared in woods along the Western Corinth Road around Fraley's, and Woodyard chose to re-form "on the brow of a hill" facing in a more westerly direction. The Twenty-first Missouri and the attached

troops laid a withering fire on the startled rebels until about 6:20.
Then, wary of trying a frontal attack, the Johnnies sought to pass
around Woodyard's right. He countered by retiring to the northeast
corner of the Seay field.

Four companies of the Sixteenth Wisconsin coming up, Woodyard
"ordered them to a position east of the field," among trees overlooking a creek behind them. The line now, he noted, faced south, "behind
a small incline, enabling my men to load and be out of range of the
enemy's fire." It was a strong line, and the rebels soon despaired of
forcing it. Therefore, around 7 o'clock, Confederate artillery opened,
and flanking movements resumed. With too small a force to contain
them, Woodyard withdrew across the branch to a hill position running
southeast from the lower end of the Rhea farm. "This was the last
formation of our regiment," Private Henry K. Rugh reminisced fifty-
five years afterward, "and I saw no more of my company that day."

In this retreat across the branch, fresh tragedy overtook the Twenty-
first Missouri. Exuberant Barney King, idol of the regiment ever after,
had been all over the line cheering on the boys. But now a rebel bullet
suddenly laid him low, and the major was soon beyond the cares of
this life. Later that spring, Steve Carnegy had the body brought home
to Canton in a leaden coffin, and in 1863 the regiment raised six
hundred dollars to erect an impressive marble shaft to Barney's
memory.

As the grieving Woodyard organized a new line, barely a half-mile
before the camps, Peabody arrived with the rest of the brigade. It was
about 7:30, and George Washburn thought Johnston's Confederates
were coming on "like a Kansas cyclone." Prentiss had both brigades
drawn up to receive the attackers, Sherman's division was evidently
about ready, and the "long roll" was audible well to the rear in other
divisions.

The new line was soon tested. Brigadier General R. G. Shaver's brigade of Hardee's corps pitched into it at once as Johnston's gunners
wheeled pieces up to bolster the attack. Peabody's brigade, firing steadily by ranks, soon drove the rebels back, and Johnston himself had to
take a hand in rallying them for a second attempt. With fresh troops,
the Johnnies came again, and the Yankee line began to buckle. Finally,
around 8 A.M., Peabody tried to save his formation by withdrawing to
within a quarter-mile of camp. Apprising Hurlbut and Wallace of his
predicament, he urged reinforcements from them without delay.

"We gradually began to fall back and reached our tents," Woodyard said, "when the ranks got broken in passing through them." The horror of that rout in the camps never left those who went through it. Peabody and Powell died there, and Captain Murrow was badly trampled by his frightened horse. Woodyard could not reassemble his terrified regiment in the rear of camp. Werly, understandably vague about his specific movements during those terrible hours, recorded that "it weighed heavily on me that I should die in such a manner, by murderous weapons." Sergeant Starr was soon writing with great frankness to Miss Headley that he had been *frightened dreadfully.*

This breakup of the First Brigade unhinged Miller's position in the Spain field. Second Brigade, led by the green-as-gourds Sixty-first Illinois, stampeded for brushier land with Brigadier General Adley H. Gladden's Southerners in hot pursuit. Colonel Jesse Hildebrand's brigade of Sherman's division, favored with extra time to get ready when Moore's resistance deflected the rebels toward Prentiss, had made little use of its good fortune. The Fifty-third Ohio panicked, setting the stage for the crumpling of Sherman's left flank. The Ohioans created an alibi that they "would have stood their ground had not their colonel dodged." The truth of the matter was clear to Sherman, who engineered the colonel's dismissal a few days later.

Soon after 8 o'clock, Surgeon Wyman and his perspiring stretcher crew reached the Landing with Colonel Moore. Belknap, major of the Fifteenth Iowa, heard directly from Wyman the grim news that Moore's leg bone had been shattered so badly that amputation was inevitable. The landing was a perfect madhouse. Hundreds of terrified stragglers were gathering. Many of their officers were coming to round them up, but it was difficult to talk sense to such men. Doc Rickey seemed to a fellow sutler "the most excited man I ever saw. He said we were whipped, and would all be driven to the river in less than twenty minutes. Says he, 'Pack up your traps and leave, . . . for what I tell you is so. I have lost everything." Doc proved substantially correct, as far as his own enterprise was concerned, for even his clerk, Rufe Wilsey, was shot in one leg and lost to the business indefinitely.

Between 8 and 9 o'clock the steamer *Tigress* put in, bringing U. S. Grant to the scene of action. After he had ridden off to assess the situation, his staff invited Wyman to bring Colonel Moore aboard to remove him from the clamor along the bank. Docked there since shortly after sunrise was the *Minnehaha,* with Colonel Hugh T. Reid's Fifteenth Iowa aboard. Later that day, after the Iowans had landed, Moore was transferred to the *Minnehaha* and the care of Reid's surgeons, Samuel B. Davis and William H. Gibbon. Davis amputated the mangled leg just above the knee that afternoon, Gibbon assisting. "The Colonel swore roundly until he got under the influence of chloroform," Gibbon recalled, "and if I am not mistaken, his first words after he came out from under its influence were of a very sulphurous character against those who had rebelled against 'the best government on earth.' "

Meanwhile, Prentiss had had little luck forming a new line behind the encampment. Woodyard's men "got much scattered, a great many falling into other regiments under the immediate command of General Prentiss; others divided to other divisions, but continued to fight." Well and good, to be sure—but this does not tell us what Woodyard did with *his* day. If he never revealed how he spent it, his officers swore later, almost to a man, that Woodyard had "retired from the field to Pittsburg Landing where he remained, and stated to the men . . . that they should return to Missouri."

George Washburn thought that "our lines became stronger all the time." Nearly a mile behind the tents ran an old sunken road through an area "shielded by a heavy growth of blackberry bushes, underbrush, and small trees." Seeing the defensive potentialities of this "natural rifle pit," Prentiss pulled together remnants of the Eighteenth and Twenty-first Missouri, Twelfth Michigan, and Eighteenth Wisconsin. This fragment of his division he sandwiched after 9:00 A.M. into the sunken road position between Hurlbut to his east and W. H. L. Wallace to his right. About two hundred men of the Twenty-first Missouri followed Prentiss into the new position, soon dubbed the "Hornets' Nest" by Confederates who learned at great cost to respect it during that long and bloody Sabbath.

Now that Prentiss had a line he could hold, he began collecting reinforcements. First to reach him was the Twenty-third Missouri Infantry, just off the boat from northern Missouri and commanded by Colonel Jacob T. Tindall, a member of the state convention. "This regiment," Prentiss "immediately assigned to position on the left." Next to it was the Eighth Iowa, "loaned" by Wallace. Soon after 10:30 there came Reid's Fifteenth Iowa, many in its ranks surely doubting the wisdom of hurrying to a place like this. On their way, they had met hundreds of fleeing men screaming such encouragements as "Don't go out there!" or "You'll catch hell!"

The Hornets' Nest appealed to Grant who had just withstood a massive rebel charge around 10 o'clock, as a matchless defensive bastion. Prentiss showed Grant "the disposition of my entire force, which . . . received his commendation, and I received from him my final orders, which were to maintain that position at all hazards." To the west, McClernand had inserted his division into the vacuum created by Sherman's collapsed left, and together their divisions put up a staunch fight to hold the ridge line near the church. To Prentiss' east, Hurlbut and Stuart tangled with the enemy around a peach orchard and a pond just west of the road to Hamburg. The noise of this three-mile battle line, George Washburn thought, was "deafening at times."

As the struggle raged on, Sherman and McClernand withdrew to positions behind the Purdy-Hamburg road. This retraction of the federal left—together with unbending resistance in the Hornets' Nest, Peach Orchard, and "Bloody Pond"—convinced Johnston the operation was running counter to his plan. Instead of shouldering the Yankees *away* from the landing, this advance was driving them slowly back on it. Directing Brigadier General Daniel Ruggles to concentrate eleven batteries of artillery on the Nest, Johnston went over to the Hamburg Road to supervise the all-important thrust along the river. This devotion to detail cost Johnston his life, and it probably cost the Confederacy a signal victory. Struck in a leg artery by a minié ball at 2:00 P. M., the brave Kentuckian soon perished near the pond from loss of blood. Beauregard took command, anxious to press the attack with the vigor characteristic of the great Creole.

Ruggles' batteries soon took their toll. Successive barrages, interspersed with infantry rushes, forced Yankees on both sides of the Hornets' Nest to fall back out of contact with Prentiss and Wallace. Stuart's line gave way at 3:00 P.M., as did those of Sherman and McClernand, and soon Hurlbut's division was also in retreat toward the landing.

Survivors of the Twenty-first Missouri huddled in the Hornets' Nest and "made a determined stand, loading and firing at will," but the cost of their gallantry was high. Around 3:00 P.M., Lieutenant Washburn was struck in the right hip by a shell fragment. George was certain the lieutenant was dead, but he soon regained consciousness. The injured man told his son to "take my money and equipment and make your escape if possible and go home to look after the family. We will be captured here unless orders are given to cut our way out."

For surely the first time, George disobeyed. With help from the others, he loaded the lieutenant on his back and started for the rear.

Wounded badly at the same time was Private John Fahey of Company
E, a twenty-six-year-old Irishman from Knox County. The Washburns
decided to take him along, George carrying first one and then the other.
It was near sundown when they reached the landing, but George's hope
of getting the sufferers to a transport bound for "home" was near to
success.

What the Washburns found at the landing beggared description, with
"thousands of dead and wounded, and their comrades who had carried
them down there, bales of hay had been placed to form tables where
Surgeons were busy amputating." Nine days later, Wilsey was home in
Keokuk telling friends he had seen "probably seven thousand men huddled in down there all disorganized." In retrospect, it seems clear the
main body of the Twenty-first Missouri was among them. A historian
observed of Sunday's fighting that "none but the steadiest and bravest
soldiers could stand such discouraging encounters without losing faith
in their leaders and confidence in themselves." Many wounded had "got
themselves to the rear, or were brought there by friends glad of an excuse to leave the fighting."

By 5 P.M., some sixty men of the Twenty-first Missouri, attached
now to Colonel William T. Shaw's Fourteenth Iowa, remained in the
Hornets' Nest. Adjutant Tobin was the ranking member there, and
with him were Second Lieutenants Richardson (C) and Whittemore (F).
Captain Cox's sixty-two-year-old first sergeant, Joseph A. Crandall, was
in the closing trap, as were First Sergeant Morrey (D), and Private
George Wilson (H)—the same who almost caught Bill Dunn at that
Schuyler County barn lot.

Beauregard found the Army of the Mississippi badly scrambled;
some units were by noon little more than debris. His right wing along
the river road to the landing he placed under Braxton Bragg. Ruggles
and Hardee commanded formations engaged with the Hornets' Nest.
Elements free to push into the gap between the Nest and the Union
right were grouped under Major General Leonidas Polk, late Episcopal missionary bishop of the Southwest. Redeployed into a right,
center, and left—instead of a front, middle, and rear—the rebels could
take better advantage of Ruggles' barrages to pinch off the Nest.

That the Confederates meant to surround this position was obvious
before 5 P.M. W. H. L. Wallace chose to extricate his troops while
there was yet time, and two regiments did make their way out to the
bluff beyond them by going down a ravine. Wallace himself was wound-

ed in the attempt, dying shortly after the battle. Colonel Tindall, trying
to pull the Twenty-third Missouri back to the bluff, was killed outright.
Convinced that his own escape was impossible, Prentiss,

> . . . having dispatched my aide, Lieut. Edwin Moore, for re-enforce-
> ments, . . . determined to assail the enemy, which had passed between
> me and the river. . . . I found him advancing in mass, completely en-
> circling my command, and nothing was left but to harass him and
> retard his progress so long as might be possible. This I did until
> 5.30 P.M., when finding that further resistance must result in the
> slaughter of every man in the command, I had to yield the fight.
> The enemy succeeded in capturing myself and 2,200 rank and file. . . .

While Prentiss kidded Beauregard over prospects for a Confederate
victory on this field, the prisoners stacked arms and passed into captivity. Surrendered with Tobin was a party of fifty-eight representing every
company of the Twenty-first Missouri. A dozen other regiments and
batteries fell wholly or partly into rebel hands. Beauregard thought it
a capital day's work, but historians would come to see in Prentiss' valiant stand the salvation of a badly shaken Army of the Tennessee.

Challenged by Prentiss to advance on the landing to find out how
many Yankees there were, Beauregard did so. While the sun hovered in
the west, Bragg wheeled the brigades of James R. Chalmers and John K.
Jackson into line for an assault across Dill's Branch and onto the bluff
around the landing. But the Yankees were ready, and there was no out-
flanking them here. Grant had turned the bluff into a giant battery from
which "on every available spot of earth an iron-lipped monster frowns."

To the cannonade from the bluff, Chalmers and Jackson could "make
no effective reply," a historian wrote. "Again and again they attempted
to scale the crest, and again and again they were forced back from the
ditch." One soldier on the bluff thought it like a "horrible dream" as
the ground trembled and the artillery "belched forth streams of fire."
Two gunboats, standing off the mouth of Dill's Branch, added their
shellfire to the weight of Grant's barrages. Soon it became apparent
that Bragg was giving it up, and Iowa soldiers were so jubilant that
"we snatched off our hats and yelled like maniacs. We had repulsed
the foe and the first day's carnage was over."

Beauregard telegraphed Richmond that "a complete victory" had
been gained. Within an hour, however, he began to have doubts. Now

he knew the Army of the Ohio was massing under cover of darkness on the east bank and that he could do little to prevent Buell's crossing. Indeed, by morning some seventeen thousand fresh and combat-wise federals would be on the west bank. Lew Wallace's Third Division would be there, too, although he would spend a lifetime explaining why he had taken the long way out, past Purdy, and arrived too late for Sunday's fighting. His veterans of Donelson would be a "deal of help" if fighting resumed.

Sunday night was a time of alarms. Gunboat crews made it a point to drop a few shells over in the army's former campgrounds about four times an hour, just to keep the new occupants awake. Several thunderstorms blew in, drenching both sides. Around the landing, all shelter was commandeered by the surgeons, and even Grant spent the night out in the storm in preference to witnessing the heartrending scenes indoors. Like many other youngsters with the army, George Washburn found himself "drafted" to assist the surgeons, "so I held the arm and leg of many boys while it was sawn off, and threw it on the pile, and saw many, many a poor boy die under the influence of chloroform and amputation. I afterwards wanted to be a surgeon, as I felt sure I could do the job just as well as those who were doing the cutting."

About midnight, George got his father aboard a hospital boat, which took him as far as Savannah. At the lieutenant's urging, the boy went back to the bluff to hunt up Marion and Uncle Wilbur Davis, both safe and sound in Company H, as it happened.

George found Colonel Woodyard with the regiment in a camp between Dill's Branch and the ground occupied later by the national cemetery. George found little time for visiting. By sunup, Grant had received nearly twenty-five thousand fresh troops from both sides of the river, and the Confederate Army of the Mississippi, more than forty thousand strong a week earlier, had dwindled to about twenty thousand tired and miserable men. The federal juggernaut could not be stopped, and Beauregard found it impossible to get his line of battle in working order before losing the Peach Orchard and Hornets' Nest. Furious fighting raged until about 2 o'clock, when Beauregard broke off the contest to avoid utter ruin. From his command post at Shiloh Church, he sent out word to abandon the struggle. Within two hours, the Southerners were out of contact and slogging through the mud on their way to Corinth.

The "Bull Run of the West" was history. The Confederates had been induced to leave *this* battlefield—at a frightful cost, to be sure. More than a fourth of Grant's army was on casualty reports, including 1,433 killed and 2,818 captured or missing. Buell's casualties in the second day's fighting came to 2,103, including 241 dead. Of the 65,000 Union troops committed at Shiloh, 13,000 were casualties. Confederate losses were also calamitous, with 1,700 dead and a total of 10,699 casualties out of a force of fewer than 45,000.

Late that afternoon, survivors of Sunday's fighting moved back to their old camps. Apparently Woodyard looked on the matter as a routine hike, for his officers later complained that "when the Regiment left Pittsburg Landing to proceed to the front, he failed to take command and made no effort to keep it together." Understandable, for the trek to the ransacked camp was a depressing one, even to romantics like young Washburn: "The entire ground over which we passed was literally covered with dead and mangled men, horses, mules, broken and dismounted artillery, wagons and ambulances disabled and mired in the mud, and the ground littered with camp equipment. . . . I now realized what war really was, and my curiosity had been fully satisfied."

Starr wrote the girl back home that by Monday night "we again held soul possession with thanks to Gen. Buel for our success." In fact, he was even willing to credit Henrietta's latest letter with turning the tide, for "in two hours after receiving it, the enemy commenced a stampede, left the field followed by our own forces."

Tuesday was a busy day on the battlefield, as burial squads interred the dead in long trenches, segregating the blue from the gray. Wounded men—many, such as Private Aquilla Barnes of Company E, had lain in the brush since Sunday—were rounded up and taken to hospital boats. Some of the distinguished dead were buried in separate plots, to be reclaimed later. Colonel Peabody's remains were buried where his tent had stood, and, within the month, a party of civilians came out to Tennessee to claim the body for reburial in his native Massachusetts.

With the help of Sergeant Major Best, Woodyard took up the administrative obligations laid on him by Moore's absence. While Pressell arranged to feed the troops, Woodyard and Best struggled to perfect casualty reports. They tentatively concluded that 64 men were missing and presumed captured, 46 were wounded, and 18 killed outright. Time would alter the figures somewhat, but it is clear that a fifth of the First Brigade's casualties occurred in the ranks of the Twenty-first Missouri. Later in the week, figures came out revised for the benefit of St. Louis papers, listing 18 dead, 58 wounded, and 62 missing. The unknown source, lauding Woodyard's "coolness and bravery," curiously echoed Woodyard's own praise of Adjutant Tobin's acting "well and bravely."

It took weeks for the true horror of Shiloh to become apparent to the regiment. Analysis of service records reveals that the total captured was actually 59 and that 17 of the wounded died within two months, bringing battle deaths to 35. Even this latter figure rose by one a year later, upon confirmation that Private Columbus Dabney of Company G had also been killed in action the first day. Forty suffered nonfatal wounds, including two who were captured. The names on the regimental rolls dwindled to 702 by April 15, a loss of 260 in a month and a half.

Among the killed were Company F's Gerrit Stegeman, the Dutch lad who had found in Moore's regiment a refuge from pranksters of the Fifteenth Iowa. His family, living back in the Old Country at Zutphen, long wondered what had become of him. At last, in October 1864, the Dutch minister to Washington petitioned Secretary of State Seward in the Stegemans' behalf: "On the 22nd March 1862 he went from Hannibal, . . . under the orders of Colonel Moore. Since then no news has been had about him. If really dead, the family would much desire to have an official document respecting it." The Secretary of War was soon able to provide the dread news.

This battle's private disasters came in bunches for some families. Private Henry Bertram of Company H, a young immigrant Braunschweiger, lost part of his left arm. His father-in-law, fifty-four-year-old John Dell of Kahoka, also German-born, was among the captured, and Bertram's brother-in-law, the younger John Dell, died of wounds two weeks after the battle.

Aquilla Barnes, dangerously wounded in his left hip, was taken to St. Louis. His stepfather, Private Joshua B. Dale of Company E also, fell prisoner in the Hornets' Nest. Before long, Mrs. Dale was reading the news at their farm back near Colony, and her anguish at learning it all from the St. Louis newspapers is easily comprehended. At length, Lucinda Dale hit upon a scheme to reach her son, writing the postmaster of St. Louis to forward her letter. She told her son that

> . . . with a acheing heart and a mother love for her darling child I take my pen to let you know that I am well at present and I do hope when these few lines comes to you they may find you a greate deal better than I suppose you are. Oh Quiller the sad news when it came to me you was wonded and among strangers I tell

you how much it greived me none but a mother can feel what I
felt and then the trouble . . . I have endured to hear from you has
been my constant inquiry.

To read in the press of a loved one's injuries was one thing, but to
hear that he was missing was quite another. Charlie Blines was taken in
the Hornets' Nest, and his family near Alexandria fearfully pondered
the import. "The word 'missing' has a serious meaning," said a brother.
"It might indicate that the person had been wounded and crawled away
and died in some hidden place." In time, the family's apprehensions
vanished; Charlie came home on parole that summer.

The case of John Dunn of Company D was peculiarly depressing. He
had been with Murrow in the Millport Guard, but when the Twenty-
first Missouri mustered, Dunn was sick at home. He reached Pittsburg
Landing on April 2 and was unable to muster before the Confederate
attack; but he fought beside his comrades until a shell fragment cracked
his breastbone and three ribs. Hospitalized at Jefferson Barracks on St.
Louis' south side, he was slow to recover, and in June the medics sent
him home unfit for duty. Attempts to get pension relief ran into objections that he had never mustered. His certificate of disability discharge
came from the Department of War in the summer of 1874—two years
after his widow had buried him at Millport.

Prisoners of the Hornets' Nest spent Sunday night huddled in an open
field and soaked in the rain. "We had no protection from the storm,"
said Henry Rugh, "no blankets or covering of any kind." The next morning, General Hardee rode back to look over the "catch." "Boys, I am
sorry to see you in this condition," he declared. "You have my sympathy
in this time of distress. I wish things were different." Blines was sure
tears were welling in the famous Confederate's eyes as he wheeled his
mount to go. Their captors marched the men down the mucky road to
Corinth and a muddy corral. Then came the introduction to prisoner
cuisine, when, as Rugh said, "They gave us some crackers and pickled
beef—we called it mule meat, it was so tough."

Following a brief stay at Corinth, the Yankees were loaded on a
freight train—sixty men to a car—and taken to Mobile. Here Lieutenants
Richardson and Whittemore and the enlisted men were separated and
sent out in groups to various Alabama locations, such as Cahaba and
Tuscaloosa. Adjutant Tobin went on with other officers to Selma, Alabama, but when he got there in late April he was a bed patient. The
record is vague, but he apparently died in early May.

At Selma, the Confederates authorized the officers to elect a delegation to go to Washington, D.C., and open negotiations for a prisoner exchange. Early in the summer, matters had progressed so far that Southern officials started to move the privates to Montgomery to start paroling. Hundreds of them drifted north by boat and train to St. Louis for stationing at the Benton Barracks "parole camp," where the long wait for exchange began. In the course of the summer, officers and some noncoms, like Sergeant Morrey, were moved to Libby Prison at Richmond, where they could be handily repatriated.

Gourmets had little good to report of their captivity. In a twenty-man cell at Tuscaloosa, Rugh's party received "one pan of corn bread a day for our rations. We appointed one man to divide it. He cut it in 20 shares—3 by 3 inches. Some blackeyed peas seasoned with a very small piece of meat and sometimes a small portion of black molasses. We ate all we got at one meal." Company C's William Bradley, recalling the stay at Montgomery, thought "the rebels treated us as well as they could. They were almost destitute themselves. We were given a square of beef and a pint of unsifted wheat for daily rations." Morrey, paroled that autumn as an eighty-five-pound scarecrow, never again criticized a Yankee mess sergeant. In future years, his children were to find it unwise to get finicky about eating, since their father had learned in capitivity that "anything tastes good if you are really hungry."

News of Shiloh's carnage hit Quincy April 9, and *Whig-Republican* readers beheld bannered headlines erroneously heralding the "Great Battle at Corinth!" and its "Terrible Slaughter." Quincyites read that the Union's "loss" was eighteen thousand, the Confederates' forty thousand. Grant was reported wounded, which was friendlier treatment than he was getting from journalists convinced that he was "under the influence" when the storm broke. Western governors mobilized their resources to care for the wounded. Richard Yates of Illinois ordered conversion of buildings in Quincy to hospital use, and Kirkwood spurred the Keokuk city fathers to prepare the Keokuk Medical College, the Estes house, and other facilities for the expected tide of casualties.

Within two weeks, the wounded of the Twenty-first Missouri were scattered from Savannah all the way up to Cincinnati, Paducah, Mound City, St. Louis, Quincy, and Keokuk. On Saturday night, April 19, the first of the Shiloh casualties reached Keokuk aboard the *Jeannie Deans.* Chief among them was Dave Moore, taken to the Deming house to begin his long convalescence. Washburn returned to camp Loomis, but when he was able to travel he found it necessary to stay there because of a resurgence of guerrilla terrorism.

For more than two months, Moore chomped at the bit in Keokuk. Artemus Ward, celebrated humorist, performed before an overflow crowd in the city the evening of April 29. Moore's attendants carried him into the opera house on a cot, while the audience rose and "loudly cheered" the "Marion of North Missouri." Soon after this, a welcome visitor arrived. Captain William W. Moore, late of the Confederate cavalry, was in the mood to call it quits, and his wounded sire helped him to "come around right." If Will would take the oath and go to Ohio to study medicine, the colonel would pay his expenses. The American people lost a rebel horseman and gained a physician. For his part, "D. Moore, Union" intended to rejoin his regiment as soon as he could strap on a wooden leg. "It is not too much to say," wrote a later Secretary of War, "that this maimed the battle-scarred veteran deserves to be honored by the people of the entire Union."

By mid-April 1862, Union arms seemed triumphant in the West, and Lincoln's eastern forces were also showing some vigor. McClellan's Army of the Potomac, after landing on the Yorktown peninsula southeast of Richmond in March, moved ponderously toward the Confederate capital. Sly Joe Johnston, rebel commander in Virginia, contested the advance, while Major General Thomas Jonathan "Stonewall" Jackson, with about sixteen thousand men, raced up and down the valley all spring, making monkeys of several former national heroes.

McClellan, frustrated by Johnston's footwork and by Lincoln's insistence on diverting troops to "protect Washington," kept up his movement on Richmond. Greatly outnumbered, Johnston gave way slowly, waiting for an opportune moment to strike. Finally, on May 31, Old Joe saw his chance. Within sight of Richmond, while McClellan's army crossed a rising Chickahominy River, Johnston counterattacked at Seven Pines with every prospect of routing the Yankees. The counterstroke miscarried, and Johnston was himself badly wounded.

President Davis then turned to his adviser, General Robert E. Lee, offering him the command in Virginia. Lee, in accepting, would revive in Yankee hearts some of the terror forgotten since Bull Run.

5

Summer of Discontent

Throughout April, the Twenty-first Missouri remained on Shiloh's "dark and bloody ground." Rumblings were developing among those convinced the regiment had been "unlawfully" sent out of Missouri, and this was affecting the conduct of many. Pleading "failing health which incapacitates me for military duty," Lieutenant Pulis of Company E threw in his hand April 10. On the Sunday after Shiloh, following a special thanksgiving formation ordered from Washington, Captain Cox wrote his resignation "for reasons of sickness" in his family. Story, seeing on April 17 "no prospect for recovery whilst in service," asked to quit. How weary Woodyard would become of such memorandums! But still they came. Lieutenant Rickey of Cox's company, suffering "palpitation of the heart and rheumatism," gave in his letter April 20. Eight days later, Lieutenant Ed Turner of Company A petitioned Yust to let him go "for the reason that my lungs are so effected and my constitution so weak . . . that I cannot perform my duty for a long time to come."

Turner, Rickey, and Pulis were let go without a murmur. So far as Woodyard was concerned, Story could have gone with them, but division headquarters blocked his application. Only in dealing with Cox did Woodyard play the spoiler. "I do not deem it prudent to recommend the acceptance of this," read his kiss-of-death indorsement.

But Woodyard had a counter-proposal. The chaplaincy was open; would Cox consider it? The ex-parson from Chambersburg would, indeed. On Tuesday afternoon, April 22, the officers met and elected Cox. In a brief letter to Dr. Elliott, Cox announced with evident enthusiasm that "I have resigned my captaincy to reassume the chaplaincy."

Surgeon Wyman, burdened with sick and wounded aboard the steamer *Iatan,* took sick April 8 with pneumonia and dysentery. A friend later noted that "though a physically powerful man, his professional duties . . . were too much for human endurance." Finding Wyman

79

delirious four days after the illness set in, Seaton had him "conveyed
on board of another boat with some others and sent away" to St.
Louis. The regiment would see him no more, for on June 3 he resigned.

Seaton became acting regimental surgeon after Woodyard had under-
gone more administrative anguish. On April 14, Doc Davis reappeared,
still campaigning for the job of assistant. To a spluttering Woodyard, he
presented his appointment, signed "D. Moore." All this dated from the
Hannibal days, and Woodyard wrote division headquarters that "I know
nothing of the matter as Colonel Moore had the whole control of matters and I was never even consulted." He bucked it back to St. Louis,
and no more was heard of it. For temporary assistant surgeon he named
Carnahan, the hospital steward. Woodyard's new "contract surgeon" was
an old friend resident in Lewis County since 1847.

Particularly exasperating was the behavior of officers determined to
force the issue in choosing a new major. On the Sunday after Shiloh, a
petition began to circulate favoring appointment of Edward A. Kutzner,
fifty-three-year-old Memphis merchant highly esteemed by Scotland
County Unionists. Woodyard, to head off this move, hastily wrote division headquarters that "I think the action premature and that Colonel
Moore . . . and myself should be consulted." Simultaneously he fired
off a letter to Governor Gamble recommending Captain Harle, "a brave,
efficient officer."

Harle, however, signed the Kutzner petition along with Seaton, thirteen lieutenants, and all captains but Farris. On April 14, Turner gave the
papers to Woodyard, and the long wait for results began.

For help with paperwork, Woodyard reached into the Sixteenth Illinois for an acting adjutant. Richard Rees, a young Welsh immigrant clerking in division headquarters, was suffering from a slight neck wound but
"able for duty." "He gives entire satisfaction," Woodyard found, "is
thoroughly qualified, and from his brave and gallant conduct during the
late battle is deserving of the position." Quincyite Dick Rees had a long
and honorable future with the Twenty-first Missouri, but he never held
the adjutant's commission. With Rees advising him, Woodyard got after
the company commanders to requisition record books, round up stragglers, inventory arms and ammunition, and fill out those fearsome "Camp
and Garrison Clothing and Equipage" reports. Whether these sullen officers loved him or not, Woodyard meant to shape them up somehow.

The fog of battle lingered. As late as April 30 Captain Farris still
wrote of the "mysterious disappearance of 2nd Lt. F. A. Whittemore"
and proposed Sergeant Schram as his successor. Woodyard, equally un-

sure of the facts and well aware of the time lag in the governor's handling of appointments, did the best thing possible under the circumstances.
Ike Schram, of Moore's original company, became an "acting second
lieutenant" of Company F at once. He would have to wait for the
commission.

Rumors of high-level changes cropped up after Halleck arrived on
April 11 to assume personal charge of all forces. "He came with much
noise and parade," a hostile soldier-historian recorded,

> and brought with him the assurance that, at the earliest possible
> moment, the rebels under Beauregard would be met and annihilated.
> But days passed into weeks and no forward movement was initiated.
> Grant was virtually in disgrace, the victim of Halleck's jealousy as
> well as of the venal and libellous assaults of a class of newspaper
> correspondents, whose employment was evidently based upon their
> ability to misinterpret and misrepresent.

But Halleck was "all business," reshuffling the troops into a Right Wing,
Center, Left Wing, and Reserve. Buell, with the bulk of his army, was
to push south toward Corinth with the Center force. Most of the Army
of the Tennessee remained in the Right Wing, under Major General
George H. Thomas, while the Left Wing consisted of Pope's Army of
the Mississippi, fresh from its campaigning around Island Number 10
and New Madrid, Missouri. Two divisions of Grant's army, under Mc-
Clernand, constituted the Reserve. As "second-in-command," Grant
lived on in Halleck's limbo, his future seemingly devoid of headlines
even as his past provided a punching bag for journalists.

The Sixth Division, in the process of reorganization, passed to Brigadier General Thomas J. McKean. An elderly West Pointer, class of 1831,
McKean had spent the winter at Jefferson City, heading the district of
central Missouri. Taking over the First Brigade was Colonel John L.
Doran, whose command included the Twenty-first and Twenty-fifth
Missouri and the Sixteenth and Seventeenth Wisconsin. Woodyard, after
moving camp to Monterey, twelve miles south of Pittsburg Landing, on
April 25, prepared for the first muster since leaving Hannibal. He found
only eleven officers present for duty. Of enlisted men he could account
for 690 present, but the sad fact was that only 538 were well enough
to stay on their feet. Company commanders reported 152 gone; presumably they were sick or wounded, but many were simply heading
for home.

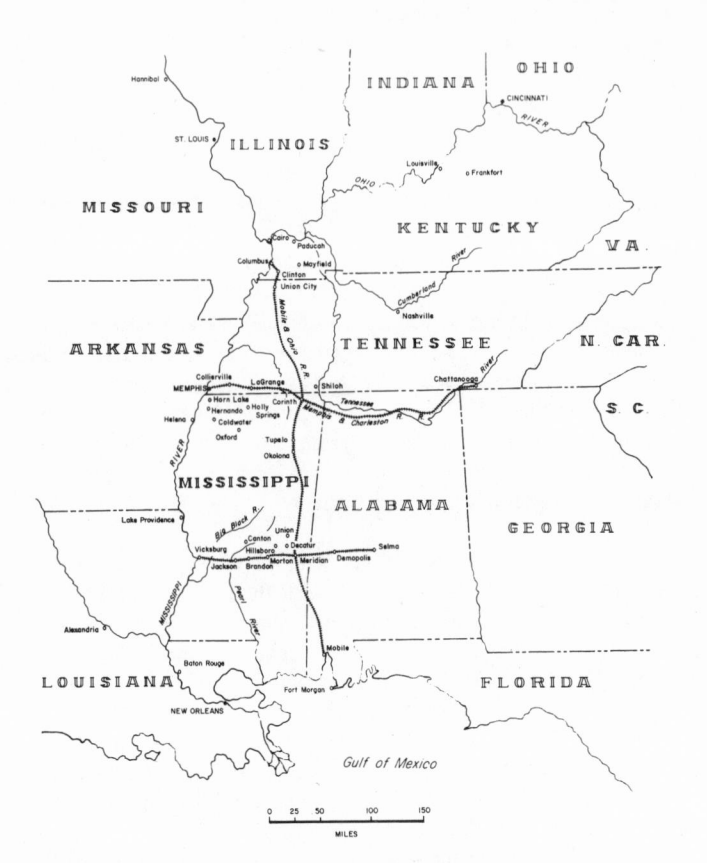

THE MISSISSIPPI VALLEY
1863 - 1864

Halleck's march on Corinth began at the end of April and carried its objective a month later. Although heavily outnumbering Beauregard, Old Brains seemed unwilling to risk a slugging match. A typical day's advance was about a mile and invariably ended with feverish erection of field fortifications to fend off nocturnal attacks. This much of Shiloh's "lesson" Halleck had learned. To many of the troops, this approach to Corinth was ponderous or even timid, but it *was* an advance and entailed small risk of the main force entrusted to Halleck.

Suffering no casualties in this slow-motion drive, the Twenty-first Missouri, its historians said, "took an active part in the siege of Corinth. On the 30th of April began the march on this formidable Confederate stronghold. It was fighting, advancing and building breastworks, until the enemy finally evacuated . . . on the 29th day of May, 1862." The regiment changed camp seven times on the twenty-mile march.

Something had to be done about Company H now that Cox was chaplain and Washburn and Rickey had left. On May 1, Quartermaster Sergeant Charles Tracy, named "acting captain" by Woodyard, took command. Private James Smith, a twenty-year-old New Yorker and ex-regular army soldier, became second lieutenant on the same basis. Sergeant John C. Smith, a Hoosier-born farmer from Luray, temporarily took over as first sergeant. Later that year, when Crandall was paroled and discharged, Smith's top sergeantcy became official.

Similarly, Captain Pearce on May 2 moved to fill the vacancy caused by Lieutenant Lester's death. His choice was a young native of Ireland, Sergeant William H. Simpson, who had "shown himself worthy a commission." Woodyard promptly conveyed the recommendations to higher headquarters. Within a month, Simpson's commission, signed by Gamble, arrived—as did those for Captain Tracy, Chaplain Cox, and Lieutenant Smith.

A different set of problems was created when Second Lieutenant Ed Fox of Company B died suddenly in camp the evening of May 19. Seaton diagnosed his affliction as "Apoplexia," and Woodyard chose a "council of administration" to inventory Fox's effects. An Adair County farmer, about forty years old, Fox left a widow and five youngsters. Woodyard, realizing that Story and Woodruff were ailing, boosted First Sergeant Jeremy Hall to "acting second lieutenant" and company commander. It took most of 1862 to get Hall commissioned, however.

Dismaying news flooded in daily. On May 18, Captain Fulton reported several "deserters," including Private Tom Roseberry of the Knox County family. Young Roseberry's departure was probably triggered by the desperate condition of brother David, dying in St. Louis of chronic dysentery. Early the morning of May 23, news spread through the army that Colonel Worthington of the Fifth Iowa had been shot by his own pickets. Private David B. Glenn of Company I, wounded at Shiloh, died in Paducah May 10. He was thirty-seven and had been among the wounded at Athens also. Word came from Quincy that Aaron Mattley's son William, of Company B, had died on April 29 after a six-week struggle with typhoid.

On the night of May 29-30, Beauregard abandoned Corinth's elaborate fortifications to fall back on Tupelo, fifty miles to the south. Werly noted that the Twenty-first Missouri, less than three miles north of town, was "put in ranks, to meet the enemy. But instead of attacking us he retreated." Pope telegraphed Washington he had taken ten thousand prisoners, a claim discounted by Confederates as "the most sensational humbug." Starr thought news of Beauregard's departure had caused "more excitement in camp than any time since we came to Tennessee. I rode into town in the evening, after I thought *all danger was past* and took a good view of the place, which is far more of a town than expected. The college on a slight elevation is one quarter mile from town and built similar to the one at Canton, but is larger and was occupied by Gen. Beauregard. Canton and Corinth are about the same size although the houses in Corinth are mostly frame ones some fine residences surrounded by large yards filled with shade trees and flowers in full bloom." Commanders began posting troops around the area, and McKean ordered the Twenty-first Missouri into camp along Elam Creek, south of town.

Adjutant Rees now found the enlisted men available for duty had dwindled to 462, down from 538 a month before. With the regiment were 21 officers, some under medical care. Rees and Woodyard had no way then of knowing that of the 317 men absent, 35 had died, and 11 had been given disability discharges that month. The weeks that followed would see more losses. Harle's first lieutenant, Joe Oliver, resigned May 31, "my health becoming much impaired" and that wounded arm having developed a weakness that rendered him "not in condition to do active duty." Halleck published formal acceptance June 12, and Oliver left the regiment. Three days later Company K was shocked by the sudden death of sixteen-year-old George Hopson. The lad, a farm boy near Quincy, had had a heart attack. A grief-ridden older brother, Frank, disappeared within two weeks.

If the regiment, in its historians' words, "laid around Corinth until about June 10th," its colonel was a busy man. Sergeant Barnabas B. Walkitt of Company H, a Keokuk fellow peeved at the army for sending the Twenty-first Missouri "south of the Hannibal & St. Joe" without his consent, asked to be reduced to the ranks. Captain Tracy "busted" the crabby noncom on June 4, provoking from Woodyard a dire warning to company commanders to stop "reducing non commissioned officers . . . without first obtaining the approval of the regimental commander."

On June 2, the division and brigade passed respectively to Brigadier

Generals John B. S. Todd and John McArthur. Todd was a Kentuckian
and kinsman of Mary Lincoln, McArthur a taciturn Scot. The brigade
adjutant, better known to the Twenty-first Missouri each week, was
Lieutenant Edwin Moore. Reshuffling soon reached higher echelons,
for on June 10 Halleck finally restored Grant to command of the
Army of the Tennessee and began dismantling the imposing army
group holding northern Mississippi. Buell, instructed to repair the Memphis & Charleston Railroad *as he advanced,* was to move on Chattanooga,
toward the eastern end of Tennessee.

Todd ordered Woodyard's camp moved on June 10 to Chewalla, a
tiny place on the Mobile & Ohio line twelve miles northwest of Corinth
and just over the line in Tennessee. Here, far off in heavy timberland,
the regiment would perform "light guard duty," its historians said. "I
have written the name, you may pronounce it," Starr wrote Miss Henrietta June 13. There were about "one dozen families living here in
this little place and they appear friendly and are tired of the war."

The Army of the Mississippi passed to Brigadier General William S.
Rosecrans on June 11, and Pope left for the East. Lincoln was giving
up on McClellan. The Department of War was planning an Army of
Virginia for Pope made up of troops "borrowed" from McClellan. Any
chance "Little Mac" had of averting this fate went glimmering when
Lee, after bringing Jackson in from the Valley, struck back at the Army
of the Potomac in the closing days of June. Sharp encounters took
place along the eastern approaches to Richmond. By the beginning of
July, McClellan's campaign had come to grief, and he was in retreat
from the Peninsula.

If McClellan needed more proof he was in Old Abe's doghouse, he
got it July 11. Henry Halleck, puffed up in the press for triumphs that
had nearly restored the Mississippi to Yankee navigators, was brought
east to become "general-in-chief," a position in which he could bring
his overweening expertise to bear in the councils of the republic.

A logical disposition of the western armies would have been to place
them under Grant, but the victorious forces were now scattered. This,
Sherman later declared, was "the most questionable strategy of the
whole war." Lincoln chose no successor to Halleck in the West for the
time being, for he was hoping to achieve unified command by giving
Halleck operational direction of *all* Union armies. The new general was
to prove a disappointment, but in this he was to be neither the President's first nor his last.

Meanwhile, guerrilla warfare was on the rise again in northern Missouri. The coming of spring had seen a resumption of bushwhacking, and in June Colonel Joe Porter reappeared. Price, sending Porter to recruit in northeastern Missouri, had assured several Union commanders a worrisome summer. Young sympathizers swarmed out to join Porter, and within a matter of days he had about two hundred recruits. Raiding Scotland County at the end of June, he collided with a superior force of state militia at Cherry Grove and retired into Knox County. Here he scattered his force for safety's sake and rode on to recruit in adjoining counties.

On June 30, Halleck sent Colonel John McNeil to head the District of Northeast Missouri. A St. Louis hatter and former member of the Missouri General Assembly, McNeil proved the answer to Porter's threat. Until he could get the hang of things, however, bad days were in store. On July 12, Porter's henchman J. H. B. Stacey raided Fairmont, administered his oath of "allegiance" to many local men, and carried into temporary captivity several well-known citizens. The next day Porter shocked the Yankees by boldly seizing Memphis. McNeil now ordered all available militiamen to converge on Scotland County, but Porter chose to clear out before it was too late. Dr. Aylward, who had tended Moore's wounded on the field of Athens, was lynched by Porter's men and left to occupy a "martyr's grave" in the Odd Fellows Cemetery at Memphis.

The Eleventh Missouri State Militia Cavalry came upon Porter near Simon Pearce's mill on July 18, along the Middle Fabius some eight miles southwest of Memphis and near the hamlet of Bible Grove. The battle of Vasser (or Vassar) Hill was a tactical victory for Porter. Among the federals wounded was Ben Northcutt's son Hosea, former bugler of the Millport Guard. If the rebels suffered fewer casualties, Porter nevertheless felt the more insecure as the fighting ended. He retreated south, as McNeil's militia, joined by a swelling force of United States Volunteers, pressed into the region to bring Porter to judgment.

The foxy rebel moved into Monroe County, fighting a series of skirmishes—losing some and winning some. In late July, he found the situation getting so hot that he chose to head south with his accumulated recruits. On July 28, however, he bumped into Colonel Odon Guitar at Moore's Mill, in Callaway County. Repulsed, Porter doubled back to the north. The end of July found him hiding out near Paris, wondering how he was going to get his enlistees across the wide Missouri.

The Twenty-first Missouri would remember Chewalla with mixed feelings. The boys recalled the countryside as "picturesque and beautiful and abounded in fruits of all kinds; but even here the 21st had its

troubles and trials." Within two weeks, four officers resigned: Captain
Roseberry (G) and Lieutenants Woodruff (B), Rice (I), and Menn (A).
Menn and Rice had been casualties of Shiloh, the former losing all his
hair from a head wound. Roseberry and Woodruff pleaded gastric ailments. Smallpox erupted, and by early July there were seventy down
with it. Seaton and Carnahan found their hands full, and many an enlisted man's nursing talents came into play. Obstinate cases of typhoid,
measles, and intestinal troubles were shipped north in considerable
numbers.

During the month of June, Woodyard received notices of thirty-two
deaths, eight of them from wounds at Shiloh. Only eighteen of the twenty-
four dead of disease actually died in June, but poor communication with
northern hospitals accounts for the variation in figures. Beneath the sta-
tistics lay personal tragedies of desolating proportions. Among the wounded was David B. Hendricks of Company D, dead at Camp Denison in Ohio
since April 27. His older brother John Samuel, unable to bear his sorrow
in the loneliness of military life, fled north on June 16. Sergeant Elias
Davidson of Company D died on June 29 at Louisville, bringing down
the curtain on a pathetic family drama. Lucinda Cunningham Davidson
had been in her grave beside their infant daughter less than a year in
the Cunningham family cemetery back in Knox County near Greensburg.
Grief-ridden old Robert Cunningham would in quieter years see his lost
daughter's family forever reunited in their companion graves back home.

All was not loss and tribulation at Chewalla. On June 25, Edwin
Moore arrived to announce that he was the new major. Woodyard's reaction has passed unrecorded, but he forthwith published orders directing that the twenty-six-year-old Briton be "obeyed and respected accordingly." The next day, Moore was mustered in on the basis of a commission from the governor, and the void left by King's death was filled. At
the same time, the second lieutenancy in Yust's outfit went to a one time
Christian University student lately reading law with Woodyard, his brother-
in-law Edward T. Nelson. Harle, having lost his officers, welcomed Sergeant
Major Best as his new first lieutenant on July 1, and Sergeant Russell moved
from Company I to headquarters as Best's replacement there.

The regimental staff assembled on Sunday, July 6, to greet David Moore.
It was three months to the day since the tragedy of Shiloh, but the colonel
was a study in red-eyed pugnacity as he hobbled along on crutches. Order-
lies Bill French and Mike ("Speckled Dick") Cashman beamed at the Old
Man's bravery in thrusting his maimed body back on "freedom's altar."
The regiment would soon need his like.

The regiment was officially following a daily routine that began with

reveille at 5:00 A.M. and ended at 9:30 P.M. Company drill took up one
early morning hour, and battalion drill followed supper at 6:00. Calls
were sounded by drums throughout the day. Moore would find fault
with several things Woodyard had done, including the location of the
smallpox hospital in camp. Summoning Seaton on July 8, Dave told him
to move the smallpox patients at least a half-mile from camp and to
place Chaplain Cox in charge of them.

Moore returned to reap whirlwinds gathering since spring. On July 9,
Captains Harle, Story, and Murrow handed him their resignations. True
enough, each had a credible complaint. Murrow's back had given trouble
since that frightened horse stomped him on April 6; Story had an ab-
scessed jaw; and Harle had a game ankle of some years' standing. One
can only guess how much their judgments were infected by physical
concerns and how much by plain disgruntlement with this protracted
war. In retrospect, resignations and desertions of that summer seem but
part of a general movement of wearied warriors from this remote encampment back to the hospitable green hills and prairies of home.

Colonel Moore and Adjutant Rees compiled a list of 234 absentees.
On July 19, the Quincy and Keokuk newspapers published it, along
with orders for the culprits to report to authorities or face court-martial.
It was little consolation to Moore, but the colonel of the Fiftieth Illinois
was advertising in Quincy for a similar crowd of missing men.

If these published messages found their marks, they did not produce
ideal results. Private Henry C. Emry, sick in bed at home near Bunker
Hill, wrote the provost marshal of Lewis County on August 9:

> I will inform you that my helth is so bad that I can not report in
> person and if I am to be taken there as a Deserter I can be found
> at my Fathers house in bead or perhaps in my grave so they can
> do as they please marking me as a deserter or give me a discharge
> or weat till I am able to go back to my Regiment for I love my
> government as well as any man living but to be taken to St. Louis
> to . . . die I think I mite as well be left here in Lewis County to
> die. I see by the papers that Col. More . . . has orded the men of
> his Regiment back to Tinesee all that is living and some of the dead
> too.

Well and good, but the colonel had no intention of babying those
still in camp. On July 10, he published orders condemning officers for
"absenting themselves from duty whenever they feel so inclined." Com-

pany commanders were served notice to arrange their routines so that at least one officer would be on duty at all times.

David Moore tried unjamming Rees' commission. Final confirmation of Tobin's death had come July 5, when two privates, AWOL from the parole camp at Nashville, showed up in the regiment. Alexander Rogers of B and William McKinney of E claimed to know that Tobin had died. Woodyard shipped them back to Nashville and passed the sad news to Moore. On July 11, Dave wrote the adjutant general of Missouri to ask that "you will please make the appointment immediately." Slips there continued to be betwixt cup and lip, however, and Rees had to be content with the first lieutenancy of Company B. He continued as adjutant on an "acting" basis. Company B had to make do a while longer with Sergeant Hall's performance as "acting" lieutenant. But it was not as if Dave Moore had not given the state bureaucracy an energetic shaking.

Another project proved more fruitful in the long run. A statewide campaign to recruit for Missouri's depleted volunteer regiments got under way in June. "Let their ranks be filled promptly," urged Gamble, praising Missouri's volunteers for their "distinction in upholding the Flag of their country against a most unnatural and wicked rebellion." Lieutenant Alex Tracy of Company F and Corporal Joshua Hagle of Company D went north on July 27 to open a recruiting station at Hannibal.

Smoldering discontent burst finally into flame. A petition sprang up from the ranks of Company G, asking Halleck to disband the regiment. Colonel Moore soon intercepted it, and that was that. Or so it seemed. Jonathan Cranmer of Company G decided to skin the cat another way, flatly refusing to show up for guard mount on July 14. He already had a reputation as a troublemaker, loudly advising his fellows to buck authority and boasting the officers would not "dare" punish him. Dave Moore did not realize that, and poor Cranmer suddenly found himself charged with "disobedience of orders" and "mutinous conduct" before a court-martial assembled for his benefit in Corinth. Found guilty on all counts, he shipped out for nine months of meditation at Alton, Illinois. Cranmer got in a last word of sorts, though. When authorities at Alton turned him loose in May 1863, he went his way and was seen no more in his regiment.

Other flare-ups followed. Private DeWitt Gallup, an Iowan of Company G, tried to go Cranmer one better, by swinging at Woodyard—and swung himself right into the stockade. It would have gone hard with the boy had not Seaton arranged his discharge for a heart ailment. Per-

haps more ominous was a plot hatched by a forty-two-year-old private,
Eri Morris, a Company F man clerking in the regimental hospital. A
lawyer, Morris was sure a legal expert in St. Louis could get the federal
district court to dissolve the Twenty-first Missouri. Why, everybody in
the regiment *knew* the outfit had been illegally mustered through fraud
and force—and that it had no business invading a "foreign country."
That St. Louis attorney would, however, require a fee, and it behooved
the downtrodden to chip in twenty or thirty cents apiece for liberation.
Corporal Joseph Morris of G, Eri's nephew, took the lead in collecting
pledges. Others, including Iowans such as Privates Isaiah Preston and
George W. Sheeks, of H and G, assisted. This campaign aborted: Colonel Moore laid hands on the pledge sheet, and malcontents found
themselves in that awkward predicament where one innocent mistake
might lead to untold grief.

Corporal George Nightingale, middle-aged carpenter from Drakesville,
Iowa, tried an end run. He wrote Governor Kirkwood to complain that
"I am not satisfied and never have been in this regiment, since we were
pressed into service at Canton, Missouri." When Kirkwood established
the quota for the Northeast Missouri Volunteers in late 1861, Nightingale had gone to Memphis and enlisted with Harle. "You know we were
recruited for a certain locality," he reminded Kirkwood, "and then the
regiment was taken to Canton and consolidated with the Second North
East Missouri [,] and in the place of disbanding our regiment according
to law . . . to disband all regiments got up for a certain locality, we
were mustered in again at the point of bayonet." He wanted to join an
Iowa regiment, "so if we gain any honor by hard fighting let our adopted
state have the praise." Kirkwood pressed department headquarters for a
remedy, but nothing came of his intervention. Nightingale, like other
Iowans who chose to avoid the way of desertion, would have to serve
his time in the Twenty-first Missouri.

The climactic explosion came Wednesday evening, August 6. Not
long after supper, Sergeant Major Russell brought Colonel Moore the
dread news of an uprising in the camp. Large groups were streaming off
into the woods to meet and discuss "whether they should lay down
their arms." It appeared the mutineers were of a mind to stage a unilateral cease-fire, and there was talk of shooting the officers and operating
the regiment without them. The Old Man immediately summoned the
major, ordering him to turn out companies A and F "on the double-
quick" to swoop down on the meeting.

Fifteen of Farris' men refused to take up arms and were left in their
tents because he could not do a thing with them. No such horseplay

held up the German lads of Company A. The mass meeting in the brush voted to stack arms and broke up before Major Moore could get there, but he met the dissidents coming back to camp. Halted and placed under arrest, several warned that the entire "camp were of the same mind." Realizing the major would not "buy," some miscreants fled into the woods. Many were rounded up, however, and before midnight Ed Moore reported to the colonel that about sixty suspects were in the stockade.

That there would be hell to pay was evident at daybreak; Ed Moore went down to the stockade to remind Sergeant of the Guard Thomas Waterhouse that the menu for this gang would be the army's delicious hardtack and good old Tennessee well water. Several outraged prisoners cut loose with hostile remarks, Isaiah Preston outdoing the others by calling Major Moore a "son of a bitch" and other "hard names." Colonel Moore held an emergency conference with the officers after breakfast to plan action against unapprehended culprits. Most officers warned that disgruntlement had been evident ever since the departure from Hannibal, and a few flatly refused to attempt further arrests. There was little profit in talking like that to a colonel with such a long memory.

Moore led the company commanders to the stockade to view the catch. The captains knew the troublemakers, he insisted, and if they would point them out he would let the followers go. Interrogations soon produced six malefactors. Ike Preston, who had been storming around about shooting the officers "the next time the regiment was in action" and amusing friends by wishing that the minié ball that took off Moore's leg had gone through his cranium—this same fellow had a sudden change of heart. Tears streaming down his face, Preston confided to the colonel that he, too, had served in the Third Ohio in Mexico and hoped Moore would "excuse" him.

No hand to "excuse" much, Dave threw the ringleaders to the wolves of military justice. Charged with mutiny were Privates Preston of H, Johnathan Blodgett of E, Barnabas Walkitt of H, Freeburn L. Dart of G, Edward Ball of F, and Ephraim Gordon of D. Other than tiring of the war and protesting violation of their rights, it is difficult to see what the Chewalla six had in common. Walkitt and Preston were Iowans. Ball and Dart were from Clark County, Blodgett from Knox, Gordon from Schuyler. At twenty-three, Walkitt was the youngest; at fifty, Blodgett was the oldest. Except for Gordon, born in Virginia in 1825, they were native to free states.

General McArthur, commanding the division, sent the six before a court-martial at Corinth in the last days of August. Captain William Hem-

street of the Eighteenth Missouri, trying the culprits one at a time, called
a parade of witnesses. One testified that the mutineers were griped mainly because "they was recruited to serve in North East Missouri, and no
where else." Another declared that the rumored plan to kill all the
officers was not really mutinous: "We were going to fight like good
fellows." And then there was the controversial muster in at Canton:
Major Moore, several witnesses declared, had promised "irons, hard
labor, and half-rations" to everyone refusing to muster. Gordon, confessing that he had accepted home guard pay back to July 15, 1861,
although he not come to duty until December 3, offered the novel
justification that having perpetrated a fraud on the government by enlisting he could not now be held legally subject to military discipline!

Verdicts and sentences came with grim uniformity. Each defendant,
found guilty, got a year at hard labor. Most of the Chewalla six later
escaped confinement or else deserted at the end of their sentences. Only
Preston came back to serve out his enlistment honorably.

To Stephan Werly, untainted by such behavior, it was altogether
appropriate that the escaped slaves around Chewalla should hold a
"Christian reunion" on Sunday, August 10. One articulate black delivered a sermon, said Werly, "and he praised and gave glory to the blood
of Jesus. Another negro, very old, white-haired man, spoke the final
prayer; and he implored God's blessing for his brother-negroes and also
for our entire regiment. I . . . felt ashamed that we white ones do not
praise the grace of God more sincerely."

Turmoil in the regiment did not prevent Colonel Moore's sending
various companies to scout the area and keep guerrillas off balance.
Pressell, rounding up horses belonging to local civilians, made it possible for the boys to cover more ground with less effort than would
have been possible for foot soldiers. Captain Fulton led Company E
to Pocahontas, ten miles west of Chewalla, on July 28, and delighted
the colonel by seizing four "wanted" Johnnies, including a major of
the Thirty-first Tennessee Infantry. Charles Tracy's Company H pulled
a daylight raid on two planters south of Chewalla on August 1, seizing
eleven bales of cotton "Contraband of War." On August 8-9, Lieutenant
Best took Company I to Pocahontas and back, reminding locals the
Missourians were keeping tabs on them.

The month of August cost several good men. Lieutenant Washburn
came back August 9, almost too lame to walk. Tennessee sunshine
wrought no miracles, and the colonel, upon Seaton's advice, let him
go. On August 15, Moore later heard, a surgeon discharged Private William Lewis of Company G, mainly because of "Physical Disability and

old age." Instead of the dapper forty-five he had claimed to be, Lewis
had been born in upstate New York in 1796 and was the oldest man
in the outfit. First Lieutenant William Simpson of Company C, successor
to the late Lieutenant Lester, had tendered his resignation July 27 and
was on his way north within a fortnight. He had been trampled by a
horse lately, Seaton said, and faced permanent disablement "unless relieved by treatment which cannot be had while in the Army." Finally,
in late August, Woodyard left with Cox for Missouri on sick leave.
Woodyard had been in and out of bed with stomach and bladder complaints, and Dr. Seaton felt that a visit to Canton's shady streets would
rejuvenate him.

Significant personnel changes took place. When Murrow left on
August 12, Lieutenant McGonigle of Edina took command of Company
D. Pennsylvania-born, he was an Irish Catholic quite in tune with Knox
Countians clustered in his company. The second lieutenancy in E went
to a young St. Louis merchant, James B. Comstock. Supported by
prominent citizens such as James O. Broadhead and John How, Comstock had gone after a commission "in the Volunteer Service," leaving
the governor to pick his spot for him. Then, on August 27, as if to
prove the Roseberrys of St. Francisville were not abandoning the
regiment, young Tom, son of the departing captain, returned. Ill since
March, he had been left at Hannibal.

On August 29, the regiment took leave of Chewalla, McArthur calling
it to Corinth. The Twenty-first Missouri mustered at its old camp on
Elam Creek August 31, while the trials of the Chewalla six were in
progress. The outfit had eighteen officers present for duty; several,
such as Woodyard and Chaplain Cox, were on sick leave. Present were
526 enlisted men, leaving about 200 absent for various reasons. In the
half-year since leaving Hannibal, 120 of the boys had died—one in every
eight who had boarded the *Die Vernon.* Simpson's resignation from
Company C was followed by the muster in of Sergeant August Gloeser
of A as Yust's first lieutenant, replacing Menn. The overall trend in
strength, however, was downward, and the importance of the Tracy-
Hagle mission to Hannibal was painfully clear.

Back in Virginia, abandonment of McClellan's peninsular campaign
was offering Lee a breathing spell. But the rebel hero chose instead to
take on blustering John Pope before reinforcements from McClellan
would get to him. Marching swiftly north in the closing days of August, Lee brought Pope to battle near the scene of the Bull Run engagement of the previous summer. Near Groveton, Lee uncorked a surprise
attack on the federal left. Deflated, Pope withdrew in haste across Bull

Run, and his retreat ended only with his Army of Virginia safely in the defenses of Washington. Pope's hour of glory, begun in those skirmishes in North Missouri with Martin Green, was now a faded memory.

Lee proceeded to invade Maryland as part of broader strategy fashioned by Davis. Simultaneously, Bragg's army lunged north from Chattanooga across eastern Tennessee. Fast-moving cavalry under Forrest and John Hunt Morgan created panic as far as the Ohio River in advance of Bragg's host. Buell's Army of the Ohio, long tied down with railway repairs in southern Tenneessee, marched frantically north to intercept Bragg before he could reach the vital base at Louisville.

Out in Missouri, Porter kept playing cat-and-mouse with McNeil. On the first day of August, one of his lieutenants raided Alexandria, provoking alarms in Keokuk and Warsaw. The next day, Porter himself led a raid across Lewis County into Canton. Four days later, he was in Kirksville, forty-five miles west, where McNeil finally brought him to bay. A three-hour battle for the town resulted in a serious defeat for Porter, from which his prestige in northern Missouri never recovered. With his force disintegrating, he fled into Knox County.

In early September, the Cunningham boys of Company D learned that their home had been a battlefield on August 28. Bill Ewing's guerrillas, slipping down to the Middle Fabius above Millport, rode across "Old Bob" Cunningham's farm intending to arrest the elderly abolitionist firebrand, burn his house, and appropriate his horses. Cunningham proved a hard man to arrest. He pitched into the gang trying to capture him, and even though one intruder shot him in the arm, Old Bob managed to wrench an attacker's revolver out of his hand. As the little civil war raged in Cunningham's yard, a strong force of the Fiftieth Enrolled Missouri Militia suddenly appeared, having galloped up from Edina. As coincidence would have it, the rescuers were partly from Company C, commanded by Captain Lucius Woodruff. Old Bob's son and namesake, Rob Cunningham, was fatally wounded as he rode into the barnyard with his comrades. It little assuaged the old man's grief that Ewing himself was among the guerrillas slain in the "affair at Cunningham's farm."

Two weeks later, Porter's struggle to recruit among homefolks came to an end. He raced through Palmyra September 12, exciting many partisans. But McNeil whipped him two days later near Newark. Collecting about a thousand recruits as he fled toward the river, Porter retired into Arkansas. He was plainly through in north Missouri.

6

"Cavalry to the Rear!"

The second September of the war was a time of crisis for Confederate arms. As it began, the rebels held the initiative east and west of the Appalachians; but by its close, Lee had suffered a sharp reverse in Maryland, and Buell had headed Bragg off from Louisville and Cincinnati. Important credit for Union success was due the people of Kentucky and Maryland, who stolidly refrained from flocking into Confederate gray or lavishing much aid and comfort on their ragged "liberators."

What caused this reversal? McClellan, reassembling his Army of the Potomac in the wake of Pope's fiasco, marched into Maryland with great energy to counter Lee's thrust to the north. The Confederates, their communications threatened by McClellan's unaccustomed speed, fell back to concentrate at Sharpsburg on the Potomac. McClellan closed in on them along Antietam Creek and, on a bloody September 17 that brought twenty-three thousand casualties and pushed Lee to the brink of catastrophe, the Confederate chieftain fought clear to retreat into Virginia. Union success at Antietam fell short of Lincoln's expectations, but he seized upon it as the psychologically opportune moment to unveil his Emancipation Proclamation. Slaves in all states still "in rebellion against the United States" on January 1, 1863, would be given federally sponsored emancipation. The American people, north of the Ohio, now had what they always seemed to crave: a moral justification for casualty lists. And should Southerners be so minded, they would have an incentive to give up rebellion in the hope of preserving the peculiar institution.

Pressed by Buell's Yankees, Bragg left Frankfort October 4 and retired south. Four days later, he offered battle at Perryville, Kentucky; Bragg stood his ground, but at a cost that obliged him to resume his withdrawal. The cautious Buell, having failed to gratify the blood-lust of Yankee journalists, found himself in hot water. Grant was starting to hunt a replacement with more get-up-and-go.

General Curtis announced on September 19, 1862, that he was commanding the "Department of the Missouri." Halleck's inability to command the western forces by remote control had impelled the President to reactivate the department, placing in it the Indian territory and the states of Missouri, Arkansas, and Kansas. Curtis, victor of Pea Ridge and prewar congressman from Keokuk, seemingly possessed impeccable politico-military credentials. It remained, however, for Conservative Missourians to learn that the new commander was far too Radical for their tastes.

Woodyard's sick leave took a predictable turn, given the political humidity. Conversations with old Radical friends like Steve Carnegy led him to fancy he was hearing the call of the people in the Eighth Congressional District. Lincoln's proclamation was enough to trigger his candidacy for a seat in Congress. Editor Philip Snyder of Quincy's *Whig-Republican*, gazing across the Mississippi upon the shaggy Kentuckian, rejoiced mightily. The Reverend Jesse W. Barrett, a Southern Methodist, had lately started a weekly paper in Canton, but his "Conservatism" was so pronounced that candidates of Woodyard's stripe were beyond tolerance on the editorial pages of his *Canton Press*. Snyder, ridiculing Barrett as "His Riverence," offered Woodyard his blessing, for whatever an endorsement from the Illinois side might be worth: "On a platform such as Colonel Woodyard stands he ought to be elected, and we wish him success not only at the polls but in punishing the rebels." The eighth district's "Unconditional Union" convention was scheduled for October 15 at Macon City.

Bragg's redeployment in July had left the defense of Mississippi to "Old Pap" Price and his Army of the West at Tupelo and Major General Earl Van Dorn's garrison at Vicksburg. It was Bragg's hope that Price and Van Dorn could put all possible pressure on Grant by cleansing the state of Yankees and carrying the war up to or beyond Memphis. To that end, Price and Van Dorn were to escalate cavalry raids and guerrilla operations to a point where Rosecrans would feel compelled to stay put around Corinth, unable to aid Buell. Rebels in Mississippi numbered little more than twenty thousand troops all told, but they could magnify their effort through vigorous initiatives.

This rising Confederate activity soon had repercussions for the Twenty-first Missouri. On September 10, the regiment marched out about seven miles southwest of Corinth and bivouacked at Kossuth, deep in the woods of Alcorn County. About the only excitement there that remains a matter of record came with Colonel Moore's furious (and ultimately successful) effort to get the captaincy of Company D for McGonigle and the second lieutenancy of B for Jeremy Hall.

U. S. Grant, in no mood to wait passively, had plans to break the Confederates in northern Mississippi. Outnumbering them by two to one, he had options. What if Brigadier General Edward O. C. Ord's ten thousand men, based on Bolivar, Tennessee, suddenly marched on Iuka, a little rail town twenty-two miles southeast of Corinth? Price would surely come up on the dead run from Tupelo to checkmate Ord. And what then, if Ord and Price were locked in battle Rosecrans suddenly dashed in on Price's left and rear? To Grant, the prospect was thrilling beyond description: the destruction of Price and the handwriting on the wall for Van Dorn!

Price and Ord came to blows at Iuka on September 19. The federal movements were uncoordinated, however, and Price pulled back before sunup. McArthur took some of the Sixth Division to Iuka, and Nick Starr, clerking for the division's adjutant general, witnessed the action. Not that he saw much. The main fighting occurred "South East of where our Division was in line." He shared, however, the disappointment of fellow Missourians who had hoped to bring Sterling Price back to Corinth as a captive.

Now it was Van Dorn's turn to set a trap. Summoning Price to a rendezvous at Ripley, some thirty miles southwest of Corinth, he merged their forces on September 28 as the "Army of West Tennessee," bent as he was on a dash into the volunteer state. His scheme was to prowl north, frighten the federals into concentrating at Memphis, and then lurch east over the Hatchie River to swoop down on the isolated Corinth garrison. The liberation of west Tennessee would wait until Rosecrans' annihilation.

Led by Major General Mansfield Lovell's division, the Confederates started north from Ripley on Monday, September 29. Their cavalry kept federal outposts under arms constantly, and Werly felt that "our regiment would be attacked by the enemy. We were ready to receive him." On October 2, Lovell crossed the Hatchie at Davis' bridge near Pocahontas and began skirmishing with Colonel John M. Oliver's brigade of the Sixth Division along the dusty trail to Chewalla, eight miles to the southeast. That evening Price and Van Dorn bivouacked around Chewalla, while Rosecrans was marshalling his scattered forces. The Forty-third Ohio marched out to Kossuth and released the Twenty-first Missouri for duty with its brigade.

After a hurried march "over bad roads in the dark night," the Missourians entered the First Brigade camp, just south of the Memphis & Charleston about two miles northwest of Corinth. It was 3:00 A.M.,

Friday, October 3. Rosecrans was preparing for the worst, and Nick Starr was "up all night writing orders" at division headquarters. Well before the sun appeared, reconnaissance reports were leaving no doubt the Corinth garrison was the Confederates' intended victim.

General McKean was back at the helm of the Sixth Division, following temporary duty in St. Louis. The Sixteenth Wisconsin, holding the line with Oliver beyond Cane Creek four miles northwest of town, was the forward regiment of First Brigade, again under McArthur and consisting also of the Twenty-first Missouri and Seventeenth Wisconsin.

Dave Moore's boys "had just got settled in their tents," said their historians, "when the bugle call to arms summoned the men to rush out and fall into line of battle." From the northwest came reverberations of occasional artillery firing, and very shortly one of McArthur's aides appeared. There was hardly time, wrote Werly, "to eat something hurriedly and get ready to meet the enemy." While the boys were at breakfast, the aide returned with orders to mount guard around an artillery battery south of camp on the Smith's Bridge road.

At the first rays of dawn, Oliver could gaze up the Chewalla pike at Van Dorn's massive line of battle, built largely around Price's troops and making ready to drive the Second Brigade across Cane Creek to clear the way for a general assault against the "Beauregard Line" of older fortifications. Price's corps, between the Memphis & Charleston line on its west flank and the Mobile & Ohio on its east, included Brigadier General Dabney H. Maury's division on the right and Brigadier General Louis Hébert's division on the left. With Old Pap were seven regiments of Confederate Missourians, mostly in Hébert's division and commanded by a brigadier well known in Moore's ranks: Martin E. Green. Lovell's division, directly under Van Dorn, stood to the southwest.

In addition to McKean's division, Rosecrans had Brigadier General Thomas A. Davies' Second Division of the Army of the Tennessee ready to fall in on McKean's right. East of the Mobile & Ohio and due north of town stood Brigadier General Charles S. Hamilton's Third Division of Pope's old Army of the Mississippi, while Brigadier General David S. Stanley's Second Division of that army gathered south of Corinth in reserve. Nor had Rosecrans been content to rest on the Beauregard line, built earlier in the year to protect Corinth from *Yankees*. Now a new line of earthworks, closer in, girdled the town, and a ring of cannon-studded redoubts guarded the main routes into town.

As a hot and cloudless Friday dawned, the rebels closed in on Oliver.

The timing was awkward for the federals, since McKean had just pulled the Sixteenth Wisconsin back to his headquarters near the First Brigade camp. Oliver made a fight of it, but one brigade was no match for the oncoming host. Oliver fell back under heavy shelling and small-arms fire. Dismantling the Cane Creek bridge, he took up a line before the old entrenchments.

Having kept a close watch on Oliver's work, Rosecrans decided around 7:30 to move McArthur up to secure the new position. The snuffy Scot, his blood up, rode out to survey the front and ordered Oliver to hold on for reinforcements. The Twenty-first Missouri, he ordered, would cover Oliver's left and move immediately onto a high ridge overlooking the Memphis & Charleston from the south and near the Beauregard line. The Sixteenth Wisconsin should go directly to Oliver. Certain that more help would be needed, McKean went to Davies and borrowed the Seventh and Fifty-seventh Illinois. Davies was under orders to maintain contact with McKean, but the latter's line at the moment was advanced far beyond the Second Division's left

Boys of the Fiftieth Illinois, seeing cavalry scouts passing by from the front, could not resist the derisive chant, "Enemy in front, cavalry to the rear!" One spunky young horseman, however, retorted hotly that "there are more rebels out there than you will want to see!"

Oliver's reinforcements were in line before 10 o'clock, the Fifty-seventh Illinois forming next to the railroad, the Seventh holding the right flank, with the Sixteenth Wisconsin in reserve. To the east, Davies and Hamilton were moving north toward the old outer breastworks. There was little time to lose, for Van Dorn was about to unleash his fury. Moore noted he "had been in position but a few minutes when the enemy opened fire upon our flank and front. We replied promptly and continued showing the most determined resistance." So withering was McKean's counterblast that the rebel advance was partly deflected toward Davies. By 10:30, however, Lovell's approach and the intensification of firing from Maury's left began to tell on the Twenty-first Missouri. Moore's line recoiled from the ridge, and a rout appeared imminent.

The colonel, on horseback, rode all over the place, urging the boys back up that hill before the Johnnies claimed it. Sergeant Gus Stevens of Company I, a color-bearer, had left the ridge too willingly for the colonel's taste, but Corporal Jesse Roberts redeemed matters. "He gallantly seized the colors," Moore gratefully noted, "and advanced on the line of battle, . . . causing great enthusiasm among the men."

Before the irate colonel could "settle" with Stevens, disaster struck.

His horse, mortally wounded, collapsed, pinning the stump of the Old Man's leg to the ground. While the brute went into its final agonies, several boys risked injury to pull the dazed commander to safety. Doc Seaton, badly shaken when his mount threw him, was of no help. Major Moore, assuming command, found "the men were giving back very rapidly." With the help of the line officers—not to mention a successful charge up the Chewalla pike by the Sixteenth Wisconsin and a series of covering volleys from the Fifty-seventh Illinois—Ed Moore "succeeded in rallying the men, who went boldly to the front and drove the enemy from the position that we occupied at the commencement."

It was getting on toward 11 o'clock, and the sun was bearing down heavily. There was no immediate relief for the Twenty-first Missouri from Confederates, for its line of battle, once restored on the ridge, faced fighting of a particularly desperate character. Enemy skirmishers were "less than 50 paces" to the front at one time, the major estimated. The advance of McArthur's line, made possible by the success of the Wisconsinites' drive, gradually took the heat off the Missourians.

Not for long, however; Lovell's infantry deployed to the immediate front as if to mount a fresh charge. Now Davies, facing Hébert's onslaught, began to recoil from the Beauregard works. This obliged McKean to withdraw McArthur about a quarter-mile, and Rosecrans moved Stanley up to cover the left rear. Major Moore, seeing the retirement, ordered the Twenty-first Missouri to fall back toward the camps. The Missourians "became scattered," and after some anxiety the major managed to re-form them on a hill position guarding McArthur's flank, on the far side of the railroad.

The grim-faced McArthur, after repelling Maury several times with aid from the First Missouri Artillery, was dismayed to see the Johnnies climbing a spur of the ridge he was holding. The Seventh Illinois now charged the intruders with bayonets fixed, but in so doing found themselves heading into a pocket created by rebel pressure on Davies. McArthur hastily ordered his line to fall back, and the Illinois colonel extricated his men "from their perilous position in good style."

Fighting to keep his line intact as he withdrew, McArthur welcomed the Seventeenth Wisconsin and Fiftieth Illinois. Colonel Doran's Wisconsinites were greeted by lusty cheers from McArthur's ranks. This gallantry, Doran noted, "drew from the enemy a galling fire . . . which was vigorously kept up till the command reached its position on the extreme right of the line. This firing having been from . . . partly in ambush, General McArthur soon rode up and requested me to send out skirmishers to reconnoiter." By early afternoon McArthur had once more arrested the rebel tide, but only after retreating a half-mile. Maury now had possession of McArthur's camps, along both sides of the railroad, after crossing a brigade of Tennesseans to the south of the Memphis & Charleston to put new life into the Confederate drive there.

McArthur decided to throw the Johnnies out of his camps before they could make themselves at home. He called for a bayonet charge, *"en echelon,"* with Doran's Seventeenth Wisconsin moving first. Then came the Seventh Illinois, Fifty-seventh Illinois, Sixteenth Wisconsin, and Ed Moore's Twenty-first Missouri, "all in fine order, sweeping the enemy before them out of the camps a distance of half a mile." As fighting intensified, McArthur called up fresh troops. Available evidence suggests that the Fourteenth and Eighteenth Wisconsin, Oliver's brigade, having been rested by midday, were now sent forward. The "reinforcements," it seemed to McArthur, were unfortunately unable to "comprehend the situation." Doran was less charitable, naming no names but reporting that the two fresh regiments "finally discharged their muskets into the Seventeenth [Wisconsin], turned and ran." McArthur thereupon withdrew his gallant troops to the position from which they had charged, to stand with their backs to the Memphis & Charleston while maintaining contact with Davies.

It was nearly 3 o'clock, and McKean and McArthur were on notice that Rosecrans would countenance no more charges without his consent. His battle plan was, as Werly grasped it, "to entice the enemy to follow us under the forts of Corinth." This necessitated pulling the division headquarters back into town, and Nick Starr was there to help. Exhausted by a hard night's work, he had "slept soundly" until noon. "I am foolish enough to believe I am getting very brave (particularly when there is no danger)," he modestly wrote the girl back home.

Price's fate was not left entirely to the inner forts. Hamilton's division, east of the Mobile & Ohio, had had little work this bloody Friday; in fact, Hamilton had held without difficulty to positions near the outer works even when Davies fell back well to his rear. This suggested to Rosecrans that Hamilton could pivot to the west, cross the railroad, crush Price's exposed left, "and close the day."

This scheme miscarried, for Hamilton's brigades grew confused in the brush east of the railroad and mounted no coordinated effort against Hébert. Moreover, Davies failed to withstand assaults on his line northwest of town along the Chewalla pike, and by 5:00 P.M. his division was giving way. An hour before, McKean had decided to pull his force back to the south side of the Memphis & Charleston. Colonel Marcellus M. Crocker's Third Brigade, guarding the division left since dawn, covered the withdrawal of outlying Ohio and Missouri artillerymen into Corinth. Iowans all, Crocker's men gave a good account of themselves, the Fifteenth and Sixteenth Iowa severely jolting the rebels with a counterattack between 4:00 and 5:00 P.M. McKean formed a line overlooking the Memphis & Charleston from the south—and awaited Rosecrans' further pleasure.

As evening shadows lengthened across this smoking and devastated scene, Price and Van Dorn were at cross-purposes. The latter urged a final assault that he hoped would finish off the Yankees, but the former was convinced that "we have done enough for to-day." Although certain that another hour or two of twilight would have secured victory this very day, Rosecrans was nevertheless sanguine over prospects for the morrow. "Things is workin'," he chortled. The upshot of a conference with the division commanders was a plan for McKean to hold College Hill, on the left, while McArthur took two brigades into bivouac at the north edge of town. Stanley's division would defend a line centered on Battery Robinet, overlooking the Chewalla pike just to the west of town. Davies, shifting to the east of the Mobile & Ohio, would face north up the Purdy Road, and Hamilton would hold his right, with flank "refused," facing northeast.

The hustle and bustle inside and south of Corinth convinced Van Dorn that Rosecrans was throwing in the towel. At daybreak, he decided, Hébert's division, astride the Mobile & Ohio, should press against Hamilton and turn the federal right. Maury would follow with a thrust toward Battery Robinet. As the Yankees broke and ran to the southeast, cavalry would be waiting to cut them down along the roads to Iuka and Tupelo.

Confederate artillery cut loose on Corinth at 4:00 A.M. Saturday. To Werly it looked "as if they would ruin and take the town, but our heavy guns soon silenced theirs." Starr, after breakfasting with the boys around the campfires, had just begun to doze

when I was suddenly awakened by the tremendous roar of Price's Canon the morning was verry dark and a more pleasant sight one cannot imagine, we could see the flash of their canon which was planted on a hill west of town, then hear the report and trace the coming shell by their light over the tops of trees until they exploded but the scene soon changed and you may believe less pleasant as they noticed the fires which cooked our breakfast and directed their aim on them which was done very accurately [.] The shell commenced exploding amongst us one solid ball coming through the air rattleing in the branches of the trees and knew that it must fall very near us but could see no one for by this time we had put out the fires. . . . Two men were wounded on the right of our break-fast-table; I was almost persuaded to be a *Christian Coward* and run but seeing all our contraband Negroes had run away from their duty, and *not* wishing to be likened unto a contraband, I remained.

It was bad enough that Van Dorn had underestimated the strength of the inner forts, to say nothing of Rosecrans' determination to go to the mat. But Hébert's turning movement did not come off as planned. Hébert had taken ill—possibly sick of being glared at by Missourians who considered him incompetent—and needed relief. It was 7 o'clock before Price found out, and 8 o'clock before a change of command took effect. And it would be 9 o'clock before the attack got going. The thickness of the "fog of battle" is evident in Maury's ignorance ten years later of the reason for Hébert's relief.

Had Dave Moore's boys known that the new commander of Van Dorn's left division was Martin Green, they would surely have clamored for duty east of the M & O tracks! But Rosecrans had other work for them. About 8 o'clock, McArthur got word to take his two brigades out of bivouac and report to McKean on College Hill, the far left of the Union line.

During Green's familiarization with the battle plan, Maury's troops took to sniping and skirmishing with Stanley and Davies. Before Price or Maury could get a grip on things, the fighting escalated into an advance by Maury's left wing. Then Green's belated attack began. Colonel Francis M. Cockrell of the Second Missouri Confederate Infantry waved his sword at Battery Powell, well to the east of the M&O. "Forward, my boys," he commanded, "we must capture that battery."

Green's Missourians charged up to the redan and seized it. The gunners, abandoning their ordnance, hitched up their limbers and stampeded to the rear. The attackers, however, ran out of ammunition and fled the scene of their triumph. The fight raged hotter to the west, where Maury won temporary possession of Battery Robinet and sent troops charging into Corinth, past Rosecrans' headquarters and on to the Hotel Tishomingo down by the railway crossover. Rosecrans kept his wits, though, and summoned reserves that trapped some of the marauders and drove the rest out of town.

By noon, it was clear that Van Dorn's reach had exceeded his grasp. Watching Price's troops falling back, he instructed Lovell to move a brigade across the Memphis & Charleston to screen the impending departure. Lamented Old Pap: "My God! my boys are running!" To Van Dorn's assurance that those stout-hearted fellows had done their "whole duty," Price could only point tearfully at the blood-spattered road to Corinth.

McKean successfully defended Battery Phillips on College Hill and Battery Williams overlooking the railroad. Only the Sixteenth Wisconsin, south of the college, had a chance at heavy combat. Lovell mounted two assaults, but, wrote McKean, "Battery Phillips and the light pieces of this division opened upon him so hotly that he hastily retired." The Twenty-first Missouri found little to do on College Hill, for Ed Moore declared later that "we were not engaged with the enemy while in this position." This, as the major saw it, was altogether fortuitous, for many of the regiment's old Springfields had about played out; indeed, after a dozen or so shots, some became impossible to load, and many of the boys spent a good deal of their time scrounging for operable weapons dropped by both armies.

When it became clear that no further attack was likely, Rosecrans started probing. McKean moved forward from College Hill about 2:30 with Oliver and McArthur. The Twenty-first Missouri, summoned to McArthur's presence at an artillery emplacement two miles southwest of the college, "scoured the woods, but found no enemy, excepting a few stragglers."

Following this, the regiment moved up the South Bridge Road for a rapid push with other troops northwest across Cane Creek. At Alexander's crossroads was Van Dorn's field hospital, word of which had come to Major Moore from the stragglers. It was dark by the time the Missourians reached the crowded hospital, but there, said Werly, "We captured the wounded and enlisted ones and held them. . . . But, oh, how many gave up the ghost and were sunk in the ground, wrapped in a blanket, before they were mustered. It is terrible to . . . see how much the poor mutilated fellows have to suffer!" The Major's total catch was "nearly 900 officers and men. We also captured 460 muskets, 400 cartridge-boxes, and a quantity of belts, &c."

To Grant's disgust, Rosecrans held to the belief the victors were too fatigued to pursue. It seemed to Grant the simplest of propositions: the *rebs* were not too tired to run. . . . All-out pursuit began Sunday morning, a day late and many a mile short. The bedraggled Johnnies, resting up Saturday night at Chewalla, started for Davis' Bridge Sunday morning. Van Dorn, however, was dismayed to find Hurlbut blocking that crossing. After a vicious fight for the bridge, Hurlbut held. The anxious

Confederates, trapped east of the Hatchie, were hourly expecting Rosecrans to catch up to them. In their extremity, they probed to the south
and discovered an unguarded bridge at Crum's Mill, six miles upstream.
Grant called off the pursuit three days later—and never forgave Rosecrans
for "permitting" the Southerners to slip away.

By Sunday noon, Colonel Moore had a new horse and was ready to
take charge. The regiment returned to its battered camp along the Memphis & Charleston. Seventeen of the boys were wounded, four seriously.
Most wounds were in arms, hands, necks, or thighs. Private Charles Postle-
wait of Company H, a Keokuk youth of Virginia parentage, received a
skull fracture. Hospitalized with a grave leg wound was Private George W.
Mendenhall of I, an Ohio-born Scotland County lad. After recuperation
at Jackson, Tennessee, he returned to the company late in the winter.
Private Mathias Myers of Company E, a native Missourian from Knox
County, worried Seaton for nearly a month before he recovered from a
neck puncture. Most seriously injured was a farm lad from Knoxville,
Illinois, Private Perry White of Company I. His death, from the effects
of a hip wound, came on October 9, making him the regiment's only
fatality of "Second Corinth."

Five men were taken prisoner during the fighting of October 3-4:
Corporal Frederick Nater (Company K) and Privates John Bernard (D),
Peter Pitts (G), William Sweeney (I), and Henry Weishaar (A). The dis-
tribution of casualties followed an interesting pattern. Seven of the
twenty-two were foreign born—Germans, with the exception of the
Belgian-born Bernard. Only Company B emerged unscratched.

Hapless Gus Stevens became another kind of casualty. On October 18,
the colonel visited upon him the expected retribution for his handling
of the colors on October 3. Reducing Gus to private, Moore awarded
his sergeant's stripes to Jesse Roberts, a twenty-two-year-old Pennsylvanian who had in Dave's estimation displayed "gallant conduct in the face
of the Enemy" by taking the colors away from Gus. Poor Stevens lived
it down, and survived to endear himself to the boys of Company I. The
original first sergeant of Company F, John A. Hart, a young Massachusetts native and one of the original Croton guardsmen, had been hospitalized in Keokuk since early May. This being too long for Colonel Moore's
satisfaction, the top-kick's stripes passed to Ike Schram, who had been
doing Hart's work for months.

This bloody contest for control of northern Mississippi terminated
Van Dorn's threat to Memphis. About seven thousand Americans were
killed, wounded, or captured—about two-thirds of them Confederates.
If Grant was not charmed by Rosecrans' total performance, the "Victor

of Corinth" nevertheless felt like crowing when he issued his message to the troops on October 25. Estimating Confederate forces at twice their actual strength, he declared them "completely broken."

For more than a fortnight, the Twenty-first Missouri lingered at Corinth, shifting camp several times. One exciting piece of news followed another. Rumors spread of an impending redeployment of Rosecrans' army—and perhaps of Rosecrans himself. Expectations grew that some regiments would go home to recruit. The Twenty-first Missouri was down to about five hundred present for duty, and the boys mixed homesickness with plain facts to "prove" that this regiment, for one, would go. Many of them had natural concerns over conditions at home. "I am anxious to hear from affairs there," Starr wrote on October 9. "Are the rebels getting any more peaceable than they were? If not, we will settle them after awhile."

Humphrey Woodyard went into the Radical convention at Macon with Quincy's *Whig-Republican* certain "that Col. Woodyard will be honored with the nomination." Unhappily, the forecast proved deceptive, and Mayor Moses P. Green of Hannibal won the nomination to Congress. Meanwhile, election commissioners from Iowa visited Corinth to take the votes from Iowans there. The Hawkeyes were holding an off-year election October 14. The sixty voting in the Twenty-first Missouri's camp were overwhelmingly generous to the Republican slate. Seaton told Keokuk friends that, having grown up as a Democrat, he had now defected to vote "the straight Republican ticket."

Losses continued, even if the Johnnies had fled. On October 9, Captain Roseberry arrived to inquire into the health of his son Tom, the drummer of Company G. Just going on sixteen, Tom was continually suffering from "camp complaints," and the captain decided to take him home. Their departure for St. Louis was not entirely amicable. While the company morning report stated laconically that young Roseberry was "taken home by his father," Moore stamped it as "desertion." Tom never returned. Lieutenant Ainslie of Company D, still suffering from his hip wound, went before a medical commission in Corinth October 17. The medics, detecting an "aneurysm" in the femoral artery, recommended discharge. Ainslie was off to Edina.

On Wednesday morning, October 22, the boys got orders to pack their gear. Homeward bound! Drummer Werly, pining for cherished faces, told his diary, "We left our camp for the depot in Corinth, from where we were to be brought by railroad to Missouri, which was promised us since a long time ago."

7

Back to God's Country

On Wednesday evening, October 22, the Missourians began loading the Mobile & Ohio train for the 480-mile journey home. Perhaps an hour was taken up serenading General Rosecrans at the Tishomingo. In any event, loading was finished by 4:00 A.M. Thursday. Through the long and frigid day that followed, they traversed the west Tennessee countryside—through Jackson, Trenton, Union City. Then, as shadows of another evening descended, they reached Columbus, where the railway terminated on the Kentucky side of the Mississippi.

At the dock waited the steamer *Tigress,* dispatched to carry the boys up to St. Louis. What memories that ship must have stirred in the colonel's breast! Surely, however, those painful reflections softened at the sight of his happy warriors crowding company by company up the gangplank. At 6:00 P.M. the *Tigress* cast off, her bow pointed north.

Sadly, one exuberant fellow was never to see his Missouri home. Vanished and presumably drowning on that dark night was Private Lewis W. Beff of Company H, a thirty-year-old farmer from the Luray community. Bravely fighting at Shiloh under John H. Cox, he had suffered a knee wound. When he did not appear at the October 31 muster, Captain Tracy recorded him as "absent without leave," but some weeks later the colonel amended this to read "drowned" at Columbus. What occasioned this change seems not to be a matter of surviving record.

Not everything was particularly enjoyable for those staying aboard. Below Ste. Genevieve, Missouri, Werly recorded that

> . . . we had sleet and a snowstorm, and the night was very cold, and we had to lie around under the snow, like poor brutes. Toward morning it turned still colder, and the poor soldiers suffered a great deal from the cold. Then the officers came and wanted to do them a favor, and they gave them whiskey to drink; many of them drank too much, and there was confusion, quarrel and a row, cursing and

swearing. I got very uneasy, and if ever I could make myself a picture of hell, it certainly was there.

Grant announced on October 26 that the Army of the Mississippi was no more and that Hamilton was to command the "District of Corinth." Four days later, the word was out that Rosecrans had taken over Buell's Army of the Ohio. Newsmen and politicians expected big things of Rosecrans; the "Victor of Corinth" would surely engineer Bragg's destruction.

Arriving in St. Louis before dawn, Sunday, October 26, the Missourians set foot in their home state for the first time in seven months. The German Methodist boys, after reaching Benton Barracks, flocked over to the First German Methodist Episcopal Church at Thirteenth and Benton for a sermon in their mother tongue preached by the Reverend Philipp Kuhl. Others found different things to do. Colonel Moore made arrangements with ordnance officers to reequip the regiment with new Springfields. The boys had acquired a variety of weapons reminiscent of those unlamented home guard days of 1861. It would take time to improve his inventory, Dave learned, but there was no hurry now.

There came a scare Monday afternoon, as the *Tigress* steamed out for La Grange. Laborers unloading the *H. D. Bacon* at the foot of Locust Street, while blowing out candles in the hold as they knocked off for lunch, scattered sparks among the hemp bales and set off a fire. Things got out of hand, and within a short time the spreading fire ravaged the *Bacon* and four other vessels. This waterfront conflagration consumed cargo and shipping valued at $175,000. "While the fire was raging most furiously," a reporter said, ". . . the flames shot up with terrific violence, and swayed fiercely to and fro as the wind fanned them into wilder fury, while dense volumes of smoke rolled up . . . and partially veiled the destruction." Werly shuddered that the *Tigress* "fortunately . . . had enough steam to escape and Providence saved us from this terrible disaster."

The next afternoon the Germans of La Grange thronged to Pittsburg Landing to welcome Leeser's company. At 5:00 P.M., the rest of the boys reached Canton. Jesse Barrett was among the greeters. The bearded and corpulent preacher-journalist beamed: "The boys look well, and are still ready to render a good account of themselves wherever duty calls them to the field. They go into quarters here at present to recruit and will in due time win new laurels on the battlefield."

The main body camped on the grounds of Christian University. Regimental headquarters made ready for the October muster, scheduled for the Friday after landing in Canton. Here Woodyard rejoined. The outfit, he saw, was in a sad condition, its weaponry in disarray and its ranks thinning. Only 530 officers and men reported for muster, although 718 names were still on rolls. There were 65 prisoners of war on parole or otherwise absent and 98 men in hospitals between Keokuk and Corinth. The regiment was at its nadir, and the necessity of recruitment was undeniable.

A parolee of Shiloh, Edward Menke of Company K, breathed his last in La Grange the day his comrades arrived. Chronic dysentery had claimed the forty-five-year-old Westphalian. Surviving him was a seventeen-year-old son, Frederick, one of Company K's wounded veterans of second Corinth. Men of Ed's company at La Grange would always remember him, and when they opened Post 166 of the GAR in the 1880s the "old boys" would name it for him.

Leeser solved one administrative puzzle after reaching home. Michael Emmons, hospitalized at Mound City before second Corinth, had disappeared. Early in November, the provost marshal at Quincy picked up a rumor that he was staying in Burlington. Upon notification of this fact, the provost marshal there investigated, only to learn that the fugitive had died November 1. Since a descriptive roll was never completed for poor Emmons and local newsmen took no notice of his death, he came near to being an "unknown soldier."

Asa Starkweather, whose recruiting in 1861 had made him familiar with the back country, put his knowledge to use. A captain of the Second Missouri State Militia Cavalry, serving as provost marshal for Canton, had been dealing through go-betweens for the surrender of "Captain" Dick Farr, who had been, as Moore said, "infesting this and adjoining counties for a long time." Moore and the provost marshal, determined to force the issue with the "Captain," hit on the idea of sending Starkweather and a dozen militiamen out to apprehend him. It did not take Starkweather long. Sounding out confidants, he proceeded to the lonely farm of a Virginia-born widow, surprised the guerrilla, and demanded his capitulation. As a local reporter told it, Farr "promptly showed fight by drawing his pistol, . . . but two discharges from their guns taking effect in his wrist and ankle quickly brought him to terms." When Farr was well enough to move, Moore shipped him to St. Louis.

With the boys mustered, Moore turned them loose for three-week furloughs. Ladies of Canton's Union Aid Society put on a welcome-home party on Monday, November 3, as the troops were making ready to disperse. Although, said the society's reporter, "we miss many loved ones who went forth with brave hearts to fight for their country, yet we remember that their lives were laid down to uphold the government made by Washington the father of our country, and we are proud of their memories. The mothers of Missouri are proud of their sons, . . . and we crown them the heroes of Shiloh and Corinth."

Tuesday was election day, and there were scores to settle—not that there were any Confederates running, but there were enough Conservative folk in the race to ignite soldierly passions. And there was a slight stacking of the deck, in that the loyalty oath required of voters was couched in terms well calculated to make certain Democrats think twice before visiting an election board. With the aid of Company I, a "Union" ticket led by Ellsberry Small took over the Scotland County courthouse. Soldier votes proved insufficient to unhorse Conservative Congressman William A. Hall, but Moses Green carried Lewis, Clark, Knox, and Scotland counties largely because of the Twenty-first Missouri and local militiamen. David Wagner, a coming man among Lewis County Radicals, won a seat in the state senate.

Federal strong-arming of Missouri produced a Republican-dominated congressional delegation. Election results elsewhere were widely discouraging to the Lincoln administration, however. Kansas and Massachusetts stood firmly Radical-Republican, but Democratic triumphs were the rule in New York, Illinois, Ohio, Indiana, and Pennsylvania. The administration kept a slight working majority in Congress but only through the help of "War Democrats." There have been many explanations for the Democratic upsurge of 1862, but Cincinnati's *Gazette* probably summarized the event well enough: "The people are depressed by the interminable nature of this war, as so far conducted, and by the rapid exhaustion of resources without purpose."

That this was a political war, Colonel Moore's soldiery never doubted. Summing up his feelings on election eve, Aaron Harlan assured Editor Howell that "the mass of the army have already passed the point at which General Frémont stood when he issued his famous proclamation in 1861, for which he was so roughly handled." Lincoln's proclamation, to Harlan's soldier-friends, embodied an idea whose time had come. Slavery and the greed that it engendered had "fostered and sustained this formidable rebellion so far. We are now in a fair way to annihilate the Institution, so let us look ahead and make preparations for the changes that must follow."

Harlan's estimate of Negro capabilities displayed an ambivalence that dismays modern Civil War buffs still convinced that the typical abolitionist was a doctrinaire patron of Negro rights and equality. Ironed out at fireside debates in the Twenty-first Missouri was a militant scheme for expropriating lands of all "rebels" in the Confederate states and confining the blacks to them. To Harlan's friends, the Negro's "natural disposition" fitted him to become the major producer of the nation's cotton, rice, and sugar. As Harlan viewed freedmen, they would all somehow become hired hands on vast industrial farms owned and managed by the federal government—or something else vaguely called "private enterprise."

This program, Harlan predicted, would deflate secessionism in Missouri. All slaves in the state would be sent south to "relearn" cotton culture, and, with their departure, the basis for the rebellion would evaporate. With the blacks gone from Missouri, he prophesied, "thirty thousand rebels would say AMEN! and a hundred thousand Union men would swing their hats and HURRAH!" He spelled out his program:

> The first thing is to decide and proclaim to the world, that we are against the institution of slavery, and in favor of *a separation of the races*.
>
> Let us colonize all we can.
>
> Let us concentrate the black population all we can.
>
> Let us do each of these things as fast as we can.

That even a religiously motivated Radical could be firmly gripped by racist stereotype was evident from the remarks of Chaplain Cox. Arriving at Corinth late in October, he learned that his regiment had just "gone to God's country." Cox applied for transportation north, but while waiting he made the most of every opportunity to be useful. For lodgings, he resorted to "putting up with the agent of the sanitary department," and from that official's quarters he essayed forth to "see the wonders of the recent battle field. Trees and dead horses, felled by cannon shot, lay scattered for miles around, while bloody bayonets, balls, rebel blankets, shell &c., are some of the evidence of a hard fought battle."

Visiting stockades where Confederate captives were held, John H. Cox came face to face, if we should credit his words, with inferior anthropoids. These lice-ridden wretches impressed him as

> . . . unconscious of having done wrong. They are utterly demoralized and in the lowest state of degradation but little better than the untutored Indan, only about one-fourth of them can read, the rest seem to be contented with "blissful ignorance." While we were gazing at

them, one of the motley crowd bawled out, "Hey, thar, you feller
with the good clothes on, do you know what they are gwine to do
with us fellers; will we be shot? His irresponsible sallow countenance
brightened up when I told him they would be treated as prisoners
of war. . . .

If the chaplain's visit to hospitals awakened more benign emotions, it
did not moderate his rhetoric. "That our sick in the hospitals in the field
do suffer for the want of kind treatment, but few who have been patients
. . . will deny," he wrote Elliott. "The inhumanity and brutality of hospital attendants and heartless surgeons has caused the death of many a good
soldier whose delicate constitution could not subsist on hard bread and
pork, while the sweetmeats, fruits, &c. furnished by kind friends at home
for the sick of the army, have gone to the table of surgeons and attendants, whose interests are in the gratification of appetite and passion instead of their country."

While the boys were at home, Colonel Moore struggled with regimental
records. Lieutenant Comstock, not having reported since being commissioned, got a caustic warning to "join your command at once." There
also came word that the last prisoners of Shiloh were being exchanged
at Aikin's Landing, Virginia. Among those on the way back to St. Louis
were Lieutenants Richardson (C) and Whittemore (F) and Sergeants Crandall (H) and Morrey (D). The lieutenants had prior to early October been
in the "prison pen" at Madison, Georgia. After a summer there, they were
ready for a Missouri autumn. Company H would not see Crandall again,
for the elderly Lewis County carpenter, who had rather "miscalculated"
his age at enlistment, received a disability discharge (for deafness) at
Camp Banks, Virginia. The others would in time regain their strength
and give a good account of themselves.

Wherever the officers went, they were followed by unfinished business.
Upon reaching Canton, McGonigle learned that a "pension and bounty
agent" from Quincy was on his trail. Ex-Private Sylvanus Decker, a fifty-
year-old veteran of Company D wounded in the left arm at Shiloh, had
lately been discharged when a surgeon found him afflicted with an "os-
seous union of radius and ulna." Before Decker could establish eligibility
for pension benefits, he needed a "final statement." Having no luck writing McGonigle, Decker enlisted expert help. A Quincy attorney, Council
Greeley, had foreseen lucrative possibilities in the coming epidemic of
soldiers' claims. He even had a "traveling agent" working up business.
At any rate, on November 12 McGonigle opened his mail to discover

Greeley's peremptory demand for the final statement and descriptive roll. McGonigle was given to understand that if he monkeyed around any longer, General Curtis would hear of it: "Now we will wait only a reasonable time to receive that roll."

McGonigle fired back a huffy refusal: "I would like to know by what authority you make a demand on me for anything connected with the military. I think it is very insolent to say the least of it." Greeley made good his threat, spilling the beans to Curtis two days later. The general did not bestir himself to strong-arm the captain about it, but in early January the papers did reach Decker.

Curtis, however, was hearing better things of another officer of the Twenty-first Missouri. John W. Rankin, a Keokuk attorney, wrote to urge a brigadier's star for the "Marion of North Missouri." Moore, he declared, kept his Northeast Missouri Volunteers in "Regimental order for months, without money and with but poor Equipments. He triumphed over enemies in his family, over obstacles that might have appalled weak men." Curtis did not do much about it, but this was far from the last that Union brass would hear of the matter.

By November 21, the companies had reassembled at Canton, with the exceptions of companies C, F, and I out in Scotland County. On November 18, the day after Company F and the regimental staff marched out for Memphis, Lieutenant Reece Allen, armed with "Special Orders 12" from Colonel Moore, served notice on the local brewery and taverns that he was until further notice sole custodian of alcoholic beverages on sale in Canton. "The Colonel Comdg. regards the necessity of this order," Moore wrote, "but in making it, he feels he is but guarding the life and promoting the proper discipline of the soldier." There remained one way to slake soldierly thirsts, as Harlan pointed out: "It seems impossible for Col. D. Moore to keep the boys from running home."

Under Ed Moore's command, the main body left Canton for Edina on Monday, November 21. The captains were directed to commandeer all teams and wagons needful and to give first priority to borrowing from "disloyal" citizens. Camping overnight at Monticello, the troops completed the forty-mile march Tuesday evening. Explained Barrett, the boys were in "the back country, where they will probably separate into detachments and spend several days in general recruiting." Lieutenant Nelson of Company A was unable to make the trip, for private grief had intruded. His father, James Nelson, a Kentucky militia captain in the War of 1812, lay dead at the family home north of Canton.

Northeastern Missouri was "bubbling over with patriotism for the

Stars and Stripes." Tracy and Hagle, working from Hannibal, had done well. New men, ultimately more than three hundred of them, were ready to take a stand. Even before Company A left Canton, young Robert Southwell had enlisted. Born in England, the sandy-haired farm lad came to duty as a teamster for Yust. Among those joining Leeser's company at La Grange were German immigrants such as Frederick Wolter and August Klusmeier. Wolter, a native of Brunswick, had been a cabinet-maker at Canton and Keokuk since coming to the New World. Young Klusmeier now followed his brothers John and Henry into the Twenty-first Missouri, after service in the militia.

Other young Missourians came to the colors in Knox and Scotland counties. David C. Ward, eighteen, an Illinois native living below Millport, thought it time to join his neighbors who had gone to war in 1861 with Murrow. Missouri-born William F. Cook of Edina enlisted in Company E. And great was the delight of Company C when Dave Justice reported to Captain Pearce on November 15, recovered and full of fight again.

Harlan was angling for more exciting work. He addressed Curtis, pouring out fears of remaining inactive all winter at Canton. He pleaded for a "secret service" detail: "I should like to have your permission to make a private military reconnoissance of any portion of the Southern States that you should think of occupying with troops previous to such occupation and report at any headquarters you may order." Soon the sage of Croton would be setting out on his travels behind Confederate lines as an undercover man for the Department of the Missouri. The thrills Harlan sought, Harlan would get.

With the exception of companies D and E, left to "talk it up" among their neighbors in Knox County, the Twenty-first Missouri trudged north to Memphis on December 1. Werly, for one, was glad to go, for his wife's family lived west of Memphis. Scotland County now had a week to look over the survivors of Moore's regiment and cheer their torn battle flag. The result, according to witnesses, was "a new impetus to the war spirit." After showing the flag in every corner of this loyal county, Moore directed a rendezvous on Canton by December 9.

And so it was that on Sunday, December 7, the regiment started its fifty-mile march to College Hill by way of Fairmont. Little though the Clark County boys then realized, on this very Sabbath Captain William McKee of the Seventh Missouri Cavalry lay dead on the battlefield of Prairie Grove, in northwestern Arkansas. McKee, saluted by his commander as "a brave man, who fell in the performance of his duty," had run into a predawn ambush and lost his life "while gallantly trying to cut his way out." A fondly remembered hero of Etna was gone.

Things were in an uproar as the boys reached College Hill. Orders from St. Louis were waiting: the Twenty-first Missouri was to report to Benton Barracks within a week. So much for expectations of winter quarters at home! Now there was "plunder" to pack and transportation to arrange. And there were new men to muster—along with some old-timers showing up once more. True to his promise to Leeser, Henry Emry was waiting in Canton, cured now of camp complaints and ready to go. It was also necessary for the regiment to accommodate Mrs. Barrett, Mrs. Woodyard, and the ladies of Canton's Union Aid Society, who wanted to present a color-flag to the regiment.

On the afternoon of December 11, the regiment marched to La Grange, where men of Company K could enjoy one last Thursday night with their families. On Friday morning, they went on to Palmyra to board a Hanni- bal & St. Joseph passenger train for Macon City. Werly lamented that he and his family "had to separate again, and I arrived late in Palmyra." Editor Snyder saluted the Twenty-first Missouri on its going: "They will soon be ready to take the field in 'as good order and well conditioned' as when they first entered the service."

Four frantically busy days followed the arrival at Benton Barracks around noon December 14. Lieutenant Tobias McQuoid, Company E, ailing with dysentery, was pronounced unfit for field duty by Seaton on December 15. McQuoid immediately tendered his resignation but agreed to stay until his letter was processed. That took two months. Company H gained an able new first lieutenant in St. Louis-born Logan Tompkins, a twenty-three-year-old bank clerk whose connections included the power- ful Blairs. Corporal Martin Easley reported to Company K after weeks of confusion over his whereabouts. The boys had not seen him since Chewalla, and Colonel Moore lifted his stripes the day after he reappeared. Another irritant plaguing many commanders was exemplified by a lad from Knox County. The tall, dark stranger said he was John S. Henry when he mustered in for Company D on December 15. Then he skipped—with his enlistment bounty and premium of twenty-nine dollars. Later, under the names "Suders" and "Saxton" he served similarly abbreviated enlistments in the Fourth Ohio and Second Pennsylvania Cavalry. Whoever he was, "Henry" was a joiner.

An exasperated Pressell learned upon arriving at Benton Barracks that regimental property, including two bales of blankets, had mysteriously vanished. As he well knew, this could bedevil him for a long time to come. Colonel Moore, while commiserating with his quartermaster, found time to fight out his own "battle of the Springfields" with Curtis' chief of ordnance. Moore won handily. Waiting for the boys as they marched down Walnut Street to the 691-ton *Maria Denning* was a huge stack of new rifled muskets, piled on the wharf and guarded by a sergeant. One by one, the troops stacked their old weapons and picked up the gleaming replacements. Moore, signing the receipt, asked the sergeant to return the favor in respect of the discarded rifles. The sergeant, however, protested his "incompetence" to give receipts. There being no ordnance officer present, and the regiment being ready to sail, Moore gave the noncom "positive instructions" to report this transaction at once to headquarters.

As the *Maria Denning* headed for Columbus, Kentucky, soldiers with St. Louis newspapers were reading of great excitement on both sides of the Appalachians. Major General Ambrose E. Burnside, now commanding the Army of the Potomac, had lately marched on Richmond from the north. He soon threw his assets away, on a blood-soaked December 13, by staging a combat crossing of the Rappahannock at Fredericksburg in the face of artillery on the heights above the town. After more than twelve thousand casualties, the chastened Burnside withdrew to the safer side of the river. Lincoln started looking for a replacement for him.

The Army of the Tennessee failed in its first attempt to seize the river bastion of Vicksburg. During December, Grant drove toward Grenada, in northern Mississippi, while sending a force under Sherman down the river to assault Vicksburg amphibiously. Sherman, however, suffered a repulse at the north edge of town on December 29, a few days after Van Dorn's cavalry laid waste to Grant's supply depot at Holly Springs, Mississippi. The federal chieftain recalled his forces. At the end of December, however, Rosecrans overtook Bragg near Murfreesboro, Tennessee. There, in a four-day battle, Rosecrans fought the Johnnies to a standstill along Stones River. When it was over, the fight was about gone out of Bragg, and the Confederates backed gingerly toward Chattanooga.

The farther west Lincoln looked, the better things were going. Confederate Major General Thomas C. Hindman, after Prairie Grove, gave up northwestern Arkansas to retire on Little Rock. McClernand's Union troops, operating in eastern Arkansas, were penetrating the countryside around Helena. On January 11, 1863, he seized Arkansas Post, some twenty miles above the mouth of the Arkansas River and more than fifty miles southwest of Helena.

8

"Oh, God, Grant Us Soon Peace!"

Colonel Moore was the busiest man on the *Maria Denning*. Two vexing problems preyed on his mind: the cases of Lieutenant Colonel Woodyard and Captain Farris. The former had declined to leave Canton, the latter had refused to join Company F in boarding the ship. Motives of both remain unclear from available records. The Old Man's reaction however, was unmistakably plain. To the commander of the St. Louis district, he sent a plea "that you arrest Captain Joseph T. Farris . . . and return him to his command." Now came a peremptory order to Woodyard, penned by Adjutant Rees, demanding his immediate return. Moore's order, Rees added, was "unanimously solicited" by the officers, who felt Woodyard should rejoin forthwith "or . . . resign your position in the service." Until he returned, Woodyard should be carried as "absent without leave" from December 10. In a matter of days, both officers were hurrying south.

Some personnel problems were handled by others. Department medics in St. Louis discharged Eri Morris, lately of Company F, "for kidney trouble" and "nervous prostration." George Matthauer of Company A remained at Canton to scout the region for some fifty AWOLs. Doubtlessly it prospered his mission that Colonel Bishop on January 4, 1863, became provost marshal of Clark County.

General Davies, commanding the District of Columbus, ordered the Twenty-first Missouri detained there upon its arrival December 20. Van Dorn and Forrest were on the rampage. Not only was Grant's depot at Holly Springs being laid in ruins this very day, but rebel horsemen were attacking outposts north and south of Memphis. Indeed, Davies explained to Moore, an early assault on Columbus itself was likely. Situated along high bluffs overlooking the Mississippi and elaborately fortified by Polk earlier in the year, this railway terminus was a vital link in the logistical system building up behind Grant's offensive into Mississippi. Brigadier General Clinton B. Fisk had four regiments of infantry (Thirty-third and

Thirty-fifth Missouri, Twenty-ninth and Thirty-third Iowa) with which to defend Columbus, and both generals had good reason to welcome Moore's regiment.

Leaving its camp gear aboard ship, the Twenty-first Missouri stood alerted for action. Werly's friends "expected to be attacked by the rebels, but such did not occur." At length, on Monday morning, Fisk ordered the Missourians to "look them up" in the general direction of Union City, Tennessee, more than thirty miles south. The Missourians reached Union City that evening. They found no trace of the rumored Confederate raiders and spent Tuesday returning to Columbus.

During the rest of Christmas week, the regiment stayed at Columbus. Some of the boys manned entrenchments; some unloaded the *Maria Denning* and put up the tents. Meanwhile, David Moore settled his problem with Farris. The captain arrived under guard from St. Louis on December 30 as the regiment was entraining for "permanent station" at Union City. The major was in charge, the colonel having left for Union City to command the post. Farris, after conferring with the major, promptly wrote a standard resignation. Dave, remembering Chewalla, intemperately denounced Farris as "unfit for any position" and washed his hands of another old comrade.

It was not that Farris was stepping out of the war. Far from it. He wanted to fight somewhere else. Company A of Iowa's Southern Border Brigade elected him its captain on February 24, 1863. "He is a staunch Union man," the *Gate City* declared fondly, "and an energetic fellow— one of whose principal recommendations is that he is cordially hated by the copperheads. Headquarters of his company are at Croton." Later, in 1864, Farris would command Company K, Sixtieth U.S. Colored Infantry.

On returning South, the boys were in Grant's Department of the Tennessee, created the previous October to embrace Cairo, Illinois, western parts of Kentucky and Tennessee, and areas of Mississippi into which Union forces expected to penetrate. The Missourians were to learn that the overriding concern of this department was Grant's determination to capture Vicksburg and restore Union control of the great midland waterway.

Little significant action developed during these last months of winter. Confederate Lieutenant General John C. Pemberton, commanding the Department of Mississippi and Eastern Louisiana from his office in Jackson, Mississippi, had ample reason to hope for quiet on his front. Surely the slashing attacks that Forrest and Van Dorn were delivering against fed-

eral communications would keep Grant off balance for months. Pemberton's principal worry, it seemed, was civilian morale. Even Richmond was
edgy about the loyalty of citizens in the war-torn western watershed. Davis
himself had made a fact-finding tour of Mississippi during December, reminding everyone in authority that defending Vicksburg was a question of
"life and death" to the Confederacy.

Intensifying Davis' fears was a stream of Union reinforcements passing
down the river toward Memphis and Helena, Arkansas. By the end of January, Grant's troops were in the forested swamps lining the Louisiana side
of the river opposite Vicksburg. The Union commander now hoped to
pass to the south and flank Vicksburg from below. This, unfortunately, entailed moving a substantial force by river transport past a four-mile gaunt-
let of artillery along the water front. Since Grant had no taste for the gamble, it remained to open a canal upstream that would enable transports to
slip through a narrow neck of land well out of range of Pemberton's guns.
However, on March 8, the river rebelled, flooding the project and much of
its equipment. Grant wearily abandoned hopes of passing by without a
scrap.

As post commander at Union City, Colonel Moore was responsible for
guarding work crews repairing the Mobile & Ohio. Ed Moore became provost marshal, with reliable Mike Cashman as his orderly. Under Dave's command, in addition to his own regiment, was a pair of cavalry outfits, Company B of the Second Illinois and D of the Fourth Illinois. A detachment
of the Thirteenth Wisconsin Infantry reported to him, as did part of the
ll9th Illinois Infantry. In the case of the latter regiment, there was an iron-
ic coincidence. Its chaplain was none other than the late lieutenant colonel of the Northeast Missouri Home Guards—Charles S. Callihan! However,
since the main body of the ll9th was at Jackson, Tennessee, it is unlikely
that Callihan ever rubbed shoulders with his former commander or ran
"competition" to Chaplain Cox at Union City.

Davies and Fisk were obsessed with protecting the railroad, crucial to
the department's mission. In fact Davies' adjutant notified Colonel Moore
on January 2 that "all citizens riding in or about your lines will be treated
as enemies and put to work on the Rail Road." Planning a task force to
Helena, Fisk persuaded Davies to trade him the Fortieth Iowa for the
Twenty-first Missouri. The latter regiment, he told Curtis, ought to stay
on the railroad: "Colonel Moore . . . is not good for field service, as he has
but one leg." How the Old Man would have hooted!

In any case, both generals were soon gone—Fisk to Helena, Davies to
Washington. Coming to head the district in January was Brigadier General

Alexander Asboth. This colorful officer, chief of staff to Frémont in Missouri, had been a leading figure in Louis Kossuth's ill-starred Hungarian revolt against Austrian rule in 1848-1849 and was an international celebrity in his own right.

Those January days at Union City brought heartening improvements. More prisoners of Shiloh were rejoining, and promotions and reassignments were coming in profusion. Sergeant Major Russell received his commission as second lieutenant of Company I, George Stine moving up to first lieutenant. Russell had already placed his order for "sword, sash & belt" priced at thirty-four dollars with a Keokuk firm. Starr was called up from Company F to become a sergeant major. At the same time, the colonel was successful in raising Sergeant Josiah W. Davis to the captaincy of B. This young Hoosier had been one of Story's original sergeants. Although Davis was boosted over the head of Jeremy Hall, no morale problem resulted. Shortly after Story's resignation, Company B had unanimously petitioned the governor to make Davis captain.

Wholesale reshuffling of two companies occurred at Union City. The slack in Company G, occasioned by Captain Roseberry's departure, was taken up as Lieutenant Blackburn stepped into the captaincy, with Allen his second-in-command. The remaining lieutenancy in G passed to Robert R. Harris, Irish-born first sergeant from Belfast, Iowa, who had come all the way with these veterans since home guard days. These promotions paved the way for Charles McMichael to become the new first sergeant. Then, on March 6, a similar change came in F. Alex Tracy assumed the captaincy formerly held by Farris, and Frank Whittemore became first lieutenant. Sergeant Peter H. Orr, a twenty-six-year-old native of New York lately farming near Deer Ridge, succeeded Whittemore as second Lieutenant.

While Seaton bore alone the duties of surgeon, the quest for an assistant continued. For a fleeting moment in January , it appeared the right man had been located. Dr. Arthur M. Thome of Primrose, Iowa, grandson of a pioneer at Athens, was willing—more or less. He would come, he wrote Gamble's adjutant general, but he did not want to abandon his practice at this time. David Moore's wire-pulling had caught Thome between two fires, idolizing as he did "that brave and gallant officer, on whom it has been my pleasure to wait after the Battle of Athens and during his confinement at Keokuk after his return from the [Shiloh] engagement." The good doctor was pestered no more.

Dr. Thome was not alone in his admiration for the Ethan Allen of 1861. Pressell, making bold to address General Curtis on February 14, assured his fellow townsman that Dave's promotion to brigadier "would give general satisfaction to all loyal Citizens in N. E. Mo. as well as along the border of our own Noble State of Iowa."

During the weeks at Union City, the prisoners returned, for the most part. They arrived individually or in pairs from Benton Barracks, and Woodyard brought about a dozen with him. Tom Richardson, middle-aged second lieutenant of Company C, rejoined, just in time to make first lieutenant. Sergeant Morrey of D, and George Wilson and Sergeant Philarmon Reynolds of H were among sixty-two returnees. By the end of February, the regiment could all but close the books on prisoner exchanges stemming from Shiloh.

Tennessee's weather made short work of expectations that the boys could spend this winter "tenting on the old camp ground." On January 15, Werly noted, "There fell in Tennessee a foot of snow, and the weather was as cold as in the north." Russell measured the snow's depth at fifteen inches two days later. Moore and Woodyard, feeling that this would never do, chose to put the men into warmer quarters. As many as could be spared from guard duty along the Mobile & Ohio went to work cutting timber for a log-cabin cantonment and stockade. Soon the regiment had a new—and certainly more comfortable—home.

Guarding Grant's communications entailed various chores. Most regularly there was the scout, a company-sized expedition to intercept enemy raiders. From time to time word came that Van Dorn was preparing to cross the Tennessee to spread havoc along the railway as far as Columbus or Memphis. Whenever this occurred, the excitable Asboth would order out someone to reconnoiter fording places to develop Van Dorn's objective. Quite another matter was the tendency of railroad work crews to let conviviality get out of hand. Russell wrote in his diary February 7 that "I was sent with ten men to [a] construction train to arrest 14 Irishmen, which I did and returned on handcars."

In a way, this situation recalled North Missouri two summers earlier. There were in Tennessee determined enemies front and rear. In February. Asboth received a denunciatory letter and petition from twenty-one leading citizens of the Union City area. Having taken the oath, they qualified as loyal, but their attitude toward blue-coated protectors was less than indulgent. This Colonel Moore from Missouri, in their eyes, was a reborn Attila the Hun. His ruffians were pillaging the countryside, burglarizing homes, and driving off livestock. There was no point in reporting this to Moore, for appeals to him were "mocked at and treated with contempt." Asboth should at least, these "loyal" Americans felt, see that "Col.

Moore . . . be removed (soon) [and] some other and more competent officer appointed to command the Post."

Asboth, explaining that "reports are current of frequent depredations
committed by soldiers of [this] command," quite appropriately asked
Moore's views. And he did not have long to wait. On March 3, Dave expressed his surprise that the "so-called 'Loyal Men' " were so quoted. He
had just grilled several, and each had denied signing that petition, so he
believed that the complaints were a bit of trouble-making by "a very bitter
Rebel who has taken the Oath and therefore claims to be 'Loyal'."

"I wish to state to you, General," Moore concluded, "that when I was
ordered here by Genl Davies it was ordered by him to treat all citizens as
enemies and place them at work on the Rail Road. Hence the hard feelings
against me." In all fairness, it must be remembered that Davies had hardly
phrased his order this way, although he had apparently given Moore considerable latitude.

On March 5, at Moore's call, the petitioners assembled at Union City.
Oddly, they were undergoing a change of heart, disinclined to make
much of the recent "petty depradations." Nor would anyone say to
Moore's face he had shown contempt toward complaints. "I gave them my
assurance of kindness and protection," Moore notified Asboth. "I asked
them if they were Union Men. They said they had taken the Oath." But
when asked if they favored emancipation, they "with one exception answered in the negative." If the illustrious Hungarian wondered how the
merchant of Wrightsville had inspired this transformation, he never bothered Moore about it.

Not that discipline in the Twenty-first Missouri approached perfection—
far from it. Perhaps it was the monotony; perhaps it was the long-smold-
ering disaffection that had flared up at Chewalla and could do so again.
Most certainly there was outside agitation, such as the older brother who
had lured young William McCullough away from Company E in early January, before he had been a month in uniform. Subsequently returned to
military custody, the youth underwent six months of hard labor at Alton,
Illinois. He came back to the regiment in the summer of 1864—to become
a good soldier for the balance of his enlistment.

All during their days in the District of Columbus, the Missourians received suggestive mail from strangers inquiring about the political climate
in the regiment and from relatives urging them to come home. Colonel
Moore minced no words in a letter to Curtis about one desertion case,
declaring that a drummer boy "was young and perhaps persuaded by some
copperheads in Illinois to desert." Corporal Sam Cameron of Company H
wrote of "letters being received in this regiment advising men to desert and

go home, and the people there would protect them." Dave Moore himself, bombarding the tristate press to persuade fifty absentees to hurry back, voiced "regrets that there is so little interest manifested by the military and citizens back at home in permitting these cowardly deserters to remain amongst them unmolested, knowing as they do the solemn allegiance they owe their country."

A vexatious case of absenteeism came the first week of March, when five men of Company H took off from Union City. Within a week, the Illinois cavalrymen caught all of them. Four months of hard labor, including a month with ball and chain, was the lot of John Yates, George Coffman, John H. Bishop, and John L. Jones. Martin Hunter beat the rap when a court-martial acquitted him later in the year. All were veterans of Moore's home guards.

Private Theodore Harrison of Company G acted up in another way. At a dress parade in Union City January 5, he persisted in jabbering, slouching, and making faces at officers. In short, Teddy was "asking for it." Blackburn, arresting him, warned Ted he would pay for this horseplay by "marking time" all morning the next day. Harrison, vowing he would see Blackburn "in Hell before he would mark time," provoked the company commander into preferring charges. A court headed by Captain Pearce pronounced Harrison guilty of "conduct prejudicial" and "using disrespectful language to superior officers." His payoff was a three-day visit to the guardhouse and a daily march to a beating drum "along the front of the Regiment upon Parade," bearing a "Disobedience of Orders" placard. Colonel Moore, reviewing the verdict, approved everything "except the drum beating," and Ted started three days of public humiliation at the dress parade of February 5.

On Wednesday, February 18, John Davis, an eighteen-year-old soldier from La Grange, raised a furor in Company K by engaging Christian Crivitz in a lengthy fuss. When German-born Crivitz appealed to Sergeant William A. Weaver to "take him away," Davis tried a string of "hard names" on Weaver. The latter, after telling Davis to "behave," left. Instead of behaving, the youth flung a brick at Crivitz, inflicting an eye injury and gaining himself a bunk in the guardhouse. Captain Best's court-martial set him up for a reprimand from "D. Moore" as well as six hours of "placarding" for three days.

Woodyard, commanding the regiment, undertook to straighten the boys out on several matters. On February 17, he issued a written condemnation of officers and noncoms who "lie out of Camp and Quarters." There would be no more boarding in town, and a regimental court-martial would attend to those persisting. Moreover, as Grant's headquarters had lately prohib-

ited "card plaing and gambling," Woodyard was going to crack down on
the vices as well.

Almost daily, it seemed to Cox, "muffled drums are beating funeral
marches." Constant were reminders of human mortality to the chaplain
as he ministered to Missouri and Illinois troops of the command. Eight of
his own died during the regiment's two months there. Particularly pathetic was the death on January 7 of a young sergeant, Patrick Cahalan. The
cause of death was unspecified in the records. Married to Ann Friel, whose
brothers James and Peter were serving with him in Company E, Pat left an
unborn son. Patrick Junior, born the following August, became a respected
Edina carpenter. Cahalan's older brother James, also an Irish immigrant,
had been wounded at Shiloh. James now disappeared, and Captain Fulton
heard no more of him.

With the resignations of Leeser and McQuoid effective in early February,
promotions were due. The extent to which Moore and Woodyard collab-
orated in the matter is highly debatable, but Moore did send recommendations to the governor that led to several commissions. Comstock succeeded
to McQuoid's first lieutenancy, in E, and First Sergeant Emanuel Bonaparte Shafer succeeded Comstock. First Sergeant Puster vaulted to the
captaincy of Company K, to the delight of his fellow Germans. In Company
D, Joshua Hagle, after a month as second lieutenant, rose a notch in February, and Sergeant Morrey became the new second lieutenant. Also, by
direct commission from Governor Gamble, a Memphis businessman, James
McFall, arrived in Union City as the new second lieutenant of Company C.

There was time for politics. Some of the boys had harbored dark suspicions Lincoln might succumb to Conservative pressure and "back down"
from the proclamation. But, Cox told Dr. Elliott,

> . . . when it did come, you should just have seen the soldiers, and heard
> their cute sayings, such as "Bully for Old Abe and his pet lambs," and
> "Hurrah for freedom in Missouri. . . ." The 2lst Missouri are emphat-
> ically a loyal regiment, and *nutiny* (mutiny), as the negroes say, is
> played out. We hail the proclamation as the wisest measure of the war,
> and now that the negro is to be free, we want them armed, so that they
> may fight for freedom, believing as we do that slavery is the sole cause
> of the rebellion.

The regiment noisily vindicated this estimate of its temper in February.
A number of things had stirred up the boys, among them the resurgence
of Democratic strength in the Ohio valley states. Radical governors were

now feuding with obstreperous "Conservative" legislators, and many in Moore's ranks saw Conservative-Unionists as did a certain Radical senator in Illinois, who fumed that "Hell itself could not spew out a more traitorous crew." Constant irritants to soldierly sensitivities were the appearances in camp of newsboys, peddling such violently antiadministration papers as Chicago's *Times,* Cincinnati's *Enquirer,* and New York's *World.*

On Thursday evening, February 19, Colonel Moore summoned his officers to discuss "the Proclamation, the Administration, and the opposition thereto." After each had presented his views, Moore and Woodyard climaxed the "speaking" with Radical tirades. Thereupon, a committee headed by Woodyard and including the chaplain and Major Moore, drafted a resolution supporting Lincoln's "use of every means for the suppression of the rebellion." Specific denunciations were offered to "Copperhead members of the Legislatures of Illinois and Indiana," along with "criers of armistice and framers of peace resolutions."

Endorsed by the officers, the resolutions went to the enlisted men the next day. The colonel presiding and Comstock clerking, the regiment, said Russell, "marched out to an open field and formed in a square to vote on resolutions. Carried unanimously almost. 29 dissenters." "Of course," Pressell told Howell, "the only obstacle in the way of those dissenting was that everlasting 'color.'" At any rate, he assured Howell, the Twenty-first Missouri was "sound on the Administration, as well as the Proclamation. The 21st is, as you know, from a slave State, and I believe the first one that has spoken out on the subject."

Even as the Missourians voted, the Conservative *Constitution* of Keokuk lay in ruins, its plant devastated by patients from local military hospitals. Provost guards broke up the riot, and a lengthy investigation ensued. To Sam Cameron, the inquiry was a pure waste of time. When word came of the disaster, he reported, "Nine out of ten said all that was wrong about it was that it was not done a year ago."

There dawned a new era for recruiters when the President signed the Enrollment Act of March 3, 1863, and the federal government moved directly into the business of conscription. Indeed, the Militia Act of 1862 foreshadowed such a move, even if that law had been designed mainly to spur local recruiting. That is, it was operable only in states failing to meet quotas for volunteers. The new law, coming as it did after Republican setbacks in the fall of 1862 and the onset of war-weariness reflected in the growing inadequacy of volunteering, set up nationwide draft machinery. It embraced all men from twenty to thirty-five, single men to age forty-five. The office of provost marshal general came into being to enforce the act through a system of provost marshals in congressional districts. This law, placing Uncle Sam's fingers on three million men, proved itself a miserable failure in some ways, for the Union got only about six percent of its manpower from this system.

As Allan Nevins has said, Congress had itself to blame for the wretched performance of the Enrollment Act of 1863. It continued the "substitute" provision enacted the previous summer, whereby any affluent person tapped for service under the Militia Act of July 17, 1862, could hire a substitute. Aside from penalizing poverty, the substitute system could shatter morale in units where a favored few were drawing double pay, one salary from the army and another from "guys back home." There was also a "commutation" privilege; the marshals would not disturb the tenor of the civilian ways of those who paid three hundred dollars. The hundred-dollar bounty of 1861 was now raised to three hundred dollars; if it encouraged enlistments, it conceivably stimulated bounty jumping. Moreover, enforcement was left to the military, with no responsibility placed on eligibles to register. Local provost marshals literally had to catch draftees, and they went from house to house like detectives to do so. If these officers were unaccustomed to lies and abuse, they got used to them. If their resistance to payoffs was weak, they could accumulate impressive tax-free assets.

As March came on, a low point in Grant's checkered career was at hand. His attempts on Vicksburg fizzled, demands for his dismissal were rising once more, and only the President stood between him and those who would bounce him for inefficiency, alcoholism, and other complaints. The man's mettle, however, would reassert itself. He came up with new schemes, to march his troops down to Grand Gulf, Mississippi, and let Rear Admiral David Dixon Porter's gunboats take their chances with the Vicksburg batteries. Once a bridgehead on the east bank could be established around Grand Gulf, the federals would operate against Vicksburg from the south and east, and the crowing rebels would find themselves in fresh distress.

Grant's drive to the south started March 29. As expected, the infantry had a difficult passage through a sodden wilderness. On the night of April 16-17, Porter ran Pemberton's batteries with a fleet of eight gunboats and three transports, losing one transport burned and one sailor killed. The next day, when Grant rode into his camps opposite Grand Gulf, everyone was understandably jubilant.

The crossing here was hazardous, Grant decided, for Confederate artillery was waiting on the east bank. But space and mobility were on his side, and he sideslipped downstream toward Port Gibson. On April 30, he crossed there. By the time Port Gibson had fallen to the advancing

Yankees on May 2, Pemberton realized he was fighting for the very life of his department. The Johnnies at Grand Gulf blew up their ammunition, spiked their guns, and fled. Particularly unsettling to them was a daring raid by Union cavalry under Brigadier General Benjamin H. Grierson, who had charged into northern Mississippi on April 17 and spread fear and devastation far and wide before galloping off into Louisiana.

Pemberton soon reaped his whirlwind as Grant pushed to the interior. So great was Richmond's alarm that Davis ordered Johnston west on May 9 to fend off this rapidly building danger. Johnston, commanding all Confederates in the west, rose from a sickbed to entrain from Tullahoma, Tennessee. Upon reaching Jackson, he found the situation deteriorating at frightening speed. The Union vanguard was only ten miles away. "Communication is cut off, " he wired Richmond. "I am too late."

Too late indeed. Sherman seized Jackson itself on May 14 and hoisted the flag over the statehouse. Two days later, Grant routed Pemberton at Champion's Hill. Torn between presidential orders to hold Vicksburg and Johnston's wiser counsel that he keep his army out of that trap, Pemberton obeyed the president and withdrew into the trap. Johnston tried to coax him out while there was time, but the stiff-necked Pennsylvanian refused. All that remained to Pemberton was an agonizing siege, a heartrending capitulation, and the lifelong scorn of compatriots.

There were repercussions well to the rear. On March 8, the Twenty-first Missouri received orders, said Werly, "to leave our comfortable quarters" and proceed to Columbus. The boys freely expected to join the coming push into Mississippi; it seemed better than watching railroad work and waiting for Forrest. On the Missourians' arrival in Columbus, however, Asboth changed things. New instructions from Grant required him to detach a force for guard duty around Clinton, Kentucky, a dozen miles east. That, said Asboth, meant the Twenty-first Missouri. Detailed to accompany the regiment were the Illinois horsemen who had been with them at Union City.

"Your position is to be regarded as an advanced post which you will hold unless attacked by too great a force," Asboth told Moore. Much of the terrain around Clinton was being flooded by the Little Obion River, and no early attack was likely. But there was the long run to consider, and Moore would need to build earthworks for Clinton's defense. There was no help for it; the Missourians, after less than an hour in Columbus, rode out six miles and detrained. The next morning, they marched to Clinton over muddy roads impassable to anything but animal and pedestrian traffic.

While the boys were making themselves comfortable at their tent city in the Kentucky mud, Colonel Moore rode out to plan fortifications for Clinton. About a half-mile west of town he found his ideal site, and on March 13 the men started their ring of earthen breastworks. If they could not live as cosily as in Union City, they would at least soon live in greater personal safety.

All the while, the struggle to make Dave Moore a general was continuing. Major Moore, having lately written General Grant to line up Missouri's Senator John B. Henderson, inspired Woodyard to put on the pressure in high places accessible to him. On March 13, Woodyard wrote Attorney General Edward Bates, the Missourian in Lincoln's cabinet, and urged him to "call the attention of the President" to this campaign in Moore's behalf. Whatever Bates could accomplish, Woodyard assured him, would greatly oblige a "Devoted and Ardent Friend."

An ominous telegram came for Seaton on April 3. It was from his mother in Keokuk: "Father is dangerously sick. Come home immediately." Myers Seaton had suffered an attack of "congestion of the brain" in the family home at Second and Times streets. Without hesitation, Doc packed his bags, sent Woodyard a request for leave, and caught a ride to Columbus. Asboth's medical director approved a five-day absence, and Seaton took a steamer for home. It took a week for Seaton to get there, barely in time to see his parent slip away.

Given the haste of Seaton's going and a lack of communication between Moore and Woodyard, there was room for misunderstandings. Aware that his only surgeon had left, but ignorant of the reason, Moore fired off a telegram to Asboth: "I gave him positive orders not to leave the post." The general promptly responded, wiring Dave everything Woodyard could have told him. Not that there was much point in hissing at Seaton. When he returned, he would lodge his resignation with Woodyard and remove himself from military jurisdiction. He considered "my infirm and aged Mother" a more inescapable responsibility than his surgeon's post.

But Moore and Woodyard were learning of another way to lose officers. Late in January, Second Lieutenant George Davis of Company K had tried to resign on account of "diseased eyes." Woodyard called Seaton into the matter, but the surgeon would only recommend a few days' change of location. Davis, "put out" at this judgment, began to sulk, By mid-April, however, Woodyard realized what was eating on the young man. Sergeant Puster was jumping over him into the captaincy! "I would most respectfully tender my resignation," he wrote Woodyard again, ". . . for the following reason, the Orderly Sergeant has been appointed and commissioned

Captain . . . over me and I cannot with credit to myself hold a commission under a man that has held a subordinate position in the company." In a sense, Davis had scant cause to complain. The company was a German outfit, after all, and Puster had leadership capacity as well as rapport with this immigrant constituency. Not until December did Davis secure acceptance of his resignation, so long did Dave Moore hold the disgruntled youth's nose to the grindstone.

The loss of Seaton, plus the vacancy for assistant surgeon, spurred efforts to revive the medical services of the regiment. On May 4 there came to Clinton Dr. William H. Knickerbocker, a native New Yorker lately practicing in Fayette, Missouri, and formerly assistant surgeon of the Second Missouri Cavalry. Transferred to the Twenty-first Missouri on April 25, Knickerbocker probably made no effort to explain that for some reason he and Colonel Lewis Merrill of the cavalry had parted on acrimonious terms. Nor is it likely that this son-in-law of Samuel C. Major, a proslavery Kentuckian and public administrator of Howard County, dwelt on the fact that his brother-in-law James P. Major happened to be a Confederate brigadier in Louisiana. In any event, Moore promptly assigned him to duty and prepared to muster him as assistant surgeon.

Dr. Abel C. Roberts arrived at the cantonment near Clinton May 9. He came recommended by the commander of the General Hospital at Keokuk, who assured Governor Gamble that if his excellency commissioned Roberts as regimental surgeon "you will have no cause to regret your action." Fourth child of a New York farm family, the new surgeon was an 1853 graduate of the University of Michigan's medical college. Removing to Fort Madison, Iowa, in 1859, and finding a community in dire need of a Democratic newspaper, he took the editorial chair of the local *Plain Dealer* and held it three years. He laid journalism aside to become a contract surgeon for the military hospitals in Keokuk, where his superior found him "a jintleman of high professional standing and of good moral character."

Two popular old-timers returned in March. Rufus Wilsey, the use of his knee restored, took over as sutler. Rickey was out of the picture. Also coming in was Joshua Dale of Company D, long-absent prisoner of Shiloh. Exchanged and cured of a bout with camp complaints, the big fellow was ready to take on the Johnnies again. His stepson Aquilla Barnes did not come with him; medics had discharged the youth.

As April began, political stirrings rose in the regiment. Sam Cameron unleashed such a blast at Democratic newsmen and defeatist politicians that Editor Howell deemed his militant remarks worthy of full exposition. The Twenty-first Missouri, Sam insisted, "has no use for Northern traitors under the cloak of Democrats, without about three hundred of them could be sent here to fill up our thinned ranks. In such an event as that, we would do all we could to train them up in the way that they should go, and would try to regenerate them from the low state of degradation into which they have fallen. . . . Men that will stay at home and do all that they can to poison the minds of the people against the Administration at such a time as this, when all the energies of the Government and people are needed to put down this unholy rebellion, [are] too mean for the damned in hell to look upon."

Lieutenant Nelson sounded off in the tristate press against convention delegates from northeastern Missouri. Messrs. Gorin, Givens, and Sayre were elected as "thorough going Union men," he claimed, "but they have betrayed their constituents, and have acted with disunionists." If, Nelson insisted, they would heed their constituents, they would resign, "that men may be elected who will reflect the sentiment of the people." These Conservative delegates, however, were deaf to such Radical intimations.

Another outburst came on May 1 among Moore's Iowans. These boys had been simmering for weeks over resolutions passed by Keokuk Democrats. These worthies, facing spring elections in the city, had voted to fight "Abolition and Secession," oppose "all attempts, come from what quarter they may, to equalize the condition of the negro with that of the white man," and to combat "introduction of negroes into Iowa." Beyond this, the Gate City Democracy urged Lincoln to seek a negotiated settlement with Richmond, starting with a six-month armistice to gain time for "sober reflection" and "cooling of passion excited by civil war." This was Conservatism Unionism in its Sunday best, strutting on the "fightin' side" of Radical soldiery. About a hundred Iowans met in camp the evening of May 1 and produced a heated condemnation of "masked traitors" who had summoned the gall to claim they were "upholding the Administration" even as they deprecated the proclamation and harped on black "inferiority." The resolution, supervised by Lieutenants Allen and Harris, passed unanimously after oratory from Sam Cameron and Chaplain Cox. The latter, in particular, brought the aroused soldiers to their feet as he contemplated with relish the "bruising" in store for "copperheads when the soldiers . . . return to their homes."

Colonel Moore gave extraordinary attention during April to the condition of his regiment. Through the regional press at home, he addressed a "cordial invitation . . . to the old soldiers of my command to re-enlist in the 21st Regiment with their friends and comrades. By so doing, you will obtain 'Bounty Pay' and not be subject to the draft. Come one, come all."

Then, too, department headquarters was still hounding Pressell about his missing regimental property. The frustrated quartermaster applied for leave in April to go back to St. Louis to talk it over, but Asboth refused permission. And it happened also that month, thanks to a command from the Department of War, that the army mustered twice. The Twenty-first Missouri's special muster of April 15 brought together only 516 men "present for duty," but the regular muster brought in 575 two weeks later. The return of more than fifty AWOLs and hospital patients helped to account for the improved strength figures.

Payday meant different things to different soldiers. On April 17, for example, the boys were privileged to draw four months' pay, and like many another family man around him Werly "sent it home out of love for my own." Only two days before he had received "pictures of my beloved family, and I put all eight faces before me, but the life in them was missing, and I could not hear their agreeable voices and a great longing for them befell me. Oh, God, grant us soon peace!"

In the East, while Burnside's force lay camped along the Rappahannock facing Fredericksburg, its commander lost his job, on January 25. The President had settled on a successor, the contentious and flighty Major General Joseph ("Fighting Joe") Hooker. Lincoln was aware that the backbiting exhibitionist might prove a less-than-ideal commander for the Army of the Potomac, but Hooker had captivated the rank and file both in the army and in Congress and seemed worthy of a chance to prove himself as a combat commander.

Organizing his 130,000 men into five infantry corps and one of cavalry, Hooker made ready to crush the rebels on the heights west of Fredericksburg by catching Lee between converging wings of Hooker's army. Leaving about 40,000 men under Major General John Sedgwick to hold Confederate attention on the Rappahannock, Hooker stole away in late April to cross the river northwest of Fredericksburg and wheel around on the rear of the enemy west of the Heights.

Catching on, Lee turned the tables. Leaving a small force to pin Sedgwick down, the Army of Northern Virginia marched off rapidly with 50,000 troops to meet Hooker in the wilderness west of Fredericksburg. As the armies came to grips, Lee suddenly divided his own smaller force by detaching 25,000 under Jackson to swing around from the south and west to hit the Yankees from their right and rear. Suddenly, the flamboyant Hooker began to waver. To the dismay of subordinates, he ordered a defensive posture that made his army around Chancellorsville a sitting duck for inferior forces. Jackson, true to his instructions, shredded

Hooker's right flank on the evening of May 2 in a surprise onslaught whose glory suffered only from the mortal wounding of mighty Stonewall himself. The next day the Yankees missed their last chance for a comeback when, by his own admission, Hooker "lost faith" in himself. Unbeaten, the Army of the Potomac nevertheless retired over the Rappahannock, leaving Robert E. Lee standing sorrowfully amid scenes of an epic but meaningless "victory." If ever that splendid Union field army in Virginia got a commander willing to slug it out until death should part the unequal combatants, grim indeed would be the outlook for Southern independence.

DAVID MOORE
(1817-1893)

Colonel, 1861-1865; brigadier general, U. S. Volunteers, by brevet, 1865

After "killing secession" in north-eastern Missouri, he was "needed south."

State Historical Society of Missouri

HUMPHREY MARSHALL WOODYARD
(1809-1864)

Lieutenant Colonel, 1862-1864

"Conservatives" quavered apprehensively when the militant Kentucky-born radical came home to be their circuit judge.

State Historical Society of Missouri

133

State Historical Society of Missouri

EDWIN MOORE
(1833-1895)

Lieutenant Colonel, 1864-1865

From western Illinois came a hard-boiled young Englishman whose military know-how proved a blessing to the regiment.

JOSEPH G. BEST
(1838-1887)

Lieutenant Colonel, 1865-1866

Out of Ulster's "garrison" came the stern youth that commanded the regiment on "Reconstruction" duty.

State Historical Society of Missouri

RICHARD MICHAEL CASHMAN
(1846-1941)

Private, Company C

Quincy's gift to the regiment, Connecticut-born "Speckled Dick" went the distance with his new-found comrades over in Missouri.

State Historical Society of Missouri

AARON WARD HARLAN
(1811-1911)

Commissary Sergeant

Surveyor, poet, historian, prospector, philosopher—he savored life as few ordinary mortals.

State Historical Society of Missouri

135

GEORGE PUTNAM WASHBURN
(1847-1922)

Private, Company H

A Clark County farm boy par-
layed his martial experiences into
supreme command of the Kansas
G.A.R.

CYRENUS Z. RUSSELL
(1840-1906)

Second Lieutenant, Company A

The slender, sober-sided kinsman
of "Higher Law," Seward became
a valued adjutant and in later life
a peerless political operator.

THE REVEREND JOHN H. COX
(1833-1902)

Chaplain, 1862-1864

Bumptious "rebel" Christians a-
roused a Methodist parson to indignation that lasted in postwar
times.

State Historical Society of Missouri

ANDREW JACKSON SMITH
(1815-1897)

Major General, U. S. Volunteers

The Missourians proudly be-
longed to "A. J. Smith's Guerrillas."

Library of Congress

9

"Good Time" at Memphis

The issue in the West was tilting toward the Union, and there was a marked southward deployment of Yankee strength. On Sunday afternoon, May 10, Asboth instructed Moore to "march for Columbus at daybreak tomorrow to embark for Memphis." Major Moore would remain at Clinton as temporary provost marshal. Pressell would stay also "to bring forward regimental property," but the brass wanted the riflemen at Memphis—and soon. Waiting at Columbus was the aging steamer *Sultana.* On Tuesday at 1:30 P.M., the *Sultana* departed, passed Island Number 10 before sundown, and pulled into Memphis the next afternoon.

This movement was taking place at the behest of General Hurlbut, commanding the XVI Army Corps in Memphis and the districts of Corinth, Columbus, and Memphis. The Memphis command was headed by a West Pointer, Brigadier General James C. Veatch, whose force consisted of four brigades. Moore, recommended to Hurlbut by Asboth as "a gallant, earnest officer," would handle Veatch's Fourth Brigade at its camp two miles south of Memphis, and he would have a potent combat team composed of his own boys: the Thirty-fourth Wisconsin, Forty-ninth Illinois, Fifth Ohio Cavalry, a detachment of the Second Illinois Cavalry, and the Seventh Wisconsin Battery.

The Twenty-first Missouri would spend eight memorable months guarding this crucial river and railway town of some twenty-three thousand inhabitants. Dating from a settlement built on the Chickasaw Bluff early in the century, Memphis was a charming cotton-market city whose elevation afforded a grand view of many miles across flatlands to the west of the Arkansas shore. The restaurants and taverns would introduce the Missourians to samples of the Memphian way of life, and the boys would surely come to agree with the soldier-historian from Illinois who looked upon this sojourn as "the 'good time' of our recollections."

Things were heating up in Missouri. Curtis, hand-in-glove with local Radicals, was becoming a nuisance in Washington. Sick unto death of

Missouri's factional disputes, the President decided to replace Curtis with Major General John McAllister Schofield, head of the Missouri State Militia. Having a good personal and political relationship with the governor, the new commander might keep Missouri's squabbles at home. Installing Schofield on May 24, Lincoln reminded him that the Radical-Conservative feud would be a heavy cross to bear and warned him to beware of "being assailed by the one side and praised by the other." Curtis went out to head the Department of Kansas.

Poisoning the atmosphere in Missouri was the issue of emancipation. Since the state was "loyal," the proclamation did not touch it. The issue, however, did. Reassembling in June 1863, the convention worked out a conservative ordinance providing "gradual emancipation" with "apprenticeship" for younger blacks, and continued slavery for those over forty. To Radical charges the delegates were no longer representative of the public mood, Conservatives pleaded guilty by denying a referendum—and by forbidding future legislatures to tamper with their solution.

The Radicals proceeded to warm up Schofield's environment. In late June, the *Missouri Democrat,* acquiring a confidential letter from Lincoln to Schofield, printed it in full. The tenor of the letter could be construed as insulting to the governor, and this led to a bitter exchange between Lincoln and Gamble. This affair jeopardized relations between Schofield and the President, much to the Radicals' glee, and it provided them with a new martyr and a fresh cause. To square himself with the White House, Schofield arrested the offending editor and touched off a freedom-of-the-press scandal. Lincoln finally told Schofield to get off the newsmen's backs and let the matter—and the President—rest.

Schofield got little rest. On August 21, guerrillas led by William C. Quantrill charged out of Missouri to massacre 150 citizens of Lawrence, Kansas. Local officials, led by Curtis and James Lane, loudly deposited the blame on Schofield's doorstep. But even to the less hysterical, it was plain that Schofield was responsible for "law and order" in Missouri, and such breakdowns as the affair at Lawrence might seem to reflect on his administration. Charles Daniel Drake and the Radicals of Missouri could hardly overlook the opportunity to embarrass Schofield and his Conservative friends.

"Out East," Hooker had little time to compose himself after Chancellorsville. At Richmond, the shape of the immediate future was decided in those mild spring days. Under the influence of Lee, the president decided to leave the Mississippi valley forces to shift for themselves while the Army of Northern Virginia hoped to extend its winning streak in the broad green valleys east of the Blue Ridge. If this was bad news for Bragg and Pemberton out West, it was grim news for Hooker as well.

In early June, Lee's army, operating behind a cavalry screen, started north, down the valley of the Shenandoah past Harper's Ferry into Maryland. Onward the gray columns plodded, entering Pennsylvania and heading for Chambersburg and Carlisle. Hooker wheeled his ponderous army around and pointed it north on a parallel course. The least he could do was head off the Johnnies before they reached New York City or Philadelphia. But he was getting jittery, and it showed in his telegrams to Washington. Lincoln, tired of his mercurial behavior, replaced him with a bewhiskered engineer, Major General George Gordon Meade.

Distrustful of Republican Radicals and heartsick over the proclamation, Meade thought he was being arrested when news of his promotion was brought to his tent! Halleck and the President forgave his ideological peculiarities, knowing he was a cool operator and not likely to lose faith in himself at some tight moment.

Such a moment was approaching, as Union horsemen and rebel infantry clashed on the western edge of the little town of Gettysburg on July 1. Both sides summoned reinforcements, and a major battle took shape. Forming up on parallel ridges running south from the town, the armies prepared to slug it out along the Emmitsburg road. On July 2, James Longstreet's Confederate corps, much against his better judgment, made a bloody attempt to roll up Meade's left flank. Longstreet failed, and the armies continued massing. The next day, Lee hurled fifteen thousand more infantrymen under Major General George Pickett against the center of the federal line, in a do-or-die attempt to put the Army of the Potomac to flight.

Pickett met disaster, and his survivors recoiled in disarray from their frightful blooding. The battle was over by sundown. More than fifty thousand Americans were casualties of Gettysburg; twenty-eight thousand of them were Southerners. That night Lee's battered army began hobbling away to the distant camps from which it had marched so full of confidence. So far as the Department of War was concerned, Meade should have launched a killer attack and liquidated Lee's forces. Meade, however, was no more anxious to pursue than Rosecrans had been after second Corinth, and within a matter of days the Johnnies were home safely in Virginia.

Moore's veterans soon learned what to expect of camping on the Horn Lake Road. The Mississippi line was only ten miles to the south in territory swarming with rebel recruiters. Competition was so vicious among those "captains" in gray that one rarely completed a company, but this did not keep them from harassing Union installations with what recruits they had.

On May 18, Moore's cavalry flushed out a small squad, traded shots harm-lessly, and chased it across Horn Lake Creek, near the state line. A month later, troopers of the Fifth Ohio met a hot reception near Hernando, Miss-issippi, some twenty miles south of Memphis, and Veatch ordered the en-tire Fourth Brigade to the rescue. Alerting his forces, Colonel Moore moved down the Horn Lake Road the afternoon of June 19. By evening, his brigade had marched fifteen miles. Overtaken by one of Veatch's aides bearing instructions to come on back, Moore chose to march over to the Hernando Road (modern U.S. 51), where the troops bivouacked in a cot-ton field. No shot had been fired.

After the Twenty-first Missouri's shortage of surgeons, its cup ran over in June. A new doctor suddenly appeared, sent from St. Louis to become "Second Assistant" to Roberts. He was a native New Yorker by the name of Frederick G. Stanley and was unable to explain what had possessed Missouri's Adjutant General John B. Gray to make an extra gift to Wood-yard's medical service. Surgeon Roberts understood, after a fashion, for he had been on duty with the regiment for six weeks—without a commission. Woodyard was not prone to look a gift surgeon in the mouth; he lowered his eyebrows and put the newcomer to work.

Lieutenant Rees suddenly found himself in growing demand. Ben Pren-tiss, his fellow-Quincyite, was commanding the District of Eastern Arkansas, and there was no one else he so much wanted as his aide-de-camp. Rees was, however, simply not available, Hurlbut twice informed Prentiss. Finally, on July 29 Hurlbut named the young Welshman "Acting AAG" of XVI Corps, and five weeks later made him aide-de-camp. Surely the importunate Pren-tiss gathered from this he could forget about Rees.

On May 31 Aaron Harlan came to camp. He was just in from St. Louis, with a string of tales to tell. His undercover work for the Department of the Missouri had hit a snag in Benton County, Tennessee, about 125 miles northeast of Memphis, when a rebel sheriff collared him. Knowing only that Harlan was an "undesirable alien," the lawman handed him to Confed-erate authorites for deportation. Harlan was sent through the lines to City Point, Virginia, in early May, and military authorities sent him in to St. Louis. Within days of his return, Harlan was off for a similar foray into Mississippi for Colonel Moore.

These weeks at Memphis brought home to Woodyard an elementary fact of life: many of his troops actively resented him. After all, in what was fundamentally Moore's outfit, he was cast in the unhappy role of "the other colonel." This being a volunteer unit, its members were more prone to flaunt insubordinate feelings than regulars would have been. On

June 24, to cite a flagrant example, Woodyard busted three corporals in Company I—Bill Edwards, Bill Lane, and Allen Myres—for "disobedience of orders." Moreover, some of the younger officers were quick to "smart off" to the bearded Kentuckian—and he was prompt in noticing. Already, back at Clinton, he had flexed his authority to place Lieutenant Jim Smith under arrest. Soon after the arrival at Memphis, Ed Nelson sassed his august brother-in-law and provoked an order to "confine himself to his quarters."

Worse yet, on July 4 Captain Pearce flouted Woodyard and took off to cut up on a grand scale. A meddlesome provost marshal returned him under guard. The furious Woodyard arrested Pearce for "leaving camp without leave" and filed charges. The next morning C. Z. Russell, brigade adjutant, laid the troublesome mess on Moore's desk. Woodyard was accusing Pearce of absence without leave, conduct unbecoming, chronic dereliction, and breaking arrest. If any of this stuck, Company C might well be due a change of captains.

Dave Moore, exasperated as much by Woodyard's overreaction as by Pearce's behavior, let things simmer for a while. Then, on July 30, he told Russell to bundle up the paperwork and send it back to Woodyard with a terse indorsement: "Respectfully returned with orders that the said Captain Pearce . . . be restored to duty." Woodyard's feelings, though not recorded, are easily surmised.

A similar tug-of-war between the colonels was going on at the same time, involving the four lads who had taken off at Union City in early March—and had been subsequently sentenced to four months of captivity. In a fit of patriotic benevolence, Woodyard restored the boys to duty on July 4, pending review of their case. "D. Moore" ran them back to the hoosegow the next morning. When the reviewing was completed, the miscreants were sent up to Fort Pickering to do their time.

But nobody acted up quite like Fife Major Kilmartin during that Fourth of July weekend at Camp Veatch. On Sunday morning, July 5, he crossly rebuffed Lieutenant Gloeser's orders to play for guard mount. He had already "played more than he was payed for," and, besides, he had "lost his fife." Principal Musician Hughes Roseberry promptly went to Kilmartin's tent and found the fife. Not to be outdone, the temperamental fife major placed himself under arrest! Obviously, an "arrested" musician could hardly play for guard mount. That afternoon, Woodyard staged an end run, "releasing" Kilmartin from arrest. However, well fortified by strong drink, Kilmartin reeled into headquarters Monday morning with a solemn declaration that Woodyard lacked authority to "release a Musician who was arrested by himself." To a layman, it might have seemed a charming legal conundrum. Lieutenant Nelson, officer of the day, hardly viewed it in that light. Instead, he ordered the besotted fifer back to his tent. Not to be outdone, Kilmartin offered the lieutenant a threshing if he would kindly step outside. Naturally, Nelson took all this straight to his big sister's husband.

Not until dress parade that evening did they quit humoring Kilmartin. While the field band was practicing, the fife major offered to beat up Charles Penick, bugler of Company B. Then, at parade time, Kilmartin "when ordered . . . to play on Parade did utterly refuse and go to his quarters." The fife major had by now done quite enough to merit trial. But after bringing charges and conferring with Veatch's judge advocate, Woodyard backed down and tried to let sleeping dogs lie.

The "Glorious Fourth" at Memphis saw the return of Major Moore and Mike Cashman. Indeed, the major had petitioned district headquarters to relieve him as provost marshal at Clinton. He had been, as he said, "receiving urgent appeals from the officers of the Regiment to join them at once." Given the deterioration of Woodyard's relations with his subordinates, the urgency of these appeals becomes clear.

In northeastern Missouri, homefolks were enjoying the quietest summer in four years. Rebel marauders and recruiters were nearly out of business. State militia commanders had a firm grip on the area, the fervent Southern partisans had disappeared into prisons or gone south, and there was in progress what Editor Howell decried as "a great exodus from Missouri lately over the plains to escape the draft. The companies doing a freighting business that way have been overwhelmed with applications from persons willing to work their passage." A fair gauge of quieter conditions was the safety with which Father McMenomy traveled between Edina and Quincy. Many lads of the Twenty-first Missouri, Catholic or not, mailed their money to the express office in Quincy, addressed to the dauntless cleric, and he would carry munificent sums back to Knox County for distribution to the families.

The paymaster failed to show up at regimental headquarters in June 1863. The department paymaster in St. Louis had lately received shocking notice that he had "overpaid" the Twenty-first Missouri by some twenty-six thousand dollars. A treasury auditor had decided that paymasters had been shelling out money without adequate "evidence" of the regiment's service, which led to a "stoppage" against the whole outfit. At the same time, the Department of War ordered a separate stoppage because of a mix-up over those new muskets picked up in St. Louis the previous December. Fortunately, the original mustering officer was now on the regimental staff, and, with Major Moore's help, these matters were in time settled.

While the Republic was rejoicing over its birthday present from Meade's valiant army, similar causes for jubilation came in the West. On July 3, Pemberton acknowledged that the drama of Vicksburg was "played out." In ceremonies on Independence Day, a forty-thousand-man Confederate army marched out of the war into the history books. The legend of "Unconditional Surrender" Grant grew taller. A few days later, with the capture of Port Hudson just above Baton Rouge, Major General Nathaniel P. Banks removed the last obstruction to federal use of the River.

During the late spring, the Confederate commander in Arkansas, Lieutenant General Theophilus Holmes, prepared to assault Helena, where Prentiss and a garrison of four thousand were holding a well-fortified river port. The attack came at daybreak on the Fourth of July, but it miscarried. The rebels afterward turned their anger on Sterling Price's faulty timing. never pausing to credit Prentiss' stout defense against a force nearly double his own.

One casualty at Helena was fairly well known in the Twenty-first Missouri. A large party of the Seventh Confederate Missouri Infantry, seeking refuge from Prentiss' artillery by huddling in a ravine, unwittingly delivered themselves into the hands of the *Thirty-third Missouri* Volunteers. Among the prisoners was Private John C. Moore—lately of Wrightsville, Missouri. He was carried away to the federal prison at Alton, and the family was notified soon after his capture.

During these same days, Moore's old veterans were also paying silent tributes to a fallen foe. Martin Green, trapped in the works at Vicksburg, was mercifully spared from witnessing the surrender. Just a week before the end, a Yankee sharpshooter picked him off, and he died instantly. Thus, wrote an admirer, "the life of this gray-haired patriot and brave chieftain was given to his country." Jesse Barrett joined in the anguish, plainly mourning the devout Southern Methodist layman rather than the "gray-haired patriot."

The revolt against Woodyard came to a head in mid-July. Sixteen, including the major and seven company commanders, petitioned Hurlbut to convene a board "for the purpose of examining into the efficiency of Lt. Col. H. M. Woodyard." The petitioners darkly hinted at treasonable conduct on Woodyard's part in the aftermath of Shiloh and blamed the Chewalla mutiny on his ineptitude. With Woodyard back in command, the plaintiffs declared, the same disciplinary dry rot was infecting the ranks now. On June 18, while in line of battle at Camp Veatch, Woodyard had disgraced himself, Hurlbut read, by giving "unmilitary commands." Complainers had heard him call out, "By the right of divisions to the rear into column . . .Battalion, about face! March!" The whole outfit had turned around and started marching, except for Company F, angrily halted by Captain Alex Tracy and told to mark time. What did Woodyard do about that? "Dress up on Company F!" he was alleged to have shouted.

Three days later, Captains Tracy, Fulton, Pearce, McGonigle, Blackburn, Davis, and Puster—signing in that order—begged Moore to secure Woodyard's resignation, "as we do not wish to resort to any harsh means." Of course, Moore checked with the "defendant," demanding a quick response. The lieutenant colonel, scrutinizing the list of signers, blandly replied that he could not resign, since his pay was under stoppage and the regiment was "hourly expecting an attack."

Alex Tracy, having gotten in too deeply to back out, took the daring step of preferring charges himself on June 26, alleging that Woodyard's unfitness had cost him "all confidence of the officers and men under his command." Having prepared the charges with a list of witnesses, including nearly every officer of the regiment except the chaplain and surgeons, Tracy lodged copies with every higher headquarters in Memphis. When Hurlbut proved rather slow to act, the sixteen officers, as earlier mentioned, sent to corps headquarters the comprehensive story of their grievances on July 26. Six days later, Woodyard pounced on Tracy, arresting him for "insubordination."

Utilizing his leverage, Woodyard arranged for three dissident captains to be sent off on detached service. Meanwhile, he and Tracy sparred, the latter having forgotten that Woodyard had been an experienced lawyer when the captain was a schoolboy. For days, Woodyard delayed forwarding the charges. Finally, Tracy demanded an immediate trial or release. Woodyard, with "deliberate speed," sent the charges to brigade headquarters on August 10. Still Tracy languished in captivity. At length, toward the end of August, Woodyard suddenly restored him to duty. In early October, he withdrew the charges, airily explaining to Veatch that since Tracy had been restored to his command he had "conducted himself . . . as an officer and soldier." Inept or not, the old boy had shown Tracy a bite to match his bark.

Life at the regimental camp settled into a comfortable routine before summer. Veatch's inspector-general looked over Moore's brigade, in which the ll9th Illinois had replaced the Forty-ninth, and found Moore's troops "in good condition and well instructed, . . . also neat and clean in appearance." There was, this official felt, an unhealthy "degree of familiarity existing between Officers and Men." But this, after all, was a brigade of volunteers, and the inspector was certain to find instances of "suspenders over blouses; mixed styles of hats and caps; sentinels with neither coats nor blouses."

The tented camp of the Fourth Brigade was a pleasant place. After the rains of May and early June, the men put up "brush arbors" over streets in camp, and these afforded a fair shield, in places, from the sunshine. Surgeon Roberts could say toward the close of summer that "diseases have been almost exclusively of miasmatic origin and attended with great debility, and often complete prostration, requiring very free use of quinine, cinchona, capsicum, and alcoholic stimulants."

What the surgeon was talking about was no mystery to Nick Starr; his sergeant major's job was a tall order for a healthy man, "so much so that I am generally writing from breakfast until dark and very often until late at night." The catch, however, was that Starr had been having "fevers" all summer, with chills about every other day. On August 5, he gave up and returned to his cot at l0 o'clock in the morning. "Had quite a number of my friends to call in to see me," he wrote Miss "Ettie," but under the circumstances "had no particular use for friends." He understood what he was up against, though: "I suppose I must have a few more high fevers until the warm weather is over and then I am certain I will be through with the fever."

Since Hurlbut was granting leaves and furloughs to 5 percent of each unit at any given time, a scramble to get home began. Werly was among the first, boarding the *Era* from Memphis on July 2l. A week later he was in La Grange, where he found "my family in fairly good health. [Thereafter] we were rejoicing together and often were allowed to feel the presence of God during our family services." The worst fault of a furlough such as this was that the end came quickly, and that parting on the night of August l8 "made our hearts bleed anew."

Quartermaster Sergeant "Duke" Wellington and Lieutenant McFall of Company C left for Scotland County the last week of July. Duke was furloughed "on account of meritorious conduct," McFall to visit his ailing wife. Then, paying fifteen dollars for his passage July 29, Lieutenant Russell took the *City of Alton* for St. Louis, where he combined business with pleasure. Putting up in St. Louis at the Everett House on July 3l, he went to the "Varieties" his first night in town. The next day he was at department headquarters arranging permission for the Moore family to visit John at his new "quarters" in Alton. On August 3, he rode the stage from Canton to Memphis: "Very hot day," he noted, " . . . tiresome ride. Stage crowded." After a friend conveyed him to the Abner Russell farm north of town the next morning, C. Z. noticed unhappily that "crops are very poor in consequence of drought."

The young man did his best to enjoy his stay at home. One day he went squirrel hunting, and on another he swung a real estate deal: "Bought 160 acres . . . at $4.00 per acre [,] all it is worth." Then, home less than a week, he confessed to his diary: "Dull place. Can't stand it long." Adding to his discontent was news that Duke Wellington and Jim McFall were both "very sick" with typhoid fever.

His vacation falling apart, Russell fitfully took off for Keokuk to visit Doc Seaton and take in a theatrical or two. Then, while riding the stage to Canton on August 19, he learned that Duke Wellington had died. The former mayor of Memphis, a man of fifty-eight, was one of Scotland County's original Masons, and the Memphis lodge saw him to his grave with appropriate honors. Much as Russell wanted to attend the rites, he was due in Camp Veatch August 24 and had to keep going.

A week before Russell's return, David Moore left for Keokuk on leave. It was necessary to go, he told Hurlbut, "that I may have repaired, or procure a new artificial foot." It was difficult to refuse a request like that. Now, while he was away, his supporters resumed the campaign for his promotion. Woodyard (who had his own motives), Ed Moore, Pressell, Best, Blackburn, and Fulton extolled the colonel's abilities and achievements in a letter to Hurlbut.

Friday—August 14, 1863—was a day that Woodyard and Doc Roberts could never forget. Two men, Privates Alexander McIntyre of Company A and John McIntire of Company H, suffered fatal wounds in shooting scrapes. The former, a native of Ireland, was carried in from town by friends and turned over to Roberts. His companions were agreed that a soldier of some other outfit had shot him with a "pistol" and was under arrest. McIntyre had lung and liver punctures, but Roberts was not at first alarmed. Indeed, even when the poor fellow died September 10, the surgeon listed "jaundice" as the cause. He conceded, however, that the wound was "without doubt a remote cause, from the depressing effect of the mental impression that it was necessarily mortal."

Over in Company H, Lieutenant Smith had been having a row with Private Andrew O'Day, a forty-two-year-old Clark County Irishman. On August 13, O'Day had wildly threatened to beat up Smith, and the

next morning his anger escalated into threatened assassination. That the
soldier was in such a frame of mind became evident before the day was
over, when he fired his musket with "malice aforethought" at McIntire,
"hitting him in the heart, thereby causing his Death instantly." Woodyard and Smith promptly impounded the offender, and as soon as
Starr could write out the charges they sent him under guard to brigade
headquarters for eventual lodging in the Irving Block Prison in town.

Moore and Woodyard were soon venting spleen on Comstock again.
This officer, taking leave in June to recuperate from chronic dysentery,
was irritatingly slow to return or account for his absence. Woodyard at
the end of August bluntly recommended that Comstock "be dismissed
the Service." Moore agreed. What had stirred them both to anger was a
copy, just received from Comstock, of a special assignment given him in
department headquarters. Moore told Hurlbut just before leaving for
Keokuk that this young officer was "evidently trying to evade duty with
his Regiment."

Adjutant General Gray agreed with Moore that it was a trifle odd
that Comstock had procured a special detail in the Department of the
Missouri "while his regiment was serving in another." Colonel Gray,
however, felt that since the lieutenant was "acting under orders, he
ought not to suffer thereby." But the matter had progressed too far for
sweeping under the rug. The absence having been reported in the *Army
and Navy Gazette,* Comstock was called to Washington to a military commission. This detail he satisfied—and came back to Memphis in late November. Apparently no longer miffed about it, Moore named Comstock
brigade adjutant on his return.

Overlooked in rejoicing over Gettysburg and Vicksburg was the resumption of Rosecrans' offensive in Tennessee. From late June through
August, the Army of the Cumberland crowded Bragg in the region
around Chattanooga. The danger posed by this thrust was grasped in
Richmond, for Chattanooga was a key railway center standing at a natural gateway leading into Georgia and the coastal plains of the lower
Confederacy.

On the Yankees came, fanning out to the south of the city for many
miles along and around a ridge that rises to the point called Lookout
Mountain, above the Tennessee River at Chattanooga. Taking alarm,
Davis ordered Longstreet's corps detached from Lee's army and sent on
a nine-hundred mile railroad journey to reinforce Bragg. Meanwhile,
Bragg retired across Chickamauga Creek, cunningly spreading a tale that
his army was "demoralized."

Rosecrans stepped up his pursuit, little dreaming his columns might each in turn run into Bragg's concentrated army and face serious risk of annihilation. When, on September 18, Longstreet began arriving, Bragg ordered a counteroffensive. During that day, the first rebels crossed the Chickamauga, and, during the night that followed, there was a tidal wave of Confederates pushing to the west over the famous creek.

On September 20, the roof fell in on Rosecrans. Quite by mistake, a hole appeared in his lines just as Longstreet charged. Naturally, the little gap became a big one in short order, and the Union right crumpled. Rosecrans morally gave up, certain the day was lost. To Virginia-born Major General George H. Thomas, however, the day had barely started. With more than half the Army of the Cumberland still on the field and reporting to him, Thomas formed up along a rise called Snodgrass Hill, and there was nothing that Longstreet or Bishop Polk could do to jar him loose. Chattanooga was saved after all, and posterity would remember Thomas as "the Rock of Chickamauga."

Since the Army of the Cumberland had gotten back in more or less good order to the defenses of the city, widespread complaints arose that Bragg had blown a marvelous chance at a sweeping victory. Even a scornful Bedford Forrest openly threatened to slap his face. On the other hand, behind Union lines, it was soon painfully clear that Rosecrans had escaped destruction by backing into a trap—for within days the Johnnies were grabbing important vantage points overlooking Chattanooga. Save for a little wagon trail over the hills to the northwest, which Brigadier General Joseph Wheeler's horsemen might disrupt, the Army of the Cumberland was in a sack.

Now it was Washington's turn to panic. On the night of September 23-24, a highest-level conference involving the President, Secretary Stanton, and General Halleck decided that if Lee could spare a corps, Meade could spare two. And Hooker was told to take the XI and XII Corps by rail to East Tennessee. This was an unprecedented logistical operation, a railway movement exceeding eleven hundred miles and involving animals, wagons, artillery, and baggage for what amounted to a field army of twenty-three thousand men. Simultaneously, Sherman was to bring the XV Corps from Memphis to the relief of Rosecrans. Almost unnoticed in this clamor of events was a Confederate withdrawal into lower Arkansas. On September 10, Price abandoned Little Rock as Major General Frederick Steele applied pressure from the north and east.

Tense situations developed around Memphis as the summer progressed. Every few days there would come an alert—and Dave Moore would hastily send out the size and type of force deemed necessary. The twenty-first Missouri seldom took part in scouts down the Hernando and Horn Lake roads, its work confined usually to patrolling a four-square-mile area between the Memphis & Jackson Railroad and the river south of town. Yet, for all the alarms and excursions, it was a rare occasion when a scouting expedition flushed out any dangerous rebel concentration.

The Twenty-first Missouri occasionally glimpsed the "unknown war." During October, the boys uncovered a clever traffic in contraband cotton. A "Lieutenant Lundy" down in Mississippi, having a good deal of the unmarketable Confederate commodity, had been smuggling it up the river by night to the barn of a kinsman, "Major" Lundy, behind Union lines. The "loyal" Major would sell the cotton in Memphis, and remit the cash to his relative. When caught, the major had sixteen bales. He did not have them long after "D. Moore, Union" spotted them.

In the twilight shadows of October 27, Lieutenant Orr of Company F fell mortally wounded—by one of his own nervous pickets. Sergeant Major Starr had little sleep that night, after Abel Roberts' sad verdict. There were reports to fill out, an inventory of effects to prepare, funeral arrangements to make. Woodyard, after securing Veatch's approval for the lieutenant's interment on the north side of town the afternoon of October 28, pulled out all stops in planning final honors to a fellow Lewis Countian. To the 119th Illinois he dashed off a request for the presence of its "brass band." However, further discussion with Lewis Countians at headquarters led the colonel to cancel his request. Orr's sister lived at La Belle, and, on mature reflection, it seemed best that Woodyard "express the remains of Lieut. Orr North." Pressell packed the belongings for shipment: Orr's sword and belt, the commission, two blankets, a valise full of clothing, a pocketbook with $53.05 in cash. Canton's *Press*, after its editorial sigh over the "sacrifice" of Martin Green, ignored *this* news.

Another political season was at hand. The state convention had ordered an election for the supreme court, timed to coincide with local judicial and special elections. James Ellison, Conservative successor to the lamented Richardson, stood for reelection as judge of the Fourth Judicial Circuit. Steve Carnegy and other Radical citizens filed candidacy papers in Woodyard's behalf. The move hardly shocked Woodyard, and for reasons not difficult to surmise he nodded indulgently—and left his hat in the ring. He would, he loftily announced, "neither seek nor refuse."

All of this rather alarmed Editor Barrett. Endorsing Judge Ellison, with whom he could find no fault whatsoever, Barrett hedged his bet perceptibly. Professing "some feeling of friendship" for Woodyard, he implored the colonel to hold his more "lucrative" position in the army and await the favor of a grateful electorate at a "future" canvass.

On August 17, Sam Cameron fired the opening gun, assuring friends at home that "the 21st Missouri is all right, and constantly pleading the doctrine of equality (not negro equality), but rebel equality. We think that rebels, North and South, require the same cure for treason, viz.: hot shot and cold steel." His comrades were in no mood for foolish distinctions among Conservatives, Copperheads, Knights of the Golden Circle. Newspapers like *The Chicago Times* and Democratic dissidents like Congressman Clement Vallandigham of Ohio were "just as vile rebels as the Confederate soldier." Such Copperheads, Sam warned should give up their dastardly ways: "They are every one marked by the soldiers, and they had better repent of their sins soon."

Woodyard, his eye on the voters, proclaimed at a thanksgiving service organized by Chaplain Cox on Sunday, September 27, that

> . . . whilst we are rejoicing over our recent victories, there is a fire in the rear. . . . It is the cry from those, worse than the traitors of the North—the copperheads crying peace! *peace! PEACE!* I myself am for peace at the right time, but we are not prepared for it now. Some of the rebel States have not, as yet, felt sufficiently the horrors of this war of theirs. The President's Proclamation must be carried out in every particular, and even then I am not for peace whilst there is an armed rebel in the land, or one slave in bondage.

Barrett, evidently grasping at straws, insisted that it was "evident from the last expression that Col. W. cannot be spared from the Army to receive judicial honors, as he is pledged to continue the war as long as there is 'one slave in bondage.' " He was to learn, however, that Woodyard the politician in no wise construed his oratory to his own disadvantage.

October 13 was election day for Iowans, and a special commissioner was present to gather the vote at Camp Veatch. The Iowa soldiers had long debated their choice between two colonels running for governor, Democratic James M. Tuttle and Republican William M. Stone. Now they were done with agonizing: it was Stone by 91-2. The soldiers were voting for the winner. Russell archly noted: "Two copperhead votes cast. Dr. Roberts and a priv. in Co. 'B'."

The commissioner was greatly impressed with the Twenty-first Missouri, its "fine soldier-like appearance," Moore's influence over the rank and file, his "strict discipline," "administrative abilities, and . . . thorough sympathy with his men in camp." Added to this, the visitor said, "the high ground taken by the Colonel and the whole regiment of unswerving devotion to the Union cause and Government, without an if or but in their creed, is worthy of commendation and of imitation by all here, or at home."

The visitor must have measured the regiment's feelings rather well, for Chaplain Cox was writing Editor Elliott that

> . . . when our enlistment expires we expect to go home and kill copperheads, for we don't desire to stop the fight until the rebellion is wiped out, and Missouri made free. . . . We believe that abolition of slavery . . . is the only true road to peace. I believe in negro equality; that is, a negro well drilled, and they take to military like a duck to water, is the equal of a rebel soldier, and more. And I am proud to say that we have not one Gamble-Schofield conservative-loyal rebel in the regiment.

The Missourians had their day at the polls on November 3. Civilians in the Fourth Circuit gave Judge Ellison a razor-thin lead of 1,832 to 1,821, each candidate carrying three counties. Schuyler, Adair, and Clark had gone for Woodyard. "Soldier vote to hear from," Barrett despondently cautioned Ellison's partisans. A week later Cox dropped the other shoe with a letter to the *Missouri Democrat*: the Twenty-first Missouri had indeed gone for Woodyard, 348-0! The boys had given a similar margin to a Radical candidate for the supreme court.

Pending the canvass, it appeared there had been a narrow but revolutionary Radical victory statewide. Morrey exulted that "this is a great triumph for Mo. as good to us as a great victory [.] We know we are sustained by friends at home and are not fighting in vain." Missouri, Starr wrote, "has become Radical and redeemed herself. [May] she be forgiven for past errors."

But then came the disappointing aftermath. A "careful" recounting deprived the Radicals of their triumph in the contest for the supreme court. Thousands of soldier votes, pronounced "irregular," were voided, some of them cast by Lewis Countians in the Twenty-first Missouri. This did not nullify Woodyard's victory, and the Secretary of State certified him in December. But the wrath of the soldiers was unbounded and shocked even Jesse Barrett. He explained defensively that "we understand that a small portion of the soldiers vote was thrown out on account of some informatity in the poll books. . . . The Board of Canvassers had but an obvious duty to perform, and however much they might feel inclined to extend to the gallant soldiers in the field the fullest opportunity for exercising the right of suffrage, they could not contravene the plain and unequivocal provisions of the laws to which they had sworn fidelity." If, however, Conservatives in Lewis County thought they had heard the last of this, they would learn how wrong they were.

And if Bragg had any idea the Yankees would leave him alone on those ridges commanding Chattanooga, autumn days would bring him much enlightenment. During October, as the Army of the Cumberland expanded to sixty thousand men, Lincoln created the Military Division of the Mississippi to provide unified command west of the Appalachians and named Grant to command it. The Army of the Tennessee passed to that feisty redhead Sherman; Rosecrans' Army of the Cumberland was given to Thomas. Before long, Rosecrans would surface again, as commander in Missouri—but Lincoln and Stanton wanted no more of him as a field commander if they could help it.

In late October, Hooker crossed the Tennessee and broke the blockade of the river below Chattanooga. Rebel horsemen were chased away north of the city, and overland communications reopened. Misreading the handwriting on the wall, Bragg released Longstreet to march north toward Knoxville, to keep a force under Burnside from sallying into North Carolina or Virginia. With Bragg's army reduced to about forty thousand effectives, he was in poor condition to face a determined Union advance.

On November 24, Grant struck, with Sherman assaulting Missionary Ridge to the east and northeast of the city, and Hooker seizing Lookout Mountain. Bragg was in trouble. True, Sherman's operation on the north end of the ridge bogged down. The next day, Grant ordered up the Army of the Cumberland in a diversionary role. Thomas was told to advance to the foot of the ridge, which should have the effect of drawing rebel strength away from Sherman. The Army of the Cumberland obediently charged the rifle-pits along the lower face of the ridge— and without orders raced to the summit and broke the rebel defense line.

Now Bragg's army disintegrated, its demoralized veterans sprinting madly toward the Georgia state line. Bragg was able to round them up for an all-winter stand around Dalton, Georgia, but the consequences of his disaster were irrevocable. Unionist mountaineers of East Tennessee were free at last of Confederate officials, and the portals to Georgia were now swinging open to the Yankee host.

Hurlbut was pressing Moore to send home a recruiting party. The muster of October 31 had turned out 587 officers and men "present for duty," a figure which stood to weaken as the winter approached. Sadly enough, there were more men "available" to go home than Moore could send. Starr "tried as hard as I knew how to procure permission to go north recruiting but the Col. thought he could not possibly spare me. . . . Which was a great disappointment." Orders came out from Corps on November 17 placing Chaplain Cox and Captains Fulton and Best in charge of recruiting. Leaving at once for the North, they were on the job by Christmas, Cox and Fulton working out of Edina, Best out of Memphis.

The campaign paid dividends, though never quite enough. By mid-January Cox was in St. Louis with fifty-six men ready for muster. The group provided an interesting sample of what was still available back home. There was John T. Kelly, nephew-by-marriage of the late Pat Cahalan. Having turned eighteen in December, Kelly joined Company D. Roaming Clark County, the chaplain "discovered" William Marion Pullins, "credibly" seventeen, and signed him for Company F. There was also Joe Morris' twenty-one-year-old brother John, whose parents had farmed near St. Francisville since coming out from Greene County, Pennsylvania, in John's childhood. He had spent some months in the Sixty-ninth Enrolled Militia, but now he was ready for "sure-enough" soldiering in Company G. Canadian-born William Driscoll, thirty-eight, joined up for Company I at Memphis the day after New Year's. Like Morris, he had militia experience, in the Second Provisional. Finally, there enlisted in Company D a seventeen-year-old Knox Countian, Porter Eden, a Kentucky-born farm lad who until this winter had been his widowed mother's chief support.

Just before he left, Woodyard began fuming over the long absence of Lieutenant Starkweather of Company K. The gentleman was due back December 20 from Nevada, Iowa, where he had gone for treatment of "partial paralysis of the right arm" and other associated ailments. Because his physician ordered him off his feet for three weeks, he took until December 28 to make it back to Camp Veatch. An enraged Woodyard arrested him at first sight and vowed to haul him before a board of officers. Starkweather was able to summon the affidavits needed to assuage the Colonel's wrath, and, on January 11, 1864, Woodyard lifted his arrest.

Aaron Harlan showed up in October. Again he had been apprehended

by Confederate lawmen, this time at Austin, Mississippi, and passed to
Union custody in St. Louis. Harlan had had all the excitement he wanted.
Still, the commissary sergeantcy was just too tame to interest him. The
superintendent of freedmen at Memphis wanted him for a clerk with the
contraband department. Colonel Moore explained that such a detail
would cause Harlan's reduction to private; would he mind? Far from it.
On December 19, the sage of Croton tendered his resignation to Moore,
"voluntarily and with the kindest of feelings." Although Harlan's name
was on Company F's roll until the final muster, he now passed from the
life of the Twenty-first Missouri.

Once the political excitement had ebbed, a new topic dominated soldierly discussions. The Department of War, dreading the impending
evaporation of that splendid army of "three-year men" mustered in 1861
and early 1862, came up with a plan to encourage the boys to reenlist
for the duration. There were some attractive provisions in the army's
offer. Every regiment qualifying would be redesignated a "Veteran Volunteer" outfit, putting it in a new class by itself. Any member of the
regiment with at least nine months of service would get a bounty of four
hundred dollars; if three-fourths of the unit reenlisted, the enlistees would
get a month's furlough for recruiting and reorganizing.

Starr was ready to sign. Overestimating Miss Henrietta's enthusiasm,
he gallantly placed the decision in her hands. "Of course," she replied,
"I shall not give my consent." Taken aback, he hastened to explain that

> should I return when my term of service expires and you be true to
> your engagement, . . . [and] we were to be married before the war
> should cease and . . . afterwards I be drafted into the army, how much
> better would that be than to remain in the Army [?] Remember war
> times may cast a different course of events on our prospects than
> could happen under circumstances in time of peace . . . If I am to face
> the fate of many before the war is closed I had much better die alone,
> by friends to mourn my loss than leave a wife to do so and make a
> widow of her.

Woodyard rose to the occasion on December 18 by naming Russell
recruiting officer for the "Veteran Service." The lieutenant found himself the center of much controversy and interrogation, and he listened
to some bizarre ideas, the most frequent of which was the assurance of
many an old-timer that he would reenlist if "they" changed the regiment to cavalry. With undisguised amusement, Russell reported to

his diary that he had discovered a "Great Mania for Cavalry Service."
There was much to be said for going to war in a saddle.

At first, business was slow. Russell had to tell the troops that
this was an infantry outfit—the Department of War liked it that way.
On December 21, Woodyard assembled the regiment and gave out some
Radical food for thought. Major Moore seconded his ideas and dismissed the Missourians to their tents. Aiding the drive was the onset of
foul weather. For more than a week into the new year, snow and sleet
pelted Memphis, and many a lad made up his mind to stay. Starr cheer-
fully observed on December 29 that "nearly *two hundred* of our regiment have reenlisted." Then, on January 7, he ran out of application
blanks. "Veteranization" was just around the corner.

This was no time of fast-moving promotions. True enough, Comstock,
before running afoul of Moore, received a commission as adjutant. And
then First Sergeant Tom Waterhouse of Company B left to become a
first lieutenant of the Sixty-fourth U.S. Colored Infantry. A considerable leap forward within the regiment was Private Ben Jenkins' sudden
rise from the ranks of Company D to Harlan's commissary sergeantcy.
Ben was forty-two, a native of Ohio living at Bonaparte, Iowa. He had
been under arms since joining Murrow in the first summer of the war.

Fifer Kilmartin, having infuriated the colonels with a self-granted
furlough in the autumn, celebrated New Year's ingeniously. He invited a group of friends to a lavish feed at Schwab's Restaurant on Adams
Street. When the boys met him there, they should have sensed something off-color about the affair, for Kilmartin was garbed as a captain!
At any rate, a good time followed, and a staggering bill for it was presented to Kilmartin. The "host" then introduced himself to the mana-
ger as "Captain Harris," promising to return and settle the bill later in
the evening.
Not inclined to cross the "captain" and his well-fed friends, the res-
taurateur went along with the arrangement. If he expected "Captain
Harris" to reappear soon, he was to be disappointed. He finally raised
a howl to the provost marshal, once he felt he had been "sold," and provost guards were soon combing Memphis for the bogus captain.

They found Kilmartin at Camp Veatch late that night. Holding a
hand of cards at a game of chance with several men of Company H, he
had gambled away three silver watches, two belonging to men of Company H and another borrowed from a bartender on Shelby Street. Adding it all up, the provost marshal ordered him "downtown." Kilmartin
managed to escape trial yet again. Colonel Woodyard dictated elaborate

charges and specifications, but the document got no further than brigade headquarters.

"I don't think we will ever get into a fight as long as we stay at this
place," Lieutenant Morrey had comforted the girl back home. But
"vicissitudes" quickly altered that prospect. In mid-January, Hurlbut
activated the Third Division of the XVI Corps, with station at Vicksburg
and commanded by Brigadier General Andrew Jackson Smith. Moreover, the main body of Veatch's force was to go down the river to join
the Third Division. Smith was determined to have David Moore commanding his First Brigade.

Eight transports, including the *Sir William Wallace*, were crowding
the levee when the Twenty-first Missouri marched to it late the afternoon of January 26. These vessels were to convey the entire brigade
to Vicksburg, but there would be much bustling and riding about before
the convoy was ready. It turned out that Hurlbut wanted the Twenty-
first Missouri aboard the *Wallace* at once, although a long wait was in
prospect. As the boys trudged up the gangplank, they realized that this
was their last operation under Woodyard. He had just received his certificate of election, and resigned. As Woodyard later recalled, while he
watched the troops embarking "for their destination in Sherman's expedition, one of the boys, seeing me on shore, called out 'Three cheers
for our old Colonel!' [and] tears coursed down their manly cheeks, for
I had been so long with them that they seemed like my own children."
Despite the ugly undertones of the recent "officers' rebellion," it
seems safe to say that Humphrey Woodyard had his partisans.

The convoy started for Vicksburg just after noon Thursday, January
28. Here began a "splendid trip," Starr wrote, during which "we saw
some very fine country and fine residences [,] others that had been
burned down." That evening, after sundown, the convoy tied up on
the Mississippi shore at a point two miles above Helena. The stopover
made it possible to post guards along the shore, enable troops to get a
secure night's rest, and send out details to restock the wood supply.

Following a brief stop at Helena after daylight, the eight ships passed
on toward the south. The Missourians still did not know why they were
shipping to Vicksburg, but they did know that their colonel was brigade commander, and Ed Moore was running the regiment. Comstock
was brigade adjutant, leaving his regimental duties to Starr. About 10
o'clock that morning there came an intimation that trouble might lie
ahead. A gunboat pulled up to the *U. S. Grant* to notify Colonel Moore
that guerrillas were active around Carthage Landing, Mississippi, and

were occasionally firing at passing ships. The word was given out, all
troops alerted, muskets loaded.

The flotilla passed the landing around noon without incident, and
the sense of urgency faded. Colonel Moore cancelled the alert, and ordered all troops to discharge their guns and lie down for the afternoon's
rest. Then, at half-past one, as the ships were abreast of Islands 70 and
71 above the mouth of Arkansas' White River, a party of rebels concealed
behind log breastworks on the east bank cut loose with a small-arms fusillade. About twenty-seven bullets struck the *Wallace* , the only vessel
hit, spreading havoc among the unsuspecting Missourians. To his dismay,
Edwin Moore had a casualty list on his hands. Many of the boys hastily
loaded, fired toward the shore, but, reported Starr, "do not presume we
hurt any of them" Lamented Werly: "That is the way it goes, when one
is thinking to be safe and misjudges the enemy." The major "thought it
policy not to leave the boat, the willows and the brush being very thick."

Sergeant Thomas J. Ryan of Company D, a twenty-six-year-old native
Ohioan, was struck in the head and died immediately. Six others were
also wounded, two suffering serious wounds that caused Roberts to doubt
their survival. Private John Collett of Company B was hit in the abdomen,
and Private Dick Friend of I had a spinal wound. Collett, twenty-two,
was a native Missourian with a wife back in Schuyler County. The
Hoosier-born Friend had been a soldier exactly one month. Neither
would see the sun rise again over the willows along the Mississippi shore-
line.

The others suffered arm or leg wounds. Corporal John P. Byrne of
Company I was so injured that he was still in a hospital when his enlistment expired. Corporal George W. Jenkins of A, Corporal Alfred Rathbun of I, and Private Orville Patten of B were the others. Patten, eighteen, had been in uniform less than three weeks. Rathbun, a New York-
born farmer living in Scotland County since 1855, must have been a little tired of such foolishness. Shot by a bushwhacker during his home
guard days, he also had been struck by a "spent ball" at second Corinth.
Now, with a puncture in his right arm, he would be out of action several
weeks.

That night, when the *Wallace* laid up at a little island near the Mississippi side of the river, Cox and McGonigle led a little party onto the
island and quietly buried Ryan. The next morning, not long after the
boat resumed its journey, the surgeon notified Major Moore that it would
be necessary to stop and bury Friend and Collett. Halting at a place de-

scribed by Russell as "Harrison's Landing in Choctaw Bend," the chaplain buried the two men in an old brickyard on the east bank.

The survivors were in no mood to respect rebel property. At 11 o'clock, the *Wallace* tied up by the Arkansas shore, and a forage party landed. Nearby was a plantation, property of Brigadier General James S. Rains of Price's State Guard. A former state senator from Sarcoxie, Rains had been among supporters of Governor Jackson chased into Arkansas by Lyon. Entering the premises, the boys "confiscated" and forthwith butchered four beef cattle. That second night out of Memphis, the regiment camped on the Mississippi side—after a steak dinner.

Camping the next evening on the Arkansas shore just a hundred miles out of Vicksburg, the regiment kept a strong guard out for a party of rebels rumored to be working the locality. Lieutenant Hagle and Sergeant William O'Connor took a squad across the river; they found no Johnnies, but returned with two black youngsters quite frightened, hungry, and footloose. One was only six, but he was destined to form a lifelong comradeship with those rough-and-ready Missourians. Little Henry Collark, who later became Joe Best's never-tiring errand boy and companion, had been born free in New Jersey. Being black, he was subject to kidnapping—and a plantation owner had him abducted while a toddler and carried south. He was still too small for serious plantation work, and thanks to his role as "mascot" of the Twenty-first Missouri, he never knew another day of servitude.

The *Sir William Wallace* and its sister ships left for Vicksburg about midnight January 31, and "just after daylight" the next morning they reached their destination. Where the Missourians were going next and what they would do if they got there, said Nick Starr, "I do not know, nor does any body else in this brigade."

10

In All Directions

Hurlbut's corps was converging on Vicksburg for a special mission. Grant and Sherman were planning two quick thrusts to halt rebel depredations against federal shipping on the Mississippi. One would consist of an expedition by Sherman across southern Mississippi to Meridian, the other a drive up the Red River in Louisiana by Banks.

Available to the Meridian expedition were Smith's and Veatch's divisions of Hurlbut's XVI Corps and two divisions of Major General James B. McPherson's XV Corps. While these pushed east from Vicksburg through Jackson, Brigadier General W. Sooy Smith, heading a column of seven thousand cavalry, would sally forth from Memphis to search out and destroy Forrest's worrisome horsemen, estimated by Sherman at possibly four thousand.

Meridian happened to be headquarters for the Confederate commander in Mississippi, Leonidas Polk. Forces assigned the good Bishop consisted of Forrest's troopers, facing Memphis, and two infantry divisions under Major Generals William W. Loring and Samuel G. French, respectively at Canton and Brandon. Working with them was a small cavalry force under Brigadier General Frank C. Armstrong. All told, Polk disposed of about sixteen thousand men with which to hold off a Yankee host nearly double that figure. Polk, thought Sherman, "seemed to have no suspicion of our intentions to disturb his serenity." Indeed, until the Yankees moved on Jackson, the Bishop discounted rumors of the impending expedition, deeming it too irrational for serious consideration.

The weather in central Mississippi hovered between clammy and balmy, and Starr "never felt more able for a big march in my life." Grass was high enough to graze cattle, and nights were expected to be warm enough that tents would not be needed. Of one thing the invaders were sure—the route ahead had been sufficiently denuded by "Sherman's torch" in 1863 that foragers would sweat to find adequate sustenance for men or animals.

As the Missourians gazed about, they found old "neighbors" from Camp Veatch gathering in Smith's division. While Moore was commanding First Brigade, the Second was under Colonel William T. Shaw of the Fourteenth Iowa, the Third under Colonel Edward H. Wolfe of the Fifty-second Indiana. But above all officers other than their own Dave Moore, the Missourians would remember General A. J. Smith as the most striking figure of the campaign. He was a bright-eyed peacetime major of the First U.S. Dragoons, "of small stature, with rather brusque, abrupt manners, sometimes verging on irascibility, yet . . . popular with his troops and [shunning] none of the hardships to which they were subjected." Born in 1815, he was the son of a brigade commander in the War of 1812 who idolized the Victor of New Orleans. West Pointer, class of 1838 (Beauregard's and Hardee's), "A. J." was at least a "condensed version" of his father's combative hero.

Sherman's columns headed for Meridian on Tuesday, February 2. The XVI Corps held the left flank, the XV the right. The Twenty-first Missouri got off at 6:00 P.M. and put in about six miles before bivouacking. Wednesday brought warm sunshine and an ideal day for the march to the Big Black at Messinger's ferry. While his brigade passed over the pontoon bridge, Moore took Comstock aside and dictated two important messages. The first informed Smith that the river crossing was secure and uneventful, the other requested Adjutant General Gray to commission Edwin Moore as lieutenant colonel.

On Thursday, having the advance and deployed as skirmishers, the Twenty-first Missouri encountered a battle line of Armstrong's cavalry on the Joseph E. Davis plantation about nine miles beyond the Big Black near Queen Hill. The Confederates were the First and Twenty-eighth Mississippi regiments, estimated by their skittish commander as "outnumbered" by at least "10 to 1." Pausing to form up under fire from an artillery piece, Major Moore advanced on the rebels late in the afternoon. A lively exchange followed before the Johnnies took to their horses. Thomas T. Gundy of Company I, his blood up over the affair, wrote a young friend: "We drove them 3 or 4 miles. We don't know how many were killed. We didn't get a man hurt in any way." The regiment halted on the plantation and camped overnight.

During the next few days, the federals marched rather steadily through the area around Jackson. The 117th Illinois ran into a bloody affray at Clinton, a few miles west of Jackson, on February 6 but succeeded in chasing off the enemy. The Twenty-first Missouri crossed the Pearl River and entered the capital on Sunday, February 7, about noon. "Jackson has been a very pretty place," wrote Welsh-born Sergeant Edwin Jones, "but is now a mass of brick walls." A rebel line of battle, formed about ten miles to the east in late afternoon, evaporated without a fight. The XVI Corps rested that night around Brandon.

Hurlbut moved Veatch's division into Morton, twenty miles farther east, on Tuesday, February 9. "Though cavalry moved on our flanks," Sherman said, "they gave us little concern, save in scaring our stragglers and foraging parties." How true those last words! On February 9, two men of Company I, Twenty-first Missouri, fell prisoners while foraging. Sergeant Jesse Roberts and Private Benjamin Cope faced long confinement at Cahaba, Alabama—for paroles were no longer easily gotten.

If raiders did not concern Sherman, still he "kept our columns compact" to offer "few or no chances for their dashes." From Morton onward, he moved in a single column, Hurlbut leading. It was around noon February 10 when the Twenty-first Missouri marched through Hillsboro. In the vicinity of this ruined village, the rebels ambushed the corps train, killing several mules. No Yankees were hit, but about a dozen of the attackers were wounded.

English-born Private Joseph Sherman of Company B, a frail youth of twenty, had to be left in the care of another outfit's surgeons at Hillsboro. He was never seen again in the regiment. Apparently, after the XVI Corps passed on through the area, enemy riders swooped down on Hillsboro and captured the ailing boy. Six months later, he was in his grave at the Andersonville, Georgia, prison camp.

On the evening of February 12, the Missourians bivouacked on Chunky Creek, twenty miles short of Meridian. The region must not have seemed especially hospitable. An Iowan spoke of these "Piney woods" as "the poorest red clay land I have ever seen. In passing a drove of muley cattle one day a soldier remarked 'it was too poor to afford horns for the cattle.'" The corps crossed the Chunky after daybreak and streamed toward Meridian. Desperate enemy riflemen tried to hold some four or five miles west of town, but Veatch's men, after a sharp encounter, scattered them. That evening the Twenty-first Missouri halted in an abandoned Confederate camp three miles west of Meridian.

Sunday, February 14, was a festive day. Late in the afternoon the Twenty-first Missouri "entered Meridian with music," as Werly said. Edwin Jones, detailed with a large party of Missourians to guard prisoners and wagons, did not get in until after dark.

Now that Sherman had gained Meridian, two matters perturbed him.

Where was Sooy Smith? And would Polk, having withdrawn into Alabama, let them wreck these railroads in peace? Sooy was late; indeed, he did not get away from Colliersville until February 11. Then, instead of making up for lost time, he began having tremors about Forrest. True, the great rebel cavalier was fearsome enough for the bravest of soldiers, but Polk's diversions of his strength had stunted his capacity for restraining the Yankee cavalry. Oddly enough, Forrest's feeble resistance bred in Sooy Smith a corrosive anxiety over the possible sinister meaning of Forrest's supine tactics!

Never mind Sooy Smith, then—the destruction of the railroads around Meridian could be handled there and then by the infantry. So for several days, the boys of the expedition indulged themselves in the strenuous team sport of prying up rails, bending them around trees, and burning heaps of ties. Meridian was a key junction of the Mobile & Ohio and Jackson & Selma lines, and Sherman's sweating vandals laid them in ruins for a dozen miles in every direction.

Giving up on Sooy Smith, Sherman ordered Hurlbut to move A. J. Smith's brigades to Marion, four miles north, on February 17. Ed Moore's Missourians were glad to go, for it had been little fun camping without tents. Temperatures had fallen nightly to near the freezing point, and on the morning of the march to Marion there was a quarter-inch of ice in the puddles. The next day brought light snow, and the Twenty-first Missouri was ready enough to get up at 4:00 A.M. on February 20 to start for Vicksburg. Indeed, the entire return trip would prove a wet and chilly one, aggravating the "rheumatiz" in Surgeon Roberts' back.

Sooy Smith's absentee troopers were destroying Mobile & Ohio tracks below Corinth with the help of local slaves, but that little prospered Sherman. On February 20 Sooy retreated on Memphis, turned back by a contingent under Forrest's brother Jeff near Columbus—eighty miles from Sherman's lines. Within a week Sooy was at Memphis, with many subordinates wishing he had worked his horseflesh as hard going *to* Columbus as he had coming *from* it. Sherman would find it increasingly difficult to be civil to cavalrymen.

Sherman took it out on Mississippians, resolving to create "a swatch of desolation" fifty miles broad, . . . which the present generation will not forget." His westward line of march would lie somewhat to the north of his eastward route, and in the coming days the region would endure much energetic foraging and judicious incendiarism. There would be no contact with the enemy, as Forrest was chasing Sooy Smith. Probably the most thrilling episode for the Missourians was their discovery

east of Hillsboro of a "148-year-old negro." Both Russell and Werly
noted the occasion in their diaries. On the morning of February 26, the
day Sooy Smith reached Memphis, the Twenty-first Missouri crossed the
Pearl to bivouac north of Canton, Mississippi.

The situation in Missouri had become unsettled again by the time
Judge Woodyard got home. On January 30, Schofield had laid down
his command in Missouri; Rosecrans, more to the Radicals' taste, succeeded him. The next day Governor Gamble, ailing with pneumonia,
unexpectedly died. Though Lieutenant Governor Willard P. Hall was
cut from the same Conservative cloth, his political establishment could
feel the ground trembling. A national election was due this year, and
there was cause to fear what *eligible* voters might send to Jefferson City.

Doing his bit to nurture Conservative hysteria, Woodyard celebrated
Washington's birthday at the courthouse in Monticello with a "hell-for-
leather" Radical speech blood curdling in partisan ferocity. The "rebellion" and its attendant horrors the judge blamed on the Democratic
party's "pandering to the slave interest" in its lust for hanging on to
power in national affairs. He paid homage to John Brown's memory
and declared ominously that whoever killed a Conservative might not
be killing a traitor but most certainly someone doing "the dirty work
of traitors." He warned county officials responsible for rejecting the
Twenty-first Missouri's poll books that the resentment of the soldiers
could explode, that there was a probability their craving for "vengeance
toward the enemy in the rear" would sooner or later bring a renewal of
"scenes of blood and terror here."

The next day Woodyard appeared at a banquet in his honor at the
Canton City Hall, amid a clamorous "Three cheers for Colonel Woodyard!" Introducing him, Carnegy cited the victory at Clapp's Ford over
a force of "two thousand thieves, marauders and murderers." Clearly
unmellowed, the new judge rose to render tribute to Cantonians who
would never return. Evoking tearful remembrances, he saluted the late
Major King, "whose likes we shall ne'er see again," and assured his hearers
that "wherever the brave boys of the 21st Missouri may be called they
will do their duty; when they enlisted they knew their rights, and knowing dare maintain them." This remark must have been aimed at those
implicated in rejecting the votes of the Twenty-first Missouri. "They
enlisted for the war," Woodyard continued, "and they have no idea of
returning until the war is over, for every one will remain until the rebellion is put down or he fills a Southern grave. But we have every reason to expect that another year will finish the work."

Shock waves billowed. Charlton Howe ecstatically hailed Woodyard's "telling, thorough-going radical speech" at Monticello. Woodyard, he gloated, was promising traitors the treatment they gave "Old John Brown." Jesse Barrett, touching this hot potato strictly by proxy, called on Madison C. Hawkins, a local lawyer vainly immune to "the morbid, sickly philanthropy of negro equality," to defend the rejection of those poll books. More heat came from a Conservative critic at Palmyra who angrily but anonymously called Woodyard "a monster whose very name is a disgrace to the judicial office." Even the dread "Robespierre never uttered a baser and more brutal sentiment."

Meanwhile, in camp near Canton, Mississippi, Major Moore was notifying corps headquarters that 354 men of his regiment had "enlisted in the Veteran Service." Still present for duty were 423 of the originals, and 50 others subsequently joining were eligible to be counted as veterans. So, the major proudly announced, veteranization was an accomplished fact, and when the regiment reached Vicksburg March 3, Dave Moore resumed command in order to supervise the transformation to "Veteran Volunteers."

The big news in camp was the furlough—the coming reward for reenlisting. The Twenty-first Missouri would go up to Memphis, draw its pay, muster in for "Veteran Service," load out for home. There were, however, 242 not making the trip, among them Werly and Tim Holman. All those who had resisted the call to veteranize or were ineligible for other reasons would remain at Vicksburg for "other work." To an ill-starred few, the decision not to reenlist meant they would see home no more.

On the evening of March 4, the excited veterans boarded the *John J. Roe* for the trip to Memphis. The *Roe* was an elderly scow, destined for immortality in river lore. As it happened, an original cub pilot on this 691-ton packet was the young Mark Twain, and his recollections of prewar life on her decks have given the *Roe* an enduring place in history. Twain had found her "dismally slow; still, we often had pretty exciting times racing with islands, rafts, and such things." Other rivermen swore that with a full head of steam "she could run all day in the shade of a big tree." In the late summer of 1864, the *Roe* would hit a snag and sink near New Madrid, and Twain would insist that "it was five years before the owners heard of it."

The Missourians marched into Camp Veatch late on the morning of March 9. Arms and equipment were turned over to Hurlbut's ordnance and quartermaster officers and arrangements made for muster in to veteran status. That ceremony was staged by Hurlbut's commissary of musters on Monday morning, March 14. Just before noon, the boys drew their pay. Late that afternoon, the Twenty-first Missouri *Veteran* Volunteers boarded the *Belle of St. Louis* for the joyous trip home.

At Camp Veatch, the veterans learned that Private John Dell, one of the originals of Company H, had died in the general hospital there on February 23 of "chronic rheumatism." Since captivity at Shiloh, he had been in frail health. Not until the summer of 1863 had he returned from a "sick-on-parole" status to attempt full duty. Vexing but less tragic was the case of Sergeant Matt Woodruff of G, who had spent the winter in his native Ohio. On furlough to Watertown in October, he had come down with dysentery and did not get back until the first week of March. Corps headquarters was itching to lower the boom on him, but Matt's company commander, Lieutenant Harris, interceded—and the charges were dropped. His reenlistment, one assumes, restored him to grace with the regimental power structure. And it got him another month's furlough!

The *Belle of St. Louis* reached the Pine Street landing in St. Louis at daybreak, Thursday, March 17. Meeting with Colonel Moore after breakfast was a representative of the Veterans Reception Committee, a civic organization dedicated to the proposition that Missouri's veterans should return to heroes' welcomes. There was to be a gala march ashore, with a militia regiment presenting arms and Frank Boehm's celebrated band providing music. Then the regiment would parade "up Chestnut street to Third, down Third to Market, up Market past General Gray's Headquarters to Fifth, up Fifth to Green, down Green to Fourth past the Commanding General's Headquarters, up Washington avenue to Tenth." On the latter street, in Turner's Hall, the boys would sit down to a lavish banquet.

The "glorious old veteran regiment" paraded through flag-bedecked streets, pausing to cheer Generals Rosecrans and Gray. There followed in the hall a maximum of sumptuous eating and an apparent minimum of unwise drinking. Various dignitaries, including Mayor Chauncey I. Filley, orated during the afternoon's prolonged speechmaking and socializing. At 5:00 P.M., Judge Samuel M. Breckinridge officiated at the presentation of a new regimental flag. Following this ceremony, the Colonel led his troops off to Benton Barracks.

Lieutenant McFall was here for another purpose. "I respectfully tender my resignation," he wrote department headquarters. His health he described as "poor and prohibiting me from doing active duty." Rosecrans approved on March 24. The military bureaucracy acted swiftly in

grinding out furloughs and boat tickets, and within two days the vaca-
tioners were leaving town. Colonel Moore, taking Surgeon Roberts and
Captain Charles Tracy's Company H, left on the *Lucy Bertram* for Alex-
andria and Keokuk on Saturday. Others followed, coming on the *Die
Vernon*. When Captain Yust's boys appeared at Canton Monday noon,
Barrett waxed enthusiastic:

> A host of friends gathered at the landing to greet their fathers, bro-
> thers, sons, or relations, and we are certain the soldiers' welcome, if
> not accompanied with the pomp and formality witnessed everywhere,
> was, at least, as cordial, earnest, and acceptable. . . . We are grateful to
> find the regiment in the enjoyment of excellent health, and though
> looking somewhat toil worn and sun-bronzed from their recent long
> march on Sherman's great raid, they have the elastic step and strong
> sinews of what they are now very properly called, VETERANS.

The boys of Company I reached Memphis to find Judge Woodyard
holding a term of court there. Russell, for one, hastened to call at the
residence of Colonel Ed Kutzner, where Woodyard was staying. Even if
the judge could entertain the "old boys" with stories of the political ty-
phoon touched off by his return, some of them must have come away uneasy. Woodyard neither looked nor felt well, suffering as he was from a
worsening kidney and bladder problem. Dr. D. B. Fowler, keeping an
anxious eye on him, cautiously pronounced him "out of danger" on
April 6.

The Union Aid Society of Canton wanted to give the veterans a send-
off, and invitations went out for them to assemble at Canton's City Hall
on Friday evening, April 15, for a reception, banquet, and ball. Every man
was due back at Benton Barracks the following Monday, and on the appointed day the troops met in Canton for the festivities.

Welcoming ceremonies had hardly begun before a chill settled on the
crowd. Spreading was the grim news that Woodyard was dead. Confirmation was at hand—the circuit judge had breathed his last in Memphis on
Thursday. There was little point in trying to entertain *these* boys, and the
carefully planned social event collapsed.

Humphrey Marshall Woodyard came home Saturday morning. Amelia
Woodyard and her sorrowing brood of three daughters and two sons saw
the husband and father to his resting-place Sunday noon. Grief-ridden
Union men of Lewis County closed ranks behind them—local Masons,
Union Leaguers, and militiamen lining up for their parts in the pageant.

Judge Ellison acted as parade marshal as the cortege set out for the family burial-ground north of Canton. The mourners halted for services at a rural Presbyterian chapel along the way, three pastors officiating. Then, after the procession reached the gravesite, the resplendent Past Grand Master Carnegy repeated the "solemn service of the Masonic Order." A squad of Woodyard's old soldiers, commanded by Joseph Best, fired a traditional salute over the casket. The militia band played its "affecting dirge" once more, and the silent throng departed.

Doc Seaton was cutting a swath in Keokuk's civic life. He came out for alderman in March. Somehow, his Republican fervor of 1862 had abated, and the good doctor announced as an "independent." To be a Democrat in Lee County at that moment was, he said, tantamount to being a Copperhead, but he would be twice-damned before he would tie up with those Radicals on the "Union" ticket. Editor Howell, regretting such standoffishness, unabashedly crowed over a landslide "Union" victory when Seaton and his Republican allies swept the field.

Knox County boys could not quite keep their minds off politics either. True enough, they had different ways of expressing themselves—ways suited to the brush country of northeastern Missouri. Just to the southwest of Colony lived a prosperous farmer, Rice McFadden, whose Southern sympathies scandalized the vacationing warriors. This was no mere persecution of opinion, for McFadden had been with Green at Athens and thereafter had done a stint in rebel gray. However, the Confederacy's recent distresses had rather chastened McFadden, and he had returned to "loyalty" by way of the oath.

As Moore's boys saw things, McFadden had helped "burn out" their folks in 1861, and it was time to return the favor. Several warned the hated neighbor to "get gone" while they were in the area. When the gentleman did not "regard" their threats, the veterans decided it was time to burn him out—and possibly shoot him on sight. On April 14 a party showed up for the "housewarming." The proprietor eluded them, with only Henry Hubble catching a glimpse of him before he took cover. But wherever McFadden hid, he could see a column of smoke towering over the clearing where his house had stood.

The flames spread to Barrett's editorial page, as the cagey editor came forth in bitter condemnation: "We are not advised of the special provocation, nor do we indeed think that anything has occurred to justify such wanton destruction, but it is said that the act was instigated by citizens, who took this opportunity to use the soldiers for the perpetration of an act which they had not the courage to attempt."

An indignant Radical notified Howe's *National American* that Barrett's attempt to blame the affair on poor, simple soldiers duped by conniving civilians would not wash. The incendiaries were from the Twenty-first Missouri, everyone should understand, and Mr. Barrett would best believe that "such good tried soldiers as Wm. McKinney, Wm. [Broyles], John B. Sexton, and Jasper Booker . . . are not to be trifled with by such rebels as McFadin, and, they desire me to correct . . . the impression given out by the Canton Press that they were instigated to do the deed by any persons living here."

Trumpeting that he had trapped his enemies into conferring "immortality of infamy to the perpetrators by emblazoning their names to the world," Barrett lapsed into an arcane quibble over the status of McFadden's property. Were the victim a traitor, he argued, the troops had destroyed "government property." Yet, he asserted, McFadden's son had recently died serving in the ll9th Illinois. That proved something to Barrett, whose readers could not know that the ll9th Illinois had never lost a soldier of that name—and who, like Barrett, were probably unaware that McFadden's son George was alive and well in Company D, Twenty-first Missouri.

The regiment's furlough was not entirely dedicated to grief and vengeance. Private Sam Phillips of Company D came home to Millport and married Corporal George Sallee's "kid sister" Julia. Judge William Beal, whose sons Jim and Dan had recently joined Company E, performed the ceremony. At La Grange, Captain Puster went to the altar. His first wife, Hermine Menke Puster, had left him a widower two years earlier with infant twin sons Robert and Edward. Now, in a Lutheran ceremony, he wed Hermine's younger sister Louisa, and his little lads had a new mother.

Numerous Scotland Countians, anxious to show their esteem for David Moore, chipped in and bought him a horse. Captain Best must have been the ringleader, for he had come to think highly (and often) of the colonel's daughter Miss Frances. At any rate, Joe was chosen to present the animal to its new master at Canton "as an expression of . . . appreciation of the faithful services which you have rendered your country and ours, and especially for your gallant conduct on the battle field." We have no description of the horse, but the colonel praised him as "elegant and beautiful" in expressing gratitude for the "high honor" thus done him.

Best was highly pleased at his winter recruiting tour with Cox and Fulton. These officers and their enlisted aides signed up eighty-four men. Indeed, one February day they had sent a contingent of nine to St. Louis, of whom only one failed to get past the medics. Three of the group—Jesse Decker, Ben DeWitt, and John H. Nelson—were "originals" who had received disability discharges but were ready for a second go. Best had constantly reminded eligible men that if they had prior service they could qualify for four hundred dollars in bounties. "If they delay . . . ," he warned, "they may get drafted, and get nothing."

And so the new men came, an intriguing lot. A young Kentuckian, James Griffin of Canton, joined in late February. Up at Prospect Grove, on the east side of Scotland County, Ohio-born William Brookhart had come to feel the Lord was "punishing" him for "evading" service. After all, his herd of prime steers had lately suffocated in driving snow. At age thirty-nine, he became a soldier of Company H, leaving Susannah Brookhart and their five youngsters on the farm. Company G acquired a stocky Scots-Irish youth by the name of James Knox Polk Wilson, a native Iowan lately resident on a Clark County farm. His half-brother Alfred Yesley had gone to Company G three months earlier. Best known among the "recruits," however, was Ben Northcutt. Since being squeezed out of his captaincy in 1862, Ben had tried in vain to find a military detail befitting his leadership talents. Now, at forty-four, he came into Company D as a private.

Company H prospered. Alfred Cameron, now of age, seized the chance to join brothers Sam and Joe in the outfit their father had helped organize. Robert Wellbaum, an Indiana-born farmer of Schuyler County, cast his lot with John H. Cox's old outfit. Better known was George Washburn, now old enough to join his older brother Marion in Union blue. Upon enlistment, George pitched in with Marion to organize an eight-man mess, which took in six other boys from home. They included Uncle Wilbur Davis, Eli Black, Charles Blackstone, Israel Elican, John H. Bishop, and John L. Jones. They "pledged to help each other and stay together when possible."

Good news and bad lurked at Benton Barracks. Governor Hall having sent his commission, Edwin Moore mustered as a lieutenant colonel and donned his silver-embroidered oak leaves. Bona Shafer rose to first lieutenant of Company E, as Ike Schram finally mustered as second lieutenant of F. But amid the congratulations there came shocks. The only chaplain the Twenty-first Missouri would ever have now resigned, effective April 21, notifying Rosecrans that he was preparing to "accept the Pastorate of a congregation, by the direction of my Church." It seems probable that Cox had come to the conclusion that in this election year Missouri was in need of pastors with a Radical turn of mind. Five days after he stepped out, Lieutenant Gloeser of Company A resigned, diagnosed as myopic by the surgeons.

Boarding the *Henry von Phul* on April 29, the regiment left St. Louis.

At Columbus, Kentucky, for want of orders, the Missourians camped on a
hill "in the rear" of the city. There was just time on April 30 for the regular muster, at which 487 officers and men reported on duty status. Some
350 were absent, including the nonveterans last seen at Vicksburg. In the
days that followed, Dave Moore rearranged personnel, reducing Henry
Kilmartin to private and banishing him to Company I and the ministrations
of Captain Best. Lieutenant Tompkins of H went off to Huntsville, Alabama, where glory called. Major General Francis P. Blair, boss of XVII
Corps, and a friend of Tompkins, wanted the young man for his aide.

"We will most likely remain here . . . waiting for our Division to return
from the Red River," Starr informed Miss Headley. There were rumors of
heavy casualties among the nonvets, who had gone with the Twenty-fourth
Missouri to serve under Banks in Louisiana. Definite word was yet to come.
Nerves were a little taut: "We have more violins in camp than anything
else," Starr complained. "They keep a continued playing from morning
till midnight all caused by being home on furlough [.] [But] against the
rebels running us out of Camp once we will have the pleasure of losing
them." Music "answers very well at home," he thought, "but in the army
it has no particular charm."

The major excitement here was a four-day scout to Mayfield, Kentucky.
Ordered to flush out marauders in the region, the Twenty-first Missouri
sallied forth on May 5. The second night out, the boys camped at Fulgham,
a twenty-mile march from Columbus and fifteen miles short of Mayfield.
Then, before daybreak May 7, nine of Moore's pickets uncovered a party
of fifty Johnnies near the Mayfield road. "If we had run," William H. Roseberry later recalled, "we would have escaped. Standing about 3 feet from
me, the captain of the Confederate squad shot me and if he hadn't I'd have
plugged him. I did hit him over the head with my musket." Disarmed,
the outnumbered Missourians fell prisoner. Loaded on secesh horses, they
were spirited away to captivity.

They were all Knox Countians of Company E, including Roseberry's
younger brother Jim, Augustus Moranville, Edgar Matlick, Thomas W.
Davis, Thomas Murphy, Andrew Haynes, Robert and William Pulis. The
last, having resigned in 1862 as second lieutenant of Company E, had returned as an enlisted man. The boys were now scattered in lodgings from
a warehouse at Cahaba to the stockade at Adairsville, Georgia, and most
of them would be captives for the duration.

Returning to Columbus, the regiment awaited reunion with its old brigade. The colonel being absent in district headquarters, Ed Moore commanded. And this must have been a stormy time, for the new lieutenant

colonel had a frightful row on May 15 with several company officers and
wound up arresting Captains Pearce and Blackburn, Lieutenants Richardson and Smith. Poor Jim Smith—in the doghouse again! Then, capping Ed
Moore's grievances, his horse disappeared. Isaac Johnston and James Hall
were detailed to look for it.

There were some pleasing chores. On May 17 Ed Moore bade farewell
to First Sergeant John J. Williams of Company K, leaving to take up a
lieutenancy in the Ninth Louisiana Volunteers, a unit of freedmen. The
same day, Moore sent to St. Louis his recommendation that Starr be
raised to second lieutenant, for possible duty in Company E under newly
promoted Bona Shafer.

There arrived at Columbus on May 17 the *John J. Roe*, as orders came
from XVI Corps directing the Twenty-first Missouri to board the ancient
vessel for Vicksburg. The reunion of A. J. Smith's division was at hand.

The army was issuing few prizes for Banks' performance in the Red
River campaign just ending. In a thin-skinned report to Secretary Stanton,
Banks blamed everybody but himself. The troops sent by Sherman under
A. J. Smith, he insinuated, "were under special orders, having ulterior ob-
jects in view, and afforded an earnest but only a partial co-operation."
Smith's report stooped to no such whining, and confirmed the prejudices
of those who thought A. J. should have commanded instead of Banks.
Among the boys of the Twenty-first Missouri attached to the Twenty-
fourth Missouri for this expedition, seven lost their lives and a dozen were
taken captive, including Philarmon Reynolds and Isaiah Preston.
Colonel Shaw, in whose brigade the nonvets had served, heartily saluted
"those heroes who had learned to fight under old Dave Moore."

11

"My God! My God!"

Unified professional guidance was coming to the nation's war effort. Lincoln had struggled to provide it, exhorting and coaxing his McClellans, Hookers, and Burnsides to more productive exertions. If the homely prairie lawyer developed into a better commander than the public had any right to expect, that was mostly a result of his keen political instinct. Lincoln never overrated his generalship but cast about from month to month for a professional warrior with the nerve to hold the armies to their appointed task until the spectre of disunion vanished.

After Vicksburg and Chattanooga, the President perceived that such a general had come. Summoning Grant, Lincoln raised him to lieutenant general on March 9, 1864, and gave him command of all federal armies. Halleck, stepping down to "Chief of Staff," operated thenceforth as a liaison officer for Grant and the President.

By early 1864, there were nearly 700,000 men in Yankee blue, against whom the Confederates could summon but 195,000. The lieutenant general chose to move on a wide front. Meade's Army of the Potomac, nearly 120,000 strong, would drive into Virginia to engage the main rebel force. Operating on Meade's flanks would be smaller armies, under Major General Ben Butler, between the James and York rivers, and Major General Franz Sigel, out in the valley. Sherman, heading the Military Division of the Mississippi, would direct operations in the Deep South. His principal formations—McPherson's Army of the Tennessee, Thomas' Army of the Cumberland, and Schofield's Army of the Ohio—were to invade Georgia, shatter Confederate resistance, and wreck the economy of the lower South. Banks turned over his command to Major General Edward R. S. Canby, who would mount an advance along the eastern Gulf Coast to afford Sherman some protection on that vital flank and ultimately a new and better line of supply through Mobile.

These enterprises required copious thinking and strenuous doing. Waiting for Meade was Lee's case-hardened Army of Northern Virginia, 64,000

veterans under the firm hand of a leader widely regarded as the greatest
Anglo-Saxon soldier of his time. And lurking in northwestern Georgia was
the Confederate Army of Tennessee, led by Johnston. In this crusty and
taciturn Virginian, long since banished from Jeff Davis' presence, Sherman
faced a worthy adversary.

In early May, the federals marched. Meade moved through the wilderness past Chancellorsville and toward Richmond. A series of heavy engage-
ments ensued, during each of which Lee succeeded in checking Meade before his hastily prepared breastworks. Bloody fighting developed at Spot-
sylvania Court House, then along the North Anna, and finally—on June 3—
at Cold Harbor, where 7,000 Yankees were killed and wounded in one
ghastly hour. For the "nervous Nellies" of the North, this was too much.
"Butcher" Grant was getting too many fine lads killed: in little more than
a month, he had taken 55,000 casualties. Grant's precursors, after less
rough handling, had usually recoiled. But not this fellow. He kept everyone marching south.

Simultaneously, Sherman marched on the rebels waiting in Georgia's
Connasauga valley between Dalton and Resaca. An attempt to trap Johnston failed, and he escaped to the south. Sherman pursued, hoping Johnston would halt and do battle. Occasionally, the great Confederate organized a strong position, Sherman would appraise it carefully—and decide to
flank it. Such tactics kept casualties low, but they brought Sherman ever
closer to Atlanta. In mid-June, a flurry of fighting in the hills above Atlanta
cost the life of the renowned Bishop Polk. On June 16, Johnston drew
his lines about forbidding Kennesaw Mountain and challenged Sherman to
slug it out right there.

A. J. Smith, lately raised to major general, reorganized. On May 30 he
named Colonel Moore to head his Third Division, and confided the First
Division to Brigadier General Joseph A. Mower. The Twenty-first Missouri,
under Edwin Moore, went into Colonel Charles D. Murray's First Brigade
with the Fifty-eighth and 119th Illinois, and Eighty-ninth Indiana. As
Starr prepared monthly returns for May, he found the regiment stronger
than it had been since spring 1862. Reporting for duty were 677 officers
and men. More than 180 were absent for various reasons, mostly legal.

Corps headquarters on June 4 recalled Smith's command to Memphis.
It so happened, however, that Confederate Brigadier General John S. Marmaduke was known to be active in that part of Arkansas just across the
river from Greenville, Mississippi, about seventy-five miles above Vicksburg—
and it seemed certain Marmaduke would attempt an ambush. Starr wrote
that "we will have the pleasure of going up pretty soon and capturing

Marmaduke (if he don't capture us) and stop this firing on boats coming down the river." Studying intelligence reports, Smith concluded that Point Chicot, where Arkansas jutted toward Greenville's waterfront, was the likely scene of the expected shenanigan. To the west of the river stood Lake Chicot, sometimes called Old River Lake because it had been the river's bed before the point was formed. Between this crescent-shaped lake and the tip of the point, a distance of some twelve miles, were countless locations where the rebels might pull the trick.

Mower's and Moore's divisions debarked around Sunnyside Landing on the Arkansas shore less than ten miles below Greenville, before dark on Sunday, June 5. Smith planned to move around the lake's west shore, flush out Johnnies infesting the point, and rejoin the fleet upstream from Greenville. The area in which the federals camped was a maze of briar patches, brush, tall weeds, cottonwoods, and bayous. If mosquitoes there were kin to those around Lake Providence, Louisiana, thirty miles down the river, they made the night hectic. Mark Twain later swore that two "could whip a dog, and . . . four of them could hold a man down; and except help come, they would kill him."

At daybreak Monday, Mower having the advance, the march around the lake started. Mower was not long in finding Johnnies. Colonel Colton Greene of the Third Missouri Confederate Cavalry, commanding Marmaduke's Missouri brigade, had formed a line of battle between the landing and Ditch Bayou, which emptied into the lake about four miles west of the landing. With the lake to his right and thick brush to his left, Mower pushed through a driving rain that turned the rutty little road into a series of mudholes.

David Moore's troops, in the rear, could tell a heavy engagement was developing. First, there were cavalry exchanges, and then Mower's skirmishers swarmed out to chase the Johnnies to the Bayou. That was as far as the Yanks got, since hostile infantry and gunners were strongly posted beyond the Bayou. Smith, seeing Mower could only push on if artillery came up, sent back to Moore for the Third Indiana Battery, whose pair of rifled guns soon convinced Green that Mower had "twelve cannon."

Still, Mower did not get the mileage he wanted out of those Hoosier cannoneers, and he spent his infantry mercilessly trying to silence Greene's half-dozen field pieces. It was probably around noon when Smith sent for Colonel James I. Gilbert's Second Brigade of Moore's division to bolster Mower's left. Finally, around 2:30 that afternoon, Colonel Greene gave up the fight. Moving out of the Yankees' way, he pulled back to the west of Lake Village, where the XVI Corps made its camp that evening.

Tuesday morning, with occasional harassment from enemy riders, Smith's troops converged on Columbia, on the north shore of the point, boarded the transports, and resumed their journey north. Edwin Moore was pleased that the regiment suffered no casualties of any kind, but there were losses in Mower's forward elements.

The Missourians found changes back at Camp Veatch. Hurlbut was out of XVI Corps; its left wing, Second and Fourth Divisions, was over in Georgia campaigning with Sherman. The rest of the corps, under Smith, was now the right wing. Major General Cadwallader C. Washburn had lately taken over the District of West Tennessee. Forrest, still pestering Memphis, had been Hurlbut's undoing. Brigadier General Samuel D. Sturgis was in upper Mississippi with a strong task force "looking up" the famous rebel.

As the Twenty-first Missouri unpacked, alarms spread through Memphis. Sturgis had run into Forrest at Brice's Cross Roads, over eighty miles to the southeast between Corinth and Tupelo—and Forrest had routed him! To Sturgis' pleas for help, Washburn responded by calling on Smith to hurry troops out toward Colliersville. This, A. J. decided, was Moore's job, and on June 12 the colonel alerted his division "to move at a moment's notice, provided with forty rounds of ammunition in cartridge-boxes, sixty rounds in charge of the ordnance officer, and three days' rations." Wolfe's brigade marched out first and met the retreating comrades at Colliersville before the end of the day. The other brigades followed Wolfe, and it was Moore's pleasure to escort Sturgis back "into Memphis without being molested by the enemy."

During the two weeks the Twenty-first Missouri remained at Camp Veatch, tragedy struck again. Tom Richardson, fifty-two-year-old first lieutenant of Company C and father of First Sergeant William J. Richardson, died of typhoid in the Officers Hospital the evening of June 11. The regiment buried the lieutenant June 13. But there were occasions for gladness and hope. Sergeant Major Starr became second lieutenant of Company E, and First Sergeant Thomas Amburn came up from A to replace him at headquarters. Amburn, twenty-six and native to Illinois, had been with Yust since 1861. Two new first sergeants made their appearance. Matt Woodruff was promoted in G, Captain Blackburn unhorsing Charles McMichael for "neglect of duty." Replacing the departed John Williams in Company K was Sergeant William A. Weaver, twenty-eight, a brick mason from Hillsboro, Iowa, and an immigrant from England's Somersetshire.

Edwin Moore gave thought to promotions in commissioned ranks. To replace McFall in Company C, desperately short of officers with the death of Richardson, Moore chose Quartermaster Sergeant Francis Marion Gough, a twenty-eight-year-old Illinoisan who had been with Pearce since 1861. Adding significantly to Gough's eligibility, no doubt, was the fact that he was McFall's brother-in-law. And then there was the vacancy for major: if the lieutenant colonel had his way, seniority would determine it. Alas! the three senior captains had the same date of rank and muster in: Yust, Pearce, Fulton. On the afternoon of June 23, they met at Ed Moore's office, drew lots, and settled the business. Fulton won. Exulted Starr: "Captain Fulton will be our major if any body will." Fulton was to him "a model and temperate man and deserves promotion." Certainly intensifying his enthusiasm was the realization that if Fulton rose to major, Shafer would become captain, and Starr would be in line for the first lieutenancy.

Governor Hall set June 21 for a special election to choose Woodyard's successor. James Ellison tried again, but Senator David Wagner of Canton, a thirty-eight-year-old Pennsylvanian who had read law with Ellison in his youth, stood against him. Jesse Barrett naturally endorsed Ellison, but it availed him little. Ellison's difficulties were summed up in the outcome at the Athens precinct. Ex-Chaplain Cox, after an all-day vigil, wrote Howell that "Hon. David Wagner, the Immediate Emancipationist, received up to 5½ p.m. *one hundred and five majority*. . . . Ellison, the rebel, copperhead, pro-slavery, bushwhacking, cut-throat candidate, received ten votes." Barrett, certain the soldier vote would widen the margin, never bothered publishing the official totals.

Could A. J. Smith, Mower, and Dave Moore handle Forrest? So General Washburn was asking, as the wreckage of Sturgis' expedition drifted into Memphis. It made sense to order Smith and his hard-bitten team into the oaken woods and canebrakes of Mississippi to see what they could do. It was a cinch that somewhere Bedford Forrest would confront those Yankee terrors, which was all Washburn could reasonably ask.

During the last days of June, A. J. Smith's troops started for the Mississippi line. Some fourteen thousand Yankees were going after Forrest, as Grierson's cavalry division and Colonel Edward Bouton's brigade of U.S. Colored Troops joined the procession. On Saturday morning, June 25, the Third Division entrained to Moscow, forty miles southeast of Memphis. Reveille sounded at 4:00 A.M. on Monday, and the Twenty-first Missouri and its comrades-in-arms were off for a nine-mile eastward trek to Smith's staging area along the Wolf River around La Grange, within three or four miles of the state line. Cloudless skies left the Yankees at the mercy of a blistering sun, while swarms of gnats tormented them and horseflies pestered their animals. Dust lay thick on the well-churned road, compounding the misery of the federal host.

Indeed, the division "lost a good many men from sun stroke," Starr recorded, ". . . a much faster way of killing men than in battle." Chief among such casualties was Lieutenant Hagle of Company D, an ambulance case for most of the campaign. To "Miss Ettie," Starr confided on July 1 that "we are camped not very far from the rebels but expect they will fall back as soon as we move. I do not think we will have an engagement until we get to Corinth." It was a blessing, he conceded, that evenings were cool and afforded "a pleasant night's rest under those large beech trees on Wolf River bottom."

Smith started probing for Forrest on a cloudy Saturday morning, July 5. Grierson's column clattered away to the east, toward Saulsbury, to turn south from there and head for Ripley, some twenty-five miles across the line. Grierson was given to understand, however, that he should establish contact every night with A. J. Smith. The infantry, artillery, and train marched directly toward the state line, bearing to the southeast, with Mower leading. Somewhere in those hills west of the Tallahatchie they surely could bring Forrest to bay.

Lieutenant General Stephen D. Lee, commanding rebel cavalry west of Alabama, had his problems. A handsome West Pointer with all the rank he needed, Lee was somewhat overawed by the renown of his chief subordinate, the daring and caustic Forrest. Besides, Confederate officialdom was constantly warning of an impending Yankee attack on Mobile, which faced Lee with the problem of deciding what priority to give the clear and present danger from Smith. This puzzlement in the Confederate command was a distinct asset to Smith's expedition, could his pickets scrapping with Forrest's skirmishers have had an inkling of it.

Despite occasional thundershowers, the Yankees trudged sweaty and begrimed through one torrid day after another. And if this was not scourging enough, rations began to run short after two or three days on the march. By the time the XVI Corps reached Pontotoc, thirty-five miles below Ripley, on the evening of July 12, Smith recognized that something drastic needed doing. Because of rebel resistance to his south, he would divert his columns eastward on Sunday morning, July 13, for widespread foraging on an eighteen-mile march to Tupelo. By the grace of God and despite Forrest, his Yankees would eat like soldiers one more time.

The advance on Tupelo was hotly contested, the Johnnies repeatedly striking at both ends of Smith's compact column. It was a dangerous time to forage, and one poor fellow of the Twenty-first Missouri fell into enemy hands. Private Joel Frazier of Company E, whose service extended back to home guard days, was apprehended near Pontotoc and taken to Cahaba.

Joel was to live a half-century more but probably did not believe it then.

With the Confederates closing in from the rear and pressing the attack, Smith prepared a showdown. If Forrest wanted a confrontation, he was going to get it. After Grierson sent word in the afternoon that he had cleared Tupelo, Smith ordered his infantry to wheel around at the deserted village of Harrisburg and face west while the train thundered by to park closer to Tupelo. Smith's aides galloped out and told David Moore to form the Third Division on a ridge facing Harrisburg. Moore's First Brigade, under C. D. Murray and containing the Twenty-first Missouri, would stand just to the south of the Tupelo road. Wolfe's Third Brigade would hook on to Murray's left, and Bouton's black phalanx would guard Wolfe's left. Gilbert's Second Brigade, camped in the rear, would double as train guards and reserves. In the evening, as Mower's troops filed in, they lined up north of the road. The position Smith chose was largely on high ground and in open country, with a heavy stand of timber to its rear. Protecting Moore's front was a "worm" fence and several ravines.

Harrisburg all but disappeared that night, as Smith's troops dismantled houses for firewood and began cooking the bountiful proceeds of the day's foraging. Many hungry stomachs were filled for the first time in a week— and not a few for the last time. The troops slept on their arms, as pickets kept bringing word through the night of an ominous rebel concentration in the woods west of Harrisburg.

Shortly after 6:00 A.M., Moore's skirmishers came in, confirming enemy preparations to attack. Then, at 7:00, the Confederates' dismounted cavalry started its charge, their objective apparently Murray's position. Historian John Fiske described the onslaught as uncoordinated, but nobody in the Twenty-first Missouri, standing between the Fifty-eighth and 119th Illinois in the heart of the brigade line, had any advance notice. "The enemy were permitted to advance in solid columns upon our line through an open field," Dave Moore said. "Our lines being concealed from their view by the brow of a hill, we were not discovered until the enemy had reached a point about twenty paces distant." Now the fiery merchant of Wrightsville gave the fateful command, bringing his forward line to its feet for the first thunderous volley.

The attackers were horrified. "My God! My God!" hundreds yelled, some dying with surprise on their faces as more fortunate comrades broke and fled. Moore counterattacked, and his shouting bluecoats pressed down the smoke-shrouded hillside delivering volley after volley into the broken ranks of the retreating foe. Colonel Thomas J. Kinney of the 119th Illinois recalled that the "Twenty-First Missouri Volunteers was formed on my right right and charged with us, they, too capturing many prisoners. I think I can say with safety that this regiment and my own captured nearly all the prisoners taken." When both brigades reached the foot of the hill down which they had pursued the rebels, Moore prudently recalled them to their original positions.

There developed no enemy counterthrust. Instead, Southern field pieces in the woods beyond Harrisburg began to play on federal lines. As one of Grierson's officers put it, "Forrest's artillery was very active, . . . throwing its shot and shell into the 21st Missouri, 58th Illinois, and 89th Indiana, until an Illinois and an Indiana battery engaged their attention." Ed Moore issued a casualty list of one killed and fifteen wounded when the fighting died down that evening. Corporal Harden Payden, a twenty-four-year-old Virginian who had gone to the colors with Joe Farris, was killed outright. Death came later to two others. Benjamin A. Simerl of Company B, whose father Samuel had been killed at Shiloh, received a severe leg wound that in time proved fatal. The Simerls were Ohioans, as was Martin Hunter of Company C, who lost a leg on this field. Hunter left a teenaged son and small daughter back on his Scotland County farm, orphans who had seen their father for the last time. George Washburn's older brother Marion was dangerously wounded. George Sheeks, lately promoted corporal, caught a shell fragment in his right hand.

The worst was over by noon, Russell noted. The Johnnies had done no better against Mower than against Dave Moore. That the Confederate loss had been severe was evident to federal officers, for Mower reported "270 of their dead" on his front alone. In reality, A. J. Smith would later learn, Lee and Forrest had lost 153 killed, 794 wounded, and 49 captured—a total of nearly a thousand. One of Forrest's regiments, 279 strong at dawn, was down to 38 the next day. Federal casualties stood at 674, including 77 dead on the field.

A. J. Smith, tangling with Forrest, had driven him from the field. Confederates labored long after to correct an impression that their hero had been defeated. Tupelo, said Lee, "was a drawn battle." But for some hours after the battle the indomitable Forrest behaved like the victim of a galling defeat. Anguished over "five hundred empty saddles," he brutally and unfairly fumed at Lee: "If I knew as much about West Point tactics as you, the Yankees would whip hell out of me every day." Words hardly born of a victor's vainglory!

Smith, pondering his next move, chose to take the shortest route back to Tennessee. Most of the hardtack issued at the start of the campaign,

"spoiled when drawn," consisted now of "worm sandwiches . . . more pal-
atable in the dark than in daylight." There were enough of these delica-
cies to last another night. Smith's ordnance officers had no artillery ammunition left—the gunners had it all. When morning came, the divisions remained in line while Grierson finished wrecking railroads around Tupelo
and teamsters moved the critically wounded into the city. A pair of surgeons
remained with these, among whom were Ben Simerl and Martin Hunter.
Later that day, they fell prisoners. Simerl lingered on with "blood-poison-
ing" and died at Cahaba in October, and a few years later the quartermaster department removed his remains to the national cemetery at Marietta,
Georgia. Disposal squads never found Hunter, who presumably lies in an
unmarked grave at or near Tupelo.

Toward noon July 15, Moore's division took the Ellistown road, heading for New Albany, twenty-five miles northwest. The march out distress-
ingly resembled the march in, for the sun continued to bake the parched
woodlands. Smith was eloquent in praising the troops, mindful that "marching over dusty roads with only one-half or one-third rations, under a broil-
ing sun, with little water, is certainly a severe test of their zeal and
patriotism."

Forrest tried his best to hurry the Yankees out of Mississippi. He might
better have conserved his strength, for he got a minié ball in one foot while
scuffling with Mower's rear guard during the first day of Smith's retirement
on New Albany. "From this date," said Smith, "nothing more was seen"
of the rebels. A supply train met the corps north of Ripley on July 19, ending the days of short rations. By July 23, the troops were back in camp
at Memphis.

One matter found Smith and Washburn in firm agreement: this one-
legged colonel from Missouri could handle a division in the hottest of
fights. Washburn singled Moore out for lavish praise in his report on the
expedition. Smith saluted both division commanders, praying that "our
country may always find such sons in her hour of need." Still the army
could spare no star for the shoulder straps of "D. Moore, Union."

Possibly shedding light on the promotion problem was a crisis in the regiment Monday morning, July 25. Ed Moore was up early to warn corps
headquarters: "I am sorry to inform you that a portion of my command
intend to mutiny and refuse to do duty to-day."

Was this another Chewalla? Perhaps not, but there were resemblances.
Agitation for a July muster out had been growing in ranks. Sergeant Andrew Briggs and Corporal Lytle Laird of F had narrowly missed reduction
to the ranks in June for writing General Smith "outside of the military chan-

nels." This stratagem, they reasoned, would keep Edwin Moore from side-tracking their claims. But the lieutenant colonel was not holding any lid on the growing clamor for an "early out." He had been importuning higher echelons for a decision since early June, convinced though he was that the musters of February 1862, which he had personally supervised, were the only legal ones, not the home guard musters of June and July 1861.

Many dissidents with home guard service affected to recall that the hallowed Lyon had led them to believe they had only to serve three years from the date of their entry into the guards. Some of them had stirred up prominent civilians to put the heat on Rosecrans and others. To officers who suggested the muster in at Athens of October 1861, as a possible compromise date—the guards having then mustered as United States Volunteers—the agitators turned a cold shoulder for two reasons. First, they maintained, Frémont himself had ratified the sacred promise. Second, they claimed, Dave Moore had been telling them, so Ed Moore heard, that "they should be mustered out . . . and further that the muster-in at Canton, Mo., on the 1st February 1862 was illegal."

Interesting! *Was* David Moore stoking the embers of mutiny in his old outfit? Evidence permits no ready answer, but the present writer senses a chasm between what Moore said to his 1861 boys and what they *said* he said. Still, if the impression got abroad in Memphis that he had abetted this mutiny, the damage done his promotion chances appears obvious. Could mere coincidence explain Moore's relief from divisional command on July 31 and his assignment to court-martial duty?

At any rate, mutiny flamed. Ed Moore, prepared for this sit-down at Camp Veatch, made thirty-two arrests. Companies A, C, and G were un-affected, while two-thirds of the offenders came from three companies—D, I, and K. Half had entered home guard service under Moore, the rest under Woodyard. Eight noncoms were in the group, among them stalwarts like Sergeants John Cunningham and Bill O'Connor of D, Martin Morton of F, Owen V. Adams of K. Unlike the Chewalla outbreak, Germans played a forward role in this one: eight men of K defied military discipline—Werly among them. Yust's Germans stood aloof in A. Company D's mutineers constituted the largest single group.

There was a quaintly American fragrance about this insurrection, in which nearly three dozen dutiful soldiers claimed personal rights and braved severe penalties for so doing. The English-born lieutenant colonel had his own ideas about these rights and the curiously American addiction to such. On July 26, he packed the offenders off to Irving Block. To his disgust, Washburn's provost marshal sent the entire gang back and demanded "charges and specifications." Starr soon had these ready, and the next day the accused were jailed.

Few stayed in the block, for authorities chose finally to make examples of three, who were convicted of mutiny and sent to Alton for dishonorable discharges at the end of their enlistments. Sergeant O'Connor, heroic color-bearer of the recent Louisiana campaign, was sent "up the river." Along with him went Buel Stevens, onetime top kick of Company I, and Alexander Rogers of Company B, a prisoner of Shiloh.

Notwithstanding this sad affair, Ed Moore sought elementary justice for those still in the ranks. On August 1, he petitioned Smith to send Captain McGonigle to St. Louis to secure copies of muster rolls made out at Athens in October 1861. Smith shot the proposal down with a terse "Not granted." It scarcely mattered, for in late August the malcontents got their answer from Washington. The Athens muster in of October 25, 1861, the 1861 boys learned, was *their* date; however, other originals of the Twenty-first Missouri not affected would wait until February 1865. Like them or not, the boys now knew their rights.

Meanwhile, General Washburn was preparing Smith for another showdown. Forrest was rumored to be gathering south of Holly Springs for a dash up to Memphis. Smith's troops were soon on the march, southeast into Mississippi, preceded by Brigadier General Edward Hatch's division of cavalry. Late Monday afternoon, August 8, the Twenty-first Missouri marched into Holly Springs with the 119th Illinois and Eighty-ninth Indiana, and camped at the southeast edge of town. During the next few days there came frequent reports of cavalry skirmishes to the east and south, and Smith felt sure he was "developing" the enemy in the direction of Oxford, thirty miles below Holly Springs.

Until August 16, Smith's infantry lay in its camps awaiting events. Then he ordered an advance on Waterford, seven miles or so farther south. "I suppose we will move with the army in front," Adjutant Starr wrote. "I hear but very little of what is going on whether they are fighting or not but now soon will learn." The boys would as soon have stayed in camp for a celebration, for the mail brought a major's commission for Fulton. Shafer now took permanent command of Company E, and Starr began dreaming of the "gold-embroidered" bars of a first lieutenant.

Smith's infantry and artillery marched on, crossing the Tallahatchie to bivouac around Abbeville on August 18. Two days of heavy rain stalled the federals, but on Saturday afternoon Smith directed Shaw to move a brigade forward to Hurricane Branch, about four miles down the Oxford road, to report to Hatch. Two cavalry regiments would lead. "Send the brigade that is in the rear," Smith instructed, and Colonel Murray's First Brigade thereby got the honor of spearheading the XVI Corps' coming march into action.

Murray's troops camped on a hill south of Hurricane Creek that night, but Hatch got them up early for an advance against Johnnies "believed to be in our front in some force." The Twenty-first Missouri took the lead, flanked by cavalry, while Shaw assembled the rest of his force for the attack. The Third Division would press forward in a "column of regiments, with their colors displayed and at distances of about 125 paces." By 7:00 A.M., Ed Moore's Missourians were in a heavy skirmish line and waiting for the division to form behind them. There was a hill to the south, held by General Chalmers' cavalry; Hatch wanted the hill cleared.

Once Chalmers' men sighted the Yankee display, their commander rapidly lost control of them. As the Twenty-first Missouri approached, sporadic firing broke out along Chalmers' line, but Ed Moore promptly responded to deal out better than he was getting. A spent ball knocked down Isaac Thacker of Company F, bruising but not otherwise damaging him. The Johnnies skedaddled. In camp below the hill that night, Ed Moore was happy to learn that Thacker was his only casualty. Oddly, neither Hatch nor Shaw mentioned the skirmish in their subsequent reports.

Recalled to the Hurricane Branch camp on August 22, the Missourians did not get to Oxford. Several other regiments did, and that evening Russell recorded that "Oxford burned to the ground." Local folks never quite got over the conflagration, in which three dozen businesses, numerous residences, the courthouse, two hotels, and the gracious mansion of former President Buchanan's Secretary of the Interior went up in flames. Smith supervised the incendiarism, Confederates heard, and in early 1866 a local grand jury indicted him. It was reasoned that since the Yankees held secession unconstitutional, Mississippi was a "loyal" state, and Smith had no cause to incinerate the town. Needless to say, not a cent changed hands and nobody went to jail.

Smith's troops had little time to sniff the ashes, for couriers reaching Abbeville brought startling news that Forrest had sneaked around Smith and captured Memphis! The XVI Corps started galloping or jogging the seventy miles back to Memphis, but when the Twenty-first Missouri got there August 30, the raiders were long gone.

Sunday morning, August 21, had indeed been a tumultuous time in Memphis. Rebel troopers, hoping to catch C. C. Washburn "sleeping late," charged into town before daybreak, scattering green troops before them along the Hernando Road. The commander of the city garrison managed to get several hundred sleepy veterans into the streets in time to ward off disaster. Dave Moore, volunteering his services, spent the day commanding forces along the Hernando Road. It was the Johnnies' good fortune that they left by a different route.

Washburn escaped to Fort Pickering—in his pajamas. The marauders made off with his uniform and captured several dozen patients at the Gayoso Street Hospital. Among these ailing unfortunates was Corporal Deroy Brown of Yust's company, under treatment for "fevers." Hurlbut, who happened to be staying at the Gayoso House, was heard to crow that while Grant had fired him for being unable to keep Forrest out of western Tennessee, it did not appear his successor could even keep the sly rebel out of his bedroom!

It was necessary to locate the Twenty-first Missouri in a new camp, over a mile north of Camp Veatch. Here, as the regiment moved in, Sergeant Ed Jones made his appearance, just in time to muster for pay. He had been away battling the chills and fevers of malaria. Also arriving was the second lieutenant's commission for Sergeant Gough. Too, there was the case of Doc Stanley, sent back to Memphis from Holly Springs in mid-August to get bandages. He was still in Memphis when the regiment returned. The lieutenant colonel did not fancy that at all and was of a mind to "take measures." However, the XVI Corps medical director made it clear that Stanley was a victim of circumstances, that the road to Holly Springs had been closed when he tried to return, and that he had been "borrowed" for emergency duty at Fort Pickering.

Starr had lately detected a little cloud over headquarters. Miss Ettie had written that Edwin Moore was resigning, or so Mrs. Moore was telling around in Canton. Much troubled, Nick had checked it out and become convinced the lieutenant colonel wanted out and would probably resign "as soon as he can." This news, we may be sure, generated staff speculation, the more so as Knox County Radicals were talking up Major Fulton for sheriff—and he was listening.

Dave Moore received news that Diademia Schnabel Moore had lately died at Alexandria. Neighbors had taken charge of Miss Frances and the boys still at home and seen to their mother's burial in the churchyard of the Sisson Chapel, on a shady hill between Winchester and Antioch, not far from Wrightsville. The colonel's reaction to the demise of his "rebel" spouse is not preserved in family tradition, but the record shows that he took no leave to go north and attend to matters left unsettled by her passing.

In the war's broader panorama, Grant was still grappling with Lee in

Virginia. The federal commander, having been Cold Harbored once, backed away from another one. Leaving a cavalry screen and an infantry-held trench system, he marched his main body in mid-June toward the James River. Some twenty-five miles southeast of Richmond, it so happened, Union engineers were laying across the James one of the longest floating bridges ever built by soldiers, a structure nearly a half-mile long. Lee had not expected this: he had thought Grant would swing around to attack Richmond's eastern outskirts by way of, perhaps, the York River Railroad. Now Grant would be coming up from the southeast, below the James. Could the Confederates possibly stop him in time?

Lee hurried through Richmond to check this move. There was little time to lose, but the rebels saved their capital and started a line of trenches around Petersburg. Lee, that master of mobility, was at last pinned down behind breastworks. Mercifully concealed from him was the ominous portent in the name of the river flowing past Petersburg to the James: it was the Appomattox.

In Georgia, after an awkward pause before Kennesaw Mountain, Sherman tried a frontal attack on June 27. If Johnston was caught off guard, he recovered to deal the Yankees a painful repulse. Sherman then skirted the defenders' right flank, crossing the Chattahoochee River to threaten the eastern approaches to Atlanta. In that city, heavily entrenched, Johnston would do battle under conditions nullifying much of Sherman's manpower advantage.

Jefferson Davis was not satisfied merely to learn that his Army of Tennessee was still intact before Atlanta. In a dozen weeks, Johnston had yielded a strip of Georgia a hundred miles long. Too many politicians were condemning Johnston for letting Sherman into the Peach State. The president at length called on Lieutenant General John Bell Hood, a maimed veteran of Gettysburg and Chickamauga, to supersede Johnston on July 17. Confederates were widely jubilant—but so for that matter was Sherman. He knew Hood was a rash fellow who would bring his little army out where the Yankees could "attend to it."

True to his reputation, Hood attacked along Peach Tree Creek northeast of Atlanta on July 20. Sherman threw him for a loss. Two days later, Hood charged the federal left in woodlands east of the city. This battle of Atlanta was a tight squeeze for an hour or so, costing McPherson his life, but it sent the bleeding rebels scurrying into Atlanta's earthworks. A siege was in prospect, but Hood had so wasted his army's morale and substance that his troops could not keep up their end of such a struggle very long—on short rations. With the Yankee trenches reaching toward Atlanta's southern outskirts, Hood abandoned the city to Sherman at the beginning of September.

The fall of Atlanta climaxed a month of good news for Lincoln. Canby, in cooperation with Rear Admiral David Farragut, assaulted forts guarding the entrance to Mobile Bay, in the first days of August. All three of these— Forts Morgan, Gaines, and Powell—were reduced by XIII Corps troops within three weeks. A rebel ironclad and a flotilla of wooden warships inside the bay were neutralized, but Mobile remained in Confederate hands. Sherman, who had hoped to gain Mobile and with it a shorter and more dependable line of communications, was going to have to fight on without that fine port.

Other good news was political. The President, shrewdly aware his election chances were less than robust because of general war weariness, decided the Republicans should "take in partners" to ward off bankruptcy. Partners were available in "War Democrats" determined to back the attack until secession was overcome. Meeting in June, the Republicans styled their gathering the "National Union" convention and nominated a fusion ticket of the President and Governor Andrew Johnson of Tennessee.

Now the regular Democrats were left with their Copperhead and peace factions. "They must nominate a war candidate on a peace platform, or a peace candidate on a war platform," Lincoln calculated, "and . . . I don't much care which they do." Meeting in August, the Democrats gripped the first horn of the dilemma, resurrecting McClellan and handcuffing him to a cut-and-run platform that Little Mac repudiated. The war was a failure, to the platform writers. Bogged down at Atlanta! Hung up before Petersburg! All those black abolitionists offered was an endless wastage of blood and treasure—just to make "Sambo" the equal of the white man. On the other hand, the Democrats offered negotiations "with a view to an ultimate convention of the States, or other practicable means, to the end that peace may be restored on the basis of the federal Union of the States." How long that tunnel—how faint that light!

It seemed in early August that the Democrats had the better mousetrap. But with the fall of Atlanta, and the attendant nationwide rejoicing, their spirits began to droop. Perhaps it was not necessary after all to write off these years of bloodletting and return helplessly to the obsolete political arrangements that had brought all this desolation. Perhaps the Union could be rebuilt on foundations envisaged in Radical nationalist thinking, that seasons such as this might never come again.

To the men of David Moore's regiment, political news from home had excitement all its own. The Conservative-Union folk had nominated a

militia general, Thomas Lawson Price, for governor, and against him the
Radicals were pitting young Colonel Thomas C. Fletcher of the Thirty-
first Missouri Volunteers. The boys of the Twenty-first Missouri took particular note of the candidate for state treasurer on Fletcher's ticket—William
Bishop of Alexandria.

General Washburn had been in correspondence involving the Twenty-
first Missouri. Sherman, it seemed, had been wanting to reunite the XVI
Corps in Georgia, where matters yet hung in the balance. Halleck, sym-
pathetic though he was to Sherman, kept reminding everyone that events
west of the Mississippi might generate major demands on Union military
resources. Since spring there had been rumors that Sterling Price would
raid Missouri "when the corn ripens." By midsummer, the threat had
materialized in northeastern Arkansas, and Steele was beginning to clam-
or for help.

When A. J. Smith reached Memphis, therefore, Washburn was on notice
to spare at least one division for Arkansas. Mower's First Division sailed
for Devall's Bluff, beyond Helena. Smith, however, remained under orders
to take the Third Division to Georgia, and on September 5 the Twenty-
first Missouri boarded the *W. R. Arthur* to proceed up the Mississippi,
Ohio, and Tennessee rivers to Chattanooga, where it could march to the
XVI Corps' camps before Atlanta. While the boys were boarding the
Arthur, Roberts tossed C. Z. Russell into the malaria ward of the Officers
Hospital. As a result, the young officer would miss one of the strangest
adventures in his regiment's career.

12

The Lost Tribes

As the *W. R. Arthur* docked at Cairo the morning of September 7, an urgent telegram from Rosecrans was waiting. The last few days, it transpired, his command had been subject to a three-way argument among Rosecrans, Sherman, and Halleck. Confident now that Smith would be diverted to Missouri, Rosecrans wanted him to mark time at Cairo. A. J. obliged him and landed his troops a mile above the town.

Rosecrans won his argument, with the aid of Sterling Price, and wired Smith on September 8 that "Grant's orders" were for the divisions under Mower and Shaw to remain in the West for operations "against Price." A day or so later, Halleck wired further orders, leaving Smith to decide how best he might come to Rosecrans' aid.

On one point A. J. Smith was adamant: he wanted no part of an infantry chase into Arkansas after Price's mounted troops. If, he reasoned, the Third Division sailed directly to St. Louis, it would be in a position to move by river, road, or rail to any point in Missouri's Ozarks the Confederates might threaten. He had no difficulty, therefore, in deciding to proceed by boat up the river.

September 14, 1864, was a memorable day in the life of the Twenty-first Missouri. Ed Moore departing on a ten-day leave to Canton, Major Fulton took command. And the boys were cheered by the arrival of that most familiar figure, the Old Man himself, fresh from special duty in Memphis. Upon reaching Cairo, Dave took over First Brigade and revealed Smith's orders to load out at daylight.

On Saturday, September 17, just at dawn, the Twenty-first Missouri landed at Jefferson Barracks, on St. Louis' south side. There were no "barracks" available to Smith's troops, however, and they had to camp along the shore. In the process of unloading, twenty-six-year-old Jim Hall of K, a La Grange butcher, fell off the steamer *Jarvis* and drowned. It is not apparent from contemporary newspapers, the Barracks cemetery roll, or from his service record that his body was recovered.

But cheerful things also happened. Hardly a day passed without some-one's family arriving to rejoice at his return. Starr did notice, though, that when relatives left for home, "scenes changed and happiness turned to sor-row, whether meeting with friends only a few short days is sufficient com-pensation for the solemnity which follows in parting, I do not know." There was jubilation in Company E, where Bona Shafer's commission as captain arrived. Going forward now were recommendations asking the first lieutenancy for Starr, and a second lieutenancy for Sergeant Sinnott. Over in Company C, Frank Gough moved up a notch to first lieutenant.

During the stay at the Barracks, there was a political scandal in Company C. Lieutenant John E. Markle of the Thirty-fourth Indiana had lately re-ceived a letter from a former hired hand. Youthful John J. Vasser, who had left the Twenty-first Missouri back at Columbus, Kentucky, the week Lincoln's proclamation took effect, had lately returned. Whatever his rea-son for returning, Vasser made clear to Markle the relationship between the proclamation and his departure: "Well John I thought I would rite you a letter to let you know what I am doing. I am in missouri now but have been down in Tenisee ever since I left your house but dont know what land we are bound for now. I think we are going to the front to fight the indians. . . . I wish I was there to work for you I think that I would not be a Slave for the Dam nigar [.] But I am here and here I must stay till my time is out then I will give you a visit. But that dont make Eny difference but 'hurrah for McClellan' that is the word with the bark on I am a dima-crat til yet and always have to be."

Markle confessed to no such feelings and immediately sent the letter to Major Fulton: "I don't know the man and don't want to know him. I think a year or two to Tortugas would be a good thing for writing the way he has." Someone at regimental headquarters, probably Starr, thought Mr. Howe would love to have the letter in his *National American*, and Vasser's indiscretion soon became public knowledge. Neither Fulton nor Ed Moore took any open reprisals, but buck private was as high as Vasser got in their regiment.

With three mounted columns cantering north, Price's "Army of Missouri" crossed into the state from Arkansas on September 19. St. Louis was sud-denly gripped by a hysteria it had not known since 1861. This was indeed Price's "last hurrah," and he meant to make the most of it. Barring his ad-vance was the small garrison of Fort Davidson at Pilot Knob, some eighty-five miles south of St. Louis. Commanding was Sherman's brother-in-law, Brigadier General Thomas Ewing, author of the infamous "Order Number 11" that had depopulated Missouri's western prairie counties in 1863.

Ewing was very certain that if Price caught him, he would be shot out of hand. Also stiffening his determination to hold was the fact that he had with him Colonel Fletcher, the Republican candidate for governor. On the other hand, the Confederate incursion was the worst of news for Fletcher's opponent: Thomas L. Price might protest daily he was no kin to Sterling, but the coincidence was a heavy political cross to bear in this year 1864.

The struggle for Davidson was a bloody affair, culminating in an almost miraculous escape by the defenders on September 28. Still, the news of Price's presence at Pilot Knob panicked St. Louis. Rosecrans called out

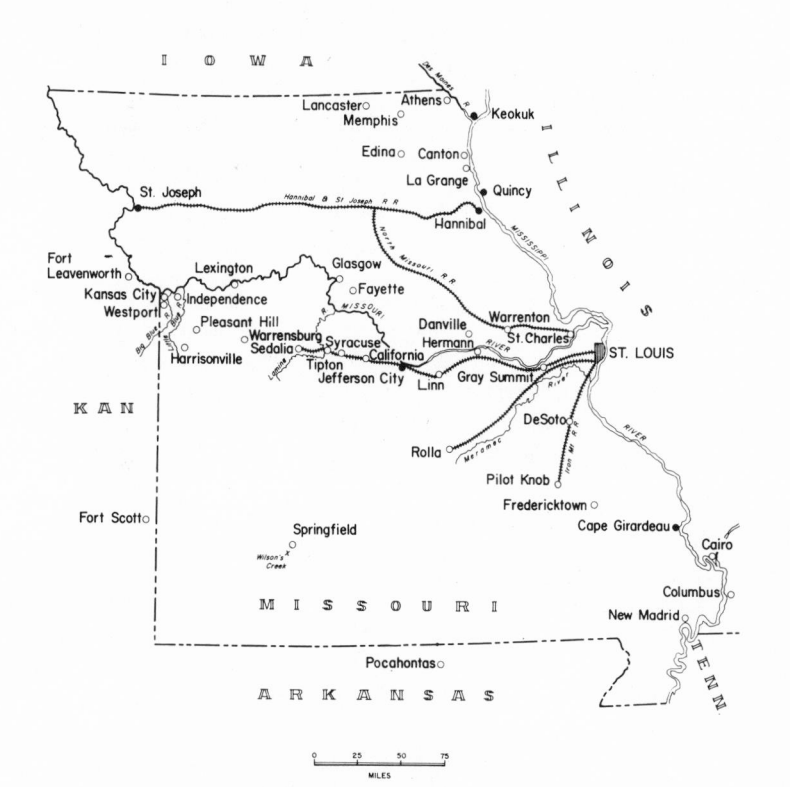

MISSOURI, 1864

(PRICE RAID)

militia to ward off the threat, and, not knowing where Price would next appear, he ordered Smith's division down the Iron Mountain Railroad, in the general direction of the oncoming rebels. The First Division, under Mower, was still in Arkansas, behind Price but hundreds of miles from any scene of likely action in Missouri.

On the morning of September 27, therefore, while the fight was in progress at Pilot Knob, Smith loaded his troops on the cars for a thirty-five-mile trip down to De Soto. As the division bivouacked there, Smith waited in vain for Price's vanguard. Price, however, in a soldier-historian's words, "failed to show up at that point but was reported moving in the direction of Jefferson City. On learning the fact the command was hastily put on cars and returned to Jefferson Barracks."

It was obvious that veteran troops under Rosecrans would be busy for a long time. The grim word came down, and Shaw told each brigadier to "hold your command in readiness to move at 7 A.M. to-morrow, October 1, 1864, taking with you all land transportation, camp and garrison equipage . . . and five days' rations." Dave Moore's First Brigade—Twenty-first Missouri, Eighty-ninth Indiana, and the Fifty-eighth, 119th, and 122d Illinois—was ready.

Rosecrans was plotting Price's destruction, in which the Twenty-first Missouri had a starring role. If things worked out, the Johnnies were going to find themselves fenced in along the Missouri River in the western part of the state. Strong Union cavalry formations under Major General Alfred Pleasonton would hang onto Price's heels, while Curtis would put up a solid wall of Kansas militiamen and United States Volunteers to complete the entrapment of the Confederates. Then A. J. Smith's infantry columns would stalk in for the kill, ending the Civil War out west.

Thomas C. Reynolds, Confederate "governor" of Missouri since Jackson's death two years earlier, dreamed of a triumphal entry into Jefferson City and a gala inaugural at the statehouse. Unfortunately, the federals were waiting to "welcome" him behind heavy entrenchments. Price looked things over from the hills to the south, and on October 7 mortally offended Reynolds by deciding to "pass by on the other side" toward Boonville, up the river some forty miles to the northwest.

In Boonville, on October 11, Price met with Missouri's leading guerrilla chieftains, William L. "Bloody Bill" Anderson, George Todd, and the perpetrator of the sacking of Lawrence, Kansas—Quantrill. "Bloody Bill" had come in fresh from his Centralia massacre of September 27. His men had raided the town, some forty miles north of Jefferson City, dragged two dozen unarmed and furloughed Union soldiers off an incoming passenger train, and murdered all but one. And before the end of the day, his men had slain more than a hundred men of Kutzner's Thirty-ninth Missouri Infantry. Repelled as he was at the barbarism of these sadistic partisans, Price welcomed them to his team. Todd's gang was asked to operate along the Pacific Railroad with the invading army, while Anderson and Quantrill remained north of the river to raid the North Missouri and Hannibal & St. Joseph lines. These undisciplined freebooters would assure the campaign a character of partisan warfare that men like Price could wage only in sheerest desperation.

When the "Army of Missouri" reached Lexington on October 19, Price knew that rougher going was ahead. For one thing, presence of federal skirmishers east of Lexington suggested enemy formations to the west. For another, Pleasonton was getting bolder in his scrimmages with Price's rear guard. What Price could not know was that Curtis was having a frustrating time getting Kansas militiamen into western Missouri. Conservatives heading some of these outfits suspected Radical boss Lane of trying to get his political foes out of the state on election day—and Conservatives just would not believe that the Price threat was all that serious.

As the Twenty-first Missouri prepared to march west, its strength stood at 18 officers and 604 men present for duty. There were 20 others AWOL, 48 present but ill, and 86 others absent ill. Among the latter were C. Z. Russell, still in bed at Memphis, and Asa Starkweather and Ed Nelson, suffering there from stubborn gastric ailments. Several losses had lately occurred. Most notable was the disability discharge of George Nightingale. He was afflicted with a lip cancer, the medics said, and had been at the Marine General Hospital in St. Louis since June. Thus ended his more than two years of disgruntled service.

The boys were watching political fireworks up home. Major Fulton was now the Radical candidate for Knox County sheriff. Ex-Sergeant Wilson Harle was trying for another term as the Conservative law-and-order sheriff of Scotland County. More exciting, ex-Chaplain Cox had emerged as the Radicals' contender for state senator in the Fifth District (Lewis, Clark, Scotland, and Knox counties). Cox had surely given the matter a lot of thought, for he mounted every platform loaded for bear. Ever alert to bitter-end militants, Jesse Barrett hotly accused Cox of favoring the "utter extermination of the people of the South, and the re-peopling of their territory with a mongrel breed, doubtless the legitimate production of his pet schemes of negro enfranchisement and practical miscegenation."

Nor did Cox rise above vituperation. His opponent, Thomas J. Matlock, he excoriated as a "copperhead." This was close to smearing, for

the erstwhile Hoosier sheriff had lately been provost marshal of Clark
County. He had even been an emancipationist candidate for Congress in
1862. Moreover, to Barrett's dismay, Matlock endorsed Lincoln and
shunned identification with the "Conservative-Union" slate; however, his
championship of white supremacy earned him Barrett's qualified support:
"Under the circumstances we feel justified in commending him to the
support of all who condemn the Radical doctrine of negro equality and
other kindred measures advocated by his Radical Reverence, Capt. Cox."

Shaw's division started its long, weary march to its bloody rendezvous
in western Missouri. Unfortunately for the progress and comfort of the
troops, cold and rainy weather set in, and the command halted at Gray
Summit, thirty miles west of St. Louis, on October 4. Nobody was hap-
pier than Surgeon Roberts, who had been compelled to leave his splendid
mare with a Carondelet nurseryman. She had a swollen leg, caused by a
"snag or something" down by De Soto, and Moore's brigade surgeon found
himself on a strange mount. Nor did his "rheumatics" much appreciate
the clammy weather.

During the three-day encampment at Gray Summit, Roberts wrote his
wife back in Fort Madison that "I, with several other officers, board with
Widow Brown who keeps a boarding house on the apex of the *Summit*.
I also staid there over night to protect the fat old widow from the soldiers
she seems to be mortally afraid of."

"Theirs being a cavalry force," Starr wrote Miss Headley, "can keep out
of our way [,] it being impossible for us to do them any damage until we
catch them." So far as Roberts was concerned, the division was "on another wild goose chase after the Rebs. We on foot and they mounted with
a chance to 'swap horses' whenever they choose. . . . So of course we will
catch them if they choose to let us." This indeed was a theme favored by
Unionist writers that fall in Missouri, and even Governor Hall repeated it in
his final address to the general assembly.

The Yankees, however, made too much of Price's mobility. Albert Castel reminds us that the Johnnies' progress up the Missouri valley—averaging
fifteen miles daily—"would have done little credit to infantry, much less
cavalry." Price, in fact, was hampered by a train of more than five hundred
teams and vehicles. It resembled, a witness said, more a "Calmuck horde"
than a serious military expedition. To the extent that A. J. Smith was unaware of this, the cavalrymen had much to answer for.

On October 7, the day Price chose to bypass Jefferson City, the Twenty-
first Missouri broke camp at Gray Summit. Smith was a good eighty miles
behind the Johnnies. Nevertheless, the stern little dragoon was determined

to close the gap. Mower's division, after marching across Missouri's boot-
heel, arrived by boat at St. Louis October 8. There, Mower bade the expedition goodbye, Sherman having summoned him to Georgia. Colonel
Joseph J. Woods of the Twelfth Iowa superseded him. The First Division
embarked for Jefferson City on October 9, by which day Shaw's troops
lay in camp along Big Berger Creek in Franklin County, some sixty miles
west of Jefferson Barracks.

By the time Woods reached Jefferson City on October 18, he was sixty miles behind Smith, then camped at Sedalia. Colonel Moore and his
staff halted a few days at the Lamine River crossing of the Pacific Railroad near Otterville, less than fifteen miles east of Sedalia, to assist the
First Division's passage through this vicinity toward the front October
19 and 20. Smith, headquartered at Sedalia, was certain the rebels were
at Lexington, more than fifty miles farther to the northwest. He would
leave nothing to chance in speeding concentration of his veteran divisions
assigned to the extermination of Price's dwindling army.

Price marched on toward Kansas City the morning of October 20.
Smith's forward elements were within thirty miles of him, so much had
his long lead faded. "The halcyon days of the Confederate invasion were
over," wrote Howard Monnett. "At long last the Federals were upon . . .
the Army of Missouri." On Friday morning, October 21, Marmaduke's
division ran into a force of Kansas and Colorado troops along the Little
Blue River, fifteen miles east of Kansas City. Marmaduke having no luck
at all with the boys in blue, Price threw in Brigadier General Jo Shelby's
Missourians. The Yankees retreated toward the Big Blue, ten miles to the
west; Price went after them, even as Pleasonton's cavalry nipped his heels.

Curtis was ready along the Big Blue, the west bank of which was studded
with breastworks and rifle pits. The Kansas militia were present in force.
Rosecrans, expecting Price to flee into Arkansas after the clash along the
Big Blue, directed A. J. Smith to turn southwest from Lexington toward
Lone Jack, twenty-five miles away. Here Smith would be in position to
make fast work of the rebels reeling southward from Kansas City.

The federal line on the Big Blue failed to hold, for Shelby breached it
on October 22. Leaving Shelby to hold the fords of the Blue against Pleasonton, Price hurried on in pursuit of Curtis. On Sunday, October 23, the
victor of Pea Ridge turned to confront the hero of Lexington, and the battle of Westport flamed along the south side of Kansas City. Outnumbered
two to one, Price was disastrously beaten in fighting that saw the destruction of Marmaduke's division and a frantic rebel retreat down roads leading to Hickman Mills, Harrisonville, and "points south."

Fortunately for Price, A. J. Smith was not waiting at Lone Jack to spring his lethal ambush. Pleasonton, while wrecking Marmaduke, had persuaded Rosecrans that Price's "whole army" was still facing him. With great misgivings, Rosecrans deflected Smith to Pleasonton's "rescue." Price owed his salvation—such as it was—to the fact that Smith's force had been diverted to a sector where the least use could be made of it.

While Union horsemen harried the Confederates to the south, there was nothing left for Smith but to concentrate around Harrisonville on October 25 and 26 and wait for orders. By now he knew he had with him what remained of the old XVI Corps. Hurlbut, after inactivating corps headquarters, had gone to New Orleans to head the Department of the Gulf, and the two divisions in Georgia had transferred to XVII Corps. And it looked as if Smith's troops might find themselves "down South" again. "You will probably go to Sherman," Rosecrans wired Smith from Warrensburg on October 28. "Grant wishes it." Verily it seemed to Smith that his orphan divisions were latter-day lost tribes of Israel—so extensive had their wanderings become. "The river is too low to transport you," Rosecrans telegraphed. "The railroad has not enough capacity." Well, the lost tribesmen could read that message loud and clear—they would have to *walk back* to St. Louis.

David Moore was uncommonly busy. There was mustering to do, and Colonel Shaw was preparing to shed his uniform and turn the Third Division over to Moore. In addition, Ed Moore's resumption of the regimental command, occuring at Jefferson City October 13, struck the Old Man as a trifle tardy, since Ed had left for Canton a month before on "ten days' leave." At Harrisonville, on October 28, the lieutenant colonel went before a court-martial and pleaded guilty to absence without leave. The court convicted him but attached "no blame or penalty."

Shaw departed for civilian life, bequeathing a problem to his successor. There were complaints from citizens of the Harrisonville vicinity over "depredations" committed by Third Division lads against livestock, liquor, and groceries belonging to local folk. Moore, fed up with civilian grievances, was almost grateful when Smith told him to move the division to Pleasant Hill, a lovely little village a dozen miles to the north.

General Smith rode up from Harrisonville at 3:00 A.M. on October 31 with word that XVI Corps would "sweep the country east and north" from Pleasant Hill on its way downstate. Other forces would be working the north bank of the Missouri. The Third Division's northeastward advance—through Jackson, Saline, and Lafayette counties—would pass through rich and loamy farmlands interspersed with numerous small tributaries of the Missouri. There were broad patches of brush and, along the creeks, abundant stands of ash, elms, black walnuts, hickories, and several varieties of oak. Here and there were hills and knobs offering magnificent views of the countryside.

Here was a region where terror and counterterror had been the rule for years. Rosecrans wanted thorough work done on rebel guerrillas as the hour approached for their disappearance into history books and folklore. Passions were running high in Union ranks because of the Centralia massacre, but fresh spasms of outrage greeted the revelation on October 26 that Major James Wilson and six of his Third Missouri State Militia cavalrymen had been wantonly slain fifteen miles southwest of Washington, Missouri. Wilson's party, captured at Pilot Knob, had been turned over to a local guerrilla leader. That worthy patriot, whom General Ewing accused of subjecting his prisoners "to every indignity which malignant cowardice could invent," gunned down the prisoners beside a state road and left their bodies to a drove of hogs. Rosecrans' chief of staff instructed field commanders to "hang every secesh soldier you catch in Federal uniform by military commission or drum-head."

The rebels were also collecting martyrs. Rosecrans executed six prisoners in reprisal for the Wilson affair on October 29 and was about to shoot a major when Lincoln stopped him. George Todd was killed by federal marksmanship at Independence on October 22, and Bloody Bill was cut down by militiamen five days later in Ray County, just across the river from the scene of the recent heavy fighting. "Smith's guerrillas" should have realized that the area swarmed with killers vowing revenge.

Just before noon October 31, the Twenty-first Missouri left Pleasant Hill. It was a clear and crisp Monday, and the leaves were largely gone from timber along the way. The boys were still brigaded with the same outfits, except that the 122d Illinois had gone. That night, after an eighteen-mile hike, the brigade camped along a creek near Oak Grove, in eastern Jackson County. On this march, near Lone Jack, Corporal John W. Frazier of Company H disappeared. Captain Shafer learned afterward that Frazier had fallen into enemy hands.

Tuesday, a day of unforgettable horrors, the Missourians left camp at 7:00 A.M. and proceeded northeast. After a twelve-hour march, they camped on the south edge of Lexington but with great uneasiness pervading the ranks. Four boys of Company H were missing. They were Marion Washburn, John H. Bishop, John L. Jones, and Eli Black—all of whom had gone into the home guards with Peter Washburn at Fairmont.

It seemed certain that guerrillas had caught them: George Washburn
would have known if his brother and their friends had skipped out for
home. The captives' fate was a mystery for months, but their comrades
half-knew it from the beginning. That very evening, the Eighty-ninth
Indiana lost its major, quartermaster, and assistant surgeon when a murderous crew in blue uniforms "arrested" them as "stragglers" at Greenton,
between Lone Jack and Lexington, led them to a thicket and callously
snuffed out their lives. Starr heard that the victims had been "shot through
the head with pistols so near that their hair was burned with powder."
The guerrillas were "killing all they catch," he wrote Miss Ettie, and "whenever a man straggles . . . he is no longer." The tentative conclusion he drew
from these atrocities was that "we shall be obliged to exterminate the
whole party in Missouri."

Glasgow, on the north bank of the Missouri sixty miles below Lexington, was at this time garrisoned by Kutzner's infantrymen. Moore's
troops arrived on November 5, a Saturday, and completed ferrying across
to go into camp there. The last couple of days' march had been a dreary
time. Before daybreak Friday, the snow had begun, Starr recalled, "and
continued nearly all day and got just as cold as was necessary. If ever I
wished I was at home it was then."

Colonel Moore was late getting to bed. He and Comstock had a pile of
work because of Smith's instructions to prepare requisitions "for everything needed . . . for another campaign in the field." Laden with requisitions, muster rolls, and payrolls, Comstock left on Sunday for St. Louis,
where General Smith was expected shortly.

Comstock was also going on a mission to General Gray, but for an entirely different purpose. Moore was fretting over the declining strength of
his favorite regiment, down to 795 men "present and absent" at the recent muster. "I do not wish to fatigue you on this subject," Moore wrote
the adjutant general, "but I am very ancious to keep up the orgination of
the Reg. It is now the best Reg at least in numbers in the Div perhaps the
largest Infantry Reg in the State, and from its long service and afficiency
I trust you will consider its claims as being amongst the first with Mo.
Troops—and that it will merit your Ernest attention."

Moore's division moved on to Fayette, ten miles to the southeast, on
November 7. Surgeon Knickerbocker was particularly pleased to visit this
seat of Howard County, where he had practiced before the war. On August
5, Euphratis Major Knickerbocker had been delivered of a daughter, Bessie,
and the Majors' Yankee son-in-law had good reason to lay aside partisan
considerations and rejoin the family circle.

Yet, this was probably the worst of times for a "mixed family" reunion. Election eve! Each company commander had his poll books and when Tuesday dawned the judges and clerks were ready everywhere. While the Third Division balloted in Fayette, the First Division was voting in camps along the Osage River a dozen miles to the east of Jefferson City.

Now came the deluge the Conservative-Unionists had dreaded. Voting 472-2 for Lincoln, the Twenty-first Missouri played its predictable role in this historic turning point. Votes elsewhere down the ticket followed the same tendency but not so nearly unanimous as the blackballing of "Little Mac." Sweeping into office were Colonel Fletcher, the state's first Republican governor; a Republican general assembly; and a strongly Radical constitutional convention. William Bishop won the distinction of becoming the first Republican state treasurer. In Scotland County, James Best drove Wilson Harle from the sheriff's office, and Major Fulton gave similar treatment to a Conservative rival in Knox County. And from Waterloo came word that John Cox had overwhelmed "my Copperhead opponent" for a seat in the State Senate.

At the war's outbreak in Clark County, "there were nine rebels to one Union man," Cox explained to Editor Howell. "We have made this change by taking the rebellion where 'Cale took the hen'; by treating rebels as rebels deserved, and by allowing nothing to exist which existed solely to destroy the Government." Senator Cox would arrive in Jefferson City with unblemished Radical credentials.

Despite David Moore's general order of November 6 putting the division on "good behavior" and forbidding straggling, incidents of violence and vandalism against civilians multiplied. Indeed, such deportment was probably unavoidable after the guerrilla atrocities and physical exertions recently endured. This area was in Missouri's little Dixie, where saviors of the Union could expect restrained gratitude. Furthermore, shoes and clothing were rapidly playing out, and bad roads and bad weather aggravated tempers. Colonel Moore tried to alleviate matters by arranging for Captain Charles Tracy to take about 150 barefooted lads by rail to St. Charles.

The division halted at Warrenton, eighty miles east of Fayette, on November 15. This was still fifty miles short of St. Louis, but on this day Woods' division reached Benton Barracks, its arduous campaign in Missouri done. During the evening, while the officers attended a ball, several enlisted men took off for home. Company E was the big loser, as Corporal William McKinney and Privates James Johnson, William Broyles, Jasper Booker, William Burk, John Sexton, and John W. Trunnell slipped away to their Knox County homes.

Dave Moore's arrival at Warrenton in the early afternoon of November 15 coincided with a telegraph from General Smith. Moore was to "march your command to Saint Louis as rapidly as possible, via Saint Charles, at which point you will find boats to cross the river." Responding at once, Moore assured Smith his troops would be in St. Charles in two days: "Our rations will hold out."

True to his word, he pushed the division to Camp Gamble, the notorious "Camp Jackson" of 1861, on schedule. The Old Man by now was as cranky as a setting hen, as his Special Orders 103 of November 20 made abundantly clear. Since, he huffily proclaimed, "troops of this command are committing nearly every species of crime, including murder, robbery, assault and battery, destruction of private property of peaceful citizens, . . . it is hereby ordered that every enlisted man of this command be kept in camp."

Preying on his mind was a shocking incident that had taken place the previous day. An officer sent by the city provost marshal arrived at Camp Gamble to report the arrest of two soldiers of Company C. Abram Purvis and Ephraim Richardson, farm boys from Scotland County, were charged with murdering Dominick Patton, a farmer in the Bridgeton community at the northwest edge of St. Louis. Anguish generated by this deed spread to parents of young Purvis and to Thomas McAllister, who had taken the Hoosier-born Richardson as an orphaned infant and reared him.

Civilians had noticed on Thursday evening, November 17, two soldiers standing by the road at the village of Cote Brilliante. Armed with muskets, they were said to be halting every wagon that came by and extorting a half-dollar at gunpoint. Some drivers paid; some whipped up their teams and sped recklessly past. Patton, however, apparently stopped to scold the miscreants. Both soldiers attempted to fire; only one gun went off, but its minié ball punctured Patton's lungs and liver. The soldiers took to their heels, but a local farmer named Joseph Haberstroh made up his mind to arrest them. Seizing a revolver and cavalry saber, he sprang to horse and galloped after the culprits. Within an hour, the indignant German had them standing in front of the district provost marshal.

Frau Albertina Flasbach, Haberstroh's sister, had meanwhile run to Patton's aid. The victim "showed me where he was shot in the side," she said. "His arm was bleeding also." Then, still holding the reins, he collapsed. The team broke into a run and kept going until someone stopped it at the Six Mile House and carried Patton inside. Ironically, it was here the young stragglers had been seen drinking rather heavily before their encounter with Patton. By 9:00 P.M. Patton had died, and the provost marshal felt obliged

to conclude that Purvis and Richardson"did wilfully, maliciously and felon-
iously, and with malice aforethought, assault one Dominick Patton . . . with
a gun loaded with gunpowder and leaden bullets, and did, then and there . . .
shoot to death, kill and murder him, the said Dominick Patton."

A Conservative reporter, studying the lads at their conviction on December 8, pronounced them "fine specimens" of young manhood: "Both of
the boys are remarkably open-faced, free-spoken, and prepossessing, and it
is difficult to conceive them guilty of the dastardly crime of which they
have been convicted, but the jury of a military commission would hardly
convict them of the offence without very pointed testimony. The many
murderous outrages committed during the past year have rendered it necessary that examples of the perpetrators should be made and if they are
guilty let them suffer." This attitude curiously echoed the remarks of a
Radical observer who anticipated that hanging the two would "have a
good effect on their comrades."

On that dreary Thursday, the court's president, Captain Alexander
Windmueller of the Forty-first Missouri Infantry, pronounced Richardson
and Purvis guilty as charged and ordered them hanged at the St. Louis
county jail at such time as the military authorities should direct. The reviewing process was not lengthy, for no mercy from David Moore or from
Major General Grenville M. Dodge, who had replaced Rosecrans, was
forthcoming.

A crowd of curious civilians and militiamen, visibly moved by Purvis'
boyish appearance, saw him led from his cell at 10:30 that Friday morning, January 13, 1865. Father P. J. Gleason of the St. Louis Cathedral,
who had baptized the youth the previous day, accompanied him. Grieving Philip and Matilda Purvis understandably declined to come in from
Scotland County's Bible Grove community to witness their son's hanging.
Abe "appeared greatly agitated and trembled violently," a reporter noted.
"Father [Gleason] assisted him in ascending the steps of the scaffold,
and on reaching the platform, knelt down with him and offered up a
prayer." As they rose, a somber Lieutenant Colonel Gustav Heinrichs,
superintendent of military prisons, read aloud the findings of the court
and the order for execution. Asked for a final statement, the poor soldier
could only say, "I am innocent of it myself. I am willing to die. I die as
a Christian." Now the executioners stepped forward to place the traditional white cape over his head and adjust the noose to his neck. Father
Gleason continued his exhortations and instructions, and Abe was heard
to murmur repeatedly: "Jesus, receive my soul! Jesus, have mercy on me!"
Then, fifteen minutes after emerging from his cell, he plunged into eternity.

It was 11:20 when Richardson came forth to his terrible moment on that platform. Father Gleason alone was here to console him, for he had no close kin. Heinrichs repeated the notification ceremony, to which the youth glumly responded: "I am ready to die." The trap door opened, and Ephraim Richardson began one last struggle with his mortality. At high noon, the ritual over, a detachment of militiamen marched out, bearing the two Scotland County soldiers to the Jefferson Barracks cemetery. The procession clattered almost unnoticed through the streets of a metropolis preparing the morrow's mammoth celebration of emancipation in Missouri. The solemn Jesuit bade farewell to the boys among graves of hundreds more who would never see the dawn of peace in this ravaged land.

At Camp Gamble, the corps was about ready for duty in the Army of the Cumberland. Indeed, Thomas wired Smith on November 19 to start for Nashville "as soon as possible." Next, there came the paymasters, to the relief of those who had suffered most from the cold since arriving in camp. Ed Moore was beside himself over the shortage of firewood in the barracks and the "poor prospect of obtaining any." He also wanted "somebody . . . held responsible for the neglect" not only of men but of animals, since the horses and mules had gone a day and a half without feed after arriving. However, the regiment would be leaving before any "proceedings" could begin.

Adding to the lieutenant colonel's unhappiness was the loss of valued officers and men. Nelson and Starkweather, their resignations approved at Memphis, "went up the river as citizens," Russell said on November 10. Election results in Knox County forced Major Fulton to hand in his resignation. Scheduled to be left in St. Louis to muster out were Lieutenants George Stine of I and Jeremy Hall of B. Private Charles Murrow, who had joined in January, died of dysentery at his Millport home on November 11. On the anniversary of his muster in, a receipt for his effects was mailed from Millport bearing the grief-ridden father's familiar signature: "Nicholas W. Murrow."

When Edwin Moore filed his complaint about forage and firewood, he also gave headquarters his reaction to the latest bombshell from General Gray. Plans were afoot to consolidate Moore's regiment with the Twenty-fourth Missouri. The latter outfit would soon be dissolving, having failed to "veteranize." To the lieutenant colonel of the Twenty-first Missouri, this would be his opportunity to depart. "I have been in the service as an officer since the 2nd May 1861," he pointed out, "and am therefore entitled to a discharge." Moreover, there were several officers in the regiment "worthy of promotion."

THE FRANKLIN ~ NASHVILLE CAMPAIGN

NOVEMBER ~ DECEMBER, 1864

There was nothing routine in those orders summoning Smith to Nashville. The Army of the Cumberland was precariously situated. Leaving Thomas with fifty thousand troops to guard his rear against the marauding Hood, Sherman had started across Georgia with more than sixty thousand, pillaging and burning a fifty-mile-wide swath from Atlanta to the coast. If the boys under Sherman stormed east with only token resistance, such was not the case with Thomas. The rambunctious Hood crossed into central Tennessee around Pulaski and Lawrenceburg on November 20, moving north with about forty thousand veterans. Elements of the IV and XXIII Corps under Schofield were first to engage Hood's Army of Tennessee, at Spring Hill on November 29. With luck and nerve, Schofield extricated his smaller force from a planned entrapment and retreated to a position along the Harpeth River at Franklin. Stung by the fiasco of Spring Hill, the rebel

chief hurled his columns at Schofield's lines on November 30. The entrenched Yankees decimated Hood's ill-used army that afternoon, and a
dozen generals in gray were among the six thousand casualties.

What was Hood to do now? Hopes for a Confederate foray into
Kentucky were glimmering, as Thomas dug in around Nashville with a
superiority of numbers and firepower that Hood dared not ignore. To
attack Thomas here was stark, staring insanity, even to John Bell Hood.
But should he bypass Thomas? The Rock of Chickamauga would surely
overwhelm him from the rear. Might Hood withdraw to Alabama? That
would surely entail dissolution of his army, as disgruntled soldiers voted
"no confidence" with their feet. It remained for the rebel host to sit
tight in their lines, hoping for Thomas to make a mistake. For that, the
graycoats had already waited a long time.

In the eastern theater, the siege of Petersburg dragged on. The major
actions that autumn occurred mainly in the valley of Virginia, where
Major General Jubal A. Early gave the Yankees a hard time until Grant
sent Major General Philip H. Sheridan after him. Early now met his
match, suffering reverses at Winchester and Fisher's Hill during September—and then meeting with final disaster at Cedar Creek in October.
Lee's army would have to do without the forage, fruits, and vegetables
of the valley.

On November 24, two dozen transports gathered on the St. Louis
waterfront to carry XVI Corps to Nashville. Dave Moore, aboard the
Wananita, would take the Third Division. General McArthur, of whom
the Twenty-first Missouri had heard little since second Corinth, was now
heading the First Division. The route of the corps would be down the
Mississippi to Cairo, up the Ohio to the mouth of the Cumberland, and
up the latter stream to Nashville. The Twenty-first Missouri, Ed Moore
learned, was to board the *Mars* the morning of November 25, a Friday.

John S. Goodwin, a thirty-four-year-old private of Company A,
missed the trip to Nashville. James Howard, living at the corner of
Lesperance and Grand Avenues, procured his arrest the afternoon of
November 24. The charge was horse stealing, and for this the soldier
was lodged in the St. Louis county jail. In vain did he insist that Private Jacob Burgett of Company C, Fifty-eighth Illinois, had turned the
"brown medium sized horse" over to him to dispose of, it being understood Burgett would pay a commission. That some third party might
own the horse apparently never occurred to Goodwin. Nor did this
lapse in judgment favorably impress the grand jury that indicted Goodwin for grand larceny.

13

Nashville

Tennessee's capital, shivering with chills of early winter on the south bank of the Cumberland, was a bustling city under siege when A. J. Smith's transports arrived at the end of November. George H. Thomas, Rock of Chickamauga, was grimly pulling together a force to deflect Hood's drive toward the Ohio. Troops were working around the clock digging a ring of entrenchments guarding the outskirts of Nashville from the river's bank on the west to its bank east of town. Manning the inner lines was the garrison of Nashville.

Nine pike roads fanned out from Nashville's side of the Cumberland, and Thomas was posting forces to cover them. Brigadier General Thomas J. Wood's IV Corps watched to the south, Schofield's XXIII to the southeast. Outlying garrisons welded into a "Provisional Division" under Brigadier General James B. Steedman marched in from Chattanooga to take up a line along the river from which they could guard the Lebanon and Murfreesboro pikes to the east.

The XVI Corps flotilla appeared along the levee around 4:00 A.M. on November 30. One of the first veterans off the boats was heard to proclaim that "We're A. J. Smith's guerillas. . . . We've been to Vicksburg, Red River, Missouri, and about everywhere else . . . and now we're going to Hades if old A. J. orders us." That evening, when Smith reported to the St. Cloud Hotel, Thomas "literally took Smith into his arms and hugged him, for he now felt absolutely sure of coping with Hood." Thomas gave XVI Corps his right flank, a three-mile line anchored on the river west of town and running south toward the Hillsboro Pike. The Twenty-first Missouri soon found itself, according to its historians, two miles southwest of the city and throwing up breastworks "to assist in repelling the attack of . . . Hood, which was hourly expected." Edwin Jones recorded that his outfit "was called into line of battle about 4 P.M. [December 2] and marched up a hill and built breastworks until 10 P.M. and layed in line of battle all night."

Little transpired on the regiment's front for nearly two weeks, but a great deal went on behind the line. There were 566 men present with the regiment as it took up its positions; 217 more were absent. Russell was among those absent with authority, but he would be mustering out at Memphis before he could rejoin. Mike Cashman missed the boat in St. Louis out of a desire to spend Christmas with the family in Quincy— and he would not be back until the holidays were past. A number of homefolks joined the regiment, however. Among them was Emily Cole Roberts, big with child, who came by boat to join Doc at his downtown lodgings.

Gains and losses came during the first days at Nashville. Nearly a hundred men of the Twenty-fourth Missouri joined the Twenty-first Missouri by attachment. As soon as state officials could get to it, they would formally muster the newcomers into the Twenty-first. And reinforcements were urgently needed, for on December 5 it was necessary to muster out 76 men, representing all companies save A and K. Among the "1861" boys departing were Philarmon Reynolds, Patterson Harper, Dave Justice, Eli Kenoyer, and William French. Harlan, still on detached service at Memphis, had to be notified by wire that he was once again a citizen.

It was not given to all to live happily ever after. John Herron, a middle-aged soldier of Company B, died of smallpox in St. Louis on December 9. He was of that gallant band who had sprung to arms with Joe Story back in that terrible first summer of hostilities. Ailing for two months, Herron had been left behind at Gray Summit. A similarly tragic end came to Hoosier-born Private Levi Bledsoe of Company E, who died at his parents' farm back in Knox County on November 26. Andrew Jackson Bledsoe and his wife Polly buried their son within sight of his home, and there Levi and his "folks" wait on the Lord a century later. In such obscurity and isolation did he pass away that not even the cause of his death is known.

Jack Trunnell, who had taken French leave at Warrenton in November, found it more difficult to get back to Company E than to leave it. A young friend from home, John Parrish, was in a general hospital at Memphis, Tennessee, and Trunnell stopped by to see if he was ready to come along. Parrish released himself from the hospital, and together they set out for Nashville. They got as far as Cumberland City, fifty miles short of their destination, but a party of Forrest's raiders took them into custody on December 9. Soon they were "paroled deserters" stuck at Benton Barracks with much to untangle.

Corporal Wilbur Davis of Company G was accidentally shot in the left side while on picket duty during the sleet and snow storm that broke over Nashville December 9. Surgeon Knickerbocker feared inflammation of the right lung, and he was right. Davis lingered on ten days before his death. Captain Charles Tracy saw that the $103 found in Wilbur's belongings went to his widowed mother back in Fairmont. George Washburn mourned a close comrade and continued fretting over the chilling silence about Marion and the Fairmont boys who had mysteriously vanished in western Missouri.

On December 8, David Moore settled a matter that had slipped the minds of nearly everyone in the Third Division. Those citizens of Harrisonville who had complained about the vandalism and pilfering of Moore's troops, now got their justice. Their claims, as "D. Moore" adjudicated them, came to $5,144, and the colonel would pay off by laying a stoppage of one dollar against every officer and man shown by the rolls to have been present for duty on October 31, 1864.

This was Moore's last act as a division commander. That very day Brigadier General Kenner Garrard arrived to supersede him. The thirty-seven-year-old West Pointer had lately headed a division in Major General James H. Wilson's cavalry corps under Thomas, and in 1863 had been the United States Army's chief of cavalry. Garrard's arrival, in fact, heralded a thorough reshuffling of Smith's corps. Now it would be known as the "Detachment Army of the Tennessee," preserving a legal connection with that army now battering at Savannah. McArthur remained at the helm of the First Division, Garrard's command was redesignated the Second Division, and a new Third Division came into being under the temporary command of Colonel Jonathan B. Moore of the Thirty-third Wisconsin. At Garrard's suggestion, Dave Moore took over his First Brigade, Kinney stepping down to his 119th Illinois.

On December 13, the army suddenly forgave Buel Stevens, Alex Rogers, and Bill O'Connor for their roles in the July mutiny. The District of West Tennessee ordered them restored to duty because of "the mitigating circumstances in these cases, and of their former good conduct." Captain McGonigle would soon bestow upon O'Connor those sergeant's chevrons the court had shorn from him. All three were anxious to muster out, but the confinement at Alton, being "bad time," delayed their freedom by more than three months.

There came notable changes at regimental headquarters on December 11, when Sergeant Major Amburn's commission as first lieutenant of Company A arrived. Yust, for the first time since Gloeser's resignation eight months before, had a lieutenant. Sergeant Greenberry Jones, a thirty-three-year-old Ohio native from the Luray community, came up from Company D to become sergeant major. With his father Robert and younger brothers Chesley and John he had gone into Wooley's company of home guards. But now he and Ches alone remained, for their father had been discharged for "age and debility," and John was in the party missing in Lafayette County, Missouri, since November.

In the armed camp of Nashville, few doubted Hood was coming. As early as December 2, Johnnies were visible west of Smith's works, and one of his batteries cut loose at the distant enemy—only to find him beyond range, "which respectful distance," Smith noted, "was retained throughout the siege, with the exception of an occasional picket-post or reconnoitering party." Three days later Edwin Jones recorded "heavy *cannonading*," from one field battery and two forts—and a "cavalry fight in plain view and in front of us."

The *Louisville Courier*, devoted to the Union but chagrined over McClellan's sad fate, snarled at Hood's army. Suspecting the rebels would be heading for Kentucky, the editor expressed doubt they would get past the Cumberland. After hearing that Breckinridge would make a diversionary raid into eastern Tennessee, the *Courier* dared "Hood and Breckinridge [to] make the attempt, and we promise them that General Thomas will annihilate both their armies."

Grant, however, was beside himself. Hood was sitting motionless outside Nashville, but Thomas was displaying no signs of assaulting him. Grant simply could not understand why Thomas would not hurl his battle-hardened legions on that rickety little army to overwhelm it. Thrice in nine days, Grant had wired firm orders for an attack "at once." Secretary Stanton prophesied that "Gabriel will be blowing his horn" before George H. Thomas ever moved.

The Rock of Chickamauga, on the contrary, neither feared the Confederates' escape nor intended to move on their works until his cavalry was ready. Nearly a thousand of Wilson's troopers lacked horses, for Sherman had stripped the command to mount the cavalry accompanying him to the sea. Wilson was "requisitioning" animals throughout the region, but this took time. Finally, on the night of December 8, Thomas thought the moment had come.

The next morning, however, freezing rain fell. "It snowed and sleeted about two inches deep," Ed Jones said. The temperature fell below zero, and stately gum trees along the Cumberland began falling victims to Union axmen in search of firewood. Upon hearing of this, Grant

shelved plans to dismiss Thomas. Two days later, however, he reiter-
ated the order to attack. Even then the area was, in Thomas' words,
"covered with a perfect sheet of ice and sleet."

As the weather moderated, it became clear that Hood's evil day was
near at hand. Late the afternoon of December 14, the principal commanders assembled at the St. Cloud. Smith, having come with Sherman's
endorsement as one who "fights all the time," got the leading role—destruction of the Confederate left along the Hillsboro Pike between Sugar
Tree and Richland creeks. This thrust should jolt Hood out of his positions. Wilson's cavalry would keep rebel horsemen off Smith's back and
be available to charge into Hood's rear area. Wood's IV Corps, standing
to Smith's left, would engage the enemy on Montgomery hill between
the Hillsboro and Granny White pikes. Behind Smith there would be
Schofield's corps, while Steedman's troops east of the city were to provide sufficient diversion to occupy the energies of Lieutenant General
Benjamin F. Cheatham, guarding the Confederate right along the No-
lensville Pike and the Nashville & Chattanooga Railroad.

December 15 began as a clammy and foggy Thursday, and morning
was well along before clearing came. Ed Jones wrote that the Twenty-
first Missouri "marched over our breastworks and advanced on the rebels" soon after 7 o'clock. Smith's troops forming in columns of regiments, Garrard placed Moore's First Brigade in the center of his line,
the Second to the left, and Third to the right. Then, at 9:00, Smith's
line of battle being ready, he ordered the advance. With heavy skirmish
lines preceding, he wheeled his veteran brigades toward the south and
east, crossed the Hardin Pike, and re-formed along the ravines emptying
into Sugar Tree and Richland creeks.

The Johnnies were still there, A. P. Stewart holding their left (facing
Smith to the west and Wood to the north), Stephen Lee the center, and
Cheatham the right. As Smith's line neared Stewart's trenches, enemy
skirmishers and cannoneers grew more active. The Twenty-first Missouri, at Dave Morre's instruction, brought up the rear of First Brigade.
And, as Ed Moore later sadly reported, it was the Missourians' lot to
spend the day merely "executing the movements of the brigade." Mc-
Arthur's division moved out onto the Charlotte Pike, with Wilson's
cavalry herding Chalmers' horsemen out of the way, and veered south
off the pike to come into line on Garrard's right. The Third Division
started the day in reserve but finished it in Schofield's sector.

Since Stewart had a battery of "Napoleons" on hills overlooking tributaries of Sugar Tree Creek, Smith trundled out four of his own bat-

teries to silence them. His barrage lasted well into the afternoon, with Hood's guns frequently responding and the rugged westerners huddling in ravines for safety. Late in the morning, McArthur, facing the rebels' hilltop fort, attacked it in a column of brigades and "the work was carried at a run," in Smith's words. General Hatch, present with a cavalry division, swept around the position to the south and helped to unhinge it. All six of the defending guns were captured.

Simultaneously with this movement, Wood charged south across Smith's front, overrunning enemy fortifications but also "crowding out" Garrard's First and Second Brigades. Thomas decided that Smith had "obliqued" more to the left than he should have, whereas A. J. had carried out orders to maintain contact with Wood's right. Since Thomas now felt the line should extend more to his right, he suspended forward movements until Schofield could march his corps around to Smith's right. And this took a good part of the afternoon.

Action intensified after 4 o'clock, with a general advance on the battered survivors of Franklin. "I would like to tell you how I felt if I could," Morrey wrote his brother back in Ohio "but I cannot: nothing like fear, though eager to see all that was going on and waiting for the order to [go] forward. . . . Then arose the awfulest shout from thirty or forty thousand men, you could not imagine it without hearing it!" Around 5 o'clock, the Johnnies everywhere broke for the rear and left the Yankees to bivouac where they stood. A Southern officer sorrowfully found his men "utterly lethargic and without interest in the battle. I never witnessed such want of enthusiasm, and began to fear for tomorrow."

Thick fog shrouding the area that night, Hood reconstructed his front along the Brentwood Hills, nearly two miles south of his original line. To the north of this front, which extended between "refused" flanks west of the Granny White Pike and along Overton's Hill east of the Franklin Pike, there lay a mile-wide stretch of relatively flat land, broken by creeks and ravines and consisting mostly of muddy old cornfields or freshly plowed ground. Cheatham switched over to Hood's left. anchored on a hill commanding the White Pike. This left Stewart in the Confederate center, facing north up the White Pike, and Lee now stood on the right. Forrest, away on a diversion ordered by Hood, was never more needed by his comrades. The new position, as a Southern historian said, was "even more precarious" than the line held at the onset of the struggle.

Thomas picked the ideal time to send Hood reeling back into the

Brentwood Hills. Grant was starting for Nashville to have it out with him and probably replace him with flamboyant John A. Logan. Grant had gotten as far as Washington when the sensational news arrived. He happily cancelled his trip. Congratulating Thomas for "your splendid success," the lieutenant general urged the taciturn Virginian to "push the enemy now, and give him no rest until he is entirely destroyed."

It was around 8 o'clock Friday morning when the federal move began. Groping through the murk to develop Hood's position, Smith found that as he approached the Granny White Pike he was moving perpendicularly across Hood's front. There seeming no percentage in that, he began pivoting on his right to face Stewart frontally. The caustic little dragoon had his problems. Since he had detached his Third Division to Schofield, who was fearful for his flank between Otter Creek and the Hillsboro Pike, Smith now held with two divisions a mile-long front from the base of a hill west of the White Pike to a ravine on the Bradford farm to the east. Maintaining contact with Wood was troublesome, as he did not advance with much energy. At first, Smith thought that Moore's brigade, on his left, ought to hold a refused position to maintain contact with IV Corps. Before long, however, the irate Smith told Garrard simply to place the Twenty-first Missouri in reserve behind Moore's exposed flank and trust it to handle any rebels trying to exploit the gap between Smith and Wood's laggards. The way Smith looked at it, there was work to be done up front, and he had little time to baby IV Corps along.

General Wood had his hands full on the left, where he and Steedman were encountering uncommon grief along the Franklin Pike. After heavy fighting, Lee stopped the Yankees cold. Meanwhile, to the west of the Franklin Pike, an artillery duel ranged on through much of the day. During the afternoon, as IV Corps brought its line up to a position more agreeable to Smith, the Twenty-first Missouri moved forward to guard the Ninth Indiana Battery. One of Stewart's officers, watching the contest from a knob where his corps headquarters was located, "could see the Capitol all day, and the churches. The yanks had three lines of battle everywhere I could see, and parks of artillery plaing upon us and raining shot and shell for eight mortal hours."

Particularly worrisome to Schofield and Smith was the Confederate defense of that hill overlooking the White Pike on Hood's left. Major General William Bate's division was perched up there, and it would surely take a strenuous effort to dislodge it. Smith's artillery gave the hill its attention, and around 3:00 P.M. John McArthur suggested that he could rush the position from the west and carry it. If so, that might finish off Hood. For this decisive moment, Thomas had labored for a fortnight.

With Smith and Schofield at his side, Thomas studied Bate's hilltop position through his field glasses. By now, the enemy line extended farther to the south of the hill than it had in the morning, since Hood had responded to the cavalry threats to his left and rear by switching troops from his right. The assault looked to Thomas like a job for Schofield, and at 4 o'clock he ordered XXIII Corps to come forward to administer the coup de grace.

It was around 4:15 when Schofield stormed Hood's flank, with Mc-Arthur's right brigade joining the effort by charging rebel entrenchments on what was known afterward as Shy's Hill. As Schofield's men awaited orders to advance, they began to yell, and the uproar spread across the entire front. Morrey recalled how "we stood with breath almost suspended after the shout died away. Then began the heaviest musketry and cannonading I ever heard. Directly afterward, the shout again commenced and the whole line rushed forward"—in a drizzling rain. There was no stopping the Yankee horde anywhere. The impulse to charge spread to Smith's front, and on to Wood's. One officer told A. J. Smith that "powder and lead were inadequate to resist such a charge."

One of Cheatham's soldiers, standing below Shy's Hill, saw Bate's men "rise like a flock of big birds and fairly fly down the hill." A rebel journalist thought Bate's retreat "the most patriotic service that could be rendered, as that saved the army." Hood, fearing historians as much as contemporaries, dolefully "beheld for the first and only time a Confederate Army abandon the field in confusion."

Thomas was not one to jump to premature conclusions about the scope of the day's victory. Sitting astride his horse and watching McArthur's men struggling along the enemy breastworks, he became perturbed. "General!" he barked at Smith, "What is the matter; are your men being captured?"

"Not by a damn sight," A. J. bristled. "My men are capturing *them,* these are rebel prisoners you see."

Lowering his glasses, Thomas began to laugh. Men did not see that very often. And his smiles broadened as aides continued dashing up to report details of the triumph from various sectors of this historic field. Cheatham's men had lost all cohesion when they found Wilson's troopers blocking the White Pike behind them. Artillery, wagons, baggage, and even rifles were flung aside in the panic. Stewart's corps also became a crazed mob in the flight to Franklin.

Hood's Army of Tennessee was now purely and simply debris—with 1,500 dead and wounded, 4,500 captured. Smith's share of the spoils included three dozen artillery pieces and the bulk of the prisoners. It fell to Moore's brigade to catch the biggest fish in the collection, when lads of the 119th Illinois and Eighty-ninth Indiana collared Major General Edward Johnson, a rotund fellow who realized that sitting on a horse made him an inviting target and had abandoned his mount. For the glorious outcome at Nashville, Union forces had suffered in casualties 387 dead, 2,562 wounded, and 112 missing. One man of the Twenty-first Missouri was among the wounded, Private Davis Goodwin of Company D, slightly nicked in the second day's fighting.

Thomas was a national hero again. Many stout fellows in his camps—George P. Washburn among them—would proudly name newborn sons for the surly Virginian who had resisted family pressures to stand with Old Glory in the hour of disunion. Surgeon Roberts was of a different turn of mind: when Emily gave birth to their son the week after the battle, to the certain disgust of his comrades Doc named the boy Edward *McClellan* Roberts.

Conformably to Grant's urging, Thomas took up pursuit at daybreak Saturday. A soldier-historian remembered that "we joined the movement south, over the Granny White Pike, seeking the retreating . . . enemy." Hood scraped together a small rear guard of infantry and cavalry, under Forrest, and Thomas conceded that this hard-pressed contingent was "undaunted and firm, and did its work bravely to the last."

"Some say the war is near over [and] some say it will never end," Starr wrote. Many "prisoners . . . had no shoes and the ground covered with snow, some were tired of fighting and some others declared they meant to fight to the last man." Indeed, one Alabama soldier in Lee's corps thought it "a touching scene to witness a thousand and more of our boys without shoes and leaving their bloody footprints on that cold and frozen ground." A veteran of the rear guard was reduced to footgear that "consisted of a pair of socks almost footless, and the uppers and soles of my shoes were tied together with strings."

The weather remained neutral, tormenting both sides. Heavy rains came, lasting for three days. John P. Morris remembered that "water dripped out of our knapsacks as we marched." It was getting on toward winter: Ed Jones recorded on December 21, as the brigade lay in camp along the Harpeth near Franklin, that it "snowed for a change." On this day, with snow pelting the miserable rebels, Hood crossed the Duck

River, thirty miles to the south. A Confederate thought that compared
to Hood's crossing of the ice-strewn Duck, "Washington's crossing of
the Delaware was insignificant." Four days later, the Johnnies were beyond the Tennessee and heading for Tupelo. There Hood turned over
his ruined army to Major General Richard Taylor and rode off to Richmond to deliver his alibi in person.

The bluecoats pressed onward, through Columbia, Lawrenceburg,
and Waynesboro to camp on the Tennessee at Clifton. This village was
only some thirty miles downstream from Pittsburg Landing and that
"dark and bloody ground" was still fresh in many Missourians' memories.
Arriving at Clifton January 2, Edwin Moore was wrestling with a thorny
problem. His regiment was "croupy" from dampness and icy weather,
and Adjutant Starr was on the verge of pneumonia. He was lodged in
a vacant house with Pressell and other quartermasters. The fireplace was
in use, making the patient tolerably comfortable, "but the fare is pretty
hard for a sick man," he observed. Amburn took over Starr's work for
the fortnight of his incapacitation.

Thomas, keeping up the pressure, ordered Smith up the river to Eastport, Mississippi, sixty miles northeast of Tupelo. On the morning of
January 3, Garrard loaded his division on transports and started them on
their way. The Twenty-first Missouri, boarding the *Norman* at noon, had
a long wait while other outfits got ready. Four days later, the boys went
into Smith's new encampment on the south bank of the Tennessee at
Eastport.

For a month, the regiment stayed here, finding life easier than on the
march out of Nashville. Brigadier General Thomas Kilby Smith, arriving
January 9 to take over the Third Division, found the weather "warm,
raining, muggy," the countryside "gravelly, the forests pine." In mid-
January fair weather returned, but a hard freeze soon came. Starr, Amburn, and Sergeant Major Jones shared a little log cabin. When it started
snowing on January 24, Nick wrote, "The snow came in the roof covering our bed and floor, the roof turns rain well but won't snow." The
others shared his feeling that "cold weather in Missouri is more pleasant
and less hard to bear than in [Mississippi] ."

Making evil weather harder to endure was a ration shortage. Even on
the march west of Pulaski, the boys had had fair warning to let up on
eating: "Rations are out of the question," Starr found. "Our men living on corn and beef. The corn they boil and make hominy of, but pretty hard fare." Fred Yust never wearied of telling friends and children
how he and his comrades lived nearly two weeks on "nothing but a pint

of corn a day. They cooked it in water and wood ashes and then divided it into three parts . . . for the next day."

Captain Puster was disturbed one day by what seemed at first a herd of whinnying horses outside his tent: it proved to be only Private Jim Griffin and his comrades. They explained to the puzzled little Bavarian that with all the corn they were eating they needed a little hay! It is unclear from Griffin's account that Puster fully appreciated such native-American wit. Blessed relief soon appeared. The fleet, off to Paducah for rations, returned to Eastport on January 26 to a wild ovation.

To harassed Edwin Moore, desperately wanting out of uniform, January was a long month. Before the first full day at Eastport was over, what seemed to Ed Jones like "one hundred drafted men" arrived. Actually, there were eighty-five, and Moore parceled them out fairly evenly. Gains came in other ways. Mike Cashman reappeared on January 15, fresh from that unauthorized vacation in Quincy. While the boys filled him in on what he had missed, Pearce asked the lieutenant colonel to overlook the youth's indiscretion. Lately "gone" a few days himself, Pearce was in no condition to point an accusing finger. Also, there bobbed up a half-forgotten face. Thomas A. Roseberry of Company E, William's older brother, had left the company a month after Shiloh. In the summer of 1863 he had departed Nathan Roseberry's Knox County farm to join the Tenth Kansas Infantry. His luck ran out, for the Tenth Kansas was now in the Second Brigade of Garrard's division— and it was certain somebody would spot him. The provost marshal brought him over on January 16. Shafer welcomed Roseberry back and urged Edwin Moore to do the same.

This just seemed no time to get tough with the old comrades. John Sam Hendricks, away since the mortal wounding of his brother at Shiloh, reported to duty of his own volition. He had long since managed to put his grief into perspective, and he was weary of dodging the provost marshals in Scotland County and at Quincy. And the regiment learned the fate of Marion Washburn and his companions. The post commander at Lexington wired news that citizens had lately discovered the bodies in a desolate and brushy hollow, north of Lone Jack, where their captors had executed them. The remains had been identified from stenciled names on shelter-halves found at the scene. Captain Charles Tracy removed from his rolls the names of Washburn, Johnny Jones, Jack Bishop, and Eli Black. George Washburn joined Israel Elican and Charles Blackstone in mourning the loss of comrades who with them had formed their eight-man mess back in early spring 1864. Now that

Wilbur Davis was in his grave at Nashville, more than half the old gang had vanished. Then, on top of all this, there came the word of Richardson's and Purvis' hangings.

In various other ways, the regiment lost staunch fellows during those weeks at Eastport. Jim Dye, of Company C, falling prisoner while working with the pioneer corps, found himself in the notorious Andersonville camp. Sad, too, was the death, from chronic dysentery, of Corporal George W. Emerson of K at his home near Barry, Illinois. Less than a week before word of Emerson's death reached Eastport, Captain Puster had issued orders making him first sergeant. Private John Tillett of Company I requested permission to go to Scotland County for "business matters requiring his personal attention." Best approved on January 26 and lived to curse the evil luck that made him do it. At daybreak the next day the steamer *Eclipse* exploded at Johnsonville, Tennessee. Most men of the Ninth Indiana Battery, on the way home to muster out, were killed or injured. Among the twenty-seven passengers lost was Tillett.

A. J. Smith, examining his subordinates' after-action reports on the Nashville operation, perceived a glaring omission. Garrard, while recommending promotion of brigade commanders, had overlooked one. "I desire," Smith wrote the Department of War, "to call the attention of the President to David Moore, colonel of the Twenty-First Missouri Veteran Volunteer Infantry, who in the commencement of the rebellion rallied around him the loyal men of North Missouri and drove from it the half-formed bands of rebels who were being organized there. . . . At the battle of Shiloh, Colonel Moore lost a leg, and ere he had fairly recovered he reported to his regiment for duty. . . . Knowing that Colonel Moore has done and suffered enough for the country to deserve it, I most earnestly recommend that he be at once promoted to brigadier general of volunteers."

Emotions were somewhat frayed by a proxy feud that broke out between the Colonels Moore in January. Exercising his de jure colonelcy of the regiment, Dave had dashed off from Nashville a short letter to General Gray on December 18 recommending Best for the major's vacancy: "Capt Best commands Co I of said Reg and is a good and afficiant officer." Unfortunately, Ed Moore preferred to take seniority into account. The senior eligible, Yust, ruled himself out because his "language is too broken and difficult to understand." Pearce, next in line, was chafing to get out of service. Third in line was Charles Tracy, whose date of rank was April 2, 1862. Best, however, was cherishing a technical seniority over Tracy and was pushing it for all it was worth.

Although his date of rank was eight weeks junior, Best had managed to get mustered as a captain before Tracy.

Such logic hardly impressed the lieutenant colonel. "I am fully satisfied you are wrong," he bluntly refuted Best. But the young Ulsterman would not let the matter drop. When a dress parade occurred on January 31, he refused to attend. Rather than line up Company I in a position inferior to Tracy's Company H, he preferred to sulk in his cabin. The lieutenant colonel promptly arrested him.

The next morning Best and the regimental commander laid their cases on the record. Explaining that his absence from formation implied "no disrespect to any officer" and entailed no intent of disobedience, Best petitioned for release. Moore, assuring the captain his behavior was "not in my estimation a very great breach of military discipline," informed him that had it not been for the squabble over relative rank "I should not have taken notice of it." Tracy held the trumps, he warned, "and if you take my advice you will not contest the matter and I will order your release."

Yet unbowed, Best responded that he was claiming only what was rightfully his and would abide by the "laws and orders governing the army of the United States." This, to Moore, was disappointingly oblique. "I cannot issue any order for your release untill you give a decision one way or the other," he insisted. "You are aware that it is very unpleasant for me to have a matter of such importance unsettled."

Realizing his hash was settled so far as *this* Colonel Moore was concerned, Joe capitulated. Tracy, however, did not have the last laugh. Upon getting wind of the fuss in its early stages, Dave Moore had fired off to Jefferson City a searing reminder that "the Col of a Reg should have the right at least to recommend for promotion in his own Reg." Seeing the point, Fletcher's new adjutant general, Colonel Samuel P. Simpson, hastily revoked the major's commission mailed to Tracy just before the arrival of Dave's letter.

News from home was often hilarious to the Missourians at Eastport. Senator John H. Cox was twisting Conservative tails. On January 19, he introduced a resolution urging Fletcher to "pardon all the military prisoners and soldiers now in the Penitentiary who are held as such by sentence of copperhead courts martial and treasonable civil authorities, for the trivial crime of killing rebels and bushwhackers." The "gentleman from Clark" produced a resolution instructing the congressional delegation to "vote for an amendment to the Federal Constitution, forever prohibiting slavery and securing to all men, without regard to race or color, absolute equality before the law." The first resolution lost, with more than a third of the senators absenting themselves. The second was such a hot potato that there were neither the votes to pass nor kill it, and the senators finally buried it in the judiciary committee.

During January, there came three first lieutenant's commissions, for Starr and two first sergeants, Jeremiah Hamilton of I and Bill Weaver of K. Two men made ready to assume the top sergeantcies being vacated. Carlton Shamp, original bugler of Company D, succeeded Weaver, while Henry Deems took over in Company I.

The time was approaching to merge with the Twenty-fourth Missouri. Of the 173 men still on that regiment's rolls, about a hundred were nearing the end of their enlistments. Much as he wanted even a smattering of reinforcements, Ed Moore concluded the price was too high. He wrote the Department of War on January 11, that consolidation would "give the Major of the 24th Mo. the same position in the 21st Mo. thereby depriving efficient and worthy officers of their rights." His proposal—disapproved—was to rescind orders to amalgamate.

On February 4, it happened—and 127 men of the defunct regiment joined their new outfit. An interesting lot they were. Major James J. Lyon, one of the two officers remaining, was a swarthy and stocky gentleman of twenty-eight, native to West Pembroke, New York. His ancestry went back to pre-Revolutionary Connecticut Lyons, as did that of the martyr-hero of Wilson's Creek. Dr. Owen H. Crandall, assistant surgeon, had gone to service as a private of the Elgin (Illinois) Light Artillery. The Twenty-first Missouri never saw much of him because A. J. Smith used him as an artillery surgeon. Two young cousins assigned to Company K were Green and Emanuel Keltner, scions of a prominent Tennessee family that had settled near Springfield, Missouri, in the 1840s and left an enduring imprint on the history of the western Ozarks. Curiously, given the soldierly inclinations of the Keltners, their family's origins went back to German Quakers of colonial Pennsylvania.

Orders came for the Detachment Army of the Tennessee to sail for New Orleans. With a "present and absent" strength of 875, Ed Moore loaded his regiment on the *Peerless* February 5. "All extra baggage must be disposed of," he had learned. There would be one wagon for regimental headquarters, one for "officers valises and mess boxes," and one for whatever enlisted men could not carry. Evidently there was "hot work" waiting on the Gulf Coast.

Three days later, the *Peerless* docked at Cairo, and the Twenty-first Missouri marched off to camp. Now came muster out of more nonvets.

Taking leave and heading for the long-neglected comforts of home were
129 old originals, whose memories reached back to Chewalla and Shiloh—
and in many cases to Lancaster, Clapp's Ford, or even Athens. Four
short-timers from the Twenty-fourth Missouri left also, after one week
in their new outfit. Chief among officers now departing was David Moore,
whose wishes to carry on ran afoul of a mustering officer. Numbers on
the rolls were well below the statutory minimum for mustering a full
colonel. So Moore bade his regiment goodbye, and with him went Edwin Moore, who could not have cared less what the law permitted in
such cases.

Among those going home were Captain Pearce and Lieutenant Frank
Whittemore. Russell, mustering out on February 8 at St. Louis, declared
to his diary: "I am a free man once more. Made final settlement with
U. S. Took train at 2 P.M. for Quincy, Ills." Others getting out were Sergeant Ed Jones of Company A; Sergeant Sam Cameron and Private Adolphus Singleton (H); Sergeants John Cunningham and Bill O'Connor and
Private Tim Holman (D); and Sergeant Mart Morton (F). Hardest hit
was Puster's Company K: Among its thirty-three brand-new civilians
were Henry Emry, August Klusmeier, William Smith, and Stephan Werly.

Dave Moore, Editor Barrett announced, had been "mustered out of
service and will enjoy a season of respite." Not for long. The old warhorse was soon in St. Louis talking with Colonel Simpson. It happened
that federal authorities were planning a few short-term regiments of
Missouri Volunteers and were looking for experienced colonels. With
his office at Hannibal, Dave set to work raising the Fifty-fifth Missouri
Infantry. The bottom of the barrel being well scraped, he failed. But
after consolidations of various partial organizations, he emerged as colonel of the Fifty-first, headquartered in St. Louis. During the summer
after the collapse of the rebellion, he was named commanding *general*
of the post of St. Louis—for he had received from the White House a
commission as brevet brigadier general. For a brief season, then, silver
stars belatedly adorned the shoulder straps of Wrightsville's merchant-
militant.

The fleet bearing Smith's detachment to New Orleans steamed away
from Cairo on February 9. Colonel John I. Rinaker of the 122d Illinois
assumed command of the First Brigade, and Major Lyon went with
Smith as "assistant inspector general." As a result, Best had to swallow
the bitter pill of serving in a regiment headed by Charles Tracy, much
as the latter was having to swallow his "vacated" major's commission.
The steamer *Brilliant* carried the regiment to Vicksburg, where the de-

tachment camped east of town on February 15. During the stay here, Tracy made one last strenuous bid to keep Lyon from flanking him in their three-way struggle with Best for the top rung. Tracy forwarded a letter to Simpson, unabashedly asking "that I be commissioned Lieut. Colonel of the 21st Mo. Infty. as such an appointment would be in accordance with the expressed wishes of the officers and men of the Command." Accompanying was a petition from Surgeons Roberts and Knickerbocker; Captains Davis, McGonigle, Shafer and Blackburn; and Lieutenants Harris, Hagle, Morrey, Weaver, Starr, Sinnott, Schram, Smith, and Allen. Best withheld his signature, as did Yust. Of course, Alex Tracy signed the petition for his brother's advancement, but the promoters should have spared themselves the effort.

The balmy mid-February weather at Vicksburg was welcome indeed. Starr described scenery "more romantic than war like" in his letters to Miss Ettie, speaking of wild magnolias and their copious foliage, the flourishing green grass carpeting the landscape, budding trees. Clearly Nick was close to mustering out, at least emotionally: "I dreampt last night that I had arrived safely at home mustered out of the army and arrived in Canton just in time to see you leave going somewhere on a visit. It being a dream the first night we camped in this place must be true, but whether indicative of my getting out of the army, or you going on a visit I cannot say. . . . I saw you wave your handkerchief on the boat as it left Canton. I want you to make your visit and get back when I do."

14

A Final Blooding

Trapped between Grant's forces in Virginia and Sherman's "vandals" storming across the Carolinas, the main armies of the Confederacy were at bay. Both Davis and Lincoln had relinquished direction of the war effort to their professionals, and Lee and Grant now faced each other as generals-in-chief of their respective armies. Columbia, South Carolina's "nest of secession," fell on February 17, suffering extensive fire damage. Johnston, summoned to command fragmentary forces still in the Carolinas, tried to arrest Sherman's progress at Bentonville, North Carolina, on March 19. This encounter simply proved there was no stopping the audacious redhead now.

During March, Lee tried without success to break Union lines menacing Richmond and Petersburg. Sheridan had joined Grant, and the Yankees numbered well over a hundred thousand. Against these, Lee could field little more than fifty thousand. His right flank gave way, and on April 2 the Johnnies abandoned Petersburg. A day later, Davis fled burning Richmond. The Army of Northern Virginia, facing starvation, lunged west in search of food supplies supposedly awaiting them at Amelia Court House, or Lynchburg, or Appomattox Court House.

Camp Chalmette—"five miles below New Orleans near the old battle-field of Jackson," as Morrey described it—became the latest stopping place for A. J. Smith's detachment on February 23. Company clerks in the Twenty-first Missouri calculated that since leaving Clifton the regiment had traveled by boat 1,882 miles.

Smith's command was in Hurlbut's Department of the Gulf, and it was shedding its connection with the Army of the Tennessee and forming a reactivated XVI Corps. McArthur's and Garrard's divisions were remaining as they were, but Brigadier General Eugene A. Carr was replacing T. K. Smith in the Third Division. The Twenty-first Missouri, under Tracy's command, would remain brigaded with the Eighty-ninth Indiana, and the 119th and 122d Illinois.

The corps was bound for General Canby's Military Division of West Mississippi, which had for its objective the reduction of Mobile, Alabama. Canby, a forty-eight-year-old Kentuckian, was becoming the army's clean-up man. In spring 1864, he had come to New Orleans to salvage Banks' expedition and convert it to new uses along the gulf. The year before, it had been his squalid luck to be commanding in New York City when the notorious draft riots occurred. Now he was to mop up Mobile, and for this he would have not only Smith's guerrillas but also Major General Gordon Granger's XIII Corps, an engineer brigade, and a siege train.

Kilmartin was at it again. On French leave to Wisconsin much of the past year, he now returned to duty. But duty, as he saw it, included a "Captain Harris" spree in the big city. This "Harris," however, fared even less well than his predecessor at Memphis a year earlier—and Kilmartin wound up in the grip of provost guards. A garrison court-martial lifted the fancy uniform and ten dollars of his next pay, but, thanks to his hospitalization, the happy-go-lucky musician mustered out in May without coming back to duty.

The bright lights were a little too much for Company G's Jake Glessner, a native Pennsylvanian whose service had begun with Roseberry's Home Guards. Hitting town at the first opportunity, Jake relieved his thirst a little too hastily. Provost guards hauled his inert form out of the elements, and a court-martial pronounced him guilty of "conduct prejudicial." The court gave him ten days of further confinement and ordered him saddled with a forty-pound knapsack four hours daily. When reviewing officers learned he was "required for duty in the field," Glessner escaped the punishment.

Starr wandered through the boisterous celebration of Lincoln's inaugural on March 4, admiring the parading fire companies and bands both civilian and martial, but the adjutant was disappointed at the lack of oratory. "Gen'l Hurlbut was to have made a speech," he related, "but I presume his friends and him had some good old wine which probably they thought better than to turn out in public." Starr had visited the city a week earlier, only to be repelled at the spectacle:

In New Orleans from an ancient habit long practiced here, but unpardonable in our northern cities, they celebrate an ancient Roman Custom on the 28th Feb. called Mar-de-Gras, in which the citizens mask themselves and all classes of society are thrown together promiscuously [sic] not knowing each other but all associate as old friends, prom-

enade, attend masquerades. . . . Some of the Federal officers and soldiers participated but the general feeling around the Army was disgust with their actions. I did not attend a Ball, nor wish to I was satisfied in seeing what I could on the streets and think masquerades in
a civilized country should cease. . . . But the French think them grand
and will follow their old habits. . . .

Like many of his comrades, Lieutenant Morrey was "tired and would
like to come home; but I take things as patiently as possible for there is
no use to fret. The better a man is satisfied, the less trouble he will have,
and I try to think of home as little as possible. A short time ago I got a
detail . . . to the Ambulance Corps . . . which I think I will like when I
get the run of things. I will have a horse to ride on the march and a man
to see to it for me, which will be easier than marching on foot; and a tent
to sleep in at night."

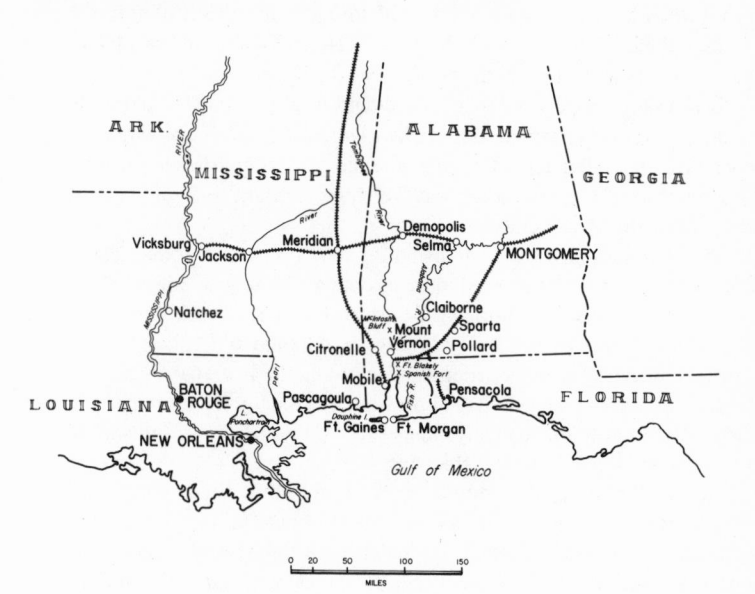

THE GULF COAST

1865 · 1866

Canby alerted Smith on February 27 for shipment to Dauphin Island, at the west side of the entrance to Mobile Bay. General Maury, commanding at Mobile, had ten thousand men, five gunboats, and artillery batteries with three hundred pieces. He was capable of a noisy defense, but Canby would move against him with forty-five thousand Yankees. Granger was at Fort Gaines, on the east side of the harbor entrance, with the XIII Corps and Grierson's cavalry.

On March 4 came Canby's order to load out for Dauphin Island. The following morning, McArthur's division embarked on the Pontchartrain side of town, and in the next few days, the other divisions followed. The Twenty-first Missouri moved out to the race track north of town to guard Smith's trains and wait for a boat. Life here, the Missourians learned, could be a trial. "The weather is warm and pleasant," Starr found, "but very frequently hard rain and the wind generally blows down a lot of our tents just when it commences raining." What the Missourians faced when their turn came to sail, a historian of the 119th Illinois pithily described: "This riding on the seas is disturbing to a well regulated stomach, but we heaved with the sea, and finally landed."

Besides Morrey, other officers were held to duty outside the regiment. A. J. Smith was in particular downright larcenous. Lyon, for whom he cherished an abiding regard, remained at corps headquarters as inspector general. Comstock, after a few days' duty as assistant to Lyon, became the corps adjutant general.

Starr had gotten wind of an intriguing development at home. The convention, flexing its Radical muscles, was about to pass a historic "ousting ordinance," authorizing Governor Fletcher to sack "disloyal" judges and county officials. David Wagner was talking up Starr for Lewis County clerk. Other friends were urging the lieutenant's case, and he admitted to his fiancee that "I do want to come home more particularly on your account than anything else." He was, however, unwilling to count unhatched political chickens.

General Smith, headquartered on Dauphin Island, directed the Twenty-first Missouri to "rejoin its division in the field near Mobile, leaving one company as a guard with the transportation of the division." Canby's quartermaster arranged for the 607-ton *Kate Dale* to call at Camp Chalmette on Wednesday, March 22. Ten years old, *Kate* had started the war as a Confederate river steamer, but the Yankees had captured her in 1863 and found her seaworthy. So would Tracy's Missourians, on that 160-mile voyage through the choppy gulf waters to Mobile Bay. Not quite everyone was able to make the trip, however. George Washburn and Israel Elican of Company H happened to be out doing the town, and it took them a week to catch up with the others. And Captain Davis' Company B, detailed to stay with the wagons, did not get up until mid-April.

The XVI Corps had gone into camp around Dannelly's Ferry, on the Fish River, a stream emptying into the bay from its east side. At the river's mouth, it was necessary to transfer to the *Reserve,* a smaller vessel that still scraped the bank at every bend. Mobile was thirty miles away to the northwest, but the Yankees, said Starr, were "thinking that taking Mobile or its adjacent forts will be a big job. The rebel gunboats keep up a constant firing but the guns from our skirmish line keep their Artillery still during the day." Weather in the piney woodlands east of the bay he found pleasant but "cooler than many March days I have seen in Missouri."

Two strongholds barred Canby's advance up the eastern shore of the Bay. Some eighteen miles northwest of Dannelly's Ferry stood Spanish Fort, a five-mile crescent of irregular bastions with a strong artillery concentration. Four miles farther up stood Fort Blakely, where additional stern resistance awaited. Canby would launch three mighty columns against the forts. Granger would move directly north along the shore from "Mobile Point" against Spanish Fort, while Smith approached from the southeast and General Steele's division of U.S. Colored Troops from the "Reserve Corps of the Gulf" undertook a rambling hundred-mile trek northwest from Pensacola to come in on Smith's right. Standing by to enter the twenty-seven-mile-long bay was a fleet of six ironclads and numerous wooden vessels under Rear Admiral Henry K. Thatcher.

The Yankees started north on March 25, along muddy trails through dense oak and pine forests, across a region drained by frequent ravines and creeks with steep banks, and dotted with occasional swampy patches. McArthur's division led the XVI Corps, running into sporadic but heavy skirmishing. Smith's forward riflemen overwhelmed the Johnnies at every stand, and the second day's march brought the corps to the creek known as Bay Minette, four miles east of Spanish Fort. Granger on the left, Smith on the right, the two corps drew their lines around the rebel battlements. Garrard's division, camping along Bay Minette, guarded Canby's trains during the first week of the siege. Federal gunners remembered the Fort as "located on the bluff opposite Mobile. When we came up a hill in sight of the fort we saw that it was built in the shape of a half moon, with the open side resting on the bluff. It was in a heavy pine forest and the trees on the inside were left standing, on the outside they were felled with the tops out from the fort, a strip around the fort about a quarter of a mile wide. The tops of the limbs had been cut with a sharp point so, if the infantry undertook to reach the fort, the points were toward them."

Now began the siege of Spanish Fort, setting a style for the final operations on Mobile Bay. The Yanks started with a "parallel" trench four hundred yards from the Johnnies. "From this parallel," A. J. Smith explained, "saps were worked forward by each brigade, and these again connected by trenches at a distance of about 200 yards from the enemy's works. From the second parallel saps were again worked forward . . . to distances varying from twenty-five to seventy-five yards, depending upon the nature of the ground." Of course, the Confederates were vigilant and artillery duels could erupt at any time. Rebel gunboats aided the gunners in the Fort until Smith deployed two thirty-pounder batteries to warm things up for the sailors.

April 2 was a busy day. Major Lyon sent an unblushing request to Colonel Simpson that "a Commission as Lieutenant Colonel of the 21st Missouri Veteran Volunteer Infantry be issued to me at the earliest opportunity." Meanwhile, Captain Tracy was court-martialing seventeen men in the camp on Bay Minette. Most were AWOL cases, involving "loss of pay and allowances" accruing during the absences, a few fines in the five-dollar category, and one reprimand. Among those processed were Alfred Harper, Isaac Longcor, and Corporal Joe Morris (G); Marshall Brewer and Isaac Thacker (F); and Fred Yust (A).

The work at Spanish Fort was soon well enough along that Garrard could join Steele's troops investing Blakely. With Steele now was Brigadier General John P. Hawkins' First Division, U. S. Colored Troops, and Brigadier General Christopher C. Andrews' Second Division of the XIII Corps. Veatch's division of this corps would soon be on hand also. Garrard's men joined the digging and skirmishing on Monday evening, April 3, with Steele on the right and Garrard the left. The Twenty-first Missouri, shorn of another company when Yust's men were detained as camp guards on Bay Minette, took up the left of the First Brigade line, along a swampy thicket extending down to the Apalachee River, a few hundred feet to the west. Here were makings of a first-class shooting scrape, for the defenders were well supplied with artillery and had grown to a force of twenty-seven hundred. General Cockrell's Missouri Brigade defended the northern half of the line, and Brigadier General Bryan Thomas occupied the southern redoubts with a brigade of Alabama and Mississippi artillery, cavalry, and infantry. Directing the defense of

Blakely was Brigadier General St. John R. Liddell, commanding the Confederate "Eastern Department of the Gulf." A Kansas colonel in Garrard's division noted that

> The opposing rifle-pits and our outer parallels were no more than eighty yards apart and it is no wonder that some of our Missourians scraped up an acquaintance with some of Cockrell's Missourians. This led to quiet little truces, when the muskets would be left in the trenches, and the blue and grey meet each other socially, half-way, to swap lies for the ten minutes, and at other times trade coffee for a Mobile paper and a plug of tobacco.

Casualties rose as rebel sharpshooters joined Liddell's Alabama Battery and a mortar outfit in the struggle to discourage Yankee diggers and skirmishers. Jake Glessner of Company G was slightly wounded in one shoulder and Corporal George Ackland of H suffered a minié ball in one foot on April 4. Ackland, son of a Clark County farmer, died of "blood poisoning" at New Orleans May 1. Sergeant Conrad Wagner of F and Private Warrenton McMillin of D were hit April 5, Wagner receiving a severe hip wound, from which he convalesced at an army hospital in Davenport, Iowa. On Saturday, April 8, John Westfall of Company H was killed instantly, and Hiram Alvis of the same company was sent sprawling when an unexploded shell grazed his head. Two other men of H, Jim Brown and Levi York, incurred wounds from which they soon recovered.

There was occasionally good news in the rear. "We heard today that Col. D. Moore had been promoted Brevett Brigadier General," Starr wrote. There was word from Scotland County boys who had gone home in February that "they are having gay times with parties and dances." The adjutant was thinking ever more fondly of northeastern Missouri, confessing to Henrietta that "I miss a good many who have gone home, . . . but none so much as Captain Cox who I miss very much."

Before daylight on Palm Sunday, April 9, the veterans facing Blakely sensed that the moment of truth was near. Until after midnight there had been thunderous cannonading and constant yelling down beyond Bay Minette. By 2:00 A.M. it had subsided. That surely had but one meaning: Old A. J. and Gordon Granger had gone in for the kill, and it was all over for the Johnnies at Spanish Fort. Then, as if to confirm the rumors, General Smith appeared at Garrard's headquarters in midmorning, with fateful news. Canby wanted those "butternuts" pried out of

Blakely—and today was as good a day as any to do it.

If Garrard needed help, there would be plenty. Granger's men, taking over Spanish Fort, freed Smith to bring up McArthur and Carr. Moreover, Smith could promise Garrard overpowering artillery support—six batteries with twenty-six guns all told, ranging from mighty thirty-pounders to old-reliable brass Parrotts.

Garrard examined the ground between him and the Confederate redoubts, a no-man's land from four hundred to six hundred yards in width. As the thirty-pounders arrived, he positioned them on the left, near the Apalachee, to keep enemy gunboats from enfilading his trenches. Then, around 2:00, he summoned the brigade commanders. Brigadier General James Gilbert, commander of the Second Brigade, joined Rinaker and Colonel Charles L. Harris, Third Brigade, for the session, which General Veatch observed, as his division of XIII Corps was standing to Garrard's right.

"I directed them," Garrard said, "to move their commands into the trenches, placing one-half in the rifle-pits of the skirmishers and one-half in those of the reserves. That at 5:30 P.M. a single line of skirmishers should advance, and as soon as it appeared that they were advancing with success that a second line of skirmishers should follow, and when the first line reached the enemy's works then the main line should charge." Rinaker would hold the left, Harris the center, Gilbert the right. Garrard chose this plan of attack because of the "terrible obstructions in my front and to avoid loss of life, and hoped to silence the enemy's guns and drive off their sharpshooters before I exposed a large mass of my men to the enemy's fire."

Brigade commanders now assembled subordinates and explained their roles. In Rinaker's brigade, there were three main assignments. Colonel Kinney's 119th Illinois, on picket, was already "to the front" and would stay there for the coming advance. Tracy's Twenty-first Missouri, down by the swamp, was to hold the left of the brigade's (and Canby's) main line, while Colonel Hervey Craven's Eighty-ninth Indiana held brigade right. The terrain would oblige the two regiments of the main line to fan out as they advanced, and Rinaker placed Colonel James F. Drish's 122d Illinois about a hundred yards to their rear, where it could cover a gap between the Missourians and the Hoosiers.

Tracy's Missourians, gazing out across this strangely quiet scene, were no longer the half-drilled malcontents with home-guard yearnings who had followed Dave Moore into "exile" three years earlier. Many of the old boys from 1861 were gone. Of the original officers, only six remained on the rolls: McGonigle, Yust, Blackburn, Alex Tracy, Pressell, and Allen. Of the 350 or so men on duty this April 9, only about 210 had been with the regiment from first muster. Sixteen original enlisted men were now officers, five of them captains. Among old hands present and awaiting the bloody charge on Blakely were the Captains Tracy, Blackburn, Puster, and McGonigle; Lieutenants Starr, Gough, Harris, Hagle, Schram, and Hamilton; and enlisted men such as Josh Dale, Matt Woodruff, Bill Matlick, Mike Cashman, Matt Roseberry, Harvey Sisson, and John Sam Hendricks.

The 119th Illinois, having the advance, soon got the word. As a sergeant remembered, "At 5 P.M. Col. Kinney come to us and told us an assault was to be made on the rebel works." The Illinoisans would count off in a single rank, with the odd numbers to lead the charge while the even numbers stayed in their pits and raked the enemy embrasures with enough musket fire to cramp the gunners. And even as Kinney spoke with his officers, Union artillery was opening a preparatory barrage to last until jump-off time. When the bugles sounded "forward," a do-or-die charge had to begin. The onsalught would be echeloned, opening on the left and spreading to the right, across the division front.

The bugles blared. Kinney's shouting and cheering skirmishers sprang from the rifle pits. Confederate pickets raced to the security of the massive redoubts behind them, while Liddell's artillerymen, little intimidated by the fusillade from Garrard's reserve skirmishers, opened a terrible "execution" with grape and canister. Watching the forward line bounding ahead over fallen trees and through ravines and patches of swamp, A. J. Smith soon concluded that the Illinoisans were going all the way—and deserved help. Garrard ordered the reserve skirmishers into the attack, and started his main line forward in their trenches for a third and massive knockout wave.

It was about 5:35 when Garrard threw the rest of the division into the action. Going out on the dead run, the boys of the Second Division raced to catch up with comrades fighting their way through the *abatis* and telegraph-wire entanglements between a ditch and the redoubts beyond it. There were two foot-bridges over the ditch that the Johnnies had not taken with them—and the Yankees were grateful beyond measure. Enemy artillerymen pulling their guns back to reload were dismayed to fine blue-clad visitors clambering through the embrasures wielding bayonets with deadly effect. First man in was the indomitable Colonel Kinney.

Panic seized the defenders as the four-mile-wide Yankee flood engulfed them. Johnnies cornered in their redoubts hoisted hands by the hundreds. Over one redoubt there flew the colors of the Twenty-first Missouri, and, if we believe Best, these were the first planted on Blakely's works. Two other outfits claimed the honor; the 178th New York of Garrard's division and the Seventy-third Colored of Hawkins' division. Higher commanders took no sides in the dispute.

The infantry onset into the rebel works put a quick end to artillery participation in the fight. Smith's gunners also fell silent, to protect friendly troops inside the fortifications. The rebel gunboat *Morgan* had to cease firing for the same reason, and joined its sister ships in flight up the Tombigbee River to Demopolis.

Cockrell's troops, seeing Hawkins' black legions coming, cast aside weapons and scrambled for the protection of white Yankees. Surrender to the Colored Volunteers was too horrible for the Confederate mentality to contemplate; however, one Missouri rebel conceded that the black Yankees "behaved well in the action." Federal commanders saluted the effectiveness of former slaves soldiering under Hawkins.

In an hour's time, all was comparatively quiet. Johnnies fleeing to the river bank west of the fort were pursued by the victors, but only some 150 rebel Missourians succeeded in swimming the Apalachee to safety on the farther shore. Jubilation reigned among the Yanks, from the newest recruit up to Canby. The latter proudly wired Grant "to report the capture this day of the rebel fortifications at Blakely with 2,400 prisoners and 20 guns." Two of the defending generals, Liddell and Thomas, were snared by Garrard's men, and Cockrell fell prisoner elsewhere in the works. The glorious outcome at Blakely did not, unhappily, make Canby "teacher's pet," since Grant had more pressing matters closer to hand. Grant's acknowledgment was a virtual yawn in Canby's face, and he later dismissed the Blakely affair with a question-begging remark that the fort, "if left alone . . . would within a few days have fallen . . . without any bloodshed whatsoever." How tragic that he had not shared his crystal ball with Canby! At any rate, an Illinois veteran remembered "how we danced over our prizes in the way of prisoners, guns, swords, flags and ordnance stores. Once again we could square ordnance accounts." Roaming the captured works, Jim Griffin was astounded to find "boys from ten to fourteen . . . cooking and doing other work" at enemy bivouacs along the bluff.

Unstinting self-congratulation embellished Kinney's report. Garbing himself with an asininity mitigated only by his heroic conduct, he

"humbly" begged the pardon of superiors "if I have committed one
of the blunders to which military men are subject, by taking the enemy's works with a skirmish line when the intention was only to feel
of his lines and learn their strength." Garrard and Smith greeted this
rodomontade with stony silence, and only Rinaker had the temerity
to support the insinuation that Canby had only meant to "feel" Fort
Blakely. No other brigadier or higher commander shared this view,
and there are grounds for doubting that Kinney's own troops saw the
matter in such a light.

While the prisoners were being sent to Ship Island near Biloxi, Mississippi, surgeons and nurses were counting the frightful cost of that
evening's glory. Garrard was able to report on Monday that 44 of his
men had been killed in the action, with 152 more wounded. The death
toll would mount as the outcome of desperate cases became known.

On Monday evening, Adjutant Starr scribbled assurances to Miss
Ettie. He had been "very busy all day arranging prisoners" and had
completed a list of casualties for publication in Howe's *National
American*. "I escaped unhurt," he declared, "but our loss has been
very severe." Nearly half the casualties in Rinaker's brigade had occurred in the Twenty-first Missouri. Killed were nine men, including
Sergeants Matt Roseberry and John J. Lewis, color-bearers in Companies G and C. Dying on the field also were Privates John Warren (C),
Joe Davis (E), William Calvert (G), George Spencer (H), Ben Palmerton
(H), Israel Elican (H), and Charles Blackstone (H). Hearing the fate of
these last two, a desolated George Washburn grieved over those comrades whose perils and fears he had shared through the past year.
Once they were eight; now George alone remained.

Horrors hardly stopped there, for twenty others were under care of
Doc Knickerbocker, Harve Sisson, and other surgeons and stewards at
the division hospital. Most worrisome were the cases of Lieutenant
Gough of Company C, First Sergeant Matt Woodruff of G, Privates
Bill Bias (C), Josh Dale and James Fahey (D), George Haggard (E),
Charles Lewis and Dillwood Fields (G), Pete Riley (H), and Columbus
Page and Bill Driscoll (I). Among those in the less serious category
Knickerbocker placed First Sergeant William H. Smith (E), Sergeant
George Coffman (H), Corporals Ed Alvis and James Peverly Smith (G),
Bill Edwards (I), Privates Oliver P. Martin and Charles Mason (F), John
Hufford (H), and John McGinley (I).

It took six weeks to learn the cost of this final blooding. Five
brave fellows died at various hospitals around Mobile and New Orleans.

Lieutenant Gough and Columbus Page passed away on Monday. At Greenville, Louisiana, on April 18, Joshua Dale succumbed to damage done his left lung in that last charge. He was the third color-bearer to die. Aquilla Barnes, his stepson, had rejoined in 1864 after recovering from that hip wound at Shiloh, and it now fell to his lot to comfort a mother twice widowed. Haggard, a transfer from the Twenty-fourth Missouri, yielded up his spirit at New Orleans on April 21. Last of the boys to perish from the carnage of Blakely was Riley, a thirty-six-year-old Irish substitute with less than four months of service, who died May 28 at Greenville.

Even for the survivors the way was hard. Charlie Lewis incurred such impairment of his left lung that doctors in Keokuk let him out with a 50 percent disablement in January 1866. Knickerbocker was of a mind to do the same thing for Bill Bias, whose recuperation from a severe head wound was long, painful, and never quite complete. However, by the time Doc gave up on Bias, the regiment was about to leave for St. Louis, and it was clear that a disability discharge would not speed his way home. Woodruff, after hospitalization for an extensive thigh wound, convalesced at his boyhood home in Ohio. But even light wounds could be troublesome, as McGinley and J. P. Smith learned. Hit in a hand by a minié ball and in one hip by a shell fragment, Smith did not get back to duty until winter. And the regiment was ready to muster out when McGinley returned after a year's absence with a "slight" leg wound.

General Maury was ready to abandon Mobile. At daybreak Wednesday the forty-five hundred defenders marched north up the Mobile & Ohio toward Demopolis, 140 miles or so away. Canby prepared to enter the city, whose inhabitants proved "happy to greet us as friends." Maury was to be allowed no rest, however, for thousands of Yankees were going after him. On Wednesday morning, Canby directed Smith to move on Montgomery, nearly two hundred miles to the northeast, and on Selma, between that place and Demopolis. As Smith's guerrillas marched overland on Montgomery, they would not fear for their flanks. Grierson's cavalry would be marauding to their east, while Steele's black troops would be mopping up along the Alabama River. Wilson's cavalry, under Sherman's immediate command, was rampaging through central Alabama, and Canby hoped that Smith's operations might mesh with Wilson's.

With McArthur marching at 9:00 A.M., XVI Corps took its leave of Fort Blakely on Thursday. Captain Yust's boys were rejoining, and only Company B was absent from that last reveille on Mobile Bay. The job of bringing up the rear and guarding wagons fell to Rinaker's brigade—a familiar chore. Smith vigorously pushed his troops northeast along the roads and, in company with Grierson, rode into the Confederacy's first capital at noon April 25. Rebel resistance had faded.

"I am out of rations," A. J. wrote Canby, "but can get along until the 27th." It might be possible, he surmised, to live off the country a few days beyond that. At any rate, his boys were in fine spirits, having learned on the way that Lee's Army of Northern Virginia had furled its colors at a place called Appomattox the very day of Blakely. A veteran of Rinaker's brigade recalled that the news had touched off a demonstration "simply indescribable."

Word had traveled slowly enough, demonstrating the condition of telegraph communications in the war-ravaged South. Keokuk's papers bannered the tidings of Appomattox on April 11, but it was another four days before New Orleans editors could do so. The news of Blakely did not reach Keokuk for ten days. The *Gate City* gave it minimal treatment, ignoring the Twenty-first Missouri's role. After all, the menace to Keokuk was long past, and those heroes who had spent nearly four years of their lives pushing that danger to the gulf had ceased to be "news."

To do him justice, Editor Howell was preoccupied with weightier matters. Two days before the news of Blakely arrived, he had published an edition with columns edged in black, announcing the assassination of President Lincoln, "the pilot in whom the people trusted." Old Abe was suddenly gone, and it remained to be seen how his legacy would fare on the hands of the War Democrat now succeeding him.

The war was not quite at an end. Johnston was on the verge of quitting, and his battered little army's surrender would terminate the conflict on the Atlantic coast. On the other hand, General Richard Taylor was still belligerent in the Deep South, and Kirby Smith was holding out beyond the Mississippi.

Proof came May 3 that the matter was receiving creative thought. Canby wired Smith to "desist from all aggressive operations." The next day Taylor showed up at Citronelle, thirty-five miles north of Mobile, to sign the capitulation of twenty-five thousand troops still in his command. With a flourish of his pen, the stalwart son of Old Rough and Ready ended the Confederate war effort between the Chattahoochee and the Mississippi. For his part, Canby cautioned

Smith to see that "strictest discipline . . . be enforced, . . . and the people at all times treated with leniency."

"Oh what a glorious termination of things on this side of the [Mississippi] River," Lieutenant Morrey wrote his fiancée. "We have some rumer of Curby Smith's surrendering his army and if this proves true we will see each other soon. God grant it may be true." The boys of Smith's corps, camped two miles north of Montgomery, were "in a verry beautiful place, . . ." Morrey thought, "shady and plenty of good water." His job as ambulance officer had grown pretty soft, now that casualties were relegated to a hideous past.

The formal end of America's bloodiest war came in New Orleans on May 26, when representatives of Kirby Smith signed their surrender to Banks, Hurlbut's successor on the Gulf. This occurred just as the Department of War was transferring Canby's Division of West Mississippi into Banks' department and preparing to supersede Banks with Canby. However, it would take some days to make the change, for Canby was busy supervising the wind-up in Alabama and Mississippi. Granger was going west, which meant that A. J. Smith would police the surrender in Alabama. McArthur's division, ordered to Selma, was the first of the XVI Corps elements to enter the pacification process.

Despite the return of peace in the Deep South, the weeks following Blakely were dreary ones for Tracy's Missourians. The boys in the ranks were restive. Home was on their minds. Various officers remained on detached duties—Comstock continuing as corps adjutant general, Lyon receiving a federal commission as lieutenant colonel of volunteers to go with his position as Smith's inspector general. Company B rejoined on May 19, after nearly a month of protecting liberated Yankees along the Tombigbee, but Yust's Company A was now on daily duty as General Smith's provost guard.

Not even the liberation of many of the old boys from rebel prison pens was free from sorrowful side effects. Of the nine Knox Countians taken at Mayfield, Kentucky, in May 1864, William and Robert Pulis had returned from parole in November; however, Bill Roseberry, paroled in Georgia, returned to federal custody in Florida on April 28 and was discharged to civil life without the pleasure of a reunion with old comrades of Company E. Edgar Matlick, Andy Haynes, Tom Murphy, Gus Moranville, Tom Davis, and Jim Roseberry—the other Mayfield captives—were among beneficiaries of an exchange protocol signed at Vicksburg in February and as such were among several thousand prisoners from Cahaba paroled near Vicksburg in mid-April. They too

mustered out in St. Louis that summer while on furlough. Released
with Bill Roseberry in Florida was Jim Dye, captured near Eastport
in January.

The timing of one's release could make a terrible difference. Corporal John Frazier of E, captured in Missouri, landed in a stockade in
Texas. His older brother Joel, taken near Tupelo, wound up at Cahaba. Both now returned to federal custody at Vicksburg. River steam-
ers were coming and going, rapidly bearing parolees north, and by the
time John arrived, his brother was on his way to Benton Barracks.
With other late arrivals, John shipped April 24 aboard the *Sultana*, the
vessel that had taken him and his comrades down to Memphis two
springs earlier.

This was the *Sultana*'s final voyage—and Frazier's. Bearing the last
contingent of prisoners from Vicksburg, the creaky and overloaded
steamer blew up at 2:00 A.M. on April 27, nearly ten miles above
Memphis. Among the 1,647 men perishing in that fiery roar and its
aftermath was Corporal Frazier. An Illinois trooper at Memphis wrote
his mother that the disaster "would make you shrink if you had saw
it." Many survivors, scalded in the explosion, clung to the wreck as
it drifted down toward Memphis. "Their cries for help were awful,"
said Fenton Hussey, but they "let the people know the sad Accident
that had befell the Sultana and her living burthen."

Tracy's Missourians would shudder at Frazier's fate, and at a
catastrophe that demolished the *Kate Dale* at Mobile six weeks after
the surrender. Lax handling of captured percussion shells by federal
troops was officially blamed for the holocaust, which claimed 130
tons of powder and ammunition in a warehouse at the corner of Lips-
comb and Commerce Streets. Between two hundred and three hundred perished in the disaster, which a witness said gave "the whole
northeast quarter of the city . . . a dilapidated appearance." The concussion knocked down horses a half-mile distant.

While the Twenty-first Missouri was at Montgomery, Johnnie Goodwin arrived from St. Louis. The charges of horse stealing on Grand
Avenue, lodged against him six months before, had never made it to
court. While he had sweated out the affair in the Gratiot Street Military Prison, his civilian attorney had lined up a telling defense. At the
core of Goodwin's case were depositions from comrades—Tom Beaver,
Otis Hoskins, and Byron Van Valkinburgh—attesting to his innocent
receipt of the horse in question. When the trial judge advocate finally
capitulated, General Dodge gave the terse order: "Release—evidence
insufficient."

Colonel Lyon had a little matter to settle with the officers on May 13. He had just received a commission as lieutenant colonel of the Twenty-first Missouri, "which I am proud to accept." The federal commission, valid for the inspector general's post, he would have revoked. But who should be major? This matter he checked to the officers, and after hashing it out they agreed to petition the governor in Joe Best's behalf. Pressell, Roberts, and five captains—Yust, McGonigle, Shafer, Blackburn, and Puster—led the group, eighteen in all. Five balked, among them Starr and two captains named Tracy. In fact, the latter two were almost certainly the officers who had informed Lyon earlier that they would never "approve" commissioning Best.

As the Union army entered upon its inevitable dissolution, the XVI Corps began to shrink and disperse. Loud were demands for mustering out, as trains and ships headed north almost daily with throngs of happy veterans becoming private citizens again. But thousands were obliged to stay in uniform, since the peace was yet to be won. Stern and humorless Radicals in Washington had no doubt that only a determined show of military muscle "at the South" could preserve what had been so painfully won.

On May 27 General Canby told A. J. Smith that, having sent McArthur to garrison Selma, he must now post forces in Mobile. Smith and Garrard conferred, and Rinaker's brigade got its orders to leave for Providence Landing, on the Alabama River sixty-eight miles west of Montgomery, where the boys would ship down to Mobile.

15

Victors in the Midst of Strife

The return to Mobile on the *W. H. Osborne* was more leisurely than April's march to Montgomery. Company A remained in Montgomery as XVI Corps provost guard, while Amburn became A. J. Smith's provost marshal. There was a tragic note: on June 3, Private William E. Demoney, twenty-nine, a native Pennsylvanian who had soldiered all the way through with Company D, fell overboard into the Alabama River and drowned before anyone realized what was happening. He had been one of Story's home guards, and was among the wounded of Shiloh. Left to mourn him were Elizabeth Timmons Demoney and their six-month-old son William, who later became a Putnam County judge and Republican leader. To John Demoney, the dead man's younger brother, Captain McGonigle confided the personal effects.

The post quartermaster had staked out a campsite for Rinaker's brigade on the western outskirts of Mobile, over two miles from the waterfront. This was strictly a tenting proposition, amid fortifications built by rebel engineers. While comforts of home were scarce, things could have been worse. Most of the brigade would be going home soon, and troops who stayed would be scattering to other locations.

Among regiments remaining was the Twenty-first Missouri. For a while, the boys hoped for an early muster out, but as summer faded into autumn the optimism would turn to mutinous despair. The war might be over; the duration was not. Morrey, for one, did not relish staying to watch his comrades chafe. "I am so lonesome here sometimes I cannot hardly live," he confided to his Kate. "The officers in the Regiment are nearly all young men and pretty fast ones too. Though there are many worse."

George H. Thomas, from his Nashville headquarters, now commanded the Military Division of the Tennessee, embracing much of the Deep South. Under him was the Department of Alabama, headquartered at Mobile. A. J. Smith, commanding in Alabama until

June 27 "by virtue of seniority," yielded his position to Brevet Major General Charles R. Woods. The newcomer had won his spurs as commander of the Seventy-sixth Ohio and was a veteran of Shiloh, Donelson, the march through Georgia, and Sherman's recent Carolinas campaign. Kilby Smith's District of Mobile, including a dozen or so counties of Alabama, started operations with Rinaker's brigade, the First Indiana Artillery, the Thirty-first Massachusetts Infantry, and the Eighty-sixth and Ninety-seventh U.S. Colored Infantry.

Tracy's men must have itched to participate fully in Missouri's constitutional referendum of June 6. Several emissaries from Jefferson City took poll books to units outside the state, but the scattering of the Twenty-first Missouri was too much for them. The proposed constitution was quite controversial, particularly because of its iron-clad oath barring dozens of "disloyal" categories from voting, public employment, and even preaching. A network of "registrars" would see that rebels, bushwhackers, and Copperheads stayed home on election days. Born of fears and rancors lingering in Radical breasts, such vindictiveness was but another of the noticeable scars etched in the American spirit by this ghastly war between brothers.

There was little enough disposition in those summer days to let bygones be bygones, least of all among Radical Missourians of native-American stock. But immigrant Germans, for all their courage and loyalty during the rebellion, were more inclined to magnanimity of spirit. Only the Germans of Company A and a number of others on special duty at Montgomery got to represent the Twenty-first Missouri in the voting. Those polled voted 142-66 in favor, with the "no" votes presumably cast mainly by Germans in close touch with kinsmen back in Missouri. Clark, Scotland, and Knox counties—in the regiment's Anglo-Saxon hinterland—gave the document landslide majorities. Despite the adverse vote of La Grange's Germans, Conservative Lewis County still gave it a thirty-one-vote lead. Disqualification of voters tainted with "disloyalty" really saved the constitution, soldiers providing its scant statewide margin of victory.

The Twenty-first Missouri began dispersing; only the return of Company A in July slowed the process. On June 7, Company F entrained to Whistler, seven miles northwest, where it spent most of the summer on guard duty. The next day, Company E left for Citronelle, farther up the Mobile & Ohio, for a similar stay. Company K moved to the Mount Vernon Arsenal, thirty miles north of Mobile, and G took the *Starlight* for a summer's guard detail at East Pascagoula, Mississippi, on the coast thirty miles southwest of Mobile. The remainder of the regiment split into detachments for assorted duties around the bay.

The officers were also stretched paper-thin over the district. Comstock left for good in June to muster as corps adjutant general, and Amburn continued until August as provost marshal. Nor would Garrard let go of Rees, using him as inspector general and judge advocate of the division. Even when Company K was relieved at Mount Vernon in August, Lieutenant Weaver had to stay as post quartermaster. Lieutenant Jones of H rode off to provost duty at Pollard, sixty miles to the northeast, in June. Colonel Lyon also kept his distance, remaining on the corps staff until leaving service in August.

Such special assignments were only part of the picture. Charles Tracy, aware that his command of the regiment was provisional and that there was no likelihood of promotion, mustered out June 11—the long-feared arrival of Best's commission as major precipitating his departure. Dan Pressell, anxious to see his folks in Keokuk, went north with him, and Martin Sinnott was the quartermaster while he was away. Starr, having received Governor Fletcher's appointment as clerk of Lewis County, also left for home in June to be sworn before doing anything so drastic as resigning his lieutenancy. Sergeant Stephen Hall of Company B took over the adjutant's work. And several enlisted men discovered compelling reasons for furloughs.

Best took formal command of the Twenty-first Missouri on June 14, and his coming had a "new broom" effect. It was he who summoned Steve Hall to the adjutant's post and elevated principal musician Thomas H. Roseberry to the sergeant major's office, replacing Greenberry Jones. During July, the new commander, in consultation with Colonel Lyon, secured captaincies for Lieutenants Jerry Hamilton of I and Jim Smith of H, and first lieutenancies for Henry Deems and Green Jones, respectively of these units.

Lyon and Best were evidently in complete agreement on the regiment's future. All the titular commander asked of Fletcher was a colonel's commission, and he would terminate his career by resigning. On August 5, he recommended Best for lieutenant colonel and McGonigle for major. Alex Tracy and Charles Morrey turned in their resignations August 14. To Morrey, who supported Tracy's brother in that struggle for the major's rating, it seemed high time to recall "important business at home." The governor commissioned Lyon and Best on August 17, McGonigle a little later.

Occasionally a fondly remembered face appeared at headquarters.

Three prisoners of the Red River expedition arrived at Mobile June 11: Isaiah Preston, Jacob Kiess, and Frederick Nater. Before long they would be northward bound. There was, however, no cordial reception for Jack Trunnell, who reported June 29. The trouble here was that Jack had been exchanged and ordered back to duty February 13! Best would try him for desertion but had to rest content with an AWOL conviction.

Three casualties of Blakely came back to Company G. Matt Woodruff, largely recovered from that hip wound, returned from Ohio by way of St. Francisville in early July. Matt had taken a side trip to Clark County, for he was in love with Carrie Springer, whose Uncle John Springer was still in Company G. Matt found the boys living in luxury, occupying a three-story hotel overlooking the beach. The convalescing top kick would enjoy sitting on the balcony, gazing out to sea "as far as the eye can reach." However, he found his office work "farther behind than when I left it three months ago." This was no compliment to Sergeant Jasper N. Whetstone, who had been trying to fill Woodruff's shoes since that bloody spring evening. Then, in mid-August, Ed and Hiram Alvis, wounded in the fighting around Blakely, returned from hospitalization.

Major Best developed fever and a general run-down feeling, and Knickerbocker suggested that he get out of town a day or so. But a week with Company E at Citronelle availed nothing, and the major checked in at the Marine Hospital in Mobile. Medics could only tell him he was suffering from "remittent fever" and needed a change of climate. Accordingly, he shipped out for home July 25, to give "the invigorating atmosphere of our northern prairies" a chance to restore him. It helped, too, that a doctor back home realized his ailment was hepatitis. By mid-September he was back at headquarters.

During Best's absence, the command devolved on Captain Yust. And the weeks the fierce-eyed Prussian headed the outfit were no idle times. Lyon, Alex Tracy, and other resigning officers departed. And it fell to Yust's lot to make a new quartermaster sergeant, by lifting Private Cyrus D. McDowell out of Company I. The thirty-three-year-old Virginian had joined in January 1864 and became conspicuous for soldierly abilities. Best found no fault with his promotion. But Yust's biggest decision came in late August, after the provisional governor declared civil authorities unable to preserve order at Sparta, eighty miles northeast of Mobile at the junction of the Mobile & Great Northern and Alabama & Florida rail lines. Since "cotton

thieves and jayhawkers" were rampant, Garrard as district commander
called on Yust to "have the best and most efficient company officer
in your Regiment ready with his company to go to Sparta." Yust
turned to Josiah Davis. Company B left under shoot-to-kill orders—
and patrolled Sparta until the following spring.

Best left another ticklish problem for Yust. A boy in Company F
had shot and killed Private James Odell of the 130th Illinois. This
was no murder case, for Private William Ray had been walking guard
that July evening when Odell failed to heed a challenge. District headquarters instituted an inquiry, but investigators felt the killing "justi-
fiable, and that Private William Ray . . . should be commended for
the prompt manner in which he executed his duty as a sentinel."

No Yankee was truly safe in the gloom of those muggy summer
nights in Mobile or in the forests outside the City. Richard McKinney,
a twenty-eight-year-old teamster of Company E, fell victim of a bush-
whack murder September 17 near Claiborne, an Alabama River town
northeast of Mobile. The killer was never brought to temporal justice. The dead man, an original soldier of his company, had returned
to service in January 1864 after being invalided out for typhoid in
1862. His wife having drowned in Knox County a month earlier,
their infant son was left to the care of relatives.

Death came less spectacularly to others that first summer of
"peace." Dysentery was the principal villain. First afflicted was
Gilbert Sammons of Company B, a native Illinoisan who had enlisted
in early 1864. He succumbed June 27. Company H's first sergeant,
William Reahard, who had mustered in with Captain Cox, died of a
lung ailment September 6. Company H also lost George W. Carberry
of Prospect Grove to dysentery July 6. George W. Freemyer, an Ohio-
born youth of Company E, died at home in Knox County July 24,
and the family laid him to rest in a woodland cemetery near Colony.
Two draftees with about a month to serve, Henry McNeese of F and
Jonathan Richardson of D, perished in early August.

There were ways to "cheat" death, however. Albert Drayton, a
young corporal of Massachusetts forebears, entered the Marine Hospital
at Mobile in June with typhoid. In early November, a message arrived at Sparta, notifying Captain Davis of Corporal Drayton's death
June 16. He had, a surgeon wrote, been buried in plot 72 at the
city cemetery. Davis thought this passing strange, and so for that matter did Drayton, long since returned to duty! Further study of the
note revealed that the name was spelled "Frayton," but no man of

that name ever had served in the regiment, let alone the company.

An investigation ensued, for *someone* was most assuredly reposing
in plot 72. The hospital's chief surgeon soon traced the error to a
part-time registrar, Chaplain Hezekiah Lewis of the Forty-sixth Illinois.
Back in early June, Lewis recalled, an elderly man in federal uniform
had been brought into Marine Hospital with sunstroke but had died
without regaining consciousness. After burying the old fellow as "unknown," Lewis tried to identify him. Other patients thought the departed one was from a "Missouri regiment." Thumbing through a
very haphazard register, Lewis found Drayton's name and outfit—and
since Drayton's dismissal had gone unrecorded, he jumped to an un-
warranted conclusion. Misreading someone's handwriting, he reported
"Frayton" of the Twenty-first Missouri as dead and thus "clarified"
the record. Although Drayton unquestionably welcomed reversal of
the registrar's decision, the quartermaster department did little to clear
things up later when it sent a headstone for "Albert Fenton." The
resident of plot 72 remains an unknown soldier.

Few men of the Twenty-first Missouri going home on furlough
would have agreed with the returned Confederate who found the
homefolk suffering "a despotism more fearful and revolting than that
which rules in the empire of the Muscovite." Certainly the war had
laid waste the culture and economy of wide areas. Masonic lodges
in the northeastern area, for example, had suffered fearfully. Political dissensions had wrecked them all in Clark County, and only the
Memphis and Colony lodges kept the "spirit of masonry" alive in
Scotland and Knox. Still, for hundreds of war-weary Missourians,
there was no place like home.

Courthouses, well stocked now with "loyal" officers, resounded
with militant oratory. Radicals of Clark County staged a mass meeting at Waterloo September 18, 1865, with Captain Roseberry presiding, Barton Hackney and John H. Cox dominating the resolutions committee. Breathing scorn at vanquished neighbors, they resolved to
"stand by each other" and insisted that "rebels and bushwhackers cannot be allowed to return, . . . to stir up strife and contention in our
now peaceful county." They stridently voted "no confidence in the
conversion to loyalty of those who left the county for their country's
good with Mart. Green, Porter, Shacklett." Six weeks later, a similar
gathering at Memphis, with Simon Pearce orating and George Stine
handling resolutions, accused Conservative-Unionists of preferring Jeff
Davis to Andrew Johnson. Adding a note at variance from the Water-

loo resolutions, this conclave went on record favoring "rule not only
by white men, but loyal white men." It was probably a rare bird in
either coop that saw in such racist rhetoric the approaching twilight
of Missouri's Radical-Republican demigods.

Major Best fought to stem the erosion of his regiment's morale. He
nagged his commanders to make noncoms wear their stripes. He announced enthusiastically A. J. Smith's memorable "General Order 28"
of July 17, authorizing the regiment to inscribe on its colors the battle honors TUPELO, NASHVILLE, BLAKELY. And before taking
off on sick leave, Best ordered up four hours of "company drill"
daily.

High Missouri Radicals agitated at the White House and Department
of War to secure the muster out of the Twenty-first Missouri. Well
they might! for letters and petitions from the ranks streamed northward. Governor Fletcher hounded Senators John B. Henderson and
B. Gratz Brown to "urge upon the Secy. of War the necessity, virtue,
and propriety of mustering out the Mo. troops, especially the 21st."
By Christmas, the Department of War was hinting that projected
troop reductions might "facilitate" release of the regiment in the prox-
imate future.

Such responses satisfied few, but there were ways besides desertion
to express one's impatience. Several anonymous letters warned Best
to get the boys out immediately—or "a piece of real estate not over
2½ miles from this place" would be reserved for him. After sniffing
around, Best decided the culprit was Scottish-born William Simpson,
a substitute in Company A known as "Big Sandy." Simpson, away
on duty with the Freedmen's Department at district headquarters,
found himself under arrest October 24. He brazened it through, however, and Best was unable to pin a thing on him.

Payday was becoming the occasion for a week-long drunk now, and
hangovers seemed a part of the regiment's equipment. Frequent reductions of noncoms for "drunkenness" or "disobedience" occurred,
the most notorious coming in August, when Alex Tracy busted four
corporals in Company F on the eve of his departure. In late September, the Fourteenth Wisconsin got orders for home, and its loud celebration devastated morale in the Twenty-first Missouri. The general
atmosphere had inspired one "distinguished citizen" outstate to write
a Mobile editor to protest retention of Yankee Volunteers in rural
Alabama. The Fifteenth U.S. Infantry, Regulars, drew good marks for
order and discipline, but this anonymous dignitary insisted that the

Department of War remove the homesick Missourians, whose presence was making local negroes "daily more troublesome."

Woodruff sensed the deterioration from the beginning. The boys of Company G at Pascagoula were constantly hitting the bottle, and fights were common among them and with local people. Frank Massey, Isaac Longcor, and Alf Harper mixed it with several civilians about daybreak July 20, Massey getting slugged and Longcor stabbed in one arm. Lieutenant Harris, coming to their aid, was threatened with murder by one assailant, who vanished after voicing the threat. Captain Blackburn, told his boys were tipsy, had them tried and fined.

Several of Woodruff's friends, having "taken up" with local girls, hounded him to come and meet their creole mistresses. Matt politely looked them over, but huffed to himself that they were "mostly Mongrells, Negroes, Mulattoes, and so on." Despite his hatred of rebels, Matt was a Conservative-Unionist unable to see black folk as more than amusing nuisances. His diary, in consequence, bristled with references to "kinkeys," "Nigs," and so forth.

On July 19 Woodruff made the acquaintance of a "verry beautiful young Spanish lady" from Vera Cruz, a "Miss Cassimere." Though mindful of "dear Carrie," he cautiously ogled the strange girl and promised to teach her to "schottische" in exchange for lessons in French. The budding romance fizzled soon, when Matt found she was residing at a house of "Illfame." He faced the ugly "truth" and began to "loose confidence."

Racism manifested itself variously with the Ninety-sixth Colored Infantry in town. The proximity of black and white troops in this environment was part of the problem, but the Missourians also reacted from national sterotypes in dealing with the Belgian-born commander of the Ninety-sixth who was also commander of Pascagoula's area, Lieutenant Colonel Octave Fariola de Rozzoli. "Frog-eater," the Missourians called him, and managed to resent nearly everything he said or did.

Fariola fed their resentments. Blackburn, soggy from drink, went boating on an August Sunday morning. He took several potshots at a schooner "to attract her attention," and before Blackburn could sober up, "Frog-eater" arrested him. Not that it did much good—the next day Blackburn broke arrest and resumed his boating. But it was also the day for legislative elections in Mississippi, and Company G was all over town "helping." Many citizens got drunk at the polls, and obliging Missourians escorted many home and put them to bed. First Sergeant Woodruff then had to "arrest the boys and put *them* to bed."

Street fights and drunken revels continued. A gang of Missourians invaded a private home in search of whisky, found none, and beat up the elderly inhabitants. "Frog-eater," keeping a weather eye on Blackburn's crowd, provoked indignation by arresting Ike Longcor and Alf Harper on September 3 for "disobedience." Alf deserted, scribbling a note to Blackburn accusing Fariola of planning to frame him. A week later, Frog-eater threw Company G out of its hotel and into a tent camp. It was certainly a relief to local authorities when Garrard recalled the company to Mobile.

The XVI Corps folded July 20. A. J. Smith, publishing his farewell orders, recalled Tupelo and Blakely—battles his Missourians knew so well. He exhorted the boys to "let the memory of what you have endured endear to you every foot of American soil. Having asserted the supremacy of the General Government in arms, assist now in creating for it a glorious future among nations."

Stripes fell like leaves as autumn began. Best signed order after order reducing corporals and sergeants for "drunkenness and disorderly conduct," "disrespect to superior officer," "trying to use dishonorable means to get out of the service." A half-dozen men passed into desertion each month, and dozens more were unaccountably absent at every formation. Chief among troops remaining in Mobile were the Missourians, the Fifteenth Infantry, and the Eighty-sixth and Ninety-seventh Colored Infantry. And a three-way guerrilla war among blacks, regulars, and volunteers provided federal officials and local folk with anxiety and entertainment that first autumn and winter of "peace."

September 30 was a memorable day for the Twenty-first Missouri. The governor, "doing right" by the new commander, raised Best to full colonel after only six weeks as lieutenant colonel. At twenty-seven, he became the last colonel of the regiment, and Dave Moore was to remind everyone fondly that this solemn youth had risen from private "through all grades up to his present position. His gallantry was always conspicuous on the battle-field." McGonigle moved up to lieutenant colonel, Blackburn to major. Three captains were made: Shane Palmer of C, Josh Hagle of F, and Reece Allen of G. Among the five new first lieutenants were Quartermaster Sergeant McDowell (C), Sinnott (E), and Schram (F). The governor completed the bundle by naming nine second lieutenants, among them First Sergeants

George Matthauer (F), Owen S. Hagle (B), and George Coffman (H).
Sergeant Major Roseberry won the second lieutenancy of G, but
Matt Woodruff, aware that the regiment's "aggregate" strength stood
only at 550, presciently observed that none of those promoted "can
Muster at present [;] dont know as they ever will."

This shiny array of potential rank hardly improved the regiment's
image. On the evening of October 1, Marshall Brewer of Company
F landed in jail for stabbing a local Negro, Edward Alexander. A
court-martial headed by Major McGonigle found Brewer innocent of
the stabbing, mainly because Alexander failed to appear. Two men
of the Fifteenth Infantry did their neighborly best to persuade the
court to put Brewer away anyhow, but in the end he was fined only
for wearing civilian clothes on the occasion of the offense. On the
night of the stabbing, two others in Company F suffered cuts and
bruises in a street row with Negro soldiers.

A new commander had come to the district, and he was unamused
at the tendency of the regulars and Missourians to pick fights with
black soldiers and citizenry—and with each other. Brigadier General
Gustavus Adolphus DeRussy was the son of a brilliant former superintendent of the U.S. Military Academy. The general himself was a
West Point "drop-out," and his Uncle Lewis DeRussy had been a colonel in gray. Gustavus, however, was "unconditionally Union" and
came up with the Fourth New York Artillery. Brevetted for bravery
in the seven-days battles around Richmond, he had won full brigadier's
rank in May 1863. He had little patience with the horseplay going on
in Mobile, and from his office at the corner of Dearborn and Government streets he eventually warned subordinate commanders to be on
guard against "acts of violence and robbery committed by enlisted
men . . . upon negroes. The most stringent measures must be adopted
to prevent such occurrences, which are reported as almost nightly.
Enlisted men must be kept in camp after Retreat, unless sent out on
some particular service which must be specified, in a written pass
signed by the Commanding Officer."

The mischief continued. Chauncey Murch of Company G, a guard
at the ordnance depot, concocted a prank for his civilian friends.
After dark one night, he laid a streak of filched gunpowder across a
street to an acquaintance's front yard. Then, without washing his
hands or brushing powder from his clothes, he ignited his surprise.
What a fiasco! He wound up in the regimental hospital with severe
burns on his face and hands. A. C. Roberts shook his head, but the
prankster slowly recovered.

On October 30, a playful fellow from Company G tanked up on "oh-be-joyful" in downtown Mobile. And according to Woodruff, the sidewalk suddenly flew up and hit him in the face. "Swore some-one had mugged him," Matt scoffed. Not so comical was a counter-feiting ring uncovered the next day, when provost guards jailed a gang of civilians and uniformed Missourians. Tom Hopson of Com-pany K deserted in the face of impending charges, but John and Fielding Sexton, both of Company D, went free after interro-gation.

The troublemakers were primed for state elections on Monday, Nov-ember 6. The commotion started with a jailbreak at St. Stephens, fifty-eight miles north of Mobile on the Tombigbee. Here Captain Jim Smith had just incarcerated three men of Company H. Why? The record is unclear, except that Corporal Joe Cameron felt the boys had gone to jail for doing only what Smith himself was doing—whatever that was. At any rate, Joe decided to spring the "St. Stephens Three"—Jasper Booker, Abe Shoemaker, and Charles Postle-wait. Joe handed an axe through the bars and left the inmates to figure things out for themselves. Somehow a door fell to pieces, and the prisoners were free. But Cameron shortly found himself under arrest for mutiny.

Tried on this and other charges ten days later, Cameron lashed out at Smith, claiming his dear old mother back in Clark County would blush to know her son was serving under such a captain. There was no point in sending Joe back to Company H; the court handed him four months at hard labor and busted him. While reviews were in progress, Joe addressed a pathetic note to General Woods, denying "the slightest idea of Mutiny, . . . being devoted to his country as his willing volunteering and conduct on the battle fields of Nashville and Blakely will testify." His excuse, "forgetfullness by indulgence in liquor," he did not defend beyond pointing to the "example and practice of many in the Command." Woods, hardly indulgent, ignored the plea, despite its endorsement from Lieutenant Jones, Sergeant Coffman, and most of the company.

Meanwhile, their comrades back in the city had celebrated election day in a characteristic manner. Missourians led by Jim Roseberry and Mike Cashman picked a scrap with the bellicose regulars. Mike was cut severely on his right hand, Roseberry so badly bruised about the face that he was unable to see by the time they got him to camp. However, Woodruff heard on the evening after the election, "a crowd has gone to the city for sweet revenge." This, or something worse, was usually available.

On the following Friday, Matthew Mauck and Jake Glessner gave their captain more reason to hit the bottle. Matt, according to Blackburn, "did while on duty as guard get drunk and leave his Post." Worse, he had taken a sling shot after Glessner. Both were loaded with "sod corn." Hooted their first sergeant: "Capt. reeling from Effects of same orders charges preferred." But before Mauck could be tried, he was gone—on December 5. A week later, Glessner went, taking his musket with him. Woodruff wondered if he meant to "fight his way" back to Clark County.

Mauck's cousin Reuben of Company D found little security even in behaving. Dining at a restaurant with some comrades and ladies the evening of November 11, he was set upon by a knife-wielding citizen who sought to vindicate the lost cause by exterminating a Yankee. He failed, but Mauck came out of the fracas with a scar on his chest.

City elections, held on December 4, featured a contest between Major C. F. Moulton and Jones M. Withers, late "major general commanding" of the troops attacking the Twenty-first Missouri's lines at Shiloh. The *Advertiser and Register*, avoiding news "tending to infractions of the public peace," paid scanty attention to the electioneering. This could hardly be said of federal troops around the city, however. Voting was oral, and few judges and clerks dared disqualify boys in blue showing up to vote. Both sides offered bribes to get Yanks to the polls—everything from a shot-glass of whisky to a bundle of cash or a new suit.

DeRussy ordered troops confined to camp for the day, but the boys swarmed off to town as if they had never heard of him. Frank Massey's younger brother Bill, Ike Longcor, and Matt Mauck got into a fight with lads of the Fifteenth Infantry, Massey getting two slashes on his left arm, Longcor a scratch on his chest, Mauck getting off unscratched in this, his farewell skirmish. For Ike this was nothing new, for he had been a casualty at Athens, years ago up in Missouri. Jim Roseberry made an agreeable holiday of it: that night he staggered in to report he had voted "6 times & got fifty dollars for it, a good days work." Little though the boys may have hoped or cared, Withers won the election.

Trouble with the Fifteenth Infantry peaked in December. A roughhouse started on Thursday, December 7, when Nate Longcor, Jack

Greathouse, and Bill Holcomb of G stirred up ten "Regs" on a street corner. The Missourians were chanting, "I'll never jump the bounty any more," which somehow offended the Regulars. The odds were grossly uneven, and the Missourians were in a fair way to have their bones picked when Mike Cashman, mounted orderly to DeRussy's commissary of musters, came riding by and saw their plight. Assessing their need for massive reinforcement, Mike spurred his horse off to camp for help.

Battle-wise rescuers were soon charging down the street, and the "Regs" fled the scene, with bricks and other missiles helping them on their way. Then, emboldened by reinforcements, the regulars turned and began chasing Company G back toward its camp. A general riot seemed in the works, and in the hand-to-hand fighting that ensued, even blacks employed by the Twenty-first Missouri pitched in to defend the regiment's honor. Doc Roberts' helper, a muscular fellow named "Governor," came out of it with an arm fracture and scraped head. Soon, however, McGonigle and an "enemy" officer of the day arranged a cessation of hostilities.

But, a week later, it started again. Thursday evening a general alarm spread through the Twenty-first Missouri's camp, and Colonel Best emerged from his tent to find a dozen regulars had chased Joe Wright of Company G in from town for laying out one of their number in a sidewalk brawl. The angry, jabbering visitors, toting fixed bayonets, looked like they meant business. Unfortunately for Wright, Best had come into the matter with an impression that the callers were "provost guards." With that understanding, he released Wright to their custody!

As soon as the regulars got Joe out of sight, they "attended" to him. They dumped him at the edge of camp and fled into the darkness. Wild indignation spread in camp, and soon got out of hand when a garbled report came that there had been a savage slingshot attack on Private George Wagner of F downtown. The boys learned *later* that Wagner, an orderly at department headquarters, had been assaulted by none other than Marshall Brewer, apparently on the suspicion that he was an "informer." Long before truth could overtake rumor, Wagner's comrades were exacting revenge from the Fifteenth Infantry.

Major Edward Grosskopff, DeRussy's inspector general, rode out to the camps with orders that both colonels get their culprits in irons. But that was easier said than done, since the number of miscreants was growing. John W. Masterson of G, determined to "have a mess of regulars," had set himself up as ringleader of fifteen assorted comrades bent on following the direct route to "revenge." Naturally, no fifteen Missourians alive could have whipped the Fifteenth Infantry, and the vengeance seekers soon fell back in a shower of bricks and other debris. The regulars needed to be a little careful, for one Missourian was unloading a revolver at them as the retreating force neared its camp. Colonel Best, alert to this situation, now called his regiment to arms, which meant a battle line of only about ninety men under the circumstances. This was Woodruff's "first appearance under arms since I recd. my wound at fort Blakely Apl. 9." Best and Grosskopff rode down to the regulars' camp to meet with authorities there, and Bona Shafer was left to command the Twenty-first Missouri in its confrontation with the angry mob outside camp. His heart ruling his head, Shafer ordered a bayonet charge, before which the regulars quickly melted. The trouble seemed over, and Shafer marched his triumphant legion back to camp.

Masterson was thought to have a concussion as well as a mangled face, and Roberts rated his chance of survival at fifty-fifty for some days. Woodruff sardonically figured that if Masterson "has not got a mess this time, he had better try again. I think however he will . . . call at some other firm for the next mess."

The next morning, it flared up again. McGonigle, Shafer, Sinnott, and Regimental Blacksmith Isaac Johnston stopped at a New Market Street tavern for cigars. There they were accosted by several noncoms and one buck private from the Fifteenth Infantry who had taken on sufficient booze to detect their natural enemies the Missourians—or "Hoosiers," as the inflamed regulars seemed to prefer. The private cheekily offered to beat McGonigle up, and the infuriated major stomped out for a guard detail sufficient to arrest the scamp.

It became necessary to arrest the entire gang, McGonigle found, and the regulars fell back in good order through the tavern to the security of an area discreetly known as the "Ladies Bedroom." A sergeant in the culprit squad was swearing loudly that "all the damned hoosiers in the city" could not arrest him, before Captain Shafer's revolver nudged his ear to induce caution. Once the prisoners were in the Twenty-first Missouri camp, the major released the noncoms on their promise to behave like "soldiers." The impudent private, however, was sent on to the provost marshal's "cross-barred hotel."

But the regulars, honoring their word to behave like "soldiers," now formed up a large group in the street, bayonets at the ready, a sergeant in command. All very military! And they marched on the Twenty-first's camp to procure their comrade's release. The "commander" of the guard even sent an "orderly" to Best to demand the prisoner, unaware that the matter was wholly out of Best's hands. Unable to get their comrade, the mutineers made ready to charge, just as their own officer of the day appeared. Time and again that official ordered him men to camp, and as often they openly defied him. Dangerous business, this! Colonel Best notified them that if *he* mobilized, the regulars *would* go back to camp.

That seemed to do the trick. The chastened offenders now backed off, furiously shouting that "you damned Hoosiers" or "you damned bloody cusses" had better free that comrade, or there would be blood on these streets. The regular officers assured Best that they would make a disposition "more just than merciful" of the mutineers, and Woodruff understood that they did. In retrospect, the whole business pointed up a certain advantage enjoyed by volunteers in such scrapping. It was almost inconceivable that a regular army officer would form up his outfit to pursue a street rumble originating at a liquor joint—but a volunteer officer might do just that.

Meanwhile, Captain Roseberry had not been so busy with Republican politics back in Clark County as to forget that his son still lay where comrades had hastily buried him at Blakely. To Rees, his next eldest, the captain conveyed a wish that Matt be brought home to the scenes of his boyhood. On December 21, Colonel Best granted furloughs to Rees, his cousin the sergeant major, and to Ted Harrison, assigned to disinter the remains and take them north. The next day the boys took a steamer across the bay and performed their heart-rending chore. It was midnight when they returned to the city. Early in January 1866, the sorrowing family and a local pastor saw the youth entombed in a hillside cemetery just west of St. Francisville.

The year ended with fewer than five hundred men still on the rolls, by no means all "accounted for." Companies A, D, E, and G were at Mount Vernon arsenal, and only Company C remained in Mobile, along with scattered parties from other companies. Lieutenant Charles Norton of D, heading a detachment mostly from G, was running the military prison in the city. B Company was still at Sparta; F at Bladon Springs, sixty miles north of town; H at St. Stephens; I at Claiborne; and K at Pollard. Now that they were so dispersed, occasions to fight with "Nigs" and "Regs" were almost gone.

Company G, arriving at Mount Vernon Chrismas eve, found it "a beautiful place." A Negro company was there, and Blackburn was careful to prevent "fraternizing." The recent battle of Mobile was enough. At least bibulous Missourians could celebrate holidays with segregated benders. "Major" Blackburn and Sutler Rufe Wilsey took off on several deer hunts that produced more hangovers than venison.

The new year brought excitement in the back country above Mobile. Well before daybreak on Monday, January 8, DeRussy ordered Captain Palmer's Company C to board the *Republic* for Montgomery Hill, a good seventy-five miles north. The trouble here, Palmer heard, lay with "jayhawking" guerrillas who had seized the steamer *Lily* and its nine hundred bales of cotton on the Tombigbee above McIntosh's Bluff. This gang, perhaps forty in all, had fired on the *Lily*, wounding her pilot and bringing her to shore. A newsman reported that

> . . . the hijackers boarded the boat, and made prisoners of . . .
> eight soldiers, whom they delivered to a portion of the force which
> left immediately with them. The sergeant was retained, and placed
> under guard on the boat. Fifteen of the gang took possession, and
> ran her down to Karney's Landing. . . . After landing the passengers,
> they proceeded down . . . to the Alabama, taking her through the
> cut off near the mouth, to Montgomery Hill, where they landed,
> and commenced taking off the Government cotton.

A Negro deckhand, having escaped, met Company C and gave the alarm. Palmer coolly planned a surprise for the ruffians at the landing: while the company stood by, a corporal and a squad of six crept down to the landing to gauge the size of the gang. The Missouri corporal, whose name we can only guess, came face to face with the guerrilla leader in the brush along the river. Before either could shoot, the "captain" skedaddled, and his gang jumped ship. This paved the way for the Missourians to take possession of the *Lily*. A Mobile editor gratefully proclaimed that "this prompt vindication of public safety reflects great credit on the gallant Captain, and we hope that the parties whose property has been saved will offer suitable testimonials of their gratitude to the captain and his brave fellows. Alas poor Missouri! Wherever her sons have cast their fortunes, they have ranked 'the bravest of the brave.' "

Others were also ranging far and wide in a struggle against depredations of cotton thieves. In the last days of January, Captain Black-

burn, with Lieutenant Sinnott guiding him, led Company G up the
Tombigbee to recapture another boatload of cotton, and Lieutenant
Amburn took Company A up that stream to chase off desperadoes
firing at passing boats. During most of February, Sinnott was away
heading an expedition into central Mississippi to run down more elu-
sive cotton "dealers."

By the end of February, the rolls were down to 470 names. Old
stalwarts were slipping away, unwilling to tarry here so long after the
war's end. Epidemics of yellow fever and other maladies around
Mobile provided additional excuses for do-it-yourself muster outs.
Bill Killen of Company D disappeared February 15. But the biggest
single day's exodus came on April 3, when Company G alone lost
six: Woodruff, John Springer, Amos James, Alonzo Cummings, Sam
Lee, David White. Such departures the Department of War would in
time forgive.

Not every Missourian found his circumstances so intolerable. Several married into local families. Among those taking Alabama wives
were Ben Moody of Company F, who departed secretly for Croton on
January 4, 1866, after wedding Laura Dunn at Bladon Springs. James
D. Rolen of the same outfit married Laura Wheelis there on March 4,
with Joe Wright and Marion Monroe in attendance. He stayed in uniform to the end, however. Jim Griffin did the same, and upon mustering out he also took home a "rebel bride," the former Mary Nettles
of Pollard.

Wherever the Missourians were scattered, temptations to human
weaknesses faced them. In the closing days, the orneriness reached up
into headquarters. On Thursday evening, March 30, Colonel Best took
a party of cronies to the race course at the south outskirts of Mobile
for an evening of cards and refreshments. Captains Josh Hagle and
Jim Smith were with him, as was Dan Pressell. Most unfortunately,
General Woods' judge advocate learned, Best "did . . . remain absent
from his Camp until a late hour of the night . . . —and while absent
did engage in gambling, drinking and noisily Quarreling with the pro-
prietors and bar-keepers of a certain saloon connected with the race
course, and also with the horse jockeys, loafers and usual company
collected in such places—and . . . did publicly and noisily announce
himself as connected with the said 21st Mo. Vols.—and did threaten
to use the Military Power of said regiment in the settlement of his
and his Officers private brawls."

The following morning, at Best's orders, Hagle and a detail from

Company I marched out to arrest the tavern's management. The civilians, realizing the irregularity of all this, unwisely stood on their rights, with the result that two were severely beaten and a large part of the saloon's equipment and stocks were destroyed. Three civilians were dragged away before word reached downtown that the Missourians were "off the reservation" again. On Friday afternoon, General Woods freed the captives and ordered Best, Hagle, Smith, and Pressell under arrest, "pending serious charges to be preferred against them"

While Best was seeking a chance to explain it all in person, Woods was intently greasing the skids for the young Missouri colonel. A thorny problem, however, was that the department lacked "a sufficient number of officers . . . with the required rank to constitute a court." Would General Thomas convene one at Mobile with generals and colonels from the military division of the Tennessee? Thomas would not. A week later, he rejected Woods' plea, explaining that since the Twenty-first Missouri was about to muster out, "It is not considered expedient to bring this officer to trial." Thus spake the Rock of Chickamauga—and thus did Joe Best and his friends avert a calamitous end to their military careers.

General Thomas had set April 19, Thursday, as muster-out day for the regiment, and Best started gathering his Missourians at Fort Morgan. In they came from Mobile, posts up country, and points around the bay. Rees, sporting captain's bars, returned to Company D after a winter's day as General Woods' aide. Last to rejoin were Lieutenant Norton and his prison guards, who arrived the morning of the appointed day after a miserable voyage through a damp fog. Others were also coming in from guardhouses and hospitals, among them Joe Cameron and others involved in the affair at St. Stephens.

Fewer than three hundred answered this last roll call at Fort Morgan. Still among them were 192 men that had mustered in at the beginning, including four original officers who had served all the way: McGonigle, Pressell, Blackburn, and Yust. Among old stalwarts of 1862 present for the closing ceremony were the Alvis brothers of Company G; August, John and Julius Bandhauer (A); James Eagelson (A); Bill Haynes (H); Jonathan Johnson (H); Bill Leedom (F); Lewis Quest (K); and George Wilson (H). Over the years 1,508 men had mustered at one time or another, and 285 of them were now dead—66 from battle causes, the others from disease, accidents, and murders. In more than four years of service, 92 had suffered nonfatal wounds, 74 had seen the inside of rebel prisons, and 208 had taken disability discharges. Colonel Best and Adjutant Hall carefully furled two national color-flags, two regimental banners, and that "veteran flag" presented by the St. Louisans—and these stand cased today with the colors of Missouri's federal regiments on the main floor of the capitol in Jefferson City.

As these happy warriors, citizens at last, embarked for St. Louis, their homefolk were witnessing a mighty tug-of-war between President Johnson and his Radical enemies of the Congress over "reconstructing" the fallen South. The President's recent veto of a civil-rights act, coupled with his open doubts of Afro-American fitness for "the privileges and immunities" of citizenship, had warmed Southern hearts but inflamed the Radicals determined to subdue this "accidental president" from Tennessee. "Old boys" of the Twenty-first Missouri would sooner or later plunge into the political wars stemming from the national bloodbath, and their "old colonel" would be ready, too. A retired Brigadier General David Moore awaited these brave lads who had "never turned their backs to the enemy, but marched steadily forward amidst the tempests of shot and shell."

16

Sound the Jubilee

How could the coming half-century of comparative peace match the excitement of the epic years now ending? The old boys would necessarily dream on the "vernal thunder of our morn" and relive in memory times pregnant with historic meaning as nothing else they would ever know. For a lucky few, satisfying careers of public or professional service would render the letdown relatively painless.

With good reason did Bruce Catton wonder how it ever became possible for Missourians to live again in peace with one another. That took time—and new concerns. The case of Father McMenomy provides a straw in the wind. Scorning the iron-clad oath required even of clergymen by the new constitution, he faced indictment in November 1865. Sheriff Fulton had to serve the summons. The trial mercifully never took place, for his bishop quietly transferred the once-militant priest to Iowa. Much to the relief of Conservatives, however, the oath soon withered under hostile judicial treatment.

Out of passions engendered by the conflict there came, on July 20, 1866, the era's most sensational homicide in northeastern Missouri. James A. Merriwether, former Confederate soldier, was shot down in Colony. Witnesses accused two veterans of Company D, Twenty-first Missouri—Henry Hubble and William Killen. The community had been buzzing with rumors that Merriwether, while peddling books in Iowa, had squabbled with a country doctor and imprudently cast aspersions on Moore's troops. Many enraged veterans were spoiling to see Merriwether come back to Colony.

Days passed, and no arrests occurred. The Conservative outcry was loud as the Radical rulers of Knox County made no move to punish anyone. Elias Wilson was circuit judge, Major Fulton was sheriff, and the prosecutor shared their political views. The regional press took predictable postures, Barrett thirsting for immediate retribution and Howe forgiving the gunmen because the victim was "an agent of the Canton

Press." "Are not these outrages to be met?" an anonymous Conservative pleaded. "Shall not the law be sustained?"

Sustained it was—after a fashion. Killen and Hubble did come to
trial November 11, 1867. Three jurors, it happened, were from a family embarked on a century of Republican militancy. Moreover, Jacob
Morris, Henry Richart, and Aaron Oldfather were veterans of the
Twenty-first Missouri, while yet another juror was the father of David
Glenn of Company I, mortally wounded at Shiloh. Colonel John F.
Benjamin, defense counsel, could not resist addressing himself "more
to the feeling and prejudices of the 'loyal' jurymen than to their un-
impassioned and deliberative judgment" and thereby won instant ac-
quittal. Conservatives railed at such rough justice, but it was the best
kind then available.

Naturally, the war's fevers still tormented the electorate of 1866.
Dave Moore, having lately wedded Steve Carnegy's widowed daughter-
in-law, entered Lewis County politics to stand for sheriff at the Radical
convention, only to suffer defeat at the hands of a former militiaman.
Howe engineered this outcome, resurrecting the canard that Moore had
been a "Secessionist in '61" and pointing to the disloyalty in his family! Obviously, this was revenge for Moore's expulsion of Howe's
guardsmen from his camp in 1861. General Moore, however, reduced
the offending newsman to silence during a chilling confrontation over
Howe's insinuation at a preelection rally in Canton.

Joe Best faced similar handling in the Scotland County Radical convention as he sought the circuit clerkship. The young colonel had
lately married "Miss Frank," Dave Moore's only daughter, but association with the erstwhile folk hero seemed to be worth no more here
than at Monticello. The convention rejected him for the original first
sergeant of Company H, John C. Smith.

Things were different in Keokuk, where the hyperthyroid intoler-
ance of Missouri's Radicalism cut little ice. Doc Seaton, still holding
the Republicans at arm's length, ran in 1866 as an independent and
regained his council seat relinquished the previous year. The Republicans accepted Doc, political warts and all, as a worthy city father,
but the *Constitution* still saw him as a black abolitionist.

Several political careers in Missouri interested the veterans. Bishop
served his term as state treasurer and passed into obscurity. In spring
1879, he died at a settlement he had helped found just east of Kahoka.
The local press took ample note of his demise, but the event rated only perfunctory treatment in Canton and Keokuk and none in Quincy.

A. J. Smith, after resigning his commission in 1869, settled in St.
Louis, where President Grant made him postmaster. When a wave of
strikes swept the city in 1877, he commanded state militiamen called
out to keep order. Throughout the eyars following, Smith was city
auditor, retiring in 1889. On January 30, 1897, a cerebral hemorrhage
claimed him, and mourning was widespread among his old "guerrillas."

Chaplain Callihan, like most of his fellow Radicals, enjoyed a brief
rise and sudden fall. In 1868-1869 he served as treasurer of Clark
County, but thereafter he devoted his life to gospel ministry and reconciliation. His death came at Kahoka in 1892, following a para-
lytic stroke.

Following his rejection by Lewis County Radicals at Monticello,
David Moore served two terms as Canton's nonpartisan mayor. In
1869, while a bedridden "noncandidate," he lost narrowly to George
Pledge, his trusty old artilleryman of 1861. But Dave's real political
glory was just around the corner. Missouri's Radicalism was running
aground on its internal contradictions and vindictiveness, and from its
riven side emerged the Liberal Republican movement of Carl Schurz
and Gratz Brown. The precipitating issue was the continued pro-
scription of those tainted with "disloyalty." In the political earth-
quake of 1870 that saw Brown nominated for governor, the Democrats "played possum" and pledged their votes to various Liberal
Republicans. David Moore of Canton jumped clear of the Radical
wreckage and wound up as a "Brown man" in the state senate.

Moore's senatorial quadrennium was his last. His Democratic
friends, fully enfranchised after 1870, shouldered aside their Liberal
Republican surrogates. Starting in 1872, the Democrats embarked on
three decades of unbroken "Conservative" rule in Jefferson City, and
when 1874 rolled around Senator Moore prudently left office. But
while he flourished in the capitol, he served as chairman of the militia committee and took a hand in senatorial redistricting. Moore also
joined the Democratic caucus that sent Frank Blair to the United
Stated Senate, and he won acclaim by sponsoring a commission to prepare a fitting monument over the remains of the late Senator Green
at Canton.

Moore was not, as it happened, the only man of his regiment to
win a seat in the legislature. Josiah Davis, after a brief career of school
teaching in Schuyler County, became an influential minister widely regarded as "a man of beautiful character and sincerity." Having captured the imagination of a rising generation of Adair County Repub-

licans, he was in 1886 "drafted" for the House. He won handily.
Two years later he quadrupled his margin for a second term. Particularly pleasing to the erstwhile captain of Company B was the presence of Steve Hall on the victorious ticket, as this old comrade repeatedly won the Adair County surveyor's office by landslide perform-
ances.

Captain Roseberry endured the stormiest career. This venerable
sachem of Clark County Radicalism became presiding judge in 1866,
and two years later Peter Washburn joined him on the three-man
court at Waterloo. Hottest issue in town was the proposed Missouri
and Mississippi Railroad. This line—planned to run north from Macon
through Knox, Clark, and other counties to Keokuk—would be an
economic godsend, and it was quite in keeping with Radical dogma
that Roseberry and Washburn welcomed its benefits to Fairmont, St.
Francisville, and other communities.

The M&M board could proceed only with financial backing from counties along its right of way. But the upheavals of 1870 complicated matters.
Prior to this time, with many Conservative landowners muzzled by the
oath, the electorate was much friendlier to bond issues—secured by taking
real property. Knox County voted a $100,000 issue in 1867, and the next
year Clark Countians voted to invest $75,000 in the road's capital stock.
By 1870 the voters were balky, and the judges grew powerless to persuade
them to approve further outlays demanded by the company.

With M&M hanging in the balance, Roseberry and Washburn on May 3,
1871, raised Clark County's subscription to $200,000—without con-
sulting the electorate. Only thus, they felt, could the money be raised
to see this vital public improvement to completion. Such highhandedness
infuriated Kahoka's intransigently Democratic *Gazette*. Indeed, following a mass meeting in Waterloo in which the judges were promised vigilante
treatment, the *Gazette* openly bade the outraged public to "set aside the
law" temporarily to "avenge . . . wrongs suffered from the subscription.

Worse was to come. The court in May 1872 accused the company
of reneging on its contracts and voided all unissued bonds. The M&M
board now shut down construction—permanently. The taxpayers were
now legally bound to pay eastern "receivers" for a railroad that would
never exist! Enraged Clark Countians abolished their three-man court
in June 1872 and created a five-man directorate to run it. This Democratic board settled with receivers for thirty cents on the dollar in
1881, and the county treasurer made final payment ten years later.
Hard-shell Democrats nurtured a lifelong delusion that their lost money

had somehow disappeared into the pockets of those "Black-Republican" judges.

Other judges enjoyed less tumultuous terms. Tim Holman, a power among Scotland County Democrats, served an unexpired term as presiding judge, by appointment of Governor Thomas T. Crittenden. In 1880, Casper Fetters, late of Company D, brushed aside a Republican opponent to capture Knox County's presiding judgeship, and held it for a decade. In 1883, Bill Cook of Company E joined him, defeating his Republican challenger Charles Morrey for western district judge. During the 1880s Frank Stutenberg of Company B failed twice to become the Republican minority on Judge Fetters' court.

The old regiment boasted several county clerks. Nick Starr, seeking a full term, won the Lewis County Radicals' nomination in 1866, while Editor Barrett scolded this "very estimable public servant" for keeping "bad political company." This was, of course, a matter of personal taste, but with many Democrats disfranchised, Starr led a victorious Radical slate to Monticello with a 798-541 bulge over a hapless "Conservative" rival. By 1870, the Democrats were pulling themselves together, and one of their first new-breed clerks appeared at Waterloo. Matt Woodruff served one term as county clerk, then retired from the office.

Woodruff's truly great moment came in early 1876, when he was chosen for the jury that heard the famous Whisky Ring case in the federal district court at St. Louis. Orville E. Babcock, President Grant's private secretary, was under indictment for conspiring with the St. Louis Internal Revenue Office to extort "contributions" from distillers in return for tax favors. Somehow, despite Matt's aversion to abolitionists, he joined those capitulating to the President's emotional plea to spare his precious Babcock. The remaining five years of Woodruff's life were relatively uneventful.

Joe Best, after a decade as a bookkeeper of the Scotland County National Bank, ran as a Democrat for county clerk in 1882. Far and away the best vote getter on the ticket, he led the Democrats to a smashing triumph. Four years later, he survived a Republican challenge that cost his party half its county offices. Saving Best, no doubt, was his war record, his recent elevation to command of a Grand Army of the Republic post near Memphis, and his service as a delegate to the Democrats' 1886 state convention. He was only forty-eight, his prospects gleaming. Then, on August 4, 1887, Best suffered grievous injuries at the Memphis fairground. Fearing his horse was commencing a runaway, he leaped from his buggy, only to fall across the wheel. Two days later, he died of internal injuries, to the intense despair of Frances Moore Best and her aging father. Three sons and two daughters mourned him also.

Republicans were not out of season entirely, but they had to pick their locations carefully. C. Z. Russell found in the southern Missouri countryside of Dade County that Republicans were more at home than north of the river. The somber, no-nonsense newcomer developed a political following. Active as a Disciples of Christ elder and editor of Greenfield's *Vedette*, he was soon a member of the Republican State Central Committee. In 1886 he was elected county clerk in a Republican sweep, and served through 1894. He spent the last years prior to his death at Greenfield in 1906 in selling real estate, writing insurance, winning an attorney's license, and cultivating the friendship of a grandson—who recalled for the present writer a switching given him by the "perturbed" former adjutant of the Twenty-first Missouri. A great-grandson still operates the insurance and abstracting agency Lieutenant Russell founded.

There were also county treasurers. In the 1870s, Henry McGonigle performed the dual roles of collector and treasurer of Knox County, and at his death in 1881 a local editor deplored "a sad and irreconcilable vacancy in our midst." A priest solemnly interred the major in historic St. Joseph's churchyard near many old Irish comrades of the thunderous 1860s. In Lee County, Iowa, veering rapidly back to its Democratic ways, Doc Roberts held the treasurer's job six years. Thereafter, he edited Fort Madison's daily *Democrat*, traveled, and enjoyed veterans' organizations and lodge work. Out in western Kansas, meanwhile, Lair Dean of Company I was looming as an important Republican of Smith County. At a special election in 1881, he became county treasurer for an unexpired term. In the next decade, he served on the state penitentiary commission, and when death came at Smith Center in 1904 he was an active realtor.

Dave and Ed Moore took turns as mayor of Canton and served on the city council. Other notable mayoralties were those of George Fulton and Martin Sinnott. Moving to Kinsley, 120 miles west of Wichita, in 1876, Fulton invested twenty thousand dollars in building the Anchor Steam Flouring Mill, and passing years gave him prominence among area Republicans. When death came in January 1890, he was the incumbent mayor, and a mourner declared that "no citizen of Kinsley stood higher in the estimation of his neighbors."

Sinnott arrived in Arkansas City, a settlement on the windblown plains southeast of Wichita, in 1878. Soon he was city marshal, and in time city clerk. Then, in 1903, the good citizens elevated the versatile Irishman to the mayor's chair. Serving three years, Sinnott returned to the clerkship. When he died at seventy-nine of pneumonia on January 8, 1925, a local editor eulogized him: "This man had a real task in life and he finished it with complete satisfaction."

Republican diehards persisted in northeastern Missouri's hostile climate. Dave Cravens of Company I was an organizer and treasurer of a McKinley-Hobart club at Arbela, Scotland County, in 1896. Nick Starr, heading Lewis County's Republicans, was a delegate to the state convention in 1884. The turn of the century saw Jonathan Johnson at the helm of Clark County's Republicans, and even a Democratic editor generously saluted him as "the solid old warhorse of his party."

Most of the boys had come from farms, and most of them returned to farms. John H. Cunningham became "one of the leading farmers of northern Knox County for half a century, and he was well known and respected all over the county." A few miles north, in Scotland County, there farmed Eli Kenoyer of D, Charles Oliver and Alf Rathbun of I, Captain Shane Palmer, Lieutenant Hudson Rice, and Gus and Buel Stevens.

Among others who followed this calling in northeastern Missouri were Bill Leedom of Company F, in Schuyler County, and Frank Downs of Company K, in Lewis. Aaron Mattley farmed on both sides of the Scotland-Clark line, and Peter Washburn operated several large tracts in southwestern Clark County. Edwin Smith of C took up farming near Athens. Just northwest of the hallowed battleground there lived Bill French, on a fifty-acre farm that he acquired on his return in 1865. An active Methodist, but not much of a joiner otherwise, Bill lived out his remaining forty-five years in quiet dignity and industry, cherishing memories of a thrilling career as "Colonel Moore's body guard."

Certainly the most successful ruralist of them all was Captain Story. In 1875 he purchased a 276-acre spread in Missouri near Moscow Mills, fifty miles southeast of Hannibal. His specialties were wheat and apples, and a relative noted on one visit to the captain's farm that he had a thousand bushels of apples ready to ship. An oldtime Whig, Story was ever afterward a staunch Republican—and was also father of a Lincoln County judge. Friends marveled at the "unusual mental calibre," splendid eyesight, and perfect hearing that endured through the ninety-nine years of his life.

There was a westward drift of ex-soldiers toward better and cheaper farms available to homesteaders. Kansas got the largest share of Moore's old boys. Adolphus Singleton of Company H farmed in the southern part until infirmities of age relegated him to town life in Yates Center. When he died in 1926, Dolph was praised for measuring up "to the highest ideals of Christian citizenship." Valiant "Uncle Jesse" Roberts farmed in southwestern Kansas until his death at Ashland in 1904. Fred Yust, developing "Kansas fever," took up a 160-acre homestead near Sylvia, northwest of Wichita, in 1874. After settling there with his brother Charles and their father Fred Senior, Fred prospered. As his farm and bank account grew, he marveled at his good fortune in "getting out of Germany at the right time" and moving to Kansas "when it and I were young." His second son, George, owner of Sylvia's weekly *Sun*, made his mark in Kansas journalism, and the oldest of his nine children, William, became librarian of the University of Chicago—and his father's biographer.

Grief was also Fred's lot at times. His youngest son, Benjamin Harrison Yust, died suddenly in 1910 while a freshman at Baker University in Baldwin, Kansas. And when the old soldier was seventy-three, his adopted country declared war on the land of his fathers. Fred had tried to keep the family bilingual, but after 1917 "he never wrote . . . another German letter." Still, as Fred lay near death at Sylvia in February 1937, the children could hear him murmur that "goodness and mercy have followed me all the days of my life."

Others dedicated their lives to Christian ministry. Ben Northcutt and Josiah Davis proved useful and popular Disciples of Christ pastors. After ordination in 1868, Northcutt served congregations in northeastern Missouri for two decades. He confined his preaching to Adair County at first in order to live at Kirksville and see his sons through the normal school. Upon retirement, he moved to Knox City, dying there in 1894. Davis became even more widely known in that region, enjoying vast popularity because he "did not allow his politics to color his friendships." Even when his active days were over, hundreds of young lovers sought him out to officiate at their weddings.

"Northern" Methodists enjoyed the ministry of John H. Cox to the turn of the century. Abandoning politics in 1866, he subdued his partisan rancors. Placing his hopes in youth for a peaceful mor-

row, he devoted himself especially to children. Not until his pastorate at Maryville in 1886 did he join the Grand Army of the Republic, and so casual was his membership that he never moved it in the
sixteen years prior to his "super annuation" and death in 1902. Comrades of Company H could not get him to the regimental reunions.
Still, embers of militancy smoldered behind the goateed kindliness.
During his heyday, at Trenton between 1889 and 1893, while building the sanctuary still in use, Cox undertook to "cleanse" the rolls of
members whose worthiness seemed nominal. He warned the congregation that "love of numbers and wealth makes the church a palace car
to furnish fashionable transportation to perdition for a lot of godless
church members." The conference obliged Cox to take the expellees
back, but he incurred no reprimand from the denomination.

"Brother Cox" had two daughters. The younger, Nan, was mother-
less from the day of her birth at Brookfield in 1884, and friends there
raised her as their own. Sadly, scarlet fever claimed Nan in her teens.
The older, Gladdice, accompanied her widowed father to his pastor-
ates at Maryville and Trenton. In the latter city, the tall and witty
young lady captivated a local editor, and at Christmas 1889 she became the bride of Charles D. Morris, himself child of a Union army
chaplain. Morris, later the Republican state chairman, lost his party's
gubernatorial nomination in 1916 after a bitter but historic primary.

The regiment enjoyed representation in other callings. Besides
Russell, Jim McFall and Peverly Smith also passed bar examinations
to practice, respectively, in Linn and Clark counties. George Washburn,
after studying architecture in Quincy, rose to become the state archi-
tect of Kansas. Various courthouses, churches, banks, and correction-
al institutions of Kansas and the Midwest still in use bear the stamp
of his design and supervision. Baker University boasts several buildings Washburn planned. Among physicians who came out of the regiment were Jess Maggard and Captain Pearce of Company C, and surgeons Roberts, Knickerbocker, Wyman, Seaton, and Stanley.

Among successful businessmen were Logan Tompkins, Jim Beal of
E, Henry Wellington of F, Bona Shafer, Ed Moore, Lewis Quest, and
Jerry Hamilton. After farming four decades in Knox County, Beal re-
tired at sixty to purchase an interest in the Citizens Bank of Edina.
When death came, fifteen years later in September 1919, he was the
bank's president. Tompkins served many years as a bank clerk in St.
Louis, rising at the end of the century to cashier of the State National
Bank. Wellington, who counted his friends by the thousands, contin-
ued his father's furniture business in Memphis until retiring in 1905.

Quest retailed furniture and provided undertaking service at Palmyra, and his son Joseph carried the business on after the old soldier's death in 1932. Ed Moore, managing his "agricultural depot" in Canton, was long regarded as a "real, enterprising, go-ahead fellow." Prior to Shafer's retirement in 1890, he ran a grocery in Edina. Hamilton, at his death in 1879, was co-owner of the Great Western Flour Mill at Memphis.

Two others associated with the regimental story merit attention. They were Henry Collark, the black child adopted as "mascot" in 1864, and Joe Rickey, the son and namesake whom old Doc appointed sutler's clerk back in the first winter of the War. After a brief time with the Twenty-first Missouri, Joe had slipped away to the Confederate army. By early 1863, however, he was a parolee learning the ropes of commodity speculation in St. Louis. After the war, he located at Fulton, north of Jefferson City, and cultivated the friendship of leading politicians. Branching out into Wall Street, he won and lost two fortunes and acquired such a reputation for sumptuous living that a gin-based cocktail was named for him.

Young Collark, coming "home" to Missouri with his friends, yearned for an education. In unceasing pursuit of his goal, he worked on Iowa farms in summers and attended school in other seasons. In time he became an educator, and a successful one. To the delight of the boys he had met in 1864, Collark appeared at their 1920 reunion in Kahoka. Like his comrades of long ago, the sixty-two-year-old schoolman was graying, and a nostalgic fascination for his martial childhood drew him again to those with whom he had shared it. He was teaching at Chandler, Oklahoma, and was a major landowner of the region.

The ex-soldiers flocked into civic and fraternal organizations. Purmort and Wellington were prime movers in the Northeast Missouri Agricultural and Mechanical Fair held at Memphis in the years just after the war. The Anti-Horse Thief Association, founded by David McKee before the War and resuscitated in 1863 at Millport, claimed the allegiance of many veterans of the Twenty-first Missouri. Nicholas Murrow, Ed Alvis, John P. Morris, Jonathan Longfellow, and Bill Matlick were but a few of those active in the association before it "went national" a decade after its revival.

The old boys joined lodges. Freemasonry revived in northeastern Missouri, with old and new enthusiasts joining forces. David Moore was active for years at Canton, as were Asa Starkweather and Ed Moore. Steve Carnegy reigned as Canton lodge's "grand old man" to his death in 1892—at age ninety-five. George Fulton, out in Kansas, and Joe

Farris, at Keokuk, maintained masonic connections all their days. The
Odd Fellows movement was also strong in the region, numbering among
its adherents Tom Amburn and Nicholas Murrow. Among leaders of
the Benevolent and Protective Order of Elks in Kansas was George
Washburn.

As the boys aged, they became involved in veterans' activities.
Tompkins, as aide to Frank Blair, was among the two dozen officers
who met at Raleigh, North Carolina, to organize the Society of the
Army of the Tennessee in the closing days of the war. Dan Pressell
and Ed Blackburn were among the early members of the society.
Much more to the liking of ex-soldiers was the Grand Army of the
Republic. So far as the Twenty-first Missouri was concerned, this
was just the pressure mechanism needed to persuade the Department
of War to forgive all those premature departures from Mobile. If the
word "deserter" stained a man's record, he was ineligible for pension-
ing. Some were falling victim to "pension sharks" claiming fraudu-
lently the power to have desertions expunged—for a fee. How much
better to have it all done as a matter of policy!

By the early 1880s, GAR posts were blooming across northeastern
Missouri. On the motion of Joe Best, veterans at Memphis named
their unit for the lamented Major Murray on June 21, 1884. Earlier,
Arbela's bluecoats had named theirs for Tom Weber, slain at Fairmont
in home guard days, and they quite understandably pressed the state encampment of 1884 to recognize eligibility of all guardsmen "thrown
out by the consolidation" of 1862. Canton's old soldiers voted to
perpetuate the memory of Major King in 1883 and chose David Moore
as their commander, Nick Starr as their deputy commander. The prominence of the Twenty-first Missouri in the region is clear from names
adorning posts in various localities. La Grange's veterans dedicated
theirs to Ed Menke; and the boys at Brashear, in Adair County, enshrined the name of Sergeant Tom Ryan, killed on the *Sir William
Wallace* at Island 71. When old comrades at Lancaster applied for
their charter, they fittingly memorialized Lieutenant Tom Richardson.
Finally, the old soldiers at Luray named their post for Aaron Brokaw,
longtime color-sergeant of Company H.

Longing for a regimental association manifested itself even as GAR
posts proliferated. After all, other outfits had theirs. Judge Holman,
active already in the Shiloh Survivors' Association, took it upon himself on August 5, 1888, to issue through area newspapers a call to assemble. The Brokaw and Weber posts would soon be staging a camp-

fire reunion at Arbela, and he proposed a special meeting there to form the "21st Missouri Veteran Volunteer Infantry Association." Tim reminded comrades that "General Moore . . . is now past 70 years of age, and in the natural course of life must ere long pay the debt of nature. Many of his old comrades who bore the brunt of the hailstorm of shot and shell through which the 21st conspicuously passed, with a devotion and gallantry seldom equalled, are now white headed men."

On August 18, the association was born, as seventy-three of the boys approved a constitution and elected Jonathan Johnson their president. Tim Holman accepted the treasurership, and the assemblage voted to make Phil Reynolds secretary and Dave Cravens vice-president.

Naturally, their thoughts focused on Dave Moore, whose presence could electrify such meetings. But the "Francis Marion of North Missouri" was not well. Circulatory afflictions kept him from attending the organization meeting, but when the boys met at Edina in August 1889 their old hero was among them. He reappeared in 1891 at Kahoka and shared the spotlight with Ben Prentiss, who never missed a chance to treat old soldiers to lengthy patriotic oratory. Dave made the opening address, and his followers acclaimed him president at the close of the session. "General Moore is growing old and the march of time has enfeebled his step," wrote a local journalist. "His 'old boys' gathered around him and grasped his hand with a warmth that betokened their high regard for their old commander. . . . The tie that binds 'those who shared their blankets and tents together and drank from the same canteen' is a mystery to all except the old soldiers."

This was Dave's valedictory. When the association met again at Edina the following year, he was not well enough to make the journey from his new home in St. Louis. Ed Moore, after chairing the meetings, was elected president. But the star of these festivities was Aaron Harlan. The Sage of Croton, now "80 past," offered a poem commemorating the recruiting trip home in 1862. The concluding stanzas were certainly the most affecting:

And when we've heard the last roll call,
Seen our last of earthly scenes,
With our old blue coat for a pall
We'll lay down to pleasant dreams.

And with that flag still waving o'er us,
That blessed emblem of the free,
We'll join in that immortal chorus
And help sound the jubilee.

Upon hearing the dreaded news that Colonel Moore had died in St.
Louis July 19, 1893, Ed Moore cancelled that year's reunion. St.
Louis, Quincy, and Keokuk newspapers generally and inexcusably ignored the old lion's passing. Barney King Post buried him in Canton's
Forest Grove beneath a plain government headstone, but the Ethan
Allen of 1861 lived on in the bodies and souls of other generations.
His children included five sons and a daughter by Diademia, two daughters by Mary Mattingly Carnegy. The Confederate sons, who apparent-
ly held their father at arm's length all his days, did generally well in
life. Bill flourished as a physician out West to the time of his death
at the turn of the century, and Gene carved out a notable career on
newspapers at Memphis and Palmyra, in Missouri, and at Toledo, Ohio.
John, an escaped POW when the war ended, became prosecutor of
Scotland County in 1889, before moving to the Indian Territory at
the opening of the Cherokee strip. He was the first mayor of Enid,
Oklahoma, and at the time of his death in 1919 was a municipal
judge. And a great-grandson of General Moore, William J. Giles, was
at this writing a leader of Enid's business community.

Once the association was launched, the clamor began for a regimental history. The 1891 reunion importuned the beloved general to
head a historical committee, including Frank Troth of Company I and
Jonathan Johnson. The Old Man's death sidetracked the project, but
in 1894 the association elected Edwin Moore historian with a mandate
to resume the work. Unfortunately, Ed died the following year before
getting anything done. Then, at the 1896 reunion in Canton, the survivors turned to Nick Starr and Tim Holman—and the third time
proved the charm. The authors brought their manuscript to the 1898
conclave, got it approved, and secured authority to print five hundred
copies. A year later, Tim Holman, having edited the manuscript and
gotten the books printed in Fort Madison for $76.50, distributed the
long-awaited copies of *The 21st Missouri Regiment Infantry Veteran
Volunteers* to the reunion at Fort Madison. Probably typical of the
old comrades' reactions was Bill Roseberry's oft-repeated endorsement:
"Good and true."

At Fort Madison, the association voted to send a delegation to the

Shiloh battlefield to assist the park commission in tracing the movements of the regiment at the Bull Run of the West. Doc Roberts, as
president of the association, headed the party, and boarding the steamer *Sidney* with him at Fort Madison on May 24, 1900, were Holman,
John Cunningham, and Noah Lane. At other points downstream,
Jonathan Johnson, Mike Cashman, George Sheeks, and Bill O'Connor
joined. Reaching the landing on Memorial Day, they traveled by
horse and buggy through old familiar scenes and staked out positions
held by the regiment that Sunday long ago. The next day the park
superintendent, D. W. Reed, lauded their work and promised their
findings would be cast into metal markers that would stud the area
from the Rhea farm to the Hornets' Nest.

The years slipped by, with the association holding meetings, usually in the county seats of northeastern Missouri. Occasionally, they
gathered at Quincy, Hannibal, or Keokuk. In 1905, they repaired to
vanishing Athens, and the celebration led naturally to much "refight-
ing—and several spurious interpretations—of the carnage enacted there
forty-four years earlier. Usually, three to five dozen of the old boys
came, and they were never hard put for conversation. They could
always lament recent deaths, such as that of Doc Roberts in 1901,
Colonel Lyon in 1912 out in California, or Jonathan Johnson in 1916.
They could bemoan the fate of Dan Pressell down in Mississippi. Dan
had opened a general store at Mayersville in Reconstruction days and
became a substantial citizen, with a brother-in-law sitting in Congress.
However, on July 31, 1883, Dan was arrested on charges of "outrag-
ing" a nine-year-old girl. Two days later, a crowd of hate-crazed whites
stormed the jail, seized the accused "Yankee," and hanged him from
an oak limb. Dan was sixty-five, and the horror of his lynching
gripped the editorial writers and the readers of major newspapers
across the nation.

And, while reliving Corinth and Tupelo, the aging warriors could
shake their heads over other tragedies. Wasn't it horrible the way poor
Joe Rickey went—swallowing that carbolic acid in 1903? And what
on earth caused Ed Moore to take that halter and disappear into the
brush on the Illinois side of the Mississippi early that June morning
of 1895? Friends from Canton found him later hanging by the neck
from the limb of a fallen tree. Moreover, wasn't it a shame the way
poor Bill Matlick was killed in the spring of 1903, getting his neck
broken in that tragic scuffle with his brother-in-law at a school-board
meeting in Sandhill? Wouldn't it have been wonderful if Captain

Story could have lived just a few more months to celebrate his hundredth birthday? And wasn't it a shame that Captain Roseberry, hounded out of Clark County, died an aged exile out in Vernon County, on the Kansas line, in 1891?

No death—except, perhaps, Abe Lincoln's—so riled the old boys as the hard fate that overtook Bill Edwards in 1901. There had been a fuss brewing between Bill and Everett Bartlett, a Memphis attorney and loan-office operator. A forger had swindled Bartlett out of seven hundred dollars, and the victim had blamed John Edwards, Bill's brother and also a veteran of Company I. Only when the real malefactor came to justice on a similar charge in Iowa did Bartlett concede error, and Bill began pressing him for public retraction of his remarks impugning John's character. Since Bartlett did not rush the vindication into print, Bill's impatience turned to anger. Before a crowd warmly partisan to his effort, Bill caught Bartlett outside the Citizens Bank on Friday afternoon, March 8, and took a horsewhip to him. The victim fled to his upstairs office, Bill in pursuit. At the head of the stairs, Bartlett whirled around with a revolver and began firing. One slug hit his tormentor's face, another his stomach. As the sheriff arrested Bartlett, a muttering throng carried Edwards to the Central Hotel, where he died before daybreak. He was fifty-eight.

Headed by Alfred Tinney, the Murray post of the GAR shrilly censured Bartlett, asking, "Where is the man among us who would not under similar circumstances take even more severe measures to punish one he believed guilty of doing a brother so serious an injury?" Public fury mounted; Bartlett, spirited away to Macon for safety, faced trial that spring at Monticello. Dave Justice, who had warned Bill to leave the man be, testified, as did W. W. Purmort. Found guilty, Bartlett received a two-year penitentiary sentence for fourth-degree manslaughter, but even this was set aside by the state supreme court the following year in a landmark decision. The court held that Bartlett, in his resort to deadly force, had gone well beyond the law's requirement by retreating to his office door. "This settles the case," the *Memphis Reveille* wearily conceded, even if it only convinced the boys of Murray post that city lawyers could always find instances to excuse their shenanigans.

When the association met at Kirksville in 1911, a familiar name appeared on the register. George Washburn, sixty-four, had laid down his busy professional life to start reliving his generation's historic experience.

Even if some outside Company H could not remember him, they recalled his late father, slumbering in his grave near Kahoka these thirty
years. They all soon knew George well and loved this charming comrade who never thereafter missed a chance to be with them.

Washburn, elected secretary-treasurer at the Kirksville reunion of
1916, remained an officer of the association the rest of his life. Bill
Bradley of Granger, late of Company C, was made president, and
Mike Cashman vice-president. When the boys met at Keokuk in July
1918, they persuaded Washburn to tell all about his role at Shiloh.
George needed no priming, for he was already active in the Shiloh
Survivors' Association. At the 1920 gathering in Kahoka, the old comrades elected him president, and he forthwith invited them to his home
town of Ottawa, Kansas, for the next meeting.

A dozen showed up at Ottawa in September 1921 for a festive reunion. Their president, whom they gratefully reelected, was now commanding the Kansas GAR—and how the boys loved the spotlight!
Among those coming from Missouri were Fred Wolter, Noah Lane,
and J. P. Morris. Lieutenant Allen came in from the old soldiers'
home at Leavenworth, and among other Kansans reporting to Washburn's living room were Quiller Barnes of nearby Williamsburg, Dolph
Singleton, and Rees Roseberry of Paola. One delightful feature was a
caravan of Ford touring cars that carried the white-bearded visitors on
a tour of the town.

The Kansas Grand Army met at Winfield in May 1922 under a pall
of gloom. Commander Washburn had just died of pneumonia, and
Ottawa's GAR post had seen him to his final rest in Highland Park.
Taps sounded all along the route of the procession from the home to
the large masonry mausoleum—as buglers stationed at distant intervals
echoed each other. Clarence Washburn, standing by the empty, purple-
draped "commander's chair," received condolences from his father's
comrades. From the Mississippi to the Rockies, aging veterans paused
in tribute to one who had left his mark on the Midwest. Indeed, a
half-century later, architecture classes from the University of Illinois
would still be touring his courthouses to see classics of their time and
type.

The dwindling legion marched on. The gathering at Wyaconda in
1922 attracted thirty; two years later, only half that number appeared
at Memphis. Starting with this meeting, Cashman became the peren-
nial president. And from 1924 the boys met at Memphis. The field

officers were all gone now, and after the recent deaths of Joe Farris and Bona Shafer, no captain remained. Indeed, of the lieutenants, there survived only Reece Allen and Bill Rickey.

Cashman welcomed the boys to the forty-second reunion, on August 21, 1929, at Memphis. Joining him were five others. Bill Leedom rode over from Lancaster, and John Morris came from Kahoka. Tom Gollihur, living in town, was there, as were Bill Roseberry, from Kirksville, and Eli Kenoyer, of Rutledge. A reporter found the courthouse "beautifully decorated, the work of people of the court house." After local pastors and singers presented a program of patriotic orations and songs that afternoon, Cashman gaveled the business meeting to order.

Should they go on? That was his question, necessitated by the advancing age of his listeners. At eighty-three, Mike and Bill Leedom were the youngsters, Kenoyer was eighty-eight. The little assemblage voted sorrowfully to disband. "So, the last gathering of this regiment . . . goes out of existence," mourned the *Reveille*. "Soon the 21st Mo. will be but a memory."

The Bureau of Pensions had forty-eight men of the Twenty-first Missouri still on its rolls. By the time of Franklin D. Roosevelt's inauguration, this number had shrunk to sixteen. And then, on June 20, 1933, friends and relatives saw Alonzo Cummings to his grave at Bloomfield, Iowa. He was eighty-nine. A week later, Lieutenant Rickey died in Clarinda, Iowa, from complications following a hip fracture. The erstwhile dentist and traveling salesman would have been ninety-nine the next January. Reece Allen having died in Colorado in 1927, he was the last of the officers.

Three more comrades—all in their nineties—died in 1934. Tom Gollihur died May 2 at his son's home in Memphis. During his younger days he had worked as a butcher, before and after a fruitless adventure as a gold prospector in Nevada. William Smith of Company K died at La Grange in August, closing a "life of ninety-three years, characterized almost to the last by physical and mental vigor." The summer being unusually hot and dry, many older folk languished, and Bill Roseberry was among these. That November, the once-robust old soldier died at Kirksville. Local folk recalled Roseberry as the last survivor of that first group of young men to volunteer at Edina in 1861—a party including Jack Trunnell, Mart Sinnott, and Bona Shafer.

After the death of Green Keltner at Springfield, Missouri, on October 4, 1936, there were but ten still living. The last man of

Company K, Keltner was also the sole survivor of the group transferred from the Twenty-fourth Missouri. Three others died that
autumn. Robert Wellbaum of Company H, life-long resident of Green-
top, north of Kirksville, died from "infirmities of old age." Bill Baker,
the last top sergeant of Company B, passed on in Oregon December
10, and six days later Bob Guthrie died in Wisconsin.

When death came to Fred Yust the next February, it robbed him
of a last pleasure he had set his heart on. The federal government
was planning an elaborate commemoration of Gettysburg for July
1938—the seventy-fifth anniversary—and every old boy in blue or gray
was offered an expenses-paid trip to the battlefield. Only one of Dave
Moore's old soldiers, Harvey Bloomfield of Company G, could go. Of
the 11,000 invited, 530 Johnnies and 1,420 bluecoats attended.

Before the end of 1937, two others of the Twenty-first would be
gone. Jim Griffin, ninety-seven, died in Canton October 30. Friends
who saw him buried in Forest Grove were aware that the last of Lewis
County's Union veterans was taking his leave. On November 7, John
Morris, dead at ninety-five in Kahoka, passed into "the treasury of
all true coin."

Bill Leedom, onetime corporal of Company F who had served "all
the way," died in Lancaster on June 27, 1938. He was the next-to-
last member of the Grand Army in Schuyler County, and as adjutant
of the Richardson post it had been his grim duty to return the charter
to national headquarters when the comrades grew too feeble for its
activities. Little more than a year after Leedom, Newton Sammons
died at Little Rock, Arkansas. The hardy old veteran of Company I
was almost ninety-four. Two others died within the next year.
Bloomfield, an original corporal of G discharged for disability after
Shiloh, "mustered out" on January 10, 1940, at Albia, Iowa. Perry
Martin of F, one of the first Croton guards, wounded at Shiloh and
Blakely, died May 22, 1940, in Oklahoma City.

Unaware he was the "rear guard" of Dave Moore's vanished host,
Mike Cashman lingered on at Quincy. He was not getting out much
to GAR meetings or visiting at the soldiers' home, but old friends often stopped by to help him while away the hours. As a plumber and
produce salesman, he had been a familiar figure as far back as most
Quincyites could recall. Life had been good, and it had often been
his privilege to feel the pulse of history. In 1936, at the dedication
of the Lorado Taft plaque commemorating the Lincoln-Douglas debate
in Quincy, he and the other survivor of that crowd did the unveiling.

Though childless, Mike was not alone. His never-tiring wife, Eva, daughter of John Kitts of Company B, watched over him.

But time, according to Isaac Watts' stately hymn, "bears all its sons away." A world Mike Cashman could never fathom had come into being. Cruel pagans perpetrating barbarities of which secession's gray legions were—God be praised!—incapable, bestrode the Old World, and the shadows of another war were even now lengthening over the American heartland. At last, on Saturday, March 8, 1941, Mike's creator drew the curtains on the final evening of his life, and Dave Moore's last skirmisher now crossed the river to report at the bivouac of our honored dead.

Bibliographical Essay

A monographic study of the Twenty-first Missouri Infantry encounters
an embarrassment of riches from its inception. Like a merry-go-round, the
subject offers numerous locations for a historian to get aboard. The following categories illustrate the variety of available sources.

FEDERAL RECORDS

The major published sources include *The War of the Rebellion: Official
Records of the Union and Confederated Armies* (Washington, D.C., 1880-
1901), 70 volumes in 128; *House Miscellaneous Document 186*, "Whiskey
Frauds," 44th Congress, 1st session; and *Senate Document 412*, "Missouri
Troops in Service during the Civil War," 57th Congress, 1st session. Many
valuable understandings can be gleaned from studying the census of 1860
as it applied to Lee County, Iowa, and the counties of Clark, Lewis, Knox,
Adair, and Scotland in Missouri.

Indispensable to this history are the holdings of the National Archives.
These embrace the book records of the regiment, command papers of
higher headquarters and jurisdictions, *Compiled Service Records of Volunteer Union Soldiers Who Served in Organizations from the State of
Missouri* (microfilm rolls 532-549), pension records of survivors, and
voluminous court-martial files well indexed and easily consulted. Attention should be given to the Hawkins Taylor Commission Musters in the
General Account Office records in the archives; this commission, sent
to identify and compensate the home guardsmen of 1861, compiled
valuable data on many who later served in the Twenty-first Missouri.

STATE RECORDS

Fruitful published sources include proceedings of the Missouri General
Assembly for the 1860s (unfortunately poorly indexed and in summary

paraphrase), *The Messages and Proclamations of the Governors of the State of Missouri*, ed. Buel Leopard and Floyd C. Shoemaker (Columbia, 1922), III-IV, and *Journal of the Proceedings of the Missouri State Convention* (St. Louis, 1861). For military data, one must consult the Office of the Adjutant General of Missouri in Jefferson City, operating one of the best military reference services in the nation. Here one may view original muster rolls of Missouri's Union forces, descriptive rolls, monthly returns, a partial set of Hawkins Taylor musters, and a rich collection of miscellaneous manuscripts.

COURTHOUSE RECORDS

Missouri's courthouses are poor hunting-grounds for genealogists, but military historians may learn much about the life circumstances of some Union veterans by examining probate records and, if the situation demands it, criminal cases filed in the circuit courtrooms.

STATE AND REGIONAL HISTORIES

A splendid literature in this category abounds, but scholars must handle older works with special care. Most pertinent to the present study were William V. N. Bay, *Reminiscences of the Bench and Bar of Missouri* (St. Louis, 1878); *Bench and Bar . . . of Missouri Cities* (St. Louis, 1884); Richard S. Brownlee, *Gray Ghosts of the Confederacy* (Baton Rouge, 1958); Albert Castel, *General Sterling Price and the Civil War in the West* (Baton Rouge, 1968); *History of Northeastern Missouri*, ed. Walter Williams (Chicago, 1913), I-III; William R. Jackson, *Missouri Democracy* (Chicago, 1935), I-II; Carl A. Landrum, *Quincy in the Civil War* (Quincy, Illinois, 1966); W. M. Leftwich, *Martyrdom in Missouri* (St. Louis, 1870); Joseph A. Mudd, *With Porter in North Missouri* (Washington, D.C., 1909); William E. Parrish, *Turbulent Partnership* (Columbia, Missouri, 1963) and *Missouri under Radical Rule* (Columbia, Missouri, 1965); James Peckham, *General Nathaniel Lyon and Missouri in 1861* (New York, 1866); Floyd C. Shoemaker, *Missouri and Missourians* (Chicago, 1943). Shedding additional light are outstate sources, such as J. Kurt van Achen's "Lives and Works of Early Kansas Architects" (Master's thesis, University of Kansas, 1966); Luther B. Hill, *History of Oklahoma* (Chicago, 1908), I-II; and *History of the State of Kansas* (Chicago, 1883).

COUNTY HISTORIES

Often replete with misinformation, these volumes do contain material whose sources have wholly or partially vanished. Indispensable to this history were Kate Ray Kuhn, *History of Marion County* (Hannibal, Missouri, 1963); *History of Lewis, Clark, Knox and Scotland Counties* (St. Louis, 1887); Christian County Centennial, Inc., *Christian County* [Mo.] : *Its First 100 Years* (Ozark, Missouri, 1959); *History of Marion County, Missouri* (Chicago, 1888); *History of Adair, Sullivan, Putnam and Schuyler Counties* [Mo.] (Chicago, 1888); *History of Dade County and Her People* (Greenfield, Missouri, 1917), I-II. The postwar migration of Missourians to Kansas and Iowa obliges some use of works such as *Portrait and Biographical Record of Leavenworth, Douglas, and Franklin Counties, Kansas* (Chicago, 1899); *History of Lee County, Iowa* (Chicago, 1879); and *Portrait and Biographical Album of Lee County, Iowa* (Chicago, 1887).

REFERENCE WORKS

In compiling a monograph of this kind, the scholar must live with dependable reference works. This list should suffice to illustrate materials most valuable: *Report of the Adjutant General of the State of Illinois* (Springfield, 1867), II (1861-1866); *Annual Report of the Adjutant General of Missouri for the Year Ending December 31, 1865* (Jefferson City, 1866); William F. Amann, *Personnel of the Civil War* (New York, 1961), I-II; *Appleton's Cyclopaedia of American Biography*, ed. James Grant Wilson and John Fiske (New York, 1887), III; atlases of *Lewis County, Missouri* (Keokuk, 1897), *Knox County* (Philadelphia, 1876), and *Howard County* (n.p., 1876); Mark M. Boatner, *Civil War Dictionary* (New York, 1959); *Campbell's Gazetteer of Missouri*, ed. R. A. Campbell, (St. Louis, 1875); *Confederate Military History*, ed. Clement A. Evans (Atlanta, Georgia, 1899), VI, VII, IX; *The Dictionary of American Biography*, ed. Allen Johnson and Dumas Malone (New York, 1928-1936), 20 vols.; Frederick H. Dyer, *A Compendium of the War of the Rebellion* (New York, 1959), I-III; Francis B. Heitman, *Historical Register and Dictionary of the United States Army* (Washington, D.C., 1903), I-II; Lurton D. Ingersoll, *Iowa and the Rebellion* (Philadelphia, 1866); Abraham Lincoln, *The Collected Works of Abraham Lincoln*, ed. Roy P. Basler (New Brunswick, New Jersey, 1953), VI; William M. Lytle, comp., *Merchant Steam Vessels of the United States* (Mystic, Connecticut, 1952);

Albert Dillahunty, *Shiloh,* National Park Service Historical Handbook
Series, No. 10 (Washington, D.C., 1955); William H. Powell, *Officers of
the Army and Navy (Volunteer) Who Served in the Civil War* (Philadelphia,
1893); Quartermaster General, U.S. Army, *Roll of Honor* (Washington,
D.C., 1866-1870), I-XXV (graves registration); *Revised Regulations for
the Army of the United States (1861)* (Philadelphia, 1861), should assuage
the reader's puzzlement at references to gold bars for captains and first
lieutenants.

Because St. Louis was the administrative nerve center of the war in
the West, a student may find it useful to consult the *St. Louis Directory
for 1864,* ed. Richard Edwards. For clarification of procedures, the reader may study F. A. Shannon, *The Organization and Administration of
the Union Army, 1861-1865* (Gloucester, Massachusetts, 1965), I-II. For
data on higher commanders, see Ezra Warner's *Generals in Blue* (Baton
Rouge, 1964), his *Generals in Gray* (Baton Rouge, 1959), and the West
Point Alumni Foundation's *Register of Graduates and Former Cadets of
the United States Military Academy* (West Point, N.Y., 1970).

GENERAL WORKS

Blending a regimental story into the big picture exacts thought and
effort, given the superabundance of primary and secondary volumes
devoted to the high and mighty. Most useful to this study were George
W. Adams, *Doctors in Blue* (New York, 1952); John G. Barrett, *Sherman's
March through the Carolinas* (Chapel Hill, N.C., 1956); *Battles and Leaders,*
ed. Robert U. Johnson and C. C. Buel (New York, 1884-1887), I-IV;
James M. Buckley, *A History of Methodism in the United States* (New
York, 1892), I-II; Bruce Catton, *Glory Road* (New York, 1952), *Grant
Moves South* (Boston, 1960), *Terrible Swift Sword* (New York, 1963),
and *Never Call Retreat* (New York, 1965); Thomas L. Connelly, *Autumn
of Glory* (Baton Rouge, 1971); Jacob D. Cox, *Franklin and Nashville*
(New York, 1882); E. T. Crisler, Jr., *The Battle of Helena* (Helena, Ar-
kansas, 1963); Grenville M. Dodge, *The Battle of Atlanta and Other Cam-
paigns, Addresses, Etc.* (Council Bluffs, Iowa, 1911); G. W. Dudley, *The
Lost Account of the Battle of Corinth,* ed. Monroe F. Cockrell (Jackson,
Tennessee, 1959); Charles Elliott, *A History of the M. E. Church in the
South-West* (Cincinnati, Ohio, 1868); James Elliott, *Transport to Disaster*
(New York, 1966); John Fiske, *The Mississippi Valley in the Civil War*
(Boston, 1901); Manning F. Force, *From Fort Henry to Corinth* (New
York, 1881); Douglas S. Freeman, *Lee's Lieutenants* (New York, 1942-

1944), I-III; Hugh C. Gresham, *Major David McKee* (Cheney, Kansas, 1937); Stanley F. Horn, *The Army of Tennessee* (Norman, Oklahoma, 1952) and *The Decisive Battle of Nashville* (Baton Rouge, 1956); Thomas P. Kettell, *A History of the Great Rebellion* (Cincinnati, 1865); John McElroy, *The Struggle for Missouri* (Washington, D.C., 1909); Shields McIlwaine, *Memphis down in Dixie* (New York, 1948); George F. Milton, *Conflict* (New York, 1941); Howard N. Monnett, *Action before Westport* (Kansas City, Missouri, 1964); Frank Moore, ed., *The Rebellion Record* (New York, 1862), I-II; Allen Nevins, *The War for the Union* (New York, 1959), I-II; John W. Pattison, *Biographical Sketches of the Officers and Members of the Twenty-Seventh General Assembly of Missouri* (Jefferson City, 1874); John Codman Ropes, *The Story of the Civil War* (New York, 1898), I-III; John B. Sanborn, *The Campaign in Missouri in September and October, 1864* n.p., n.d.); Thomas L. Snead, *The Fight for Missouri* (New York, 1886); Regis de Trobriand, *Four Years with the Army of the Potomac,* trans George K. Dauchy (Boston, 1889); Mark Twain *Life on the Mississippi* (New York, 1874).

BIOGRAPHICAL WORKS

Available studies deal almost exclusively with high personages, but one member of the regiment emerges with his own biography. Frederick Yust was commemorated by his son William F. Yust in *Fred Yust, Kansas Pioneer* (Winter Park, Florida, 1937). Other useful works include Stephen Ambrose, *Halleck* (Baton Rouge, 1962); Freeman Cleaves, *Rock of Chickamauga* (Norman, 1948); Henry Coppée, *General Thomas* (New York, 1912); J. F. C. Fuller, *The Generalship of Ulysses S. Grant* (Bloomington, Indiana, 1958); U. S. Grant, *Personal Memoirs of U. S. Grant,* ed. E. B. Long (New York, 1962); Robert S. Henry, *"First with the Most" Forrest* (Indianapolis, 1944); Max L. Heymann, Jr., *Prudent Soldier: A Biography of Major General E. R. S. Canby* (Glendale, California, 1959); John Bell Hood, *Advance and Retreat* (Bloomington, 1959); William M. Lamers, *The Edge of Glory* (New York, 1961); Lloyd Lewis, *Sherman: Fighting Prophet* (New York, 1932); B. H. Liddell Hart, *Sherman* (New York, 1958); Andrew N. Lytle, *Bedford Forrest and His Critter Company* (New York, 1931); Logan U. Reavis, *The Life and Military Services of General William Selby Harney* (St. Louis, 1878); John M. Schofield, *Forty-six Years in the Army* (New York, 1899); William T. Sherman, *Memoirs* (New York, 1875), I-II; W. G. Smith, *Life and Letters of Thomas Kilby Smith* (New York, 1898); William M. Sweeny, *A Biographical*

Memoir of General Thomas William Sweeny (n.p., 1907); Kenneth P. Williams, *Lincoln Finds a General* (New York, 1941).

UNIT HISTORIES

Many of the three thousand-odd Union regiments have been subjects of historical writing by their "alumni," very few by modern professional historians with access to official files and freedom to tell the story whole. Writers of first-generation accounts produced mementoes rather than monographs, making do without documentation kept confidential for the lifetimes of those involved, and such writers emphasized real or imagined triumphs and pleasures while ignoring life's seamier sides. Such a history is the valuable *The 21st Missouri Regiment Infantry Veteran Volunteers* by Nehemiah D. Starr and Timothy W. Holman, a building block essential to the present study (Fort Madison, Iowa, 1899). Bringing wider and often deeper understandings are histories of units who served with the Missourians and saw the same things. Chief among these are D. Leib Ambrose's *History of the Seventh Regiment Illinois Volunteer Infantry* (Springfield, 1868); the present writer's *The Eighteenth Missouri* (Indianapolis, 1968); Ephraim McD. Anderson's *Memoirs: Historical and Personal, Including the Campaigns of the First Missouri Confederate Brigade* (St. Louis, 1868); William W. Belknap's *History of the Fifteenth Iowa Veteran Volunteer Infantry* (Keokuk, 1887); R. S. Bevier's *History of the First and Second Missouri Confederate Brigades, 1861-1865* (St. Louis, 1879); John Hancock and William H. Tucker's *The Fourteenth Wisconsin Infantry: Corinth and Shiloh* (Indianapolis, 1895); Charles F. Hubert's *History of the Fiftieth Regiment Illinois Veteran Volunteer Infantry in the War of the Union* (Kansas City, Missouri, 1894); Lyman B. Pierce's *History of the Second Iowa Cavalry* (Burlington, 1865); *Roster of Iowa Soldiers in the War of the Rebellion* (Des Moines, 1908), I; and Henry H. Wright's *A History of the Sixth Iowa Infantry* (Iowa City, 1923).

HISTORICAL SOCIETIES

Because the regiment originated in that corner of the state bordering on Iowa and Illinois, the writer felt obliged to explore holdings of historical societies in all three states. Apart from the State Historical Society of Missouri and the Western Historical Manuscripts Collection in the Library of the University of Missouri at Columbia—the richest sources of archival matter—the author found essential materials in the Missouri Historical Society of St. Louis, among them the "Notebook of an Unidentified Traveller" who recorded in 1866 valuable contemporary impressions of northern Missouri. The Iowa Department of Archives and History, Des Moines, holds in its Samuel J. Kirkwood Papers and Southern Border Brigade Files documents crucial to an understanding of the guerrilla war of 1861 in the border region. The Kansas Historical Society made available information on George P. Washburn and provided access to useful newspapers. Several manuscripts of direct bearing on this monograph were in collections of the Illinois State Historical Society and the Illinois State Historical Library in Springfield.

VOLUNTARY ORGANIZATIONS

Members of the regiment were basically men with civilian interests, in churches, lodges, veterans' organizations. Notable among the sources from the latter group are *Report of the Proceedings of the Society of the Army of the Tennessee,* various annual meetings between 1870 and 1910 being of special value (Cincinnati, various dates of publication); *Proceedings of the Reunion Held by the National Association of the Battle of Shiloh Survivors,* April 2-10, 1921 (n.p., n.d.); *Roster of the Department of Missouri Grand Army of the Republic* (Kansas City, Missouri, 1895); Military Order of the Loyal Legion of the United States, *War Papers and Personal Reminiscences* (Missouri Commandery; St. Louis, 1892), I, *War Sketches and Incidents* (Iowa Commandery; Des Moines, 1898), III, *War Papers* (Wisconsin Commandery; Milwaukee, 1914), IV, *Essays and Recollections* (Illinois Commandery; Chicago, 1891), I. Since the regiment's only chaplain was a "northern Methodist," highlights of his career are visible in the *Minutes of Missouri Annual Conference of the Methodist Episcopal Church,* various years, 1864-1904. Many members of the regiment were prominent in masonic affairs, and vital data on their careers come from *Proceedings of the Grand Lodge of the Most Ancient and Honorable Fraternity of Free Masons of the State of Missouri Convened in St. Louis,* various communications from 1840 to 1890. Following the pattern of veterans elsewhere, these old soldiers formed their own association, the story of which may be followed in the regional press and in the *Reunion Proceedings of the 21st Missouri Veteran Volunteer Infantry Association, 1888-1902* (Fort Madison, 1903).

PERIODICALS

Voluminous periodical literature exists, most of it tangential to the monograph but nonetheless enlightening. Of most use were specific volumes of the *Missouri Historical Review* (7, 11, 12, 15, 16, 20, 31, 44, 45, 49, 65); *Annals of Iowa* (5, 6; 3d Series, 7, 9, 14, 36); *Confederate Veteran* (2, 14, 16, 19); *Southern Historical Society Papers* (6, 8, 13, 32); *Civil War History* (1, 6); *Michigan History Magazine* (27); *Military Affairs* (34); *Transactions of the Kansas State Historical Society* (7); *Iowa Journal of History and Politics* (25); *Current History* June 1968); *The Alabama Review* (July 1970).

NEWSPAPERS

Far and away the chief repository of newspapers bearing on this work is the State Historical Society of Missouri. Notable among its holdings on the Civil War era are Canton's *Press;* Columbia's *The Missouri States-man;* Edina's *Sentinel, Knox County Democrat,* and *Knox County Herald;* Fayette's *The Howard County Advertiser;* Fulton's *Callaway Weekly Gazette* and *The Missouri Telegraph;* La Grange's *National American, Herald-Democrat,* and *Indicator;* Lexington's *Weekly Union;* Liberty's *Tribune;* Louisiana's *Journal;* Memphis' *Reveille* and *Democrat;* Palmyra's *Missouri Whig* and *Spectator;* St. Louis' *The Missouri Democrat, The Missouri Republican, Anzeiger des Westens,* and *Central Christian Advocate.* For postwar activities and obituaries, the researcher must widen the above list to embrace Gorin's *Argus;* Greenfield's *Dade County Advocate;* Hannibal's *Courier-Post;* Jefferson City's *Missouri State Tribune;* Joplin's *Globe;* Kahoka's *Gazette-Herald, Clark County Courier,* and *Clark County Democrat;* Kirksville's *Daily Express* and *Weekly Graphic;* Lancaster's *Excelsior;* Lockwood's *Luminary;* St. Louis' *Globe-Democrat* and *Post-Dispatch;* and Springfield's *Daily News.*

In many ways, out-of-state newspapers are of great utility. This category consists mainly, but not wholly, of Iowa and Illinois journals. Those most helpful for wartime information are Bonaparte's *Record-Republican* (Iowa); Burlington's *Hawkeye* (Iowa); Chicago's *Tribune;* Cincinnati's *Fazette* (Ohio); Davenport's *Democrat* (Iowa); Chicago's *Tribune;* Cincinnati's *Gazette* (Ohio); Davenport's *Democrat* (Iowa); Des Moines' *Iowa State Register* and *Capital;* Louisville's *Courier* (Kentucky); Mobile's *Advertiser and Register* (Alabama); New Orleans' *The Daily Picayune* (Louisiana); New York's *Tribune.* Quincy's *Daily Whig and Republican* and *Daily Herald* (Illinois); Warsaw's *Bulletin, Hancock New Era,* and *Public Record* (Illinois). For the later lives of the veterans, see Arkansas City's *Daily Traveler* (Kansas); Ashland's *Clipper* (Kansas); Kingman's *Leader-Courier* (Kansas); Kinsley's *Mercury* (Kansas); Ottawa's *Herald* (Kansas); Smith Center's

Kansas Pioneer and *Smith County Pioneer;* Yates Center's *Woodson County Advocate* (Kansas); Albia's *Monroe County News* (Iowa); and Bloomfield's *Davis County Republican* (Iowa). All of these may be consulted either in Topeka or Des Moines, or in the Civil War Collection at Central Missouri State University.

LOCAL HISTORIANS

Needless to say, a book of this kind inevitably rests upon the cumulative endeavors of many generous and helpful individuals. The late Ben F. Dixon of San Diego, California, a towering authority on the history and lore of his native Clark County, established an enduring claim on the gratitude of this historian, who will long cherish the documentation provided him as well as memories of a day-long guided tour of Clark County's historic spots with "Uncle Ben" one warm Saturday in August 1969. Three of his paperbacks, privately printed in San Diego, were of tremendous value to this writer: *The Battle of Athens: Fourteen Contemporary Reports* (n.d.), *Martin Green's Boomerang* (1966), and *"Farthest North" 1861* (1969).

Kenneth I. Doud of Athens, descended of pioneer settlers on what was to become a historic battleground, gave unsparingly of his broad knowledge of regional history and his rich collection of Missouriana to place the author in touch with indispensable information. His sister, Bertha Parke, deserves thanks for her hospitable efforts to promote a visiting researcher's familiarity with Clark County. Lawrence and Mary Stephenson Waganer of La Grange generously devoted time, thought, and hospitality to acquaint the writer with Lewis County's Civil War memories. Jack Brumback of Memphis, Scotland County historian and collector of Civil War memorabilia, energetically unearthed data essential to this project. For information on Knox County's role in the war, the author relied frequently on S. J. Wilkerson, able postmaster-historian of Novelty. Without local historians to guide him, the stranger faces an uphill struggle in the quest for helpful contacts and materials.

INTERVIEWS

Thanks to local historians, this writer was able to interview many local people with valuable information concerning the old soldiers. Among them were Bernice Bailey of Canton (granddaughter of Eli Kenoyer and John S. Hendricks); Alvina Accola Barkley of La Grange (granddaughter of Stephan

Werly); Lula Powell Barry of Trenton (splendid source of memories of Chaplain J. H. Cox); Letty Bertram of Canton (daughter of Henry Bertram); Gary Butikofer of Quincy (great-grandson of William Smith); Edna Matlick Childers of Sandhill (collateral descendant of Edgar and William H. Matlick); Lindsey Downs of La Grange (son of Francis M. Downs); Ernest French of Athens (grandson of Philarmon Reynolds and William French); Helen Gibbons of Edina (grandniece of John H. Cunningham); Margaret Bertram Glasgow of Canton (granddaughter of Henry Bertram); Olive Hodges of Fort Madison (granddaughter of James K. P. Wilson); Sterling Hubble of Knox City (grandson of Henry Hubble); Callie Klusmeier of La Grange (daughter of Henry Klusmeier); Nelle Northcutt Nelson of Knox City (granddaughter of B. F. Northcutt); M. Hugh Pearce of Brashear (grandnephew of Captain Simon Pearce); Laura Morrey Rouner of Mountville, Pennsylvania (daughter of Lieutenant C. C. Morrey); Oren Russell of Greenfield (grandson of Lieutenant C. Z. Russell); Hazel W. Stookey of Newton, Kansas (daughter of George P. Washburn); and Peter Story of Willmathsville (grandnephew of Captain Joseph Story).

PRIVATE COLLECTIONS

Thanks also to the local historians, this writer gained access to several private historical collections. Ben Dixon provided letters and other materials from the papers of Colonel Joseph G. Best in possession of Best's granddaughter, Frances Barber Morrison of Downey, California. Mr. Dixon also secured copies of many valuable papers on the origins of the home guards and other matters in the William Bishop papers owned by Colonel Bishop's great-grandson Clayton Bishop of Eustis, Florida. Clara Sprouse and Roy Starr of Farmington, Iowa, gave the writer access, respectively, to a letter by Oliver Boardman of the Sixth Iowa Infantry shedding light on the battle of Athens and to a ledger of the Shreve & Scott wholesale house detailing provisions sold to the First North East Missouri Home Guards in the summer of 1861.

LETTERS AND DIARIES

Materials in this category remained largely ungathered when this research began. One diary of peripheral interest had been published: *The Civil War Diary of Cyrus F. Boyd*, ed. Mildred Throne (Iowa City, 1953). Early in his work, this writer was pleased to hear that Professor F. N. Boney of the University of Georgia would publish *A Union Soldier in the Land of the*

Vanquished (University, Alabama, 1969), a diary account of the regiment's sojourn on the Gulf Coast in the first year of Reconstruction. Manuscript diaries relating to experiences shared by the Missourians became available, among them those of Sergeant Lemuel Burke (119th Illinois) in the Illinois State Historical Library; Sergeant Lafayette Ruffin (First Missouri Light Artillery), loaned by his great-grandson Robert E. Kennedy of St. Louis; and Corporal John M. Keltner (Twenty-fourth Missouri), generously loaned by his granddaughter, Hope Keltner Hedgpeth of Nixa, Missouri.

From the Twenty-first Missouri, however, important materials soon appeared from private holdings. One of these, the Civil War diary of Stephan Werly, was edited by Mrs. Waganer with copies for the author and the State Historical Society of Missouri. Mrs. Ben H. Jones of La Belle, Missouri, through the good offices of Mr. Brumback, loaned the diary of Edwin Jones, compiled during the war by her late father-in-law. Oren Russell permitted research in C. Z. Russell's diary. Mrs. Rouner offered the present writer copies of several wartime letters written by Lieutenant Morrey, and Frances Starr of St. Louis secured for the author's use a trove of letters from 1862-1865 written by her grandfather N. D. Starr, adjutant of the Twenty-first Missouri.

CORRESPONDENTS

Besides those favoring the author with interviews were other relatives of the old soldiers who responded generously to inquiries for information and documentation: Anna Cahalan Boone of Edina (granddaughter of Patrick Cahalan); Frank Brookhart of Williamstown (grandson of William Brookhart); June Moore Call of Keokuk (great-granddaughter of David Moore); Mrs. Galen Chadwick of Birmingham, Alabama (granddaughter of C. C. Morrey); Jessie Morrey Condoide of Columbus, Ohio (grandniece of C. C. Morrey); Dean Cunningham of Chillicothe, Illinois (great-grandson of John H. Cunningham); Maude Barnes Diestelhorst of Tulsa, Oklahoma (daughter of Aquilla Barnes); William J. Giles of Enid, Oklahoma (great-grandson of David Moore); Robert Killen of Lincoln, Nebraska (great-grandson of William R. Killen); W. C. Langdon of Beaumont, Texas (great-grandson of Seth Langdon); Dotaline Matlick Kreeger, Maxine Forker Grabowski, Essie Matlick McPherson, and Edna Matlick Childers, whose "Our Family" (Leawood, Kansas, mimeo., 1965) proved a goldmine of information on the Matlicks and Scotland County's early days; Carl Menke of Keokuk (son of Frederick Menke and grandson of Edward Menke); Mrs. Charles H. Naylor of Holt Summit, Mo. (granddaughter of C. C. Morrey; and Ethel M. Roseberry of Kirksville (daughter of William H. Roseberry).

Index

ABOUT THE AUTHOR

Leslie Anders is professor of history at Central Missouri State University. He did his undergraduate work at the College of Emporia and received his A.M. and Ph.D. from the University of Missouri. Professor Anders is the author of *Education for Service: Centennial History of Central Missouri State* and has also contributed to many professional journals. His special interest is military history.